DISCARDED

Evolutionism in Cultural Anthropology

A CRITICAL HISTORY

Robert L. Carneiro
American Museum of Natural History

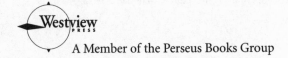

A Member of the Perseus Books Group

Westview Press books are available at special discounts for bulk purchases in the United States by corporations, institutions, and other organizations. For more information, please contact the Special Markets Department at the Perseus Books Group, 11 Cambridge Center, Cambridge MA 02142, or call (617) 252–5298, (800) 255-1514 or email j.mccrary@perseusbooks.com.

Published in 2003 in the United States of America by Westview Press, 5500 Central Avenue, Boulder, Colorado 80301–2877.

Find us on the World Wide Web at www.westviewpress.com

Library of Congress Cataloging-in-Publication Data
Carneiro, Robert L. (Robert Leonard), 1927–
    Evolutionism in cultural anthropology : a critical history /
Robert L. Carneiro
        p.   cm.
    Includes bibliographical references (p.) and index.
    ISBN 0–8133–3765–8 (hardcover)—ISBN 0-8133-3766-6(pbk.)
    1. Social evolution.   2. Ethnology—Philosophy.   I. Title.
GN360 C37   2003
303.4—dc21
                                                                                2002015342

The paper used in this publication meets the requirements of the American National Standard for Permanence of Paper for Printed Library Materials Z39.48–1984.

10   9   8   7   6   5   4   3   2   1

The photograph of V. Gordon Childe is used by permission of William J. Peace, to whom acknowledgment is made. The photograph of Julian Steward is used by permission of G whom grateful acknowledgment is also made.

Contents

Illustrations

Preface

The preface to a book should tell the story of how it came to be written. The story is often one of convolutions and contortions, of gropings and stumblings. Seldom is it one of smooth sailing. Still, the more convoluted the story, the more interesting it is likely to be, and the more it warrants being told. Moreover, as the story unfolds, the reader will be better able to assess the merits of the end result. These reasons, at least, are my justification for recounting here the peculiar origins and tortuous journey of this book.

The first thing to be told is that this is a book I never intended to write, and that I agreed to write almost against my will. Moreover, once I had started it, there were at least a dozen times when I regretted having done so, since I could have followed an easier course. However, as the book bumped its way along, it gradually gathered momentum, and by the time it neared completion, it had picked up a full head of steam. So, though resisting it initially, I grew increasingly accepting, and when it finally came to an end, I was well satisfied that I had tackled it after all.

But enough preface to the preface. Let me proceed to tell the story of this volume.

Some years ago, at an annual meeting of the American Anthropological Association, Karl Yambert, a senior editor at Westview Press, approached me with the idea of bringing out a volume of several of my previously published articles. It was the sort of idea an author would hesitate to broach to a publisher but one that, when it was broached to *him*, he could scarcely afford to turn down. Without a moment's reflection, then, I agreed.

The next question was, What articles should be included in the book? My writing has been pretty well limited to two areas of anthropology: South American ethnology and cultural evolution. I did not want to mix the two, so I suggested to Karl that the "anthology" (to give the proposed book a name) be restricted to articles on cultural evolution. That having been settled, the next step was to propose candidates for inclusion in the volume. But the articles in my preliminary selection ran to over 500 pages, well in excess of the 400-page limit Karl had set. A substantial cut had to be made. It was easy enough to eliminate two or three marginal articles, but that still left the anthology about seventy pages too long. What to do? At that point, an idea occurred to me that seemed to solve the problem. To understand why I thought so, we have to go back in time.

The year 1968 saw the publication of Marvin Harris's *The Rise of Anthropological Theory*, a volume that immediately established itself as the preeminent textbook for courses on the history of anthropology and ethnological theory. Not long after its appearance, it occurred to Raoul Naroll that a history-and-theory book on anthropology might be written that could successfully challenge Harris's volume for supremacy in its field. However, instead of writing the entire book himself, as Harris had done, Naroll proposed to farm out its chapters to specialists in the various subjects he felt should be covered in the book. In this division of labor, it fell to me to write the chapter on nineteenth-century cultural evolutionism.

I was happy with the assignment and immediately set to work with enthusiasm and high hopes. Months of work followed, but when the chapter was finally done, I felt I had put together a systematic and detailed account of the subject. The chapter seemed to me to be a clear and comprehensive treatment of the classical evolutionists, principally Spencer, Tylor, and Morgan. Moreover, I took pains to present the ideas of these men in their own words. The result was a work often at odds with the pronouncements of Franz Boas and his disciples about the early evolutionists.

The finished volume, with Raoul Naroll as editor and including the work of ten contributors, bore the title *Main Currents in Cultural Anthropology*. The book had been done under contract to a distinguished publisher (Appleton-Century-Crofts), but as it was going through production, A-C-C was bought by another publisher and promptly killed. The new publisher saw to the completion of the print run, but showed no further interest in or allegiance to the volume. It was never advertised or properly distributed, with the result that, to all intents and purposes, *Main Currents in Cultural Anthropology* "fell dead off the press."

For Naroll and his contributors it was a great disappointment. For me personally, it meant that the considerable effort expended in researching and writing my chapter on "Classical Evolutionism" had gone for naught. Virtually no one I have talked to in the thirty years since the book's publication has ever heard of it—let alone known of the existence of my chapter.

The book went quickly out of print, and with its demise, Naroll arranged to have the copyright of the individual chapters revert back to their authors, to do with what they could. At various times in the ensuing years I had entertained the idea of trying to rescue my chapter from oblivion and having it appear, by itself, as a slim volume. But nothing ever came of it.

Now, however, in the midst of a discussion with Karl Yambert about the anthology's excessive length, I suddenly saw my chance! I made the suggestion that Westview Press consider publishing my chapter on "Classical Evolutionism" as a separate volume of modest size.

Happily, Karl was receptive to the idea. Westview might be willing to do just that. However, he attached the proviso that in order to bring my treatment of classical evolutionism "up to date," something on twentieth-century cultural evolutionism should be added to it. It was, quite frankly, a suggestion I was not overjoyed to hear. I had hoped to see "Classical Evolutionism" reappear in print with no further work on my part. Still, if that was the price I had to pay to get my chapter republished, I was ready to pay it. Grudgingly, perhaps, but ready nonetheless, since I saw this as the solution to two problems at once: "Classical Evolutionism" would finally see the light of day, and, by removing it from the list of candidates for the anthology, the size of that volume would drop to the 400 pages we had agreed upon. At that point, then, it all looked like clear sailing on a calm sea.

But then, to my surprise, Karl gave me the choice of which book I wanted to do first. The anthology would have required very little work. All I would be expected to do was write an introduction to it, and then add a brief "epilogue" to each article, telling what had led me to write it, and describing what impact (if any) its publication had had.

This, then, was the "anthology," demanding a minimum of effort from me. The "slim volume," on the other hand, would require some "fattening up," as I strove, as instructed, to "bring it up to date." Now, I should note that when Karl first said he wanted me to add something to it on twentieth-century evolutionism, I had replied that I could easily do so in "thirty or forty pages." Far more prescient than I, Karl had responded, "Take a hundred."

Fine. But I still faced the choice of which book to work on first, the "anthology" or the "slim volume"; the easy one or the harder one. And, in a moment of "irrational exuberance," I chose the harder one. In justifying my choice, I have to say that I did not realize at the time that it really *was* the harder one. After all, how much work would it take to bring cultural evolutionism into the twentieth century?

However, not long after I set to work on it, a disconcerting feeling came over me. I became aware that I could not possibly do justice to twentieth-century cultural evolutionism in thirty or forty pages—certainly not the kind of justice I knew the subject deserved. Dealing with the early Boasian reaction to classical evolutionism alone took almost a dozen pages! Far more work was in store for me, I realized, than I had ever envisioned. And so I was forced to confront the stark reality that, like the saber-toothed tiger, I had innocently wandered into the La Brea tar pit, and now found myself in it hip-deep. Clearly, a radically different approach was called for. I had no option but to give my treatment of twentieth-century evolutionism its head. I therefore took off the reins and let the horse run free, wherever it would go. The only thing left to me was to run after it, trying as best I could to hold on to its tail.

And so it was that "thirty or forty" pages soon became one hundred . . . then two hundred . . . then three hundred . . . and still no end in sight. When the horse finally came to a halt, it had galloped for 417 manuscript pages—now mercifully reduced to 214 book pages. Of course, this was *in addition* to the 74 book pages of the original "Classical Evolutionism."

So now the two sections of the book were at last finished and con-joined—twentieth-century evolutionism with classical evolutionism—and the skein was finally complete. However, there was an anomaly that was glaringly apparent. The original chapter, the one that had started all the trouble, to which my treatment of twentieth-century evolutionism was supposed to be a mere appendage, now found *itself* the appendage to a much longer companion piece. In a manner of speaking, the cart had be-come the horse.

Naturally, when work on the manuscript began, a deadline was set for its submission. But as the manuscript grew longer and longer, as furlongs turned into miles, deadline after deadline came and went—unmet. New ones were set, only to be broken. Repeatedly and unconscionably I took ad-vantage of Karl Yambert's good nature and infinite patience. And countless times I berated myself for being foolish enough not to have chosen the an-thology—the easy book—to work on first. Had I done so, I kept telling my-self, it would long since have been finished and in the bookstores.

As the months passed, I continued to upbraid myself for having picked the wrong book to work on. But then one day, a slow realization began to grow in me. As the manuscript became longer, and its coverage wider and deeper, I began to find comfort in the fact that it was taking on a solid com-prehensiveness. It was reaching into corners and crannies, and dealing with more aspects of the subject, than any work I knew of. After a while, it even seemed to me that the volume would allow—indeed, *invite*—comparison with any book purporting to cover the field of cultural evolutionism. Fi-nally, the day arrived when I became convinced that I had done the right thing after all. I was *glad* I had made the "wrong" choice and had put the "slim volume" ahead of the "anthology."

So much for the history of this book. Now one or two of its features re-quire comment. Readers will quickly notice my extensive use of quotations.

This is not happenstance but a matter of conscious design. My graduate training in anthropology was under Leslie A. White at the University of Michigan, and his influence on me will become readily apparent in the pages that follow. One aspect of White's teaching and writing that struck me from the start was that in discussing a theorist's opinions, White never simply *alleged* that he had said thus and so. Invariably he was meticulous in quoting the person's very words. What particularly impressed me was the contrast between White's practice in this regard and that of various members of the Boas school, who were all too ready to impute "errors" to the classical evolutionists without bothering to quote them directly. Ever since those graduate school days, I have tried in my own writing to emulate Leslie White by never paraphrasing when I could quote.

My passion for quotation, though, goes beyond the desire for accuracy. It contains an element of the aesthetic. It has always seemed to me that a page of text without a single name or date or place, with no quotation marks and no proper nouns, is a featureless desert. On such a page one may encounter the ruminations and excogitations of the author, but not how his ideas dovetail or clash with those of other authors. The liberal use of quotations, it seems to me, is one way to bring such a textual desert to life, to make it appear inhabited and inviting. And that is what I have tried to do. However, if the reader finds in the following pages *too many* quoted passages—too many landmarks meant to punctuate and enliven a dreary landscape—then it will be a case of good intentions having gone awry through excessive implementation.

Finally, I come to the acknowledgments. The reader will already have noted the gratitude I feel to my editor, Karl Yambert, for giving me such a long leash, and for being so sparing of spur and lash. It is under such an understanding editor that every author wishes he could work.

To Joyce Marcus I feel another kind of gratitude. She read every chapter of the book as it was finished, and offered her perceptive and incisive comments. But beyond specific suggestions, she repeatedly provided reassurance and encouragement. To have at my back the unswerving support of someone whose scholarship I admire as highly as I do hers is beyond rubies.

1

The Early History of Evolutionism

Before dealing with cultural evolutionism proper, it seems useful to sketch briefly the history of the general notion of evolution. The word "evolution" itself derives from the Latin *evolūtio,* from *e-*, "out of," and *volūtus,* "rolled." It meant, literally, an unrolling, and was applied especially to the opening of a book. Roman books were written on lengths of parchment and rolled onto wooden rods, so that to be read they had to be unrolled or "evolved" (McCabe 1921:2).

In the seventeenth century, "evolution" began to be used in English to refer to an orderly sequence of events, particularly one in which the outcome was somehow contained within it from the start. This use of the word reflected the prevailing philosophical notion of the nature of change. It had been widely believed, at least since the time of Aristotle, that things changed in accordance with an inner principle of development. This principle was sometimes thought to be embodied in a seed or germ. Gottfried Leibniz called these germs "monads," and thought that encapsulated within them were all the characteristics that objects animated by them would eventually reveal (Leibniz 1898:44n., 373, 419). Moreover, the development or unfolding of a monad was, for Leibniz, largely a matter of the operation of internal forces; surrounding conditions played little or no role (1898:44n., 105).

This view of the nature of change was widespread in European philosophy during the eighteenth and early nineteenth centuries. Immanuel Kant, for example, spoke of the "germs . . . implanted in our species [by Nature]" as being "unfolded to that stage of development which is completely conformable to her inherent design" (Kant 1969:52–53). And Georg Hegel wrote that "the principle of *Development* involves the existence of a latent

1

germ of being—a capacity or potentiality striving to realize itself" (Hegel 1956:54). And he, too, viewed this development as not affected by external influences, but rather as one "which expands itself in virtue of an internal unchangeable principle" (1956:55).

Well into the nineteenth century, then, the prevailing conception of evolution was, as Arthur Lovejoy expressed it, that "the 'germs' of all things have always existed . . . [and] contain within themselves an internal principle of development which drives them on through a vast series of metamorphoses through which they ascend the 'universal scale'" (Lovejoy 1936:274).

It was in this sense that the term evolution was first used in biology by Charles Bonnet in his *Considérations sur les Corps Organisés* (1762). Being a "preformationist," Bonnet believed that all parts of the embryo were already completely formed before conception, and that prenatal development consisted only of the unfolding and expanding of a preexistent germ. It was to this supposed process that Bonnet applied the term "evolution." In his usage, "evolution" was opposed to "epigenesis," the doctrine that held that the ovum and the sperm contained none of the physical features of the developed adult, but that these arose only gradually after fertilization (Osborn 1927:118–121; Fothergill 1952:45–46; Miall 1912:289–290).

Perhaps it was because the term "evolution" still retained something of this notion of preformation that Jean-Baptiste Lamarck failed to use it in 1809 in his famous work *Philosophie Zoologique,* the first serious biological treatise to affirm the theory of the transmutation of species.

"Evolution" was, however, used freely by Auguste Comte in his *Cours de Philosophie Positive* (6 vols., 1830–1842) and again in his *Système de Politique Positive* (4 vols., 1851–1854). Comte gave the term no explicit definition, but used it in the general sense of progress or growth, without implying that the end product of evolution was always, or necessarily, contained in its beginnings.

Until the 1850s the use of the word "evolution" was relatively uncommon in England. Thus, when John Stuart Mill, a follower of Comte, wrote *A System of Logic* in 1843, in which he, like his predecessor, dealt with the possibility of a science of history, he employed the term only once (Mill 1846:578).

In the 1850s, the word evolution began to appear more commonly, but still generally retained the old idea of an unfolding of something immanent. For example, the American theologian William G. T. Shedd, who used the term some forty times in his *Lectures upon the Philosophy of History,* wrote: "The progressive advance and unfolding which is to be seen all along the line of a development, is simply the expansion over a wider surface of that which from the instant of its creation has existed in a more invisible and metaphysical form" (Shedd 1857:27; see also pp. 18, 26).

Herbert Spencer and the Concept of Evolution

A definition of evolution that was both rigorous and nonmetaphysical was not formulated until around the end of the 1850s. It is generally supposed that the first person to offer such a definition was Charles Darwin. But this supposition is incorrect. The word evolution, as such, does not even appear in the first five editions of *The Origin of Species*. Not until the sixth edition, in 1872, did Darwin employ the term. And then he used it only half a dozen times, without any specific definition (Darwin 1872:201, 202, 424; Peckham 1959:264, 265, 751).

The reason Darwin finally decided to use "evolution," after first ignoring it, was that by 1872 the term, in a scientific sense, had gained wide currency. And the man who had given it that currency was Herbert Spencer. When Spencer first began to deal with evolution, the term was still obscure. He stripped it of its metaphysical elements, defined it with "almost mathematical . . . precision" (Allen 1890:2), demonstrated its universal application, and left it as the guiding principle of all the historical sciences.

Herbert Spencer

Let us see how the concept of evolution developed in Spencer's hands. His first use of the term seems to have been in *Social Statics* (1851). As far as I have found, he used the word only once here (on p. 440) and made no attempt to define it. He applied it to those kinds of changes in society that he spoke of more frequently as "progress" (e.g., on p. 63), and meant by it only development in the general sense. No more specific meaning was given to the term. Nevertheless, it is clear that Spencer already held a nonmetaphysical view of evolution as it applied to society, for elsewhere in *Social Statics* he wrote that "civilization no longer appears to be a regular unfolding after a specific plan; but seems rather a development of man's latent capabilities under the action of favourable circumstances" (Spencer 1851:415). At that time, then, Spencer paid no special attention to the term evolution. In 1852, when he wrote his famous essay "The Development Hypothesis," he used the term only once, and merely as a synonym for "development" and "transmutation" (Spencer 1891a:1). All three terms were applied to the gradual transformation of species, which Spencer, seven years before Darwin, openly espoused in opposition to the doctrine of special creation.

In the years immediately following 1852, Spencer continued to concern himself with changes in natural phenomena. His writings for those years show the concept of evolution gradually taking more definite shape, and becoming elaborated in two ways. First, Spencer discerned additional aspects of the evolutionary process itself, and second, he saw evolution as being manifested by more and more classes of phenomena.

Increase in complexity, generally thought of as the hallmark of the Spencerian concept of evolution, was suggested to Spencer by reading Karl E. von Baer's observation that embryological development proceeded from homogeneity to heterogeneity (Spencer 1926:I, 384). In various articles published in the mid-1850s, Spencer traced this change toward progressively greater complexity in a number of discrete phenomena, such as manners, fashion, government, science, etc. (1896:II, 9–11). Then in "Progress: Its Law and Cause," published in 1857 and a landmark in the history of evolutionism, Spencer generalized the evolutionary process to the entire cosmos:

> The advance from the simple to the complex, through a process of successive differentiations, is seen alike in the earliest changes of the Universe to which we can reason our way back; and in the earliest changes which we can inductively establish, it is seen in the geologic and climatic evolution of the Earth, and of every single organism on its surface; it is seen in the evolution of Humanity, whether contemplated in the civilized individual, or in the aggregation of races; it is seen in the evolution of Society in respect alike of its political, its religious, and its economical organisation; and it is seen in the evolution of all . . . [the] endless concrete and abstract products of human activity. (Spencer 1857:465)

In 1858 Spencer conceived the idea of surveying the fields of biology, psychology, sociology, and morals from an evolutionary perspective. In its original draft this plan included one volume to be entitled *The Principles of Sociology*. By 1860 Spencer's scheme had crystallized further, and he issued a prospectus announcing the future publication of what came to be known as the "Synthetic Philosophy." In this prospectus *Principles of Sociology* had been expanded to three volumes, which would deal, Spencer wrote, with "general facts, structural and functional, as gathered from a survey of Societies and their changes: in other words, the empirical generalizations that are arrived at by comparing the different societies, and successive phases of the same society" (Spencer 1926:II, 481).

Thus, before any other of the classical evolutionists had published on the subject, Spencer already had a clear notion of a comparative science of society based on evolutionary principles.

The initial volume of Spencer's "Synthetic Philosophy," which appeared in 1862, was *First Principles*. In this work Spencer devoted a great deal of attention to the concept of evolution, and, step by step, carefully built up to his formal definition of it:

> Evolution is a change from an indefinite, incoherent homogeneity, to a definite, coherent heterogeneity; through continuous differentiations and integrations. (Spencer 1863:216)

By 1862, then, Spencer had formulated an explicit, objective, unequivocal, and general concept of the process of evolution.

While in *First Principles* Spencer presented examples of how evolution had manifested itself in nature generally, he left to *The Principles of Sociology* (3 vols., 1876–1896) the detailed exemplification of how evolution had occurred in human societies.

The Evolutionary Views of Tylor and Morgan

Here we may leave our examination of evolution as a general process and see how the concept was applied in the emerging science of anthropology. We may begin by comparing the Spencerian formula of evolution with the concepts held by the other two major cultural evolutionists of the nineteenth century, Edward B. Tylor and Lewis H. Morgan.

In the preface to the second edition of his *Primitive Culture*, Tylor wrote as follows:

> It may have struck some readers as an omission, that in a work on civilization insisting so strenuously on a theory of development or evolution, mention should scarcely be made of Mr. Darwin and Mr. Herbert Spencer, whose influence on the whole course of modern thought on such subjects should not be left without formal recognition. This absence of particular reference is accounted for by the present work, arranged on its own lines, coming scarcely into contact of detail with the previous works of these eminent philosophers. (Tylor 1920:I, vii)

And Tylor was right. *Primitive Culture* was a very different work from *Principles of Sociology*. As Alexander Goldenweiser was to observe, "When compared with the first volume of Spencer's [*Principles of*] *Sociology*, Tylor's classic work, *Primitive Culture*, was less a contribution to evolutionary thinking than an attempt to trace the life history of a particular belief, namely, animism" (Goldenweiser 1925a:216). Indeed, throughout much of his published work, especially his earlier writings, Tylor showed himself to be a good deal more of a cultural historian than an evolutionist. His concern was largely with tracing the history of myths, riddles, customs, games, rituals, artifacts, and the like, rather than with laying bare the general process or stages in the evolution of culture as a whole.

Though Tylor did use the term evolution (e.g., 1871:I, 1, 22, 62; II, 401, 406, 408), he did so sparingly, and attempted no formal definition of it. Moreover, he applied it to almost any succession of specific forms, and did not restrict the concept to changes involving increased heterogeneity, definiteness, or integration, as Spencer had.

The contrast between Spencerian evolutionism and Tylorian historicism appears most strikingly in a little-known article by Tylor entitled "The Study of Customs." This article, which appeared in 1882, was a review of "Ceremonial Institutions," a part of Volume 2 of Spencer's *Principles of Sociology*. Some years before, Tylor had engaged in a long and bitter controversy with Spencer over priority in originating the theory of animism, and he took this opportunity to assail Spencer once more, criticizing him severely for offering conjectural explanations of certain ceremonial practices.

For example, noting that high-order samurai in Japan wore two swords, Spencer had suggested that the second sword represented one taken as a trophy from a fallen enemy, and later worn as a badge of honor. But by a more thorough study of the sources, Tylor was able to show that Spencer was wrong. The two swords worn by a samurai were different types of weapons. The short *waki-zashi* served to cut and thrust at close range, whereas the longer *katana*, which was unsheathed with a great sweep, was used to attack enemies at a greater distance.

Tylor proceeded to challenge Spencer's interpretations of the origins of handshaking, tattooing, the wearing of black in mourning, etc., offering his own explanations of these practices. These explanations strike the reader as sounder and more convincing than those offered by Spencer, and appear to be based on a broader and deeper knowledge of the documentary evidence.

Tylor thus revealed himself to be better acquainted with the historical sources, and more critical in handling them, than did Spencer. But at the same time that he showed himself a superior cultural historian, Tylor also revealed the limitations so often associated with historical particularism. His concern with the minute details of culture history arrested his attention and kept him from grappling with the broader problems of the evolution of sociocultural systems. Thus, although Tylor's work was generally sounder than that of Spencer, it was also narrower. Venturing less, he achieved less. His evolutionism, such as it was, was of the limited Darwinian sort, that is, descent with modifications, and lacked the sweep and power of Spencer's. We might epitomize the two men by saying that Tylor appears to us as a master of *facts*, Spencer as a master of *theory*.

Tylor's concern with the history of discrete cultural elements rather than with the evolution of entire social systems is rarely recognized today. Yet it was the hallmark of most of his scholarly work, at least during the early and middle years of his career. Not until 1889, when he wrote his famous article "On a Method of Investigating the Development of Institutions," did Tylor attempt to wrestle with more general and systematic kinds of change in human societies.

Like Tylor, Lewis H. Morgan rarely used the term evolution. Indeed, Bernhard J. Stern (1931:23) even claimed that Morgan "carefully avoided" the word, and that "nowhere in his books" does it appear. However, as Leslie A. White (1944:224) has noted, this is not true: "Evolution" appears twice in the first four pages of the Holt edition of *Ancient Society*. But as White also notes, Morgan did not use the term often, nor did he give it any formal definition. He did, however, speak frequently of "progress," "growth," and "development," seeming to prefer these terms to "evolution." Indeed, as White (1944:224) again points out, each of the four parts of *Ancient Society* is entitled "Growth of . . . ," instead of "Evolution of . . . ," as they might have been.

Morgan was less tied to the details of history than Tylor. Though he chose to discuss the evolution of Aztec, Greek, and Roman societies specifically, rather than the evolution of society in general, as had Spencer, he nevertheless paid more attention to broad changes in whole social systems than did Tylor.

Two quite different conceptions of evolution seem to have coexisted in Morgan's mind, even though he never distinguished them explicitly. The closest he came to doing so was in a brief passage early in *Ancient Society* where he wrote that inventions and discoveries "stand to each other in progressive . . . relations," whereas, on the other hand, institutions stand to each other in "unfolding relations." The distinction Morgan made between them was that "while the former class have had a connection more or less direct, the latter have been developed from a few primary germs of thought" (Morgan 1964:12).

Morgan seems to have meant that inventions and discoveries are linked in such a way that each successive one is determined—overtly, directly, and mechanically—by the one immediately preceding it. Social institutions, on the other hand, appear to Morgan to grow out of ideas implanted in the human mind from the beginning, and to do so more in accordance with some master principle than as a response to external conditions. Thus we find in Morgan the curious contrast of a modern and scientific conception of evolution existing side by side with an older and metaphysical one.

2

The Reconstruction of Cultural Evolution

Having noted something of how the classical evolutionists conceived of the evolutionary process, we may now consider how they went about reconstructing the evolution of culture. We shall look first at the data available to them for doing so, and then at the methods they employed in carrying it out.

Three sources of evidence were at hand: archaeology, history, and ethnography. All three sources were drawn on freely, but not equally. By the 1860s, when the classical evolutionists began to write, the work of prehistorians such as Jens Worsaae, Gabriel de Mortillet, Édouard Lartet, and Jacques Boucher de Perthes had firmly established the fact that all early levels of culture were characterized by a crude stone technology and a correspondingly simple social life. The general course of cultural development from simplicity to complexity was, therefore, indisputable. However, since the archaeological record was still so limited, it could do no more than suggest the conditions of life of prehistoric man. Thus while archaeology proved the direction in which cultural evolution had proceeded, it could provide only a few of the details.

Recorded history, on the other hand, offered very rich documentation of changes that had occurred during the previous 3,000 years or so. If history were studied with the aim of discovering general trends in cultural development, and not viewed merely as a succession of unique events, then it could be of immense help to anthropology in carrying out its cultural syntheses. The history of Greece between the time of Homer and the time of Pericles, for example, revealed a considerable degree of evolution. Even greater changes were manifested by Rome during the thousand years between the eighth century BC and the second century AD as it grew from a confederacy of a few small tribes to a large empire.

But history had its own limitations. By the time of the introduction of writing, most societies in the Mediterranean region were already organized into states. Thus, history afforded very little evidence of the preceding band, village, tribal, and chiefdom levels of organization. The evidence of history was insufficient for reconstructing the events leading from primordial times to the rise of civilization. History, like archaeology, had to be supplemented from the only remaining source of cultural experience: the great number of non-Western, largely preliterate human societies. These societies varied in their level of culture from such exceedingly simple peoples as the Yahgan and Bushmen to the highly complex Aztecs and Incas. Consequently, they seemed to span much of the range through which cultural evolution had proceeded.

But just how was the evidence afforded by this vast array of peoples to be used in reconstructing cultural development? The logic by which this was done was that embodied in the comparative method, and we must now see how this method was understood and applied by the classical evolutionists.

The Comparative Method

The comparative method was already in use by the time anthropology came into existence. Indeed, it had been applied with great success by the two sister sciences of biology and philology. It was said of Cuvier, the founder of comparative anatomy, that "he developed the correlation principle . . . to the point where it was thought possible to reconstruct the whole of an unknown animal from the structure of one part" (Eaton 1951:300).

Linguistics had also witnessed the triumph of the comparative method. The men who founded comparative philology in the early 1800s, Rasmus Rask, Franz Bopp, and August Friedrich Pott, began to show, by a systematic comparison of modern Indo-European languages, that it was possible to reconstruct their common ancestor. And it was also possible to retrace the steps by which the various Indo-European languages had evolved from this early form (Pederson 1931:248–258; Fiske 1891:584). Indeed, so impressive were the accomplishments of the method when applied to linguistics that Max Muller was led to declare, "The comparative method is the truly scientific spirit of our age, nay of all ages" (quoted in Ginsberg 1961:195).

There was no question, then, that the comparative method was a powerful tool. And, with its demonstrated successes, it gained wider recognition and respect. Thus the historian Edward A. Freeman affirmed that "the establishment of the Comparative Method of study has been the greatest intellectual achievement of our time. It has carried light and order into whole branches of human knowledge which before were shrouded in darkness and confusion" (Freeman 1873:1).

It should be no surprise, then, that in the early days of anthropology the classical evolutionists seized upon the comparative method as a means for carrying out their own reconstructions. What is surprising, perhaps, is that rarely do we encounter in their writings anything like a formal discussion of how the method is to be applied. Usually the comparative method remains entirely implicit in their work. In fact, the only approximation to an explicit presentation of the method that I know of occurs in the early pages of John F. McLennan's posthumous work, *Studies in Ancient History*, Second Series (1896:8–21). (However, see Starcke 1889:1–3, and Fiske 1891:584–588.) The tenets of the comparative method probably seemed so obvious and reasonable to the classical evolutionists that they thought it unnecessary to restate or defend them.

However, it seems desirable for us to try to ferret out these principles and make them explicit. Only in that way can we judge if the classical evolutionist who applied them was validly reconstructing evolution, or, as Goldenweiser thought, "merely chasing his own tail" (1933:133). I shall try to arrange these principles in what seems to me their logical order. Moreover, besides formulating them, I shall illustrate their use by quoting appropriate passages from the writings of the early evolutionists.

The Possibility of a Social Science

Our analysis needs to begin with the fundamental issue of whether or not anthropology could be a science. The classical evolutionists were convinced that the culture of mankind had come into being entirely through natural causes. Consequently, they felt that its development was subject to explanation in terms of scientific laws and principles.

This view was, of course, relatively new, and very much at variance with prevailing opinions. According to the more traditional view of man, it was impossible to explain the course of human history without taking account of divine intervention. And since this intervention was essentially arbitrary, not to say capricious, there was no likelihood that strict regularities of the type found in physical phenomena could ever be discovered in the realm of human behavior.

Even when the idea of divine intervention in human affairs began to recede, there still was a great reluctance to accept the possibility of a social science. The men who then had the record of man's past achievements in their custody, the literary historians, found many reasons to believe that the data of history could never be reduced to a science.

Thus, James Anthony Froude wrote: "There are laws for his digestion, and laws of the means by which his digestive organs are supplied with matter. But pass beyond them, and where are we? In a world where it would be as easy to calculate men's actions by laws . . . as to measure the orbit of Neptune with a foot rule, or weigh Sirius in a grocer's scale" (Froude 1909:23). And Charles Kingsley, in his inaugural lecture as Professor of Modern History at Cambridge, said to his audience: "I only ask that . . . the hope [be] given up, at least for the present, of forming any exact science of history" (Kingsley 1860:53).

A major reason why historians were disinclined to accept the possibility of a social science was their allegiance to the doctrine of free will. As Froude wrote in 1864: "When natural causes are liable to be set aside and neutralised by what is called volition, the word Science is out of place. If it is free to a man to choose what he will do or not do, there is no adequate science of him" (Froude 1909:11). With views such as this in mind, John Stuart Mill observed: "Among the impediments to the general acknowledgement, by thoughtful minds, of the subjection of historical facts to scientific laws, the most fundamental continues to be that which is grounded on the doctrine of Free Will, or, in other words, on the denial that the law of invariable Causation holds true of human volitions" (Mill 1886:607–608).

Another reason why historians were unable to accept the idea of a social science was their preoccupation with history as the sum of individual biographies. Thus according to Ralph Waldo Emerson in his essay "History" in 1841, "civil and natural history, the history of art and of literature, must be explained from individual history, or must remain words" (Emerson 1940:131). As Herbert Spencer noted: "The possibility of Sociology was not only not conceived by historians, but when alleged was denied. Occupied as they had all along been in narrating *events* in the lives of societies, they had paid little or no attention to the evolution of their organizations" (Spencer 1926:II, 253).

By the fourth decade of the nineteenth century, though, the historian's reluctance to entertain a science of culture was beginning to be challenged. The method of science, so successful in astronomy, physics, biology, and linguistics, began to be applied to human behavior as well. In his pioneer work, *Cours de Philosophie Positive* (1830–1842), Auguste Comte argued that the scientific method could be applied to the study of society, and called this new science "sociology."

John Stuart Mill, Comte's first major follower in England, entitled the last section of his *System of Logic*, "The Logic of the Moral Sciences." In this section he dealt with such basic issues as whether human actions are subject to causal laws, and concluded his analysis by stating that "History . . . does, when judiciously examined, afford Empirical Laws of Society" (Mill 1846:578). This work of Mill's played an important role in England in laying the groundwork for the acceptance of the legitimacy of a science of society.

Perhaps the best example of the new attitude emerging among students of history as a result of the influence of Comtean positivism were the views of Henry Thomas Buckle. No better statement can be found of the premise underlying social science than the following passage from the early pages of Buckle's *History of Civilization in England:*

> In regard to nature, events apparently the most irregular and capricious have been explained, and have been shown to be in accordance with certain fixed and universal laws. This has been done because men of ability, and, above all, men of patient, untiring thought, have studied natural events with the view of discovering their regularity: and if human events were subjected to a similar treatment, we have every right to expect similar results. (Buckle 1857:6)

Turning to the classical evolutionists themselves, we find E. B. Tylor stating in *Researches into the Early History of Mankind,* "The early Culture-History of Mankind is capable of being treated as an Inductive Science" (Tylor 1870:162).

A few years later, when he came to write his major work, *Primitive Culture,* Tylor entitled the first chapter "The Science of Culture," and in it he argued that "our thoughts, wills, and actions accord with laws as definite as those which govern the motion of waves, the combination of acids and bases, and the growth of plants and animals" (Tylor 1871:I, 2). A few pages later he stated with equal assurance that "rudimentary as the science of culture still is, the symptoms are becoming very strong that even what seem its most spontaneous and motiveless phenomena will, nevertheless, be shown to come within the range of distinct cause and effect as certainly as the facts of mechanics" (Tylor 1871:I, 17).

In *The Study of Sociology* Herbert Spencer also argued for the possibility of a social science, saying that "sociology is proposed as a subject to be studied after scientific methods, with the expectation of reaching results having scientific certainty" (Spencer 1886:54). Near the end of the first volume of *Principles of Sociology,* after surveying and synthesizing a great deal of ethnographic data, Spencer concluded: "The inductions arrived at . . . show that in social phenomena there is a general order of co-existence and sequence; and that therefore social phenomena form the subject-matter of a science" (Spencer 1890:585).

This opinion continued to be an axiom of classical evolutionism. Thus, years later, James G. Frazer wrote: "Anthropology . . . aims at discovering the general laws which have regulated human history in the past" (Frazer 1913a:160).

The Uniformity of Nature

Another tenet implicit in the work of the classical evolutionists was that of the uniformity of nature. It was always assumed—and occasionally made explicit—that the laws of culture operating in the recent present had also operated in the distant past. This principle, like many others of the comparative method, was of course by no means unique to anthropology. It was basic to all the historical sciences. One of the earliest exponents of it was the geologist Charles Lyell. So important did Lyell consider this principle to be in his own science that his famous work, *Principles of Geology,* bore the subtitle: "being an attempt to explain the former changes of the earth's surface, by reference to causes now in operation" (Lyell 1830:I, title page).

The clearest statements of this principle by a classical evolutionist were made by E. B. Tylor. Tylor was ready to assert that "the same kind of development in culture which has gone on inside our range of knowledge has also gone on outside it" (Tylor 1871:I, 29). He issued the challenge that "If any one holds that human thought and action were worked out in primaeval times according to laws essentially other than those of the modern world, it is for him to prove by valid evidence this anomalous state of things" (1871:I, 29). He concluded his argument by saying: "That the tendency of culture has been similar throughout the existence of human society, and that we may fairly judge from its known historic course what its pre-historic course may have been, is a theory clearly entitled to precedence as a fundamental principle of ethnographic research" (1871:I, 29).

The Principle of Continuity

Closely akin to the principle of the uniformity of nature was the principle of continuity. According to this principle, the present was an outgrowth of the past, so that the cultures of today were necessarily derived from the cultures of the past by a continuous process. In the history of culture there had been no interruptions or discontinuities. As John Stuart Mill expressed it, "the proximate cause of every state of society is the state of society immediately preceding it" (Mill 1846:575).

Tylor made this point repeatedly. In *Researches into the Early History of Mankind* he remarked, "the past is continually needed to explain the present" (Tylor 1870:2). And in *Anthropology* he wrote: "No stage of civilization comes into existence spontaneously, but grows or is developed out of the stage before it. This is the great principle which every scholar must lay firm hold of, if he intends to understand either the world he lives in or the history of the past" (Tylor 1916:20).

From Simplicity to Complexity

It is in the nature of things that simplicity precedes complexity. Nor was this merely a matter of logical necessity but of empirical fact: Paleontology and archaeology combined to show that, with few exceptions, what was earlier stratigraphically was also simpler structurally. Thus it was possible for the early evolutionists to hold firmly to the view that complex cultures had had simpler antecedents.

Herbert Spencer's exposition of the process of evolution had stressed the progression from simplicity to complexity, from homogeneity to heterogeneity. Other classical evolutionists, although not always using Spencerian terminology, generally concurred. Tylor, for example, wrote that "history, so far as it reaches back, shows arts, sciences, and political institutions beginning in ruder states, and becoming in the course of ages more intelligent, more systematic, more perfectly arranged or organized" (1871:I, 15). He also noted that "on the whole it appears that wherever there are found elaborate arts, abstruse knowledge, complex institutions, these are the results of gradual development from an earlier, simpler, and ruder state of life" (1871:I, 20).

E. B. Tylor

Morgan expressed the same view: "All the facts of human knowledge and experience," he wrote, "tend to show that the human race, as a whole, have steadily progressed from a lower to a higher condition" (Morgan 1964:58). And John F. McLennan observed that "the higher . . . in every case passed through the lower in becoming itself" (McLennan 1896:26).

The Objective Rating of Cultures

But how was the "higher" to be distinguished from the "lower"? The classical evolutionists believed this could be specified objectively. They held that for any two cultures it was possible to say which was the simpler and which the more complex. Although the use of the terms "higher" and "lower" in comparing cultures sometimes carried moral overtones, a factual distinction was nevertheless primarily intended. Thus Spencer wrote that it was by means of "structural traits" that one could "distinguish lower and higher types of societies from one another; and distinguish the earlier stages of each society from the later" (Spencer 1886:331).

And Tylor asserted in *Primitive Culture* that the "standard of reckoning progress and decline is not that of ideal good and evil, but of movement along a measured line from grade to grade of actual savagery, barbarism, and civilization" (Tylor 1871:I, 28). Elsewhere in the same work Tylor indicated how this could be done:

> The principal criteria of classification are the absence or presence, high or low development, of the industrial arts, especially metal-working, manufacture of implements and vessels, agriculture, architecture, &c., the extent of scientific knowledge, the definiteness of moral principles, the condition of religious belief and ceremony, the degree of social and political organization, and so forth. Thus, on the definite basis of compared facts, ethnographers are able to set up at least a rough scale of civilization. Few would dispute that the following races are arranged rightly in order of culture: Australians, Tahitians, Aztec, Chinese, Italian. (1871:I, 23–24)

The comparison of societies was thus not a matter of personal predilection but of objective fact. Moreover, if the appropriate criteria were specified carefully enough, such comparisons might attain a certain precision. And if individual societies could be rated objectively and precisely, then the entire course of cultural development, in its varying degrees, could be represented with at least fair accuracy.

These possibilities helped to foster a view of the nature of cultural evolution that was very different from the one that had prevailed just a few decades before. Let us look more closely at this new conception of evolution, suggesting its causes and indicating its consequences.

Evolution Not an Inherent Tendency

Robert A. Nisbet once argued that "immanence is the core attribute of the whole theory of [nineteenth-century] social evolution" (Nisbet 1969:170). In my opinion, this view is very wide of the mark. By the time most classical evolutionists began to write, the notion of cultural evolution (or in fact any evolution) as an unfolding of immanences was in full retreat. Gaining ascendancy over it was the view that evolution was, to a large extent, the response of an existing social system to external conditions. As Spencer put it: "Evolution is commonly conceived to imply in everything an *intrinsic* tendency to become something higher. This is an erroneous conception of it. In all cases it is determined by the co-operation of inner and outer factors" (Spencer 1890:93). And Tylor spoke of explaining social evolution "by the action of new conditions upon the previous stage whence it was derived" (Tylor 1878:123).

To be sure, traces of a belief in development as intrinsic can be found in the writings of some evolutionists. Thus, Auguste Comte asserted that "our Evolution can be nothing but the development of our nature" (Comte 1875:III, 5). And we have already noted that Morgan held to a view of evolution in which social institutions were latent in, and grew out of, "germs of thought." But this essentially metaphysical notion was a relic of the past, and was accompanied in Morgan's thought by a more modern and useful conception of evolution.

Why was the older idea of evolution losing ground? Basically, because it proved to be inadequate as an explanation. Assigning the motive power of evolution to something as inscrutable as a "germ" left the causes of the evolutionary process inaccessible to understanding. Darwin's explanation of organic evolution in terms of an objective, external process like natural selection had been enormously successful, and had brought remarkable order and comprehension into biology. It was to explanations of this type that the early anthropologists were powerfully drawn.

With the emphasis now shifted from internally driven metamorphoses to changes occurring through the interaction of societies with surrounding conditions, the great range and variety of cultures to be seen in the world became much more intelligible and explainable. Similar cultures were essentially similar responses to similar conditions. Dissimilar cultures occurred because the conditions of existence of societies throughout the world differed in certain respects.

This point was often stressed by nineteenth-century anthropologists in accounting for the regularities of evolution. Morgan, for example, noted that "human necessities in similar conditions have been substantially the same" (Morgan 1964:15). And Tylor invoked the "general likeness in the circumstances of life," although at the same time noting that hand in hand with it went a "general likeness in human nature" (Tylor 1871:I, 5).

The Psychic Unity of Man

This "general likeness in human nature" we need now examine. It is obvious that the occurrence of cultural parallels throughout the world implied not only a similarity of external conditions, but also an essential sameness in the psychological makeup of human beings. This was the famous doctrine of the "psychic unity of man."

Almost every classical evolutionist accepted this position. For instance, Theodor Waitz wrote: "we are irresistibly led to the conclusion that there are no specific differences among mankind with regard to their psychical life" (Waitz 1863:327). And Tylor held that "the mind of uncultured man works in much the same way at all times and everywhere" (Tylor 1870:90).

Morgan expressed this view more than once. Thus he spoke of "the uniformity of the operations of the human mind in similar conditions of society" (Morgan 1964:6), and said that "the operations of the mental principle have been uniform in virtue of the specific identity of the brain of all races of mankind" (1964:15). Again, he noted that "The human mind, specifically the same in all individuals in all the tribes and nations of mankind, and limited in the range of its powers, works and must work, in the same uniform channels, and within narrow limits of variation" (1964:220).

James Frazer stated that "the legitimacy of the Comparative Method rests on the well-ascertained similarity of the working of the human mind in all races of men" (Frazer 1913a:172).

The most effusive advocacy of the doctrine of psychic unity came from the pen of Daniel G. Brinton. To Brinton, the existence of independent cases of ethnographic parallels "prove[s] beyond cavil the ever-present constant in the problem, to wit, the one and unvarying psychical nature of man, guided by the same reason, swept by the same storms of passion and emotion, directed by the same will towards the same goals, availing itself of the same means when they are within reach, finding its pleasures in the same actions, lulling its fears with the same sedatives" (Brinton 1895:246).

Curiously enough, though, most nineteenth-century evolutionists, who at some point proclaimed the psychic unity of all races, at other times qualified this view, and sometimes even came close to contradicting it. These inconsistencies are very revealing, and we shall have occasion to examine them at a later point.

Differential Evolution

The classical evolutionists clearly recognized that since external conditions had sometimes fostered evolution and sometimes hindered it, human societies had evolved differentially. That is to say, societies had developed at different rates and to different degrees.

Sir Henry Maine, for example, noted in *Ancient Law* that "societies do not advance concurrently, but at different rates of progress" (Maine 1871:116). And John F. McLennan remarked that "the variety of forms of life—of domestic and civil institutions—is ascribable mainly to the unequal development of the different sections of mankind" (McLennan 1896:9). Again, Frazer observed that "Mankind . . . advances in *échelons;* that is, the columns march not abreast of each other but in a straggling line, all lagging in various degrees behind the leader" (Frazer 1913a:169).

Differential evolution was of supreme importance to evolutionary reconstructions. Had evolution *not* been differential—that is, had all societies
evolved to the very same level—then little or nothing about the *course* of
their development could be inferred by comparing them.

The classical evolutionists were quick to see that the great variety in cultural level existing among surviving peoples could be used to help ascertain
their course of development. McLennan wrote that "So unequally has the
species been developed, that almost every conceivable phase of progress may
be studied, as somewhere observed and recorded" (McLennan 1876:4–5).
And Morgan observed: "Mankind . . . must have become subdivided at a
very early period into individual nations. Unequal progress has been made
by their descendants from that day to the present" (Morgan 1871:479).

John Fiske, a follower of Herbert Spencer, put the matter succinctly and
drew the obvious conclusion: "There is a general path of social development along which, owing to special circumstances, some peoples have advanced a great way, some a less way, some but a very little way; . . . by studying existing savages and barbarians, we get a valuable clew to the
interpretation of prehistoric times" (Fiske 1891:586).

Frazer also saw the historical implications of differential evolution very
clearly: "As savage races are not all on the same plane, but have stopped or
tarried at different points of the upward path, we can to a certain extent, by
comparing them with each other, construct a scale of social progression and
mark out roughly some of the stages on the long road that leads from savagery to civilization" (Frazer 1913a:172).

Contemporary Primitives and Ancestral Cultures

Given the existence of this differential evolution, contemporary primitive
societies could be equated, generally and approximately, with earlier stages
in the development of modern complex cultures. This was the essence of
the comparative method. As Fiske wrote: "The point of the comparative
method, in whatever field it may be applied, is that it brings before us a
great number of objects so nearly alike that we are bound to assume for
them an origin and general history in common, while at the same time they
present such differences in detail as to suggest that some have advanced further than others in the direction in which all are traveling" (Fiske 1891:585).

McLennan, who was perhaps the most sanguine of the classical evolutionists in this regard, thought that the comparative method gave anthropologists "the means of historically tracing back the condition of man, by a
series of irresistible logical inferences from well-established facts" (McLennan 1896:18n.).

Frazer put the matter as follows: "Even in the comparatively short space of time, a few thousand years at most, which falls more or less within our ken, there are many deep and wide chasms which can only be bridged by hypotheses, if the story of evolution is to run continuously. Such bridges are built in anthropology as in biology by the Comparative Method, which enables us to borrow the links of one chain of evidence to supply the gaps in another" (Frazer 1913a:172).

Moreover, since existing societies exhibited many gradations in complexity, it was thought possible, by comparing a great many of them, to reconstruct the course of cultural evolution in rather fine detail. Tylor, for example, wrote that "the conditions of man at the lowest and highest known levels of culture are separated by a vast interval; but this interval is so nearly filled by known intermediate stages, that the line of continuity between the lowest savagery and the highest civilization is unbroken at any critical point" (Tylor 1910:116).

And McLennan observed that "if the phases of the progress—arising from inequality of development—which have been observed and recorded are sufficiently numerous; if they are interconnected; still more if they shade into one another by gentle gradations, then manifestly it may be possible by an induction of the facts and by careful reasoning to draw a clear outline of the whole course of human progress" (McLennan 1896:9–10).

This equation of contemporary primitive cultures with earlier stages of modern complex societies was thus a cardinal principle of the classical evolutionists. But it was also one of the tenets most sharply criticized by their successors and antagonists, the anti-evolutionists. Accordingly, it seems desirable to quote additional statements of this position, even at the risk of overdocumentation.

Perhaps we should first point out that the nineteenth-century evolutionists were not the first to posit this equation. It had been done at least as early as the previous century. Adam Ferguson, in speaking of the American Indians, had written that "in their present condition . . . we are to behold, as in a mirror, the features of our own progenitors" (Ferguson 1819:147).

Among the classical evolutionists, we find General Pitt-Rivers asserting in 1867 that "the existing races, in their respective stages of progression, may be taken as the bona fide representatives of the races of antiquity" (Pitt-Rivers 1906:53). And in 1870 Sir John Lubbock wrote: "The condition and habits of existing savages resemble in many ways, though not in all, those of our own ancestors in a period now long gone by" (Lubbock 1870:1).

Writing in *Primitive Culture*, Tylor said: "Savage life, carrying on into our own day the life of the Stone Age, may be legitimately claimed as representing remotely ancient conditions of mankind, intellectual and moral as well as material" (Tylor 1871:II, 324). It was for this reason, according to Tylor, that "the European may find among the Greenlanders or Maoris many a trait for reconstructing the picture of his own primitive ancestors" (Tylor 1871:I, 19).

This theme recurs in many of Tylor's writings. In *Anthropology*, for instance, he wrote that "to look at a savage of the Brazilian forests, a barbarous New Zealander or Dahom[e]an, and a civilized European, may be the student's best guide to understanding the progress of civilization" (Tylor 1916:25). And he argued that "finding various stages of an art among the lower races, we may arrange these stages in a series probably representing their actual sequence in history" (Tylor 1871:I, 57).

On this issue Morgan stated that "the history and experience of the American tribes represent, more or less nearly, the history and experience of our own remote ancestors when in corresponding conditions" (Morgan 1964:7; see also p. 22). Indeed, it seemed to Morgan that the evidence provided by surviving primitive peoples was so vital in this regard that "if men in savagery had not been left behind, in isolated portions of the earth, to testify concerning early conditions of mankind in general, it would have been impossible to form any definite conception of what it must have been" (1964:57).

Frazer once again concurred, writing: "Modern researches into the early history of man, conducted on different lines, have converged with almost irresistible force on the conclusion, that all civilized races have at some period or other emerged from a state of savagery resembling more or less closely the state in which many backward races have continued to the present time" (Frazer 1918:I, vii). For this reason, Frazer thought it justified to say of the modern savage:

> an examination of his customs and beliefs . . . supplies the same sort of evidence of the evolution of the human mind that an examination of the embryo supplies of the evolution of the human body. . . . so a study of savage society at various stages of evolution enables us to follow approximately, though of course not exactly, the road which the ancestors of the higher races must have traveled in their progress upward through barbarism to civilization. In short, savagery is the primitive condition of mankind, and if we would understand what primitive man was we must know what the savage now is. (Frazer 1913a:162–163)

Despite a general agreement that valid evolutionary inferences could be drawn by comparing surviving primitives, there was also an awareness that the method had certain limitations. This qualification was probably best expressed by Herbert Spencer:

If societies were all of the same species and differed only in their stages of growth and structure, comparisons would disclose clearly the course of evolution; but unlikenesses of type among them, here great and there small, obscure the results of such comparisons. . . . we may infer that out of the complex and confused evidence, only the larger truths will emerge with clearness. While anticipating that certain general conclusions are to be positively established, we may anticipate that more special ones can be alleged only as probable. (Spencer 1899:242, 243)

Modern Primitives Not Primeval

While the classical evolutionists were thus clearly convinced that surviving savage tribes could be equated with an earlier stage in the evolution of modern civil society, they did not believe that contemporary savages represented the earliest and simplest level of culture ever known. In fact, almost to a man, they denied this explicitly.

Spencer wrote that "there are reasons for suspecting that men of the lowest types now known, forming social groups of the simplest kinds, do not exemplify men as they originally were" (Spencer 1890:93). Speaking of the Lower Status of Savagery, the lowest of his seven stages of cultural development, Morgan said: "No exemplification of tribes of mankind in this condition remained to the historical period" (Morgan 1964:16). He later noted that to reach "this earliest representative of the species, we must descend very far below the lowest savage now living upon the earth" (1964:422–423).

Tylor expressed the same belief. In *Researches into the Early History of Mankind* he wrote that "it does not seem likely that any tribe known to modern observers should be anything like a fair representative of primary conditions" (Tylor 1870:378). And later he remarked that "the least cultured savages have themselves advanced far beyond the lowest intellectual and moral state at which human tribes can be conceived as capable of existing" (Tylor 1910:116).

McLennan held the same view: "A *really* primitive people in fact exists nowhere. For many thousands of years now, the various races of men have been in the school of experience, all making progress therein" (McLennan 1876:52).

Frazer specifically warned of the misconception involved in equating contemporary savages with primal man: "The savages of to-day are primitive in a relative, not in an absolute sense. They are primitive by comparison with us; but they are not primitive by comparison with truly primaeval man, that is, with man as he was when he first emerged from the purely bestial stage of existence. Indeed, compared with man in his absolutely pristine state even the lowest savage of to-day is doubtless a highly developed and cultured being" (Frazer 1913a:163). (See also Bagehot 1868:452, and Ratzel 1896:22.)

Primal Human Society

The early evolutionists were not always ready to speculate about the nature of primal human society, which, they all agreed, surviving savages did not represent. Maine, for example, wrote that "I have never myself imagined that any amount of evidence of law or usage, written or observed, would by itself solve the problems which cluster round the beginnings of human society. 'The imperfection of the geological record' is a mere trifle to the imperfection of the archaeological record" (Maine 1883:205–206). It had not been his objective in writing *Ancient Law,* Maine said, "to determine the absolute origin of human society." Indeed, he added, "I must confess a certain distaste for inquiries which, when I have attempted to push them far, have always landed me in mudbanks and fog" (1883:192).

Tylor generally preferred not to conjecture about primordial human society. Even in his famous essay "On a Method of Investigating the Development of Institutions," in which he attacked the problem of the supposed priority of matriliny over patriliny, Tylor made it clear that his solution to this problem still did not penetrate back to the earliest social conditions of mankind. On this question he wrote:

> Thus the present method confirms on an enlarged and firm basis the inference as to the antiquity of the maternal system arrived at by the pioneers of the investigation, Bachofen and McLennan, and supported by the later research of a generation of able investigators. . . . By this it is not, however, meant to imply that the maternal form of family as here set forth represents the primitive condition of mankind. . . . It seems probable that this maternal system arose out of an earlier and less organised and regulated condition of human life. (Tylor 1889:256–257)

Frazer made it clear that he too disliked conjectures about primal social conditions: "To construct a history of human society by starting from absolutely primordial man and working down through thousands or millions of years to the institutions of existing savages might possibly have merits as a flight of imagination, but it could have none as a work of science. . . . About the social condition of primaeval man . . . we know absolutely nothing, and it is vain to speculate" (Frazer 1913a:164, 165).

To be sure, some anthropologists—notably Morgan and McLennan—were quite ready to speculate about the earliest form of human society, especially with regard to marriage and the family. But, contrary to the general supposition, such speculations were by no means universal among the classical evolutionists.

Survivals

As an adjunct to the use of the comparative method in reconstructing cultural evolution, several nineteenth-century anthropologists employed the concept of "survivals." Although most closely associated with the work of Tylor, this notion was not original with him. Shortly before Tylor's discussion of it, Sir John Lubbock had written, regarding the customs of contemporary primitive peoples, that "they illustrate much of what is passing among ourselves, many customs which have evidently no relation to present circumstances, and even some ideas which are rooted in our minds, as fossils are imbedded in the soil" (Lubbock 1870:1).

However, it was Tylor who coined the term "survival," and who gave the concept its clearest formulation. Survivals, he said, "are processes, customs, opinions, and so forth, which have been carried on by force of habit into a new state of society different from that in which they had their original home, and they thus remain as proofs and examples of an older condition of culture out of which a newer has been evolved" (Tylor 1871:I, 14–15).

Tylor believed that the existence of survivals placed "all along the course of advancing civilization way-marks full of meaning to those who can decipher their signs" (1871:I, 19). And he argued that for this decipherment a knowledge of contemporary primitive societies was of inestimable value. Since "savage and barbarous tribes often more or less fairly represent stages of culture through which our own ancestors passed long ago," he wrote, "their customs and laws often explain to us, in ways we should otherwise have hardly guessed, the sense and reason of our own" (Tylor 1916:401).

McLennan also made much of the concept of survivals. He remarked that "we are able to trace everywhere, frequently under striking guise, in the higher layers of civilisation, the rude modes of life with which the examination of the lower makes us familiar, and are thus made sure of the one being a growth from the other" (McLennan 1896:21). Like Tylor, he noted that a study of primitive cultures helped to make sense out of what otherwise would seem obscure practices in advanced societies. Thus he wrote that "it is not too much to say that there is no phase even of our modern civilised life but has some features which, when pointed out, will appear puzzling and strange to one ignorant of primitive facts, but which becomes suddenly significant when these facts are explained" (1896:19–20).

The evolutionist who extracted most from survivals, however, was Frazer. He noted that "long after the majority of men in a community have ceased to think and act like savages, not a few traces of the older ruder modes of life and thought survive in the habits and institutions of the people" (Frazer 1918:I, vii). And it was precisely instances of this sort that Frazer sought out and built upon in his study *Folk-lore in the Old Testament*. In this work he noted that "many references to beliefs and practices [in Biblical times] . . . can hardly be explained except on the supposition that they are rudimentary survivals from a far lower level of culture. . . . such relics of ruder times . . . are preserved like fossils in the Old Testament" (1918:I, vii).

The concept of survivals was also implicit in Morgan's work on the evolution of kinship. As Idus Murphree pointed out, "Morgan found that kinship terminologies grew out of systems of marriage and that long after the disappearance of the familial relations underlying them, obsolescent ways of naming kin held on, leaving a record of social conditions which no longer existed" (Murphree 1961:287).

3

The Characteristics of
Cultural Evolution

Let us now consider what the classical evolutionists had to say about various aspects of the process of cultural development. The characteristic that most impressed them was probably its overall regularity. Thus Tylor asserted that "the institutions of man . . . succeed each other in series substantially uniform over the globe" (Tylor 1889:269). And Sir John Lubbock, in almost the same words, said that "the institutions of man develop with considerable uniformity all over the globe" (Lubbock 1911:vi). Morgan likewise affirmed that "the experience of mankind has run in nearly uniform channels" (Morgan 1964:15).

Rectilinearity

Impressed as they were by cultural advance, the early evolutionists were by no means unaware of retrogression. Hence, in no sense can their evolutionism be described as rectilinear, that is, onward and upward in an unvaryingly straight line.

Herbert Spencer wrote in *Principles of Sociology* that "while the current degradation theory is untenable, the theory of progression, in its ordinary form, seems to me untenable also. . . . It is possible, and, I believe, probable, that retrogression has been as frequent as progression" (Spencer 1890:93). And in a later volume of the same work Spencer said: "There is no uniform ascent from lower to higher" (Spencer 1897:609; see also 1890:93–96).

Tylor expressed a similar opinion. In *Anthropology* he wrote: "It does not follow . . . that civilization is always on the move, or that its movement is always progress. On the contrary, history teaches that it remains

27

stationary for long periods, and often falls back" (Tylor 1916:18). In *Researches* he said, "We know by what has taken place within the range of history, that Decline as well as Progress in art and knowledge really goes on in the world" (Tylor 1870:183). And in *Primitive Culture* he noted that "culture gained by progression may be lost by degradation" (Tylor 1871:I, 34).

Yet, even admitting this, the conclusion was still inescapable that evolution had predominated over regression. As Tylor declared, "the history of the lower races, as of the higher, is not the history of a course of degeneration, or even of equal oscillations to and fro, but of a movement which, in spite of frequent stops and relapses, has on the whole been forward" (Tylor 1870:193). In *Primitive Culture* he again observed that "so far as history is to be our criterion, progression is primary and degradation is secondary; culture must be gained before it can be lost" (Tylor 1871:I, 34).

The predominance of evolution over regression was something nineteenth-century anthropologists thought necessary to affirm very forcefully, especially in their earlier writings. This was done in order to combat the still-current view that there had been a general cultural decline from an initial golden age of higher culture.

By the late 1870s, though, the degradation theory was virtually defunct. As Morgan wrote in *Ancient Society*, "The theory of human degradation to explain the existence of savages and of barbarians is no longer tenable. It came in as a corollary from the Mosaic cosmogony, and was acquiesced in from a supposed necessity which no longer exists. As a theory, it is not only incapable of explaining the existence of savages, but is without support in the facts of human experience" (Morgan 1964:14; see also p. 427).

Unilinearity

An assertion frequently made about nineteenth-century anthropologists is that they believed evolution to be unilinear. John Gillin, for example, has said that "in its classical form, the evolutionary theory held that *all* cultures inevitably must pass through the *same* stages of development" (Gillin 1948:600). And statements as categorical as this recur in the writings of many modern anthropologists (e.g., Steward 1953a:324, Linton 1936b:314; see also Boas 1930:102, and Goldenweiser 1922:21). Indeed, even in their own day the early evolutionists occasionally had this accusation leveled at them. Speaking specifically of Morgan and McLennan, Sir Henry Maine once wrote: "Both writers seem to me to hold that human society went everywhere through the same series of changes" (Maine 1883:201). Let us see how these allegations square with the facts.

Considerable evidence exists on this point in the form of explicit statements by the principals involved. And the net weight of this evidence is that the classical evolutionists, although they often chose to stress the regularity of cultural development, nevertheless did not believe that every society had to evolve through the very same series of stages. Their evolution was thus no more unilinear than it was rectilinear.

Let us begin with Maine himself, whose hands should be clean on this score. We find him saying: "So far as I am aware, there is nothing in the recorded history of society to justify the belief that, during that vast chapter of its growth which is wholly unwritten, the same transformations of social constitution succeeded one another everywhere, uniformly if not simultaneously" (1883:218–219).

The same view was expressed by other evolutionists as well. Spencer specifically denied that cultural evolution could best be represented as a unilinear development, saying: "Like other kinds of progress, social progress is not linear but divergent and re-divergent. Each differentiated product gives origin to a new set of differentiated products" (Spencer 1897:331). And Tylor maintained that "the state of things which is found is not indeed that one race does or knows exactly what another race does or knows, but that similar stages of development recur in different times and places" (Tylor 1870:371).

After presenting his theory of the origin of divine kingship, Frazer introduced a note of caution: "I am far from affirming," he wrote, "that the course of development has everywhere rigidly followed these lines: it has doubtless varied greatly in different societies: I merely mean to indicate in the broadest outline what I conceive to have been its general trend" (Frazer 1905:151).

McLennan was one of the two writers cited by Maine as a unilinear evolutionist. And it is true that he did make such statements as "the history of human society is that of a development following closely one general law" (McLennan 1896:9), and again, "all the races of men have had, to speak broadly, a development from savagery of the same general character" (McLennan 1876:407). But it is clear that McLennan is referring to preponderances that allow of exceptions, not to ironclad necessities. Indeed, here and there in his writings he specifically qualifies his statements to indicate that he did not believe in a perfectly inflexible development, common to all peoples.

Thus, prior to a discussion of his theory of the primacy of sexual promiscuity and of the tracing of kinship through females, he warns us that this is "not to assume that the progress of the various races of men from savagery has been a uniform process, that all the stages which any of them has gone through have been passed in their order by all" (1876:127–128). Once again, a few pages later, in connection with his argument that early human society, affected by similar influences, moved "toward one uniform type in all its parts" (1876:132), McLennan nevertheless tells us that he holds this view "without supposing the course of human events to have been uniform" (1876:131).

Finally, let us look at Morgan, the other evolutionist accused of unilinearity by Maine. Referring to the traits he used to mark the beginning of his cultural stages—traits such as the use of stone implements, pottery, the bow and arrow, fire, iron smelting, and the like—Morgan says: "It is difficult, if not impossible, to find such tests of progress to mark the commencement of these several periods as will be found absolute in their application, and without exceptions upon all the continents. Neither is it necessary, for the purpose in hand, that exceptions should not exist" (Morgan 1964:16).

In view of this evidence how is it possible that the nineteenth-century evolutionists have been indicted—not to say convicted—of being unilinearists? The harshest answer, and probably the truest, is that those making the charge simply never bothered to read their works. Or if they looked at them at all, it was at best a hasty perusal. Naturally, the early evolutionists were not about to qualify every statement of an evolutionary regularity by saying that it did not *have* to apply to all peoples and at all times. But, as we have seen, they readily acknowledged the occurrence of exceptions. Thus, if there is to be a conviction in this case, it should be for perjury, and the verdict should not be entered against the evolutionists, but against their adversaries.

Before leaving the subject of unilinearity, however, it is necessary to point out that, in a very restricted and specific way, some classical evolutionists *did* propose unilinear sequences. When Morgan wrote, "It can now be asserted upon convincing evidence that savagery preceded barbarism in all tribes of mankind, as barbarism is known to have preceded civilization" (1964:5), he was making a unilinear assertion of a certain sort. Moreover, the assertion was entirely correct, and has never been refuted by Boas, Lowie, Radin, or any other anti-evolutionist. In order to refute this statement, at least one case would have to be adduced of a society having evolved directly from Savagery to Civilization, without passing through the intermediate stage of Barbarism. And this has never been done because no such exception has been found.

A closely related sequence of stages was proposed by Herbert Spencer in discussing political evolution. He saw the process as one involving the successive compounding of social units. Thus in the course of evolution human societies could be distinguished, he said, as having passed through the stages of Simple, Compound, Doubly Compound, and Trebly Compound societies, corresponding roughly to what we now call autonomous villages, chiefdoms, states, and empires.

About the process of compounding Spencer wrote: "We have seen that social evolution begins with small simple aggregates, that it progresses by the clustering of these into larger aggregates, and that after being consolidated, such clusters are united with others like themselves into still larger aggregates" (Spencer 1967:48). And then he added these important words: "The stages of compounding and re-compounding have to be passed through in succession. No tribe becomes a nation by simple growth, and no great society is formed by the direct union of the smallest societies" (Spencer 1967:52).

The issue involved here, to put it very simply, is the difference between saying that a society at Stage A *must evolve into* Stage B, and saying that a society at Stage B *must have passed through* Stage A. The first proposition is incorrect; the second is true without exception.

The Skipping of Stages

When dealing with sequences other than the ones just cited, the classical evolutionists clearly recognized the possibility of variation from culture to culture. Tylor, for instance, saw that in the general sequence "Stone Age > Bronze Age > Iron Age," it was possible for some societies to skip a stage. Thus he wrote that "Most of Africa . . . seems to have had no Bronze Age, but to have passed directly from the Stone Age to the Iron Age" (Tylor 1916:280). And he also said that "in . . . districts, such as Polynesia and Central and South Africa, and America (except for Mexico and Peru), the native tribes were moved directly from the Stone to the Iron Age without passing through the Bronze Age at all" (Tylor 1910:118).

Well into the nineteenth century it was still widely believed that a pastoral stage had generally preceded an agricultural stage. Morgan, for instance, characterized Old World societies in the Middle Status of Barbarism as having "domestic animals yielding them a meat and milk subsistence, but probably without horticultural and without farinaceous food" (Morgan 1964:452). And Tylor seems to have believed that, by and large, pastoralism antedated agriculture (Tylor 1916:219–220).

Yet it cannot be affirmed that the classical evolutionists saw this as a universal sequence. They were too well aware of world ethnography for that. Thus Spencer noted that the "keeping of animals has not everywhere preceded agriculture. In the West, considerable civilizations arose which gave no sign of having had a pastoral origin. Ancient Mexicans and Central

Americans carried on crop-raising without the aid of animals of draught; and lacking horses, cattle, and sheep as they did, there was no stock-farming. . . . Of course a like industrial history is to be recognized among the South Sea Islanders" (Spencer 1897:332–333).

The Law of Evolutionary Potential

Spencer also pointed to a phenomenon akin to the skipping of stages, namely, the leapfrogging of one culture over another during the process of evolution. He suggested that a society with a simpler organization might be in a better position to take the next evolutionary step than one whose organization, while more advanced, was at the same time more nearly fixed and therefore less able to change. He expressed this view in several ways: "Though structure up to a certain point is requisite for growth, structure beyond that point impedes growth" (Spencer 1886:64), and "Re-adjustments become difficult in proportion as adjustments are made complete" (1886:65), and again, "The multiplying and elaborating of institutions, and the perfecting of arrangements for gaining immediate ends, raise impediments to the development of better institutions" (1886:65).

Among the several examples Spencer offered of this process was the development of railway carriages. Noting that American carriages were more efficiently designed than those used in England, he attributed this to the fact that in England, where railroads began, railway carriages had been slavishly modeled after stagecoaches, whereas in America, where railroads came in later, the disadvantages of the English practice could be seen, and railway carriages were designed, from the beginning, according to functional criteria rather than in imitation of an existing conveyance (1886:66–69).

It will be recognized that we have here a clear adumbration of Elman R. Service's "Law of Evolutionary Potential" (1960). Service tells us that in formulating this principle he had been anticipated by Thorstein Veblen and Leon Trotsky. Veblen had spoken of "the merits of borrowing" and "the penalty of taking the lead," while Trotsky had referred to "the privilege of historic backwardness" (Service 1960:99). In Spencer, then, we have a third, and even earlier anticipation of Service's law.

Rates of Evolution

Leaving aside the details of how the process occurred, what did the classical evolutionists have to say about the rate at which culture had evolved? On this score there was virtual unanimity: Cultural advance had become progressively faster. Tylor found man's progress "infinitely slow in the beginning, and increasing by degrees with redoubled velocity" (Tylor 1871:I, 30). Pitt-Rivers remarked that "progress moves on in accelerating ratio . . . the earlier processes take longer than the later ones" (Pitt-Rivers 1906:33). The same view was implied by Maine when he described "the fewness of ideas and the slowness of additions to the mental stock as among the most general characteristics of mankind in its infancy" (Maine 1880:225).

Morgan put the matter as follows: "The first inventions and the first social organizations were doubtless the hardest to achieve, and were consequently separated from each other by the longest intervals of time. . . . In this law of progress, which works in a geometrical ratio, a sufficient explanation is found of the prolonged duration of the period of savagery. . . . Human progress, from first to last, has been in a ratio not rigorously but essentially geometrical" (Morgan 1964:39).

Spencer also looked at cultural acceleration mathematically. In *First Principles* he wrote: "From the beginning . . . complication had advanced at an increasing rate" (Spencer 1896:452), and added later, "A part-cause of Evolution is the multiplication of effects; and . . . this increases in geometrical progression as the heterogeneity becomes greater" (1896:470).

But Spencer saw this acceleration not only in terms of the forces that generated change, but also in the factors that opposed it: "While the power of the evolving influences augments in a duplicate ratio," he wrote, "the power of the opposing influences diminishes in a duplicate ratio; and hence the fact that at the outset it took a thousand years to achieve a degree of improvement which is now achieved in one year" (1897:327–328).

Finally, Daniel G. Brinton, who spoke of "very slow movements in earlier times and lower conditions, [and] singularly rapid advances in later high conditions," went on to suggest that, roughly speaking, "three different rates of evolution had characterized human societies: arithmetic progression during savagery, geometric progression during Barbarism, and saltatory progression during civilization" (Brinton 1902:78).

Diffusion and Evolution

The belief is commonly held that the classical evolutionists "explained everything by independent invention." W. H. R. Rivers, for example, said of them that "where similarities are found in different parts of the world it is assumed, almost as an axiom, that they are due to independent origin and development" (Rivers 1911:490). This view, however, is a distortion of the facts. Let us examine the evidence.

Rarely did an early evolutionist state that in cases of cultural similarity the presumption was in favor of independent invention. In fact, to find such a statement at all, one must descend to the second echelon of classical evolutionism. The German ethnologist Adolf Bastian was probably the one most inclined to this view. Bastian objected to the ready use of diffusion in explaining instances where a "similarity of ideas was discovered" among primitive peoples. Instead, he felt that, "according to the psychological axioms of ethnography and the methods of comparative etymology, the explanation should be first sought in the most general and elementary laws," rather than by borrowing (Bastian 1881:90–91, quoted in Gumplowicz 1899:46).

Somewhat more tempered were the remarks of the Dutch ethnologist S. R. Steinmetz. According to Steinmetz, "the concordance of two peoples in a custom, etc., should be explained by borrowing or by derivation from a common source only when there are special, known and controlling reasons indicating this; and when these are absent, the explanation should be either because the two peoples are on the same plane of culture, or because their surroundings are similar" (quoted in Brinton 1895:247).

Brinton, who quoted Steinmetz's remarks approvingly, can be put in the same camp, while Sir John Lubbock at times also showed a predisposition toward theories of independent invention (e.g., Lubbock 1913:549).

The majority of classical evolutionists, however, and certainly the leading figures among them, had no such bias. Indeed, they frequently alluded to the great importance of diffusion and invoked it repeatedly to explain separated occurrences of the same trait. Again, let us look at the record.

In *Systems of Consanguinity and Affinity*, Morgan wrote that "amongst contiguous nations there would be a free propagation of arts and inventions, which would tend to the general advancement of society throughout the entire area in which these influences were felt. Nations are apt to share in the more important elements of each other's progress" (Morgan 1871:448). The same view was repeated in *Ancient Society*, where Morgan said: "Wherever a continental connection existed, all the tribes must have shared in some measure in each other's progress. All great inventions and discoveries propagate themselves" (Morgan 1964:40). In fact, Morgan went so far as to argue that "original ideas, absolutely independent of previous knowledge and experience, are necessarily few in number. Were it possible to reduce the sum of human ideas to underived originals, the small numerical result would be startling" (1964:58).

Morgan even leaned toward diffusion rather than independent invention to account for the widespread occurrence of clans: "Whether the gens originates spontaneously in a given condition of society, and would thus repeat itself in disconnected areas; or whether it had a single origin, and was propagated from an original center, through successive migrations, over the earth's surface, are fair questions for speculative consideration. The latter hypothesis, with a simple modification, seems to be the better one" (1964:320). We thus encounter the striking anomaly of Morgan turning out to be more of a diffusionist than Lowie, for Lowie was to write of the clan: "The classification of relatives characteristic of the sib is a very natural one under certain conditions, so that the improbability of parallel and independent sib formation does not hold" (Lowie 1920:122).

Morgan was also well aware of how diffusion could enhance the cultural inventory of particular peoples. Noting, for instance, that the ancient Britons were familiar with the use of iron, he wrote that "the vicinity of more advanced continental tribes had advanced arts of life among them far beyond the state of development of their domestic institutions" (Morgan 1964:17).

A similar recognition of the role of diffusion can be found in the writings of other early evolutionists. For example, Frazer, after asserting his belief in the psychic unity of man, nevertheless warned that "we must always be on our guard against tracing to it a multitude of particular resemblances which may be and often are due to simple diffusion, since nothing is more certain than that the various races of men have borrowed from each other many of their arts and crafts, their ideas, customs, and institutions" (Frazer 1913b:I, vi–vii).

Of all the classical evolutionists, though, none paid more heed to the workings of diffusion than Tylor. Tylor's statement in *Primitive Culture* that "civilization is a plant much oftener propagated than developed" (Tylor 1871:I, 48) is frequently quoted. Even earlier, in *Researches into the Early History of Mankind,* Tylor had written: "On the whole, it does not seem to be an unreasonable, or even an over-sanguine view, that the mass of analogies in Art and Knowledge, Mythology and Custom, confused and indistinct as they at present are, may already be taken to indicate that the civilizations of many races . . . have really grown up under one another's influence, or derived common material from a common source" (Tylor 1870:377).

Tylor had occasion to note that in accounting for cultural similarities between separate areas or peoples, "three ways are open, independent invention, inheritance from ancestors in a distant region, [and] transmission from one race to another; but between these three ways the choice is commonly a difficult one" (1870:374).

In making this choice in any given instance, Tylor did not always incline toward independent invention. For example, he was more than open-minded about the possibility of trans-Pacific diffusion. In *Anahuac,* his first book, Tylor already favored a historic connection between Asia and Mexico (Tylor 1861:244). Some years later, in his article "On the Game of Patolli in Ancient Mexico and Its Probably Asiatic Origin," he concluded that because of detailed similarities between *patolli* and *pachisi,* the presence of the former in Mexico "seems to prove that it had made its way across from Asia. How it came is uncertain, though the drifting across of Asiatic vessels to California offers the readiest solution. At any rate, it may be reckoned among elements of Asiatic culture traceable in the old Mexican civilization, the high development of which in metal work, architecture, astronomy, political and religious institutions, etc., seems to be in large measure due to Asiatic influence" (Tylor 1879:128).

Tylor concluded this article with the following words: "Now if any item of culture, even a matter so trifling as a game, can be distinctly made out to have passed over from Asia and established itself among the rude tribes of North America, this opens a way by which various features of their culture may be fairly accounted for as due to Asiatic influence" (1879:128).

The fact is that Tylor, at least during his earlier years, actually *preferred* diffusional explanations to those that invoked independent invention. In *Researches into the Early History of Mankind*, for instance, in contrasting explanations of cultural similarities based on independent invention with those based on diffusion, Tylor says: "In the one case it has no historical value whatever, while in the other it has this value in a high degree" (Tylor 1870:5). And speaking of independent invention later in the same volume, Tylor remarked: "The more difficult it is to account for observed facts in this way, and the more necessary it becomes to have recourse to theories of [cultural] inheritance or transmission to explain them, the greater is their value in the eyes of the Ethnologist" (1870:374). There is no question that these were the words of a dedicated historicist, not of a rabid evolutionist.

As I argued earlier, it is a matter of record—although generally unperceived by anthropologists—that during the first three decades of his career Tylor was strongly historical in his outlook and the tenor of his work. Only with the publication of "On a Method" in 1889 do we find his approach changing from a historical-particularistic one to a functional-developmental one.

As far as I know, Tylor never explicitly recanted his earlier preference for history and his leanings toward diffusion. Nonetheless, such a change can be inferred from occasional passages in his later writings. For example, in revising his article "Anthropology," for the eleventh edition of the *Encyclopaedia Britannica* (1910), Tylor inserted a passage not found in the version of that article that had appeared in the ninth edition (1878). In the later version Tylor wrote: "Anthropological researches undertaken all over the globe have shown the necessity of abandoning the old theory that a similarity of customs and superstitions, of arts and crafts, justifies the assumption of a remote relationship, if not an identity of origin, between races" (Tylor 1910:119). And he added: "American man, for example, need not necessarily owe the minutest portion of his mental, religious, social or industrial development to remote contact with Asia or Europe, though he were proved to possess identical usages" (1910:119).

This was certainly a very different Tylor from the one who in 1879 was ready to accept an Asiatic origin, not only for *patolli*, but for "the high development . . . in metal work, architecture, astronomy, political and religious institutions" of ancient Mexico as well.

We can say, I think, that in his later years Tylor came more into the mainstream of classical evolutionism as far as this issue was concerned. He did not deny the occurrence of diffusion, to be sure, but he played down its role in the growth of the world's cultures. He became less concerned with tracing the distribution and diffusion of individual traits, and more interested in determining the factors that led to their origin and development. Tylor was therefore coming closer to the general position of the classical evolutionists on the question of origins, a position well summarized by Edward Westermarck as follows: "It is not a sufficient explanation of a custom to say that it has been derived from ancestors or borrowed from neighbours. This only raises the question of how it originated among those who first practiced it; for a custom must have had a beginning. It is with questions of this sort that the evolutionary school of sociologists have pre-eminently occupied themselves" (Westermarck 1921:I, 6–7).

It was, then, the evolution of cultural elements in general, rather than how individual peoples had obtained particular traits, that chiefly interested the classical evolutionists. Of course when the problem at hand was how certain societies had come by certain traits, then they were prepared to invoke diffusion when it seemed the more likely explanation. But by and large the early evolutionists did not pursue the history of ethnographic details as an end in itself. It was only a means to an end, and that end was the reconstruction of cultural development as a general process.

4

The Determinants of
Cultural Evolution

We have seen how nineteenth-century anthropologists proposed to reconstruct cultural evolution. We have also noted some of their observations with respect to its general course. Next we need to consider their ideas regarding the determinants of this evolution.

Explicit and consistent theories of cultural determination are not to be found among the writings of classical evolutionists. However, a variety of causal explanations are encountered in their work. The earlier writers indeed tended to emphasize the intricacy of causation in culture, thereby virtually denying the possibility of anything like a unitary theory. John Stuart Mill, for example, said that "the circumstances . . . which influence the condition and progress of society are innumerable, and perpetually changing; and though they all change in obedience to causes, and therefore to laws, the multitude of the causes is so great as to defy our limited powers of calculation" (Mill 1846:549). At one point in his *Introduction to Anthropology* Theodor Waitz stated that "it would be difficult or impossible to give a sketch of the progressive development of society in various directions, influenced as it is by so many and various causes" (Waitz 1863:361).

So impressed was Sir Henry Maine with the complexity of causation in cultural development that he remarked: "The difference between the stationary and progressive societies is . . . one of the great secrets which inquiry has yet to penetrate" (Maine 1871:22). And he seemed to have retained this attitude, for twenty years later we find him saying: "No universal theory, attempting to account for all social forms by supposing an evolution from within, can possibly be true" (Maine 1883:285).

Charles Darwin also was perplexed by cultural causation. Thus he wrote in *The Descent of Man:* "The problem . . . of the first advance of savages toward civilization is at present much too difficult to be solved" (Darwin 1871:I, 167).

Sometimes the views expressed about cultural determination were actually contradictory. We find, for example, Lester F. Ward saying on one page that "the machine is only the material embodiment of intellectual conceptions, and it is these that lie at the foundation of all material progress" (Ward 1885:124), and on the very next page asserting that "the true interpreters of human history now understand that it is to material progress, i.e., to science and [technical] art, that what moral progress has actually taken place is indirectly due" (1885:125).

In addition to obvious inconsistencies, we also find changes in attitude and interpretation occurring among certain scholars over the course of a lifetime. In a later section we shall examine such a change in the views of Herbert Spencer.

Inherent versus External Determinants

We can distinguish two broad types of theories of cultural determination, *inherent* and *external.* Theories of inherent causation, as here understood, portray culture as evolving through the operation of forces intrinsic in human beings themselves. Such theories tended to stress the factors of race, psychology, ideas, individuals, great men, geniuses, and the like. The other type of theories, which emphasized the role of factors external to the human organism, looked toward environment, subsistence, technology, economics, warfare, and the like in seeking the principal determinants of culture.

The notion that cultural evolution was the working out of forces residing within the human psyche has a long pedigree in the history of metaphysics. The high-water mark of this view occurred in the eighteenth century, when the French Enlightenment saw cultural advances as being reflections of the Progress of the Human Mind. Theories of this sort, though, continued to be expressed well into the nineteenth. We find Auguste Comte, for example, speaking of an "inherent tendency toward change in the Order of nature" (Comte 1875:II, 36), and referring to an "instinct of progress," an "instinct of political improvement," and so on (1875:I, 51–58).

Even later and more sophisticated writers, such as Tylor, occasionally lapsed into this manner of expression. As late as 1910 Tylor wrote that "it is now certain that there has ever been an inherent tendency in man, allowing for differences of climate and material surroundings, to develop culture by the same stages and in the same way" (Tylor 1910:119).

By the mid-nineteenth century, though, the notion of evolution as internally generated was on the wane. In biology, Charles Darwin spoke out against it. Thus, when dealing with the views of the Catholic zoologist St. George Mivart, Darwin wrote: "Mr. Mivart believes that species change through 'an internal force or tendency,' about which it is not pretended that anything is known. That species have a capacity for change will be admitted by all evolutionists; but there is no need, as it seems to me, to invoke any internal force beyond the tendency to ordinary variability" (Darwin 1872:201).

In anthropology, the belief that cultural evolution was due to an intrinsic proclivity in human beings was also being challenged. Theodor Waitz, for example, argued in his *Introduction to Anthropology* that "people which have never been under the necessity of abandoning a nomadic life, who possess no beasts of burden, should not be reproached with an incapacity for civilization, as the assumption of an innate impulse for culture and labour, without being driven to it by necessity, is a mere fiction" (Waitz 1863:356).

Later in the same work Waitz restated this view even more forcefully:

In the primitive man there is no tendency to progress. The modern idealistic doctrine of the necessary development of the human mind out of itself, is a fiction, which may flatter man's vanity, but which is contradicted by actual facts. There can be no doubt that it is man's thought which produces and preserves civilization; this thought, however, does not originate by itself, nor does it move by itself, nor is it the function of *one* mind, but is the combined activity of all individuals living together, produced by surrounding media, and nourished and matured by the historical events which befall them. (1863:380)

Herbert Spencer was equally forthright in rejecting the idea of evolution as the expression of an inherent tendency. In *First Principles* he wrote, "Evolution is not necessary, but depends on conditions" (Spencer 1896:588), and in *Principles of Sociology* he said that "Evolution does not imply a latent tendency to improve, everywhere in operation" (Spencer 1897:609).

But though the principle of internal causation was falling out of favor in nineteenth-century anthropology, we cannot disregard it altogether. In one guise or another it appeared in the writings of many classical evolutionists. Thus, before proceeding to discuss theories of external causation, we need to consider those in which the causes of cultural development were thought to come from within man himself.

Psychic Unity as an Active Agent

The psychic unity of man, though not always thought of as a dynamic factor, was sometimes employed as "an active spontaneous principle," as Kroeber (1935:564) once put it. That is to say, psychic unity was occasionally deemed the prime mover in accounting for parallel evolution among cultures.

The theorist with whom this use of psychic unity was most closely associated was Adolf Bastian. Bastian saw certain elementary ideas—*Elementargedanken,* as he called them—arising spontaneously out of the human mind among all groups of men. These elementary ideas, which were relatively few in number, he compared to chemical elements or plant cells, suggesting that they were the basic building blocks of culture (Baldus 1968:23). Similarities among cultures were to be explained largely as independent manifestations of these fundamental ideas. Parallel evolution was attributed to the successive emergence of these ideas among separate peoples.

However, Bastian's theory of evolution involved more than simple psychic unity. In addition to *Elementargedanken,* common to all of mankind, he recognized *Völkergedanken*—ideas specific to particular peoples. These *Völkergedanken* were generated out of the interaction between elementary ideas and the particular geographic environments (*geographischen Provinzen*) in which peoples lived (Baldus 1968:23; Goldenweiser 1930:476; Lowie 1937:35–36). Thus a recognition of the influence of external factors tempered Bastian's doctrine of cultural evolution as a manifestation of inherent ideas.

Something like a belief in psychic unity as a determinant of evolution can be found in Morgan's *Ancient Society:* "A common principle of intelligence," wrote Morgan, "meets us in the savage, in the barbarian, and in civilized man. It was in virtue of this that mankind were able to produce in similar conditions the same implements and utensils, the same inventions, and to develop similar institutions from the same original germs of thought" (Morgan 1964:467).

Tylor also seemed at times to ascribe a causative role in cultural development to the similar functioning of the human mind among various peoples. Thus he once wrote: "No ethnical relationship can ever have existed between the Aztecs and the Egyptians; yet each race developed the idea of the pyramid tomb through that psychological similarity which is as much a characteristic of the species man as is his physique" (Tylor 1910:119).

The explanation of cultural parallels as simply the product of thought was not, however, always true of Tylor. Thus, in his article "On a Method of Investigating the Development of Institutions," he explained the widespread occurrence of such customs as the mother-in-law taboo and cross-cousin marriage not in terms of psychic unity, but of the operation of recurring sociological determinants.

Tylor was here following his own dictum that "the uniformity which so largely pervades civilization may be ascribed, in great measure, to the uniform action of uniform causes" (Tylor 1871:I, 1). But it was clear that the uniform action of the human mind was not enough to account for cultural similarities. The *circumstances* in which men lived must also be similar in order for these similarities to occur.

Let us look at the problem from another angle. The salient feature of cultural development was, after all, the fact that different peoples had attained very different levels of culture. Now, if the human mind worked the same way among all peoples, its operation was powerless to account for these differences. If it was indeed a *constant*, the human mind could be canceled out of any equation purporting to explain such differences. Being variables, cultural differences had to be explained by means of other variables. And the only other variables involved were external conditions, cultural and natural.

However, some advocates of psychic unity were reluctant to grant a strong determining role to external factors. And on those few occasions when they faced the issue squarely and forced themselves to make a choice, it was the doctrine of psychic unity that usually gave way.

A striking example of this is afforded by Daniel G. Brinton, who, as we have seen, could be an eloquent spokesman for psychic unity. However, two pages after speaking of "the one and unvarying psychical nature of man" (Brinton 1895:246), he had some rather different things to say. He began by stating: "The . . . proofs of the psychical unity of the whole species have multiplied so abundantly that some maintain strenuously that it is not ethnic or racial peculiarities but solely external conditions on the one hand and individual faculties on [the] other, which are the factors of culture-evolution." However, Brinton added, "the position just stated seems to be erroneous" (1895:248). The true interpretation, as he saw it, was as follows: "All members of the species have common human mental traits; that goes without saying; and in addition it seems to me that each of the great races, each ethnic group, has its own added special powers and special limitations compared with others; and that these ethnic and racial psychic peculiarities attached to all or nearly all members of the group are tremendously potent in deciding the result of its struggle for existence" (1895:248).

Thus, curiously enough, along with an often-stated belief in psychic unity, there coexisted in Brinton's mind a less commonly expressed, but still distinct, belief in the *inequality* of races. "I must still deny," he wrote, "that all races are equally endowed—or that the position with reference to civilization which the various ethnic groups hold to-day is one merely of opportunity and externalities" (1895:248).

And if the races were unequal, which were the less favored ones? Said Brinton: "The black, the brown and red races differ anatomically so much from the white, especially in their splanchnic [visceral] organs, that even with equal cerebral activity, they never could rival its results by equal efforts" (1895:249). Indeed, some ethnic stocks were even "of a nature to disqualify them for the atmosphere of modern enlightenment" (1895:249). Thus, Brinton was led to conclude that "we can speak of the *Volksgeist* and *Völkergedanken,* a racial mind, or the temperament of a people, with as much propriety and accuracy as we can of any physical traits which distinguish it from other peoples or races" (1895:249).

We see, then, that in the compass of four pages Brinton has come a full half-circle. From a strong assertion of psychic unity he has reverted to a full-fledged racial determinism. Remarkably, then, with a few strokes of the pen he succeeded in reducing a major principle to its negation!

It may seem difficult to understand how the same individual could hold both these views simultaneously. Yet this is but another example of the inconsistencies so often found in the thinking of the early evolutionists. And it could hardly have been otherwise. Anthropology was still in its infancy, and only gradually did it relinquish its heritage of metaphysics and folk prejudice. It was to be expected, therefore, that ambiguous, discrepant, and even contradictory theories should sometimes exist side by side in the same mind. Indeed, we shall see this as a recurring theme throughout our discussion of theories of cultural determination.

In passing, we may note that theories of psychic unity and those of racial determinism were alike in one respect: They both sought to account for cultural phenomena in terms of inherent psychological tendencies. But in another respect they were opposite: While psychic unity was invoked to account for cultural *similarities,* racial theories were used to account for cultural *differences.*

Racial Determinism

Brinton was by no means alone among those early evolutionists whose adherence to psychic unity masked an underlying racial determinism. As a matter of fact, the closer one looks at the writings of the classical evolutionists the clearer it becomes that, almost to a man, they believed in the inequality of the races. And this belief inevitably affected their view of cultural dynamics. Let us consider some examples.

We noted earlier that at one point in *Ancient Society* (1964:15) Morgan argued for "the specific identity of the brain of all races of mankind." However, a few pages later, he refers to the American Indian as being "possessed of inferior mental endowments" (1964:41). The peoples most favorably endowed intellectually, according to Morgan, were the Aryans. This family, he held, "represents the central stream of human progress, because it produced the highest type of mankind, and because it has proved its intrinsic superiority by gradually assuming the control of the earth" (1964:468).

Morgan believed in inequality not only *between* races, but also *within* them. Thus, speaking of political confederation, which he regarded as "the ultimate [i.e., highest] stage of organization among the American aborigines," he stated that "its existence would be expected in the most intelligent tribes only" (1964:112).

On rare occasions Tylor also revealed a belief in native differences among races. In *Anthropology* he wrote: "There seems to be in mankind inbred temperament and inbred capacity of mind. History points the great lesson that some races have marched on in civilization while others have stood still or fallen back, and we should partly look for an explanation of this in differences of intellectual and moral powers between such tribes as the native Americans and Africans, and the Old World nations who overmatch and subdue them" (Tylor 1916:74). Later in the same work Tylor granted that members of the white race might be least able to bear extreme heat, but added that this was offset by their being "gifted with the powers of knowing and ruling which give them sway over the world" (1916:113).

General Pitt-Rivers went so far as to claim that "the savage is morally and mentally an unfit instrument for the spread of civilization, except when . . . he is reduced to a state of slavery" (Pitt-Rivers 1906:54).

From a worldwide survey of primitive art, A. C. Haddon concluded that innate psychological differences between peoples influenced their art. Noting that "the diverse races and people of mankind have different ideas and ideals" (Haddon 1902:7), he went on to say that "the conclusion that forced itself upon me is that the decorative art of a people does, to a certain extent, reflect their character. A poor, miserable people have poor and miserable art" (1902:9).

In *Principles of Sociology* Spencer alludes to "superior races" and "inferior races" quite frequently (e.g., Spencer 1890:51). Moreover, more than most other classical evolutionists, Spencer was prepared to use innate racial or ethnic differences to account for differences in cultural attainment. For example, he spoke of "the independence of the Greek nature," and believed that it was because of this innate trait of character that the ancient Greeks "did not readily submit to the extension of sacerdotal control over civil affairs" (1897:265).

On the other hand, speaking of the Aztecs and Incas, Spencer said that "extreme servility of nature made the peoples of ancient America yield unresistingly to an unqualified political despotism," and also "made them submit humbly to the enormously developed priesthoods of their bloody deities" (1897:132). Spencer maintained as well that "the innate feelings and aptitudes of a race have large shares in determining the sizes and cohesions of the social groups it forms" (Spencer 1899:366; see also p. 368).

Yet Spencer did not believe that the mental differences between races were really basic, and accordingly took issue with the "reigning school of mythologists," led by Max Müller, for assuming "a fundamental difference in mode of action between the minds of the superior races and the minds of the inferior races" (Spencer 1890:681). Nor did Spencer impute anything like a "prelogical mentality" to primitive peoples. On the contrary, he declared that "the laws of thought are everywhere the same: . . . given the data as known to him, the primitive man's inference is the reasonable inference" (1890:98). Furthermore, despite some of the passages just quoted, Spencer only occasionally resorted to alleged racial differences in mentality to explain differences in culture.

The view that the races were not equally endowed, but that, despite the existence of real mental differences among them, they were nevertheless *essentially* the same, was also voiced by Frazer. In *Psyche's Task* Frazer first asserted "the natural, universal, and ineradicable inequality of men," adding that "different races [are] differently endowed in respect of intelligence, courage, industry, and so forth," and concluded that "no abstract doctrine is more false and mischievous than that of the natural equality of men" (Frazer 1913a:166–167). However, he went on to say:

> I have laid stress on the great inequalities which exist not only between the various races, but between men of the same race and generation; but it should be clearly understood and remembered that these divergences are quantitative rather than qualitative, they consist in differences of degree rather than of kind. The savage is not a different sort of being from his civilized brother: he has the same capacities, mental and moral, but they are less fully developed: his evolution has been arrested, or rather retarded, at a lower level. (1913a:172)

What we have found to be true of Spencer and Frazer was also true of Morgan and Tylor. While they evidently believed in some racial differences in intelligence, as we have seen, they generally refrained from relying on these differences to account for differences in culture. Indeed, Alfred Russel Wallace, in reviewing Tylor's *Primitive Culture* when it first appeared, concluded: "One of the most important results of Mr. Tylor's researches, and that which is most clearly brought out in every part of his work, is that for the purpose of investigating the development of man's mental nature race may be left out of the equation, and all mankind treated as essentially one" (Wallace 1872:70).

Thus we see that "racism" among the classical evolutionists was usually qualified in two respects. First, the difference between races was not generally seen as one of kind, but rather one of degree; and second, relatively little use was made of alleged racial differences in accounting for differences in cultural achievement. Auguste Comte's summary of the issue might well have been accepted by most of the later nineteenth-century evolutionists: "Differences of race at no time did more than affect the rate of our social evolution, and they never changed its character or the course which it took" (Comte 1875:II, 377).

Finally, in discussing cultural determination by race, let us look at the anthropologist who most nearly freed himself of this belief, and who spoke out most forcefully against it, namely, Theodor Waitz. Despite occasional qualifications, Waitz was unusually consistent in arguing that race played no role in producing differences in cultural attainment. Opposing the views of Samuel G. Morton and Louis Agassiz, Waitz held "that the psychical endowment of the various races was most probably originally the same, or nearly so; that the earlier or later emergence of individual peoples from the primitive state essentially depended on the natural and social conditions in which they were placed" (Waitz 1863:351).

Waitz was aware, of course, of the wide differences in level of culture between peoples of various races, but thought it unjustified to account for these differences in terms of race. He argued that "the assumption of a specifically different endowment of races is at least unnecessary to explain the differences in their civilization" (1863:353), and held, in fact, that positing such differences "cuts the matter short *ab initio,* thus leaving the various phenomena of progressive civilization unexplained" (1863:329).

As further arguments against racial interpretations, Waitz noted that "peoples which occupy the lowest place in humanity, and approach the primitive state, do not all belong to the same, but to different races; ... within every race there are peoples of different degrees of development" (1863:325). And he also stated: "The few thousand years we are in advance of them [the so-called lower races] in civilization, are, considering the great antiquity of the earth, too short a period for us to form a decisive judgment of the capacity of all mankind" (1863:320).

To account for the very low cultural position of the Fuegians, Australian aborigines, and Bushmen, Waitz said: "Of all these peoples it can be shown that external nature and their social condition rendered progress next to impossible, living as they did in a sterile stony country, which, on account of surrounding enemies, they were unable to quit" (1863:325).

Finally, in arguing against the prevailing belief in the innate superiority of Europeans, Waitz contended that "in order to prove that natural superiority of the white race over all others, particular stress has been laid on the circumstances that wheresoever they came in contact with the latter, they invariably became their masters. But this superiority, as can be easily shown, is not owing to the race as such, but to their civilization. Gunpowder, brandy, faithlessness, and cruelty, were pretty much the chief means by which the aborigines of their respective countries were subjected" (1863:327).

Human Perfectibility

A strong Lamarckian strain marked the social theories of several early evolutionists. Auguste Comte, for example, wrote that "every kind of improvement, static or dynamic, that has been realised in the individual, tends to perpetuate itself by generation in the species. Thus by Heredity, modifications that were at first artificial are rendered spontaneous" (Comte 1875:I, 493).

Spencer argued this point more insistently than anyone else. He held that from the earliest times a process had been at work slowly adapting human nature to the needs of social life. This adaptation occurred by the direct action of circumstances on the natures of men, causing modifications in their character that were then transmitted to their descendants by heredity. Thus, slowly, these modifications accumulated in a population, generation after generation. But the qualities so developed were not always the same among all societies. As the circumstances varied, so would the outcomes. For example, men living in rugged mountain terrain tended to develop independent natures, which was not the case among peoples living on extensive plains (Spencer 1883:II, 560–561, 1899:373, 395).

Spencer also felt that the psychological preconditions for certain institutions had to be present before the institutions themselves could arise. He thus argued that "for the development of [legal] contract, human nature has to undergo appropriate modifications" (Spencer 1897:511). The capacity for civilization also had to be gradually attained: "The constitutional energy needed for continuous labour, without which there cannot be civilized life . . . is an energy not to be quickly acquired; but is to be acquired only by inherited modifications slowly accumulated" (Spencer 1899:270).

Spencer believed, however, that the ability to undergo these modifications was not the monopoly of any race. Such changes in character could occur among any people, provided only they were subjected to the proper conditions over a long enough period of time. This was the doctrine of human perfectibility, which held out the prospect that any society might some day climb as high as any other. Several early evolutionists seem to have held this view. Morgan, for instance, alluded to "the improvable character of . . . [man's] nascent mental and moral powers" (Morgan 1964:422).

Waitz affirmed the same belief, only more explicitly. He began by noting that "the development of mankind in the course of time produces a favourable predisposing influence on the psychical endowment of the progeny, which increases with the progress of civilization, which predisposition must be less the nearer a people is to the primitive state. This partly explains why we see so many peoples apparently stationary, whilst others proceed rapidly from a certain point" (Waitz 1863:351–352). (So the existing races were not equal after all!) But then Waitz went on to maintain that "the greater natural inclination and capacity for civilization manifested by some peoples, is nothing original, but something acquired in the course of their development, which, under favourable circumstances, might have been equally acquired by peoples who appear at present less capable of civilization" (1863:352).

Individuals as Determinants

It is characteristic of earlier social thought that a major causal force in cultural development was seen to be the actions of individuals. As Charles Kingsley declared, "history is the history of men and women, and of nothing else. . . . if you would understand History, [you] must understand men" (Kingsley 1860:4, 5). And John Stuart Mill wrote that "the laws of the phenomena of society are, and can be, nothing but the laws of the actions and passions of human beings united together in a social state" (Mill 1846:550).

In the writings of Herbert Spencer we can trace a change in interpretation that begins with precisely this view. In his first book, *Social Statics*, Spencer asserted that the nature of the units determines the nature of the aggregate. As he put it, "there is no way of coming at a true theory of society, but by inquiring into the nature of its component individuals. To understand humanity in its combinations, it is necessary to analyze that humanity in its elementary form—for the explanation of the compound, to refer back to the simple. We quickly find that every phenomenon exhibited by an aggregation of men, originates in some quality of man himself" (Spencer 1851:16).

Two decades later Spencer still held the same view. Thus in *The Study of Sociology* he wrote: "That the properties of the units determine the properties of the whole they make up, evidently holds of societies as of other things" (Spencer 1886:51). And later in the same volume he said: "Nothing comes out of a society but what originated in the motive of an individual, or in the united similar motives of many individuals . . . not even an approach to an explanation of social phenomena can be made, without the thoughts and sentiments of citizens being recognized as factors" (1886:382).

But in the course of examining a vast amount of ethnographic data while preparing to write *The Principles of Sociology*, Spencer's thinking on this issue appears to have undergone a change. We now find him writing that "social phenomena depend in part on the natures of the individuals and in part on the forces the individuals are subject to" (Spencer 1890:14). He spoke also of "the reciprocal influence of the society and its units—the influence of the whole on the parts, and of the parts on the whole" (1890:11). And again, he said: "the characters of the environment co-operate with the characters of human beings in determining social phenomena" (1890:35).

Finally, Spencer noted that "the ever-accumulating, ever-complicating super-organic products, material and mental [i.e., culture], constitute a further set of factors which become more and more influential causes of change" (1890:14).

Thus we observe a growing realization on Spencer's part that an explanation of social evolution in terms of individual behavior alone was inadequate. The cultural matrix in which individuals live and the environing conditions impinging on them had to be brought to bear in order to create a satisfactory explanation of evolution.

The Influence of Great Men

If it was the prevailing view in society at large that individuals changed the course of culture, then it was only reasonable to find it asserted that great individuals changed it most profoundly. Charles Kingsley for one argued that "instead of saying that the history of mankind is the history of its masses, it would be much more true to say, that the history of mankind is the history of its great men" (Kingsley 1860:44).

Similar opinions were voiced by other men of letters of the time. John Stuart Mill declared: "If there had been no Themistocles there would have been no victory of Salamis; and had there not, where would have been all our civilisation?" (Mill 1886:615). Thomas Carlyle summarized this point of view by saying: "Universal History . . . is at bottom the History of the Great Men who have worked here" (Carlyle 1935:1).

None of the classical evolutionists was ever a staunch supporter of the Great Man Theory. The very nature of their science predisposed them more toward the opposite view. Still, a few of them occasionally attributed considerable influence to great men.

Charles Darwin, for instance, wrote in *The Descent of Man* that "obscure as is the problem of the advance of civilisation, we can at least see that a nation which produced during a lengthened period the greatest number of highly intellectual, energetic, brave, patriotic, and benevolent men, would generally prevail over less favoured nations" (Darwin n.d.:145).

Waitz spoke of "the emergence of highly gifted individuals from the mass of the people, who as rulers, heroes, lawgivers, transform the position of their people, change its relations with other nations, regulate its internal constitution, expand its horizon in science and art, improve their morals, and direct their attention to nobler objects" (Waitz 1863:363; see also pp. 324 and 381).

However, opposition to the belief in the surpassing importance of great men began to emerge early in the nineteenth century. One of the first salvos fired against it came from what might seem an unexpected quarter: the essayist, historian, and statesman Thomas Babington Macaulay.

In his essay on the poet and dramatist John Dryden, written in 1828, Macaulay made certain observations about the Great Man Theory that strike us today as surprisingly modern. Referring to the controversy that once raged over whether Newton or Leibniz had invented the infinitesimal calculus, Macaulay noted that general agreement had been reached that both men had made the invention independently and more or less simultaneously. He went on to say that "mathematical science, indeed, had then reached such a point that, if neither of them had ever existed, the principle must inevitably have occurred to some person within a few years" (Macaulay 1877:324).

Nor was this an isolated instance of Macaulay's perspicacity. "We are inclined to think," he added, "that, with respect to every great addition which has been made to the stock of human knowledge, the case has been similar; that without Copernicus we should have been Copernicans" (1877:324).

Clearly, then, Macaulay viewed inventions and discoveries not as fortuitous and uniquely inspired creative acts on the part of a few geniuses, but rather as predictable, indeed, inevitable, syntheses occurring periodically within an advancing stream of culture. The role of the great man in this process he expressed in the following terms:

> Society indeed has its great men and its little men, as the earth has its mountains and its valleys. But the inequalities of intellect, like the inequalities of the surface of our globe, bear so small a proportion to the mass, that, in calculating its revolutions, they may safely be neglected. The sun illuminates the hills, while it is

still below the horizon; and truth is discovered by the highest minds a little before it becomes manifest to the multitude. This is the extent of their superiority. They are the first to catch and reflect a light, which, without their assistance, must, in a short time, be visible to those who lie far beneath them. (1877:324)

Among the early evolutionists, Auguste Comte had suggested that we "attach too high a value to personal genius" (Comte 1875:II, 371). But it was Herbert Spencer who mounted the strongest assault against the Great Man Theory.

In *Social Statics* Spencer already showed his skepticism of this theory, arguing that social changes "are brought about by a power far above individual wills. Men who seem the prime movers, are merely the tools with which it works; and were they absent, it would quickly find others" (Spencer 1851:433). In "The Social Organism," published in 1860, Spencer stated further that "those who regard the histories of societies as the histories of their great men, and think that these great men shape the fates of their societies, overlook the truth that such great men are the products of their societies" (Spencer 1891b:268).

Renewing his attack on the Great Man Theory in *The Study of Sociology* (1886:30–37) and in *Principles of Sociology,* Spencer marshaled his most impressive evidence against it. He showed, for example, how unrealistic it was to think of the Spartan constitution as being the product of the mind of Lycurgus (Spencer 1899:376n.–377n.). He also argued that it was not the personal initiative of Cleisthenes that brought about democratic organization in Athens, but rather that Cleisthenes' political reorganization was prompted by, and was successful only because of, the large numbers of non-clan-organized persons living in Athens at the time (1899:424–425). Moreover, he argued persuasively that a militant type of society tends to foster the notion of personal causation in social transformation, and thus prevents, or at least retards, the rise of scientific notions of impersonal causation (1899:599–600).

Spencer did not stop at saying that great men did not create social and political institutions. He held that their rise was not a matter of deliberate choice at all: "Society is a growth and not a manufacture" (Spencer 1897:321). He also denied that recognition of "advantages or disadvantages of this or that arrangement furnished motives for establishing or maintaining" a form of government, and argued instead that "conditions and not intentions determine" (Spencer 1899:395).

In none of the other nineteenth-century evolutionists do we find a detailed examination of the Great Man Theory, let alone such a concerted effort to refute it.

Ideas as Prime Movers

The next view of cultural determination we have to consider is that which makes ideas the driving force of evolution. Here we will deal with idealist theories of all types, not merely those based on innate ideas or ideas believed to arise spontaneously.

Although of ancient origin, the notion of the primacy of ideas in determining culture reached its high-water mark in the eighteenth century, the Age of Rationalism. Lord Monboddo, for example, said that "as intelligence is of the essence of man, and that which distinguishes him from other animals on this earth, I consider his history to be that of the operations of his intellectual faculty, which are all guided and directed by religion; and it is by these that his character, sentiments, manners, customs, and institutions are produced" (Monboddo 1779–1799:IV, 1).

Leaving out allusions to divine guidance, the writers of the French Enlightenment also saw cultural evolution largely as a product of the human mind. The very titles of their works proclaimed this. Thus Turgot's celebrated discourse at the Sorbonne in 1750 was entitled "On the Successive Advances of the Human Mind" (1949), and Condorcet's famous work of 1795 was called *Sketch for a Historical Picture of the Progress of the Human Mind* (1955). Following in the same tradition, Auguste Comte wrote in his *Cours de Philosophie Positive:* "It is unnecessary to have to prove to the readers of this work that ideas govern and overthrow the world" (Comte 1852:44).

John Stuart Mill, a follower of Comte, expressed very similar opinions. In *A System of Logic* he wrote that "the evidence of history and the evidence of human nature combine, by a most striking instance of consilience, to show that there is really one social element which is thus preponderant, and almost paramount, among the agents of the social progression. This is, the state of the speculative faculties of mankind" (Mill 1846:585). And again Mill said: "Every considerable advance in material civilization has been preceded by an advance in knowledge; and when any great social change has come to pass, a great change in the opinions and modes of thinking of society has taken place shortly before" (1846:585).

While Sir Henry Maine seldom had much to say about the forces that moved culture, he once did express a belief in the influence of archetypal ideas, suggesting that "primitive society was brought into shape by the influence of dominant types [of ideas], acting on the faculty of imitation" (Maine 1883:281). "The communities which were destined for civilisation," he went on, "seem to have experienced an attraction which drew them towards one exemplar, the pure clan, generally exogamous among the Aryans, generally endogamous among the Semites, but always believing in purity of paternal descent, and always looking back to some god or hero as the first of the race" (1883:281–282).

The most notable instance of the use of ideas as templates for cultural development was that of Adolf Bastian and his *Elementargedanken*. Having already dealt with Bastian under the heading of "Psychic Unity," I will merely add here Ludwig Gumplowicz's assessment of the role of ideas in Bastian's work: "The fundamental characteristic of Bastian's investigations is the endeavor to attribute all social phenomena to human thought. . . . With him thoughts are always primary and deeds are an emanation from them" (Gumplowicz 1899:38–39).

Akin to Bastian's "elementary ideas" were Morgan's "germs of thought." These germs, which Morgan refers to time and again in *Ancient Society,* had originated in the infancy of the human race, and out of them had grown many complex institutions. Morgan believed that the brain of modern man was the same as that of his savage and barbarous ancestors, and that "it has come down to us laden with the thoughts, aspirations and passions with which it was busied through the intermediate periods" (Morgan 1964:59).

Because of the way in which the early human brain was organized, Morgan thought it possible to say that "the principal institutions of mankind have been developed from a few primary germs of thought; and . . . the course and manner of their development was predetermined, as well as restricted within narrow limits of divergence, by the natural logic of the human mind and the necessary limitations of its powers" (1964:23).

The fullest expression of this notion to be found in Morgan's writings is probably the following:

> Out of a few germs of thought, conceived in the early ages, have been evolved all the principal institutions of mankind. Beginning their growth in the period of savagery, fermenting through the period of barbarism, they have continued their advancement through the period of civilization. The evolution of these germs of thought has been guided by a natural logic which formed an essential attribute of the brain itself. So unerringly has this principle performed its functions in all conditions of experience, and in all periods of time, that its results are uniform, coherent and traceable in their courses. (1964:59)

These germs had not animated all aspects of culture equally, however. According to Morgan, "the original germs of thought, which have exercised the most powerful influence upon the human mind, and upon human destiny, are these which relate to government, to the family, to language, to religion, and to property" (1964:59).

Implanted as they were in the human mind, these germs of thought still required the application of special intelligence in order to become actualized in cultural forms. The idea of the gens, for example, struck Morgan as something "essentially abstruse," and therefore as necessarily being "a product of high intelligence" (1964:320). He also believed that the formation of confederacies by North American Indians must have been "a question of intelligence and skill" among those who achieved them, since "other tribes in large number were standing in precisely the same relations in different parts of the continent without confederating" (1964:112).

Morgan explained the flowering of Athens as a result of "ideas which had been germinating through the previous ethnical period" (1964:219). And speaking of the Ganowanian (Dakota-Iroquois) type of kinship system he said: "The system is under the absolute control of the fundamental conceptions upon which it rests, and if changed at all, the changes must be in logical accordance with these conceptions" (Morgan 1871:212).

Tylor was also very much concerned with ideas, their evolution, and their influence. The major portion of *Primitive Culture* is devoted to tracing the development of human thought from magic to science. Here and there in his other writings, Tylor also indicates the large role he assigns to intellectual factors in human history. In *Anthropology*, for example, he says: "While . . . [man] feeds himself as the lower animals do, by gathering wild fruit and catching game and fish, [he] is led by his higher intelligence to more artificial means of getting these" (Tylor 1916:214). And elsewhere in the book he notes that "man's power of accommodating himself to the world he lives in, and even of controlling it, is largely due to his faculty of gaining new knowledge" (1916:51).

Further evidence of Tylor's emphasis on the role of ideas and their ways of expression in determining cultural advance was the fact that he believed that writing rather than city-building was the cause and hallmark of civilization. In his article "Anthropology" in the *Encyclopaedia Britannica* he argued that "in the growth of systematic civilisation, the art of writing has had an influence so intense, that of all tests to distinguish the barbaric from the civilised state, none is so generally effective as this" (Tylor 1878:123). He expressed the same view in his book *Anthropology*, maintaining that "the invention of writing was the great movement by which mankind arose from barbarism to civilization. How vast its effect was, may be best measured by looking at the low condition of tribes still living without it" (Tylor 1916:179).

Morris Opler has taken pains to show that Tylor was not a materialist, as Leslie A. White (1949b:364–367) presents him, but rather an "intellectual determinist" (Opler 1965a:79–80). In support of this view, Opler quotes a number of passages from Tylor's writings, including some of those cited above. George W. Stocking, Jr., has also spoken of Tylor's "tendency to explain all contributions to culture in terms of conscious, rationalistic processes" (Stocking 1963:791). But it is mistaken to think of Tylor as an idealist determinist only. The truth is that Tylor was *both* an idealist *and* a materialist. At times he espoused ideas as the basic determinants of culture, and at other times he stressed the role of material objects and processes. And the very same thing was true of Morgan. When we come to examine materialist interpretations of cultural evolution we shall consider further the extent and significance of these inconsistencies in their writings.

Returning to the expression of idealist conceptions, we find that Waitz, like Tylor, considered "the progress of knowledge" to be one of the principal causes of the development of civilization: "Its effects in this direction are so great that it cannot possibly be over-estimated," he said (Waitz 1863:377), and added that "it is essentially the development of knowledge which is the moving power, all other forces being secondary" (1863:379).

Waitz's idealism, however, was rational rather than metaphysical, a fact that distinguished him from many German thinkers of his day. He did not believe in a *Zeitgeist* impelling culture forward. "There is no agent, real and substantive, which can be considered as the spirit of a people or of humanity; individuals alone are real," he wrote (1863:324).

Frazer offers us what is undoubtedly the most unqualified acceptance of the determination of culture by ideas to be found among any of the early evolutionists. In *Psyche's Task* he wrote: "The more we study the inward working of society and the progress of civilization, the more clearly shall we perceive how both are governed by the influence of thoughts which, springing up at first we know not how or whence in a few superior minds, gradually spread till they have leavened the whole inert lump of a community or of mankind" (Frazer 1913a:168).

The weakness of this view as an explanation of cultural advance became fully apparent as Frazer continued: "The origin of such mental variations, with all their far-reaching train of social consequences, is just as obscure as is the origin of such physical variations on which, if biologists are right, depends the evolution of the species, and with it the possibility of progress. Perhaps the same unknown cause which determines the one set of variations gives rise to the other also. We cannot tell" (1913a:168).

Herbert Spencer is generally regarded as the epitome of nineteenth-century rationalism. John Herman Randall, for example, called him "a son of the Age of Reason" (Randall 1926:331). And speaking of the role played by ideas in Spencer's social theory, Talcott Parsons has claimed that Spencer "saw the emotional or affective components of human motivation mainly as disturbances of the correctly rational operation of the intellect," adding that "this essentially is to say that he did not understand the sense in which cognitive and affective components must be integrated" (Parsons 1961:viii).

Yet, as prevalent as is the view that Spencer was preoccupied with ideas and virtually dismissed emotions, it happens to be wrong. As early as *Social Statics* Spencer had spoken of "the law that opinion is ultimately determined by the feelings and not by the intellect" (Spencer 1851:429). His fullest expression of this view came fifteen years later, in an article written to contrast his views with those of Auguste Comte. One passage in this work summarizes Spencer's views on cultural causation so clearly and forcefully that it deserves to be quoted in full:

Ideas do not govern and overthrow the world: the world is governed or overthrown by feelings, to which ideas serve only as guides. The social mechanism does not rest finally on opinions; but almost wholly on character. Not intellectual anarchy, but moral antagonism, is the cause of political crises. All social phenomena are produced by the totality of human emotions and beliefs; of which the emotions are mainly pre-determined, while the beliefs are mainly post-determined. Men's desires are chiefly inherited; but their beliefs are chiefly acquired, and depend on surrounding conditions; and the most important surrounding conditions depend on the social state which the prevalent desires have produced. The social state at any time existing, is the resultant of all the ambitions, self-interests, fears, reverences, indignations, sympathies, etc., of ancestral citizens and existing citizens. The ideas current in this social state, must, on the average, be congruous with the feelings of citizens; and therefore, on the average, with the social state these feelings have produced. Ideas wholly foreign to this social state cannot be evolved, and if introduced from without, cannot get accepted—or, if accepted, die out when the temporary phase of feeling which caused their acceptance, ends. Hence, though advanced ideas when once established, act on society and aid its further advance; yet the establishment of such ideas depends on the fitness of the society for receiving them. Practically, the popular character and the social state, determine what ideas shall be current; instead of the current ideas determining the social state and the character. The modification of men's moral natures, caused by the continuous discipline of social life, which adapts them more and more to social relations, is therefore the chief proximate cause of social progress. (Spencer 1891c:128–129)

Historical Materialism

A consistent materialist interpretation of cultural evolution is not to be found among the classical evolutionists. Of the nineteenth-century thinkers who dealt broadly with the culture process, only Marx and Engels and their disciples held to an explicit and thoroughgoing historical materialism.

To be sure, anthropologists at times invoked materialism in their interpretations. Thus, for example, we find Friedrich Ratzel, the anthropogeographer, writing: "The material lies at the base of the intellectual. Intellectual creations come as the luxury after bodily needs are satisfied. Every question, therefore, as to the origin of civilization resolves itself into the question: what favours the development of its material foundations?" (Ratzel 1896:26). But such interpretations tended to coexist with nonmaterialistic ones.

The exact proportions of materialism and idealism in the writings of the classical evolutionists, especially those of Morgan and Tylor, have recently been the subject of considerable discussion (see White 1948:141–142, 1949b:361–367; Opler 1962, 1964a, 1964b, 1965a, 1965b, 1966; Harding 1964; Leacock 1964; Manners 1965a, 1965b, 1966; Stocking 1963, 1965; and Harris 1968:211–216). It is not my intention here to adjudicate the issue or to try to determine the correct proportions of the two views in Morgan, Tylor, or anyone else. Rather, I would like to show that the classical evolutionists were moving toward a greater recognition of the role of material conditions in cultural advance, and that they expressed this with some frequency. That they also expressed idealist views must be taken, as I have said before, as expectable. The classical evolutionists were in the pioneer stage of their science, and their thought was still burdened with excessive amounts of rationalism, romanticism, and metaphysics inherited from an earlier age.

We may begin our survey of historical materialism in cultural evolutionism by noting some additional evidence of this inconsistency. Earlier in this chapter we quoted Comte as saying that social change arose from ideas, and this was in fact his predominating view. But at times he also adopted a materialist position, or at least pointed to the importance of material factors in evolution. Thus he noted that "material progress, long by an inevitable necessity the exclusive object of man's care, furnishes him with the basis on which he is eventually able to build all higher improvement, physical, intellectual, and ultimately moral" (Comte 1875:II, 147).

Undoubtedly the sharpest contrast between idealism and materialism to be found in any nineteenth-century evolutionist is provided by Lewis H. Morgan (see White 1948:141–142). We have already examined Morgan's idealism. Let us look now at his materialism.

It is worth noting at the outset that Frederick Engels, in the preface to his *Origin of the Family, Private Property and the State*, wrote: "Morgan, in his own way . . . discovered afresh in America the materialistic conception of history discovered by Marx forty years ago" (Engels 1942:5). And indeed no reasonable person could read the first three chapters of *Ancient Society* without being impressed by the enormous influence Morgan attributes to the material elements of culture. In later sections of this chapter we shall see what role Morgan assigned to subsistence and economic factors. Here we will limit ourselves to noting what Morgan had to say about the effects of technology.

Of pottery making, which Morgan considered to mark the beginning of the period of Barbarism, he wrote: "The introduction of the ceramic art produced a new epoch in human progress in the direction of an improved living and increased domestic convenience" (Morgan 1964:20). To expanding energy sources Morgan also gave great credit for cultural advance: "The domestic animals supplementing human muscle with animal power, contributed a new factor of the highest value. In course of time, the production of iron gave the plow with an iron point, and a better spade and axe. Out of these, and the previous horticulture, came field agriculture; and with it, for the first time, unlimited subsistence. The plow drawn by animal power may be regarded as inaugurating a new art" (1964:30).

Lewis Henry Morgan

It is very clear that Morgan saw these improvements in technology as necessary thresholds for the further advancement of culture: "The most advanced portion of the human race," he wrote, "were halted . . . at certain stages of progress, until some great invention or discovery, such as the domestication of animals or the smelting of iron ore, gave a new and powerful impulse forward" (1964:40). In fact, according to Morgan, had mankind not invented iron tools, it would have remained indefinitely at the stage of Barbarism (1964:43).

But the working of iron did come, and this event, said Morgan, "must be held the greatest event in human experience, preparatory to civilization. . . .

Furnished with iron tools, capable of holding both an edge and a point, mankind were certain of attaining to civilization. The production of iron was the event of events in human experience, without a parallel, and without an equal, beside which all other inventions and discoveries were inconsiderable, or at least subordinate" (1964:43).

As a statement of historical materialism, this passage could hardly have been surpassed by Marx himself. Indeed, one can argue that in some respects Morgan was *too* materialistic. Thus, in assigning the Polynesians to a position in his system of cultural stages he relegated them to the Middle Status of Savagery (along with the Australian aborigines) because they lacked two elements of material culture: pottery and the bow and arrow. Thus he paid insufficient attention to the fact that a number of Polynesian societies were organized into chiefdoms and even kingdoms (1964:16).

And surely it was too much to claim that "the most advanced tribes were arrested at this barrier [the Upper Status of Barbarism], awaiting the invention of the process of smelting ore" (1964:453), or that "until iron and its uses were known, civilization was impossible" (1964:468). The ancient high cultures of Mexico, for example, stood in direct contradiction to these assertions. Morgan's curious and dogmatic underrating of Aztec civilization is, however, another story (see Morgan 1950).

Yet even here Morgan was inconsistent, for the transition from Barbarism to Civilization, which he believed to have occurred only in the Old World, he measured not by metallurgical attainments or by the construction of cities, but by the invention of the alphabet (Morgan 1964:17).

Less frequently and emphatically than Morgan, but nevertheless occasionally, Tylor pointed to technology as a major element in the evolution of culture. For instance, he began the chapter on "Arts of Life" in his *Anthropology* with the words: "The arts by which man defends and maintains himself, and holds rule over the world he lives in, depend so much on his use of instruments" (Tylor 1916:182). Later in the chapter he observed: "It was a great movement in civilization for the water-mill and its companion contrivance the wind-mill to come into use as force-providers" (1916:204).

Spencer never thought of himself as a materialist. In fact, he considered the opening chapters of *First Principles* to be a "repudiation of materialism" (Spencer 1926:II, 75). Moreover, occasionally in his writings one finds passages in which he expresses an anti-materialist position. Thus in *The Principles of Psychology* he wrote: "Were we compelled to choose between the alternatives of translating mental phenomena into physical phenomena, or of translating physical phenomena into mental phenomena, the latter alternative would seem the more acceptable of the two" (Spencer 1883:I, 159).

But despite repeated disclaimers, materialistic and mechanistic interpretations suffuse much of Spencer's writings. For him, the universe consisted basically of matter and energy, and was to be explained in terms of their interactions. In the last section of *First Principles*, for example, Spencer wrote: "The deepest truths we can reach, are simply statements of the widest uniformities in our experience of the relations of Matter, Motion, and Force" (Spencer 1896:570).

In view of his underlying philosophy of mechanism, it is not surprising that Spencer should have perceived the fundamental importance of the harnessing of energy to the evolution of culture. He was, indeed, one of the very first to do so. In *First Principles* he wrote:

> Based as the life of a society is on animal and vegetal products, and dependent as these are on the light and heat of the Sun, it follows that the changes wrought by men as socially organized, are effects of forces having a common origin with those which produce all . . . other orders of changes. . . . Not only is the energy expended by the horse harnessed to the plough, and by the labourer guiding it, derived from the same reservoir as is the energy of the cataract and the hurricane; but to this same reservoir are traceable those subtler and more complex manifestations of energy which humanity, as socially embodied, evolves. . . . Whatever takes place in a society results either from the undirected physical energies around, from these energies as directed by men, or from the energies of the men themselves. (Spencer 1937:197–198)

And elsewhere Spencer noted that "human progress is measured by the degree in which simple acquisition is replaced by production; achieved first by manual power, then by animal power, and finally by machine power" (Spencer 1897:362).

Environmental Factors

From at least the time of Montesquieu, the impact of the physical environment on human societies had been amply recognized. Indeed, something of a reaction against this view had ensued. Thus, the classical evolutionists, while well aware of environmental influences on culture, were generally cautious and tempered in the way they expressed this relationship.

Theodor Waitz, for example, observed that "it is surrounding nature which first determines the direction of . . . [a people's] activity, for on it depends what means, instruments, and skill are requisite to satisfy their daily wants, and what difficulties they have to contend with" (Waitz 1863:334).

But he also noted that the impact of environment on culture "is . . . usually the more powerful the nearer a people is to the natural state, and diminishes in influence in proportion as human art and science gain power over it" (1863:329).

Carefully avoiding any overstatement of the role of environment, Waitz asserted that "geographical conditions alone do not constitute positive impulses to civilization" (1863:342). It was the interplay between cultural and natural factors, and not the single operation of the latter, that determined the course of evolution. Thus Waitz wrote that "the desert, the prairie, or the ocean are limits which confine the spreading of tribes or peoples, or ways which favor it, according as the camel, horse, or ship are available for service. The degree of civilization of the people itself alone proves decisive" (1863:342).

Spencer was somewhat readier to credit environment with having a molding effect on institutions. He argued, for example, that rugged mountain terrain, like that of Greece, fostered the development of confederacies rather than of strongly centralized monarchies (Spencer 1899:373, 395). He also noted how environment, in conjunction with subsistence, affected settlement pattern and social life:

> Where pasture is abundant and covers large areas, the keeping of flocks and herds does not necessitate separation of their owners into very small clusters: instance the Comanches, who, with their hunting, join the keeping of cattle, which the members of the tribe combine to guard. But where pasture is not abundant, or is distributed in patches, many cattle cannot be kept together; and their owners consequently have to part. (Spencer 1890:692)

Summarizing his views on how a new environment joined with the existing culture in readapting a society to altered circumstances, Spencer wrote: "While spreading over the Earth mankind have found environments of various characters, and in each case the social life fallen into, partly determined by the social life previously led, has been partly determined by the influences of the new environment" (Spencer 1897:331). A modern cultural ecologist could hardly put the matter more succinctly.

Subsistence as a Determinant

Turning to subsistence specifically, we find many of the classical evolutionists expressing a clear appreciation of its role in the development of culture. Waitz wrote:

It is easily seen how great must be the difference it makes in the character of a people, whether the chase, fishing, gathering of fruits, or the breeding of cattle and agriculture constitute the essential subsistence of a people. . . . the first important result of a hunting life is, the scattering of the population in small masses which require a large area, which by itself renders any advance in civilization impossible. (Waitz 1863:334)

What rendered civilization possible, according to Waitz, was agriculture: "It is the cultivation of the soil which may be considered as the first and necessary stage from which civilization proceeds" (1863:336). And again he wrote: "Among the elements of civilization, agriculture unquestionably occupies the first place: it is the chief basis of it, nor can true civilization grow out of any other soil" (1863:353).

We have already noted Morgan's recognition of the effect of technology on social evolution. He was also very much aware of the great impetus given to culture by advances in subsistence. Thus we find him saying that "the great epochs in human progress have been identified, more or less directly, with the enlargement of the sources of subsistence" (Morgan 1964:24), and suggesting that "the successive arts of subsistence . . . from the great influence they must have exercised upon the condition of mankind" (1964:15) afforded the most satisfactory bases for erecting his broad stages of cultural development.

Speaking of pastoralism, Morgan said: "When the great discovery was made that the wild horse, cow, sheep, ass, sow and goat might be tamed, and, when produced in flocks and herds, become a source of permanent subsistence, it must have given a powerful impulse to human progress" (1964:452).

Morgan was no less emphatic than Waitz in attesting to the effect of agriculture on cultural growth. He wrote, for example, that "the acquisition of farinaceous food by cultivation must be regarded as one of the greatest events in human experience" (1964:43). And he thought that the "new era" following the invention of agriculture "had immense influence upon the destiny of mankind" (1964:28). Later he stated that "from the increased abundance of subsistence through field agriculture, nations began to develop, numbering many thousands under one government, where before they would be reckoned by a few thousands" (1964:458).

Tylor held a similar view. His most notable passage in this regard is the one in which he referred to "those edible grasses which have been raised by cultivation into the cereals, such as wheat, barley, rye, and by their regular and plentiful supply have become the mainstay of human life and the great moving power of civilization" (Tylor 1916:215).

Economic Determinants

Though certainly not strict economic determinists, the classical evolution-ists tended to regard economic factors as powerful shapers of culture. Fore-most among them in this regard was perhaps Herbert Spencer. Spencer's analysis of the role of commerce and industry in widening the base of Athenian oligarchy, and thus paving the way for Greek democracy, was acute and convincing. Let us examine it in some detail.

Unlike Morgan, who had written that "more successfully than the re-maining Grecian tribes, the Athenians were able to carry forward their ideas of government to their logical results" (Morgan 1964:219), Spencer held that it was necessary "to exclude the notion that popular government arose in Athens under the guidance of any preconceived idea" (Spencer 1899:391). Rather, it seemed to him that "in seeking the causes of change which worked through Solon, and also made practicable the re-organiza-tion he initiated, we shall find them to lie in the direct and indirect influ-ence of trade" (1899:391).

In analyzing this effect, Spencer made much of the fact that the increas-ing number of persons drawn to Athens went mostly into commerce and industry rather than into agriculture, and noted that these multitudes tended to break down the existing social structure. "The introduction of a property-qualification for classes, instead of a birth-qualification," Spencer added, "diminished the rigidity of the political form; since acquirement of wealth by industry, or otherwise, made possible an admission into the oli-garchy, or among others of the privileged" (1899:392).

Turning from the reforms of Solon to the so-called revolution of Cleis-thenes, Spencer said: "The relatively detached population of immigrant traders, had so greatly increased between the time of Solon and that of Kleisthenes, that the four original tribes forming the population of Attica had to be replaced by ten. And then this augmented mass, largely composed of men not under clan-discipline, and therefore less easily restrained by the ruling classes, forced itself into predominance at a time when the ruling classes were divided" (1899:424).

"In various ways, then," Spencer continued, "increasing industrial activity tended to widen the original oligarchic structure. And though these effects of industrialism, joined with subsequently accumulated effects, were for a long time held in check by the usurping Peisistratidae [followers of the tyrant Peisistratus], yet, being ready to show themselves when, some time after the expulsion of these tyrants, there came the Kleisthenian revolution, they were doubtless instrumental in then initiating the popular form of government" (1899:393). "Practically, therefore," Spencer concluded, "it was the growing industrial power which then produced, and thereafter preserved, the democratic organization" (1899:424–425).

Further generalizing this process, Spencer wrote: "Industrial development . . . aids popular emancipation by generating an order of men whose power, derived from their wealth, competes with, and begins in some cases to exceed, the power of those who previously were alone wealthy—the men of rank" (1899:422).

Lewis H. Morgan was scarcely less aware of the determining effect of economic factors than Spencer, and a good deal more sanguine in giving it expression. To the institution of property in particular he assigned an immense role. In *Systems*, Morgan had already written that "it is impossible to overestimate the influence of property upon the civilization of mankind. It was the germ, and is still the evidence, of his progress from barbarism, and the ground of his claim to civilization. The master passion of the civilized mind is for its acquisition and enjoyment. In fact governments, institutions, and laws resolve themselves into so many agencies designed for the creation and protection of property" (Morgan 1871:492).

He repeated this opinion in *Ancient Society*, remarking of property that "its dominance as a passion over all other passions marks the commencement of civilization. It not only led mankind to overcome obstacles which delayed civilization, but to establish political society on the basis of territory and property" (Morgan 1964:13). "It was the power that brought the Aryan and Semitic nations out of barbarism into civilization," he also noted (1964:426).

But beyond its effects on society in general, Morgan saw property affecting particular institutions. Thus, property "introduced slavery as an instrument in its production" (1964:426), and then later "caused the abolition of slavery upon the discovery that a freeman was a better property-making machine" (1964:426).

In the accumulation of property Morgan even saw the basis of monogamy. Thus he wrote: "Property, as it increased in variety and amount, exercised a steady and constantly augmenting influence in the direction of monogamy. . . . With the establishment of the inheritance of property in the children of its owner, came the first possibility of a strict monogamian family" (1964:426).

Social Determinants

Another class of determinants employed by the classical evolutionists in accounting for certain elements of society was other elements of society. Morgan, for instance, raised the question of whether the family in its present form was a permanent fixture in society and concluded: "The only answer that can be given is, that it must advance as society advances, and change as society changes, even as it has done in the past. It is the creature of the social system, and will reflect its culture" (1964:420).

Moreover, while Morgan often spoke of property as a great force in determining the form of society, he also said: "The customs upon which . . . rules of proprietary possession and inheritance depend, are determined and modified by the condition and progress of the social organization" (1964:445).

Spencer, for his part, saw the values and attitudes of individuals, not as shaping the society, but as reflecting it. Thus he wrote in *The Study of Sociology* that "for every society, and for each stage in its evolution, there is an appropriate mode of feeling and thinking . . . [which] is a function of the social structure" (Spencer 1886:390).

The most systematic attempt by any nineteenth-century evolutionist to account for certain social features by the presence or absence of certain other social features was unquestionably that of E. B. Tylor in his article "On a Method of Investigating the Development of Institutions" (1889). Here Tylor wrote that "in the one simple fact of residence we may seek the main determining cause of the several usages which combine to form a maternal or paternal system" (Tylor 1889:258). He also believed that "the effect of [marriage by] capture in breaking up the maternal system, and substituting the paternal for it, has thus to be taken into account as a serious factor in social development" (1889:260). And again he noted that "it seemed obvious that . . . 'cross-cousin marriage,' as it may be called, must be the direct result of the simplest form of exogamy" (1889:263).

Finding substantially more societies with both exogamy and the classificatory system of relationship than could be expected by chance alone, Tylor considered this statistical finding to be "the measure of the close causal connexion subsisting between the two institutions" (1889:264).

War as a Determinant

The importance of warfare in cultural evolution, especially in giving rise to the state, had long been recognized. Adam Ferguson, for example, wrote that "without the rivalship of nations, and the practice of war, civil society itself could scarcely have formed an object, or a form" (Ferguson 1819:42–43), and Comte observed that "the decisive formation of large societies came to pass naturally from the spontaneous tendency of military activity to establish universal domain" (Comte 1875:III, 49).

Among the classical evolutionists this recognition became fuller and firmer. Thus in his *Introduction to Anthropology* Theodor Waitz wrote:

Wars require, above all, a union of force, which is not easily effected without it. Whether this union be loose or only temporary, . . . still an important step has been gained. Individuals who formerly lived in a state of isolation are now animated by a common interest, and united in common action, so important for the social development of a people. One of the most important effects of war is this, that the commanding and obeying elements temporarily subsisting in war become permanent after its termination; for though the wars of savages do not immediately lead to the establishment of despotism, still the relations between master and servant, between conqueror and conquered, are established, relations which, in various forms and degrees, are found in all the higher stages of civilization, and seem, in fact, indispensable to its development. (Waitz 1863:346–347)

Or, as Walter Bagehot put it: "It is war that makes nations" (Bagehot 1868:470).

Morgan and Tylor occasionally referred to war and its role in political development. In accounting for the origin of confederacies Morgan wrote: "A tendency to confederate for mutual defense would very naturally exist among kindred and contiguous tribes. . . . The state of perpetual warfare in which they lived would quicken this natural tendency into action" (Morgan 1964:109). Commenting on the effects of war during the Upper Status of Barbarism, Morgan said:

The localization of tribes in fixed areas and in fortified cities, with the increase in the numbers of the people, intensified the struggle for the possession of the most desirable territories. It tended to advance the art of war, and to increase the rewards of individual prowess. These changes of condition and of the plan of life indicate the approach of civilization, which was to overthrow gentile and establish political society. (1964:458)

Referring to small, autonomous, egalitarian communities ruled by the customs of the ancestors rather than by a strong political leader, Tylor remarked: "Everywhere in the world, in war some stronger and more intelligent rule than this is needed and found. The changes which have shaped the descendants of wild hordes into civilized nations have been in great measure the work of the war-chief" (Tylor 1916:430). Elaborating on this point, Tylor added: "Throughout history, war gives the bold and able leader a supremacy which may nominally end with the campaign, but which tends to pass into dictatorship for life" (1916:431).

Tylor called organized armies and confederations of tribes "two of the greatest facts in history" (1916:432), and he summarized his views on the influence of war by saying: "It is one of the plainest lessons of history that through military discipline mankind were taught to submit to authority and to act in masses under command" (1916:434).

The writer who most consistently and emphatically stressed the role of warfare in social evolution, however, was Herbert Spencer. In *Principles of Sociology* he wrote:

> In the struggle for existence among societies, the survival of the fittest is the survival of those in which the power of military cooperation is the greatest; and military cooperation is that primary kind of cooperation which prepares the way for other kinds. So that this formation of larger societies by the union of smaller ones in war, and this destruction or absorption of the smaller un-united societies by the united larger ones, is an inevitable process through which the varieties of men most adapted for social life, supplant the less adapted varieties. (Spencer 1899:280)

Elsewhere in the same work Spencer observed: "We must recognize the truth that the struggles for existence between societies have been instrumental to their evolution. Neither the consolidation and re-consolidation of small groups into large ones; nor the organization of such compound and doubly compound groups; nor the concomitant development of those aids to a higher life which civilization has brought; would have been possible without inter-tribal and inter-national conflicts" (1899:241).

Natural Selection

It is perfectly clear from the passages just cited that Spencer was invoking the principle of natural selection as a mechanism in explaining the evolution of culture. The use of this principle by classical evolutionists is today usually branded as "Social Darwinism" and dismissed out of hand. But the issue is not that simple. To begin with, we must distinguish between two very different meanings of Social Darwinism. First of all, it may refer to a society's conscious policy to weed out its "unfit" members by allowing them to suffer and die without any special effort being made to improve their lot. Social Darwinism in this sense is clearly a matter of politics and not of science. It is a program, not a proposition. As such, one is free to reject it as abhorrent to one's personal philosophy.

But there is a second view of Social Darwinism that focuses on competition between societies over the course of history. According to this view, those societies that were better adapted for the struggle are the ones that survived and flourished, whereas those less well adapted declined or disappeared. This is a scientific theory. It is either true or false. Palatable or not, its adequacy is to be measured and tested by surveying the historical evidence, not by examining one's conscience. It is only with the use of Social Darwinism in this latter sense that the present section will be concerned.

The principle of natural selection was first presented to the world by Charles Darwin in *On the Origin of Species*. In this work, though, Darwin applied the principle only to organic evolution. He had nothing to say about how natural selection might apply to the development of human society. It was actually the writer Walter Bagehot who in 1867 first seized on this principle and applied it explicitly and forcefully to social evolution.

Speaking of natural selection Bagehot wrote: "As every great scientific conception tends to advance its boundaries and to be of use in solving problems not thought of when it was started, so here, what was put forward for mere animal history may, with a change of form, but an identical essence, be applied to human history" (Bagehot 1868:458). "There is no doubt of its predominance in early human society. The strongest killed out the weakest, as they could. And I need not pause to prove that any form of polity is more efficient than none; that an aggregate of families owning even a slippery allegiance to a single head, would be sure to have the better of a set of families acknowledging no obedience to anyone, but scattering loose about the world and fighting where they stood" (Bagehot 1867:529).

A few years later, in *The Descent of Man* (1871), and with acknowledgments to Bagehot, Darwin himself applied the doctrine of natural selection to the evolution of society. Human sociality itself, which Darwin thought instinctual in modern man, he saw as having grown out of the operation of this principle: "In order that primeval men, or the ape-like progenitors of man, should become social, they must have acquired the same instinctive feelings, which impel other animals to live in a body. . . . Such social qualities . . . were no doubt acquired by the progenitors of men in a similar manner, namely, through natural selection" (Darwin n.d.:132).

Darwin saw natural selection acting not only on individuals, but on societies as well. Thus he wrote: "A tribe including many members who, from possessing in a high degree the spirit of patriotism, fidelity, obedience, courage, and sympathy, were always ready to aid one another, and to sacrifice themselves for the common good, would be victorious over most other tribes; and this would be natural selection" (n.d.:135).

In this passage and elsewhere, in accounting for the survival and success of a society, Darwin tended to place the emphasis on the personal qualities of its members rather than on the content of its culture. Moreover, he believed that once acquired during an individual's lifetime, these personal qualities were transmitted to the next generation in a Lamarckian manner:

"the intellectual and moral faculties of man . . . are variable; and we have every reason to believe that the variations tend to be inherited" (n.d.:130). "It is, therefore, highly probable," Darwin continued, "that with mankind the intellectual faculties have been mainly and gradually perfected through natural selection" (n.d.:131).

While choosing to stress the importance of qualities such as courage and intelligence, Darwin recognized that cultural improvements, especially in technology, would also convey an advantage to societies in the struggle for existence. He wrote, for example, that "if the new invention [in subsistence or defense] were an important one, the tribe would increase in number, spread, and supplant other tribes" (n.d.:131).

Competition and natural selection were seen by Darwin as continuing to operate in the modern world: "it is chiefly through their power that the civilised races have extended, and are now everywhere extending their range, so as to take the place of the lower races" (n.d.:137). But at the same time, Darwin saw the process operating with diminished severity. "With highly civilised nations," he wrote, "progress depends in a subordinate degree on natural selection; for such nations do not supplant and exterminate one another as do savage tribes" (n.d.:145).

Spencer disliked Darwin's phrase "natural selection" because "selection," he said, "connotes a *conscious process,* and so involves a tacit personalisation of Nature" (Spencer 1895:748). He proposed instead the expression "the survival of the fittest," which he felt was free of teleological connotations (Spencer 1872:263–264). But whatever the label, Spencer, as we have seen, made extensive use of the concept in accounting for the increase in size and organization of political units. Furthermore—and much to the dismay of some of his readers—he was unflinching in the way he expressed the operation of natural selection in human history. Thus he once wrote: "As, throughout the organic world, evolution has been achieved by the merciless discipline of Nature, 'red in tooth and claw'; so, in the social world, a discipline scarcely less bloody has been the agency by which societies have been massed together and social structure developed" (Spencer 1908:355).

Most classical evolutionists made at least some use of the concept of natural selection in explaining social evolution. Thus Daniel Brinton observed that "the great law of Natural Selection, of the destruction of the less fit, exercised its sway to preserve that horde which, on the whole, was better adapted for preservation and gave it power over the land" (Brinton 1902:48).

In *Ancient Society,* Morgan wrote that "the organization into classes upon sex [referring to the section system of some Australian aborigines], and the subsequent higher organization into gentes upon kin, must be regarded as the result of great social movements worked out unconsciously through natural selection" (Morgan 1964:50).

Morgan also saw natural selection at work in the rise and spread of forms of the family. Speaking of the "punaluan" family, a form of group marriage that he thought had arisen during the period of Savagery, Morgan wrote: "Commencing . . . in isolated cases, and with a slow recognition of its advantages, it remained an experiment through immense expanses of time; introduced partially at first, then becoming general, and finally universal among the advancing tribes. . . . It affords a good illustration of the operation of the principle of natural selection" (1964:360).

The gens too was considered by Morgan to have conferred a selective advantage on societies possessing it. This advantage was not only cultural but also biological. Thus he argued that "when the gens had become fully developed in its archaic form it would propagate itself over immense areas through the superior powers of an improved stock thus created" (1964:321).

Although Sir Henry Maine did not often discuss the mechanisms of social change, he too made occasional use of natural selection. In combating Morgan's and McLennan's notion of original promiscuity, for example, he invoked the principle in this way: "The inference that they point to[,] an absolute promiscuity[,] must be received with the greatest hesitation . . . because the evils which such a condition would draw with it [i.e., the infecundity alleged to accompany promiscuity] would possibly lead to the extinction or the dangerous weakening of the societies which practiced it" (Maine 1883:209).

The spread of exogamy was likewise explained by Maine in terms of natural selection: "I cannot see why the men who discovered the use of fire and selected the wild forms of certain animals for domestication and of vegetables for cultivation," he wrote, "should not find out that children of unsound constitutions were born of nearly related parents. If such children, left to themselves, are really weakly, the fact would be forced on notice by the stern process of natural selection, affecting either the individual or the tribe" (1883:228). In arguing that the prototypical clan was probably exogamous, Maine suggested that "the practice of taking its wives from a distance, however this came about, increased its physical vigour and caused it to prevail in the struggle for existence" (1883:281).

Tylor also accounted for the origin and spread of local exogamy through the operation of natural selection. In one of his most famous passages he wrote:

Among tribes of low culture there is but one means known of keeping up permanent alliance, and that means is intermarriage. Exogamy, enabling a growing tribe to keep itself compact by constant unions between its spreading clans, enables it to overmatch any number of small . . . groups, isolated and helpless. Again and again in the world's history, savage tribes must have had plainly before their minds the simple practical alternative between marrying-out and being killed out. (Tylor 1889:267)

Tylor saw natural selection acting not only on societies as wholes, but on separate cultural elements as well. Thus he wrote that "from time to time institutions of past ages which have lost their original purpose, and become obsolete or hurtful, are swept away" (Tylor 1878:122). His most trenchant statement of this view appeared in *Primitive Culture*, where he wrote: "History within its proper field, and ethnography over a wider range, combine to show that the institutions which can best hold their own in the world gradually supersede the less fit ones, and that this incessant conflict determines the general resultant course of culture" (Tylor 1871:I, 62).

The idea that in cultural evolution competition was no longer between individuals, or even societies, but rather between elements of culture, found a strong adherent in John Wesley Powell. It is true that in recoiling from Spencer's notion of bloody and unremitting conflict between societies, Powell wrote: "The struggle for existence between human individuals is murder, and the best are not selected thereby. The struggle for existence between bodies of men is warfare, and the best are not selected thereby. The law of natural selection, which Darwin and a host of others have so clearly pointed out as the means by which the progress of animals and plants has been secured, cannot be relied upon to secure the progress of mankind" (Powell 1888:303).

However, in another paper, Powell argued that in cultural evolution man

transfers the struggle for existence from himself to his activities, from the subject, man, to the objects which he creates. Arts compete with one another, and progress in art is by the survival of the fittest in the struggle for existence. In like manner, institutions compete with institutions, languages with languages, opinions with opinions, and reasoning with reasoning; and in each case we have the survival of the fittest in the struggle for existence. Man by his invention has transferred the brutal struggle for existence from himself to the works of his hand. (Powell 1885:193)

Morris Opler (1965a:73) has implied that Tylor's frequent use of the principle of natural selection invalidates Leslie A. White's (1949b:364–367) depiction of him as a historical materialist. Opler appears to believe that natural selection and technological determinism are contradictory and irreconcilable principles of explanation. But this is surely not the case. The two are in no way opposed. Natural selection is, in fact, entirely compatible with almost any view of cultural determination.

Two separate questions are involved here. One is, which factors are predominant in determining cultural development? The other is, how do these factors operate? Whatever determinants are deemed most potent in molding culture, they still can be seen as operating by conferring a selective advantage on certain traits, or on societies bearing those traits. If this is so, then the traits or societies thus favored would tend to displace those not so favored by the clear operation of natural selection.

Even someone who believed that so subtle and tenuous a class of determinants as ideas are what really mold cultures might still argue, with perfect validity, that the way in which certain ideas triumph is by winning out over other ideas through a competitive process that can unambiguously be labeled natural selection. Indeed, one of the classical evolutionists argued precisely this.

We have already cited James Frazer's strong assertion of the primacy of ideas. Immediately following the passage quoted earlier, in which he stressed the determining "influence of thoughts" arising "in a few superior minds," Frazer says of such thoughts: "We cannot tell [how they arise]. All we can say is that on the whole in the conflict of competing forces, whether physical or mental, the strongest at last prevails, the fittest survives. In the mental sphere the struggle for existence is not less fierce and internecine than in the physical, but in the end the better ideas, which we call truth, carry the day" (Frazer 1913a:168).

Conclusion

The reign of classical evolutionism, which we have just surveyed, was marked by bold and vigorous theorizing. Anthropology was founded on fresh evolutionary ideas, and these ideas gave it purpose, direction, and propulsion. The great amounts of cultural data that were then rapidly accumulating were synthesized into a picture of cultural development revealing its full scope and sweep.

To be sure, the classical evolutionists were not without their shortcomings. Preconceptions, errors of fact, and faulty judgments marred some of their work. And the anthropologists who followed them seized on these inadequacies, magnified them beyond their true proportions, added some preconceptions of their own, and gave to the world a distorted picture of what cultural evolutionism had been. As a result, evolutionism was discredited and suffered an almost total eclipse. For decades, the early evolutionists were belittled or ignored, and no one chose to follow in their footsteps.

The generation of scholars who succeeded the evolutionists had a much narrower view of the science of culture. They seemed to cultivate, and in fact to prize, a negativism and skepticism. Accordingly, during the years in which they dominated the profession, the pursuit of broad temporal generalizations was largely abandoned. But in time, anti-evolutionism ran its course, and once again cultural evolutionism quickened the pulse of the discipline. The reaction against evolution, and its eventual resurgence, forms a major part of the history of twentieth-century anthropology. It is to a recounting of the many aspects of this history that we now turn.

5

Anti-Evolutionism in the Ascendancy

The Boasian Backlash

The story of cultural evolutionism in the twentieth century can best be said to begin four years before the century itself. In 1896, in a brief communication in which he cautioned against the dangers of a slipshod use of the comparative method, Franz Boas nonetheless affirmed that "The fundamental idea of this method, as outlined by Tylor and in the early writings of Bastian, is the basis of modern anthropology, and every anthropologist must acknowledge its soundness" (1896a:742).

Very shortly thereafter, however, Boas began to express grave doubts about this method. Indeed, later that same year, in an oft-cited article entitled "The Limitations of the Comparative Method of Anthropology," he explicitly rejected the use of it for establishing evolutionary sequences, declaring "we must . . . consider all the ingenious attempts at reconstruction of a grand system of evolution of society as of very doubtful value" (1896b:905). Moreover, he advised anthropologists to "renounce the vain endeavor to construct a uniform systematic history of the evolution of culture" (1896b:908).

And anthropologists took heed of Boas' advice. So faithfully did they follow it, in fact, that Goldenweiser was to write, with perhaps a bit of gloating, "The triumphal phase of evolutionism was . . . of short duration. With the accumulation of adequate anthropological material the concept of uniformity and of stages was shaken and then collapsed altogether" (1931:659–660).

Thus began an anti-evolutionary tide that was to sweep over the whole field of anthropology for more than fifty years. Boas was only one man, but so powerful a voice was his as professor of anthropology at Columbia University—virtually the only anthropology department in the United States in the early twentieth century—that his opinion carried the day.

Many of the anthropologists trained by Boas went on to found anthropology departments of their own, and transmitted to their students the message they had absorbed from their master. And so it was that anti-evolutionism became firmly entrenched in cultural anthropology, and was destined to last until—if we must pick a date—1959. That was the year of the Darwin centennial when numerous conferences were held describing the enormous impact that evolution had had on biology since the publication of *On the Origin of Species*. As a result, many anthropologists began to realize that a principle so powerful and so fruitful in biology and other sciences was worth reconsidering in their own.

But that is jumping ahead of the story. Let us go back to the Boasian reaction to cultural evolutionism and consider some of the arguments raised against the pronouncements of the classical evolutionists.

There were, to be sure, errors to be corrected. Morgan's sequence of the evolution of marriage and the family—which saw its beginnings in unregulated promiscuity, proceeding through a stage of group marriage, and culminating finally in strict monogamy—was challenged on the basis of its being purely hypothetical. No surviving primitive society showed any vestige of unregulated promiscuity or group marriage.

Another valid Boasian criticism involved the evolution of art. The British ethnologist A. C. Haddon had "tried to demonstrate the existence of one-way sequences from the realistic to the geometric, and Boas wrote his paper on Eskimo needle cases to show that it was equally possible for art to develop from the geometric to the realistic and representational" (Mead 1964:7).

Still another issue that Boas and his followers focused on was the mistaken notion of Bachofen, McLennan, and Morgan that in the history of social institutions, clans had preceded family organization. In 1905, John R. Swanton carried out a comparative study of North American tribes that, according to Robert Lowie, "proved beyond a reasonable doubt that in North America the clanless condition preceded unilateral descent" (1947:145). This finding was hailed as a great victory—the overthrow by means of hard evidence of a postulated evolutionary sequence.

However, the anti-evolutionism prevalent among American anthropologists at the time blinded them to the fact that what Swanton had actually done was to *reverse* the purported evolutionary sequence. He had shown that in the evolution of human social life, the family had *preceded* clan organization. But instead of rejoicing at the discovery of this new evolutionary sequence, the Boasians took pleasure in the fact that Swanton had refuted an old one. It is hardly too much to say that Boas and his followers, for years to come, found it more noble to overthrow an erroneous evolutionary sequence than to establish a valid one.

In their attacks on evolutionism, Boas and his followers tended to focus on a relatively narrow segment of social organization, such as marriage, the family, and clans, failing to consider the great political movement that had carried societies from tiny bands to huge states and empires, such as Herbert Spencer (1967:48–53) had outlined in his sequence of stages designated by the terms Simple, Compound, Doubly Compound, and Trebly Compound. This line of development, duplicated in its essential features by Elman Service's sequence of Band, Tribe, Chiefdom, and State more than half a century later, was never alluded to by Boas or any of his followers. And there were other parallels and regularities in cultural evolution that were there to be found if only they had been looked for.

The sweeping away of faulty evolutionary sequences, with no effort being made to replace them with better ones, appears to have been a source of satisfaction for Boas. Certainly it did not seem to cause him any great regret, for in 1904 he wrote: "The grand system of the evolution of culture, that is valid for all humanity, is losing much of its plausibility. In place of a simple line of evolution there appears a multiplicity of converging and diverging lines which it is difficult to bring under one system" (1904:522).

This statement might be said to have ushered in the era of historical particularism, which came to be recognized as the hallmark of Boas' approach to the practice of anthropology. The great number of facts he amassed in the field and in the library during his career, when organized at all, were strung together in unique individual histories. They were apparently not meant to serve a higher purpose. As Lowie observed, "Probably more familiar than any of his contemporaries with the ethnography of the world, ... [Boas] has never traced the sequence of culture history as a whole" (1937:147).

Writing in 1925, Alexander Goldenweiser, one of Boas' most prominent students, remarked that "If the guiding principles of the [Boasian] historical school were to be condensed into a brief catechism," it would be "the rejection of evolution" in its "crude classical form" (1925a:247). While no one could object to the rejection of anything "crude," one might at least hope that something constructive would be forthcoming to counterbalance this rejection. But Boas' contemplation of evolution contained nothing positive to accompany the negative. No hint was evident of any desire to seek out and embrace those elements of classical evolutionism that remained sound and illuminating.

Six years later, in an article in the *Encyclopedia of the Social Sciences* surveying the entire field of social evolution, Goldenweiser had no difficulty in

pointing out errors in the sequences of the nineteenth-century evolutionists. But at the same time, he could not point to a single valid evolutionary
sequence set forth by Boas or any of his students. It is clear, then, that at this
time the interests and efforts of American anthropologists lay elsewhere.

It is no exaggeration to say that during the first half of the twentieth century, Boasian anthropologists had largely repudiated cultural evolutionism.
If further testimony be needed, we can cite the remarks of several other
Boas students. Bernhard Stern, for one, was convinced of "the inherent
weakness of any evolutionary classification of culture" (1931:135). Melville
Herskovits declared that as far as economic interpretations of culture were
concerned, the evolutionary approach "is to be regarded as the most important single factor standing in the way of an adequate use of data from
nonliterate societies" (1960:56). And Robert H. Lowie concluded his article
"Social Organization" in the *Encyclopedia of the Social Sciences* with the
statement: "The only safe inference is that social phenomena pursue no
fixed sequences, or at least that their sequences are so intricate as to elude
perception" (1931:148). Finally, Berthold Laufer, not actually a student of
Boas but greatly influenced by him, asserted that the theory of cultural evolution is "the most inane, sterile, and pernicious theory ever conceived in
the history of science" (1918:90).

Small wonder, then, that Edward Sapir was moved to say that "evolutionism as an interpretative principle of culture is merely a passing phase in the
history of thought" (1920:378).

Writing in 1937, four decades after Boas' landmark article of 1896, Sol
Tax assessed the results of the onslaught on cultural evolution in the following way: "Never, thereafter, did evolutionism seriously raise its head in
America" (1955b:475). And with evolutionism dead in the water, Boasian
anthropology also turned its back on the broad vistas of ethnological theory in general, and pursued instead what Elman Service characterized as a
"raw, ethnographic, barefoot empiricism" (1971b:9).

In a later section, we shall examine in more detail some other specific
criticisms raised against evolutionary theory by members of the Boas
school, and the attempts of Leslie White to deal with them. First, though, let
us cross the Atlantic and examine the fate of cultural evolutionism in England during the early years of the twentieth century and in the decades that
followed.

Diffusionism in British Anthropology

With the death of Herbert Spencer in 1903 and the retirement of E. B. Tylor
from his professorship at Oxford in 1909, England entered the twentieth

century with its two leading evolutionists at the end of their careers. And with their passing, the study of cultural evolution in that country, if not entirely eclipsed, was at least greatly overshadowed. But before surveying the attenuated form in which British evolutionism survived, let us look at the kind of anthropology that began to replace it.

The most interesting figure in this theoretical sea change was W. H. R. Rivers, who, though trained in psychology, in 1898 had led the famous Cambridge Anthropological Expedition to the Torres Straits, lying between Papua New Guinea and Australia. In 1911, in an article entitled "The Ethnological Analysis of Culture," read before the British Association for the Advancement of Science, Rivers proclaimed his conversion to diffusionism. He began, though, by describing the status of British anthropology as he had found it: "The theoretical anthropology of this country is inspired primarily by the idea of evolution. . . . The efforts of British anthropologists are devoted to tracing out the evolution of custom and institution. What similarities are found in different parts of the world it is assumed, almost as an axiom, that they are due to independent origin and development" (1911:490).

Rivers proceeded to "confess" that until lately he too had been "obsessed" by "a crude evolutionary point of view" (1911:495). However, as a result of his recent fieldwork in Melanesia he had begun to have second thoughts on the subject. "It became evident," he said, "that the present condition of Melanesian society has come into being through the blending of an aboriginal population with various people from without" (1911:493–494). For example, he believed that kava drinking and betel nut chewing had not developed indigenously in Melanesia but had reached it from other culture areas. In other words, they had *diffused* there, and in his address to the British Association he went on to describe "the history of my own conversion" to diffusionism.

Three years later, in 1914, came Rivers' magnum opus, *The History of Melanesian Society*, in which he attempted to account for the present distribution of material traits and social customs in Melanesia by an elaborate scheme of diffusion.

Rivers was a sober and discriminating diffusionist by comparison with two English diffusionists who followed him, G. Elliot Smith and William J. Perry. Unlike Rivers, Smith and Perry can be described as *arch-diffusionists*. The two men set forth their views in separate books, Smith in *The Ancient Egyptians and the Origin of Civilization* (1923) and *The Diffusion of Culture* (1933) and Perry in *The Children of the Sun* (1923). Summarizing Smith's and Perry's so-called "heliolithic theory," A. L. Kroeber wrote:

Primitive culture is conceived as essentially stagnant, inclined to retrogression as much as to progress. It is contended that at one time and place in human history, namely in Egypt around 3000 B.C., an unusual constellation of events produced a cultural spurt leading to the rapid development of agriculture, metallurgy, priesthood, concern with the after life and mummification, writing and other cultural institutions. From this center of origination this great cultural complex was carried in whole or in part, with secondary embellishments and degenerations, to Mesopotamia and the Mediterranean world, to India, Oceania, Mexico and Peru and in fragmentary form even to remote peoples who remained otherwise primitive. (1931:141)

Although Kroeber held that Smith's and Perry's outlandish theory had performed a useful service to anthropology by "helping to clear the ground of the older school of evolutionism" (1931:142), it was in fact a case of the antidote being more lethal than the "poison" it was meant to combat.

By deriving all higher culture from a single source, with no convincing explanation of *how* it had originated there, Smith and Perry did anthropology a disservice. In focusing entirely on the *spread* of culture and virtually ignoring its *origin*, they cast a deep shadow over attempts to understand the dynamics of how cultures grow. After all, whatever diffuses has first to be evolved, and the study of this originating evolutionary process should command priority.

This extreme diffusionism attracted only a tiny handful of anthropologists. Flaring up briefly, arch-diffusionism lay quiescent for some three decades before once more it reared its head, this time with a slightly different region—Mesopotamia—being anointed as the great culture-giver of the world (Heine-Geldern 1956).

As interest in the "heliolithic theory" was declining, another approach to anthropology was beginning to emerge. This approach—which was soon labeled functionalism—regarded cultural evolution with indifference if not disdain.

The Functionalist Reaction

Functionalism, as a way of studying human societies, arose almost simultaneously in the theoretical writings of two men, Bronislaw Malinowski and A. R. Radcliffe-Brown. Expressing functionalism's basic credo, Malinowski declared that a society's culture is not "a loose agglomeration of customs . . . a heap of anthropological curiosities, but a connected living whole . . . all its elements are interconnected and each fulfills a specific function in the integral scheme" (1929b:864).

The functionalism of both men emphasized how sociocultural elements worked here and now, rather than how or when they had come into existence. However, their respective brands of functionalism differed in certain respects. Malinowski's centered on the ways in which a society satisfied the biological needs of its members; Radcliffe-Brown's focused on how customs and institutions together worked to maintain the social order in some kind of equilibrium. In the writings of neither of these men do we find the open hostility to cultural evolution that we see in Boas or some of his followers. The attitude of Malinowski and Radcliffe-Brown toward cultural evolution was generally skeptical, sometimes disdainful, and, on occasion, almost condescending.

Malinowski

Malinowski was more anti-evolutionist than Radcliffe-Brown. He had little interest in the origin of institutions or in historical reconstructions based on inference. Much of nineteenth-century cultural evolutionism he rejected as belonging to "the limbo of untrammeled conjecture" (quoted in White 1987:14)."It was Malinowski's proud boast," Edmund Leach (1957:126) tells us, "that he had taught anthropologists the futility of the pursuit of conjectural history."

One of the bases of Malinowski's distaste for the classical evolutionists was their use of *survivals:* "The method of evolutionary anthropology [he said erroneously, except in the case of James Frazer] was based primarily on the concept of survival" (1931:624). Malinowski was steadfastly opposed to any use of survivals in an attempt to reconstruct earlier stages of human history. Virtually every trait in a society's inventory, he held, had a current role to play in maintaining its viability.

Thus, speaking of technology, Malinowski found it "improbable that any culture should harbor a great many irrelevant traits, . . . handed over as survivals, useless fragments of a vanished stage" (1931:624–625). And if that was true with regard to technology, "Still less is it likely that customs, institutions or moral values should present this necrotic or irrelevant character" (1931:625).

When his theoretical guard was down, though, Malinowski occasionally left the door open a crack for modest evolutionary reconstructions. In *Coral Gardens and Their Magic,* for example, he says that "the ethnographer ought to keep his eyes open for any relevant indications of evolutionary lags or historical stratifications" (1935:I, 459). However, such reconstructions as he might allow he would push well into the indefinite future: "Until the nature of the various cultural phenomena, their function and their form are understood and described more fully," he said, "it seems premature to speculate on possible origins and stages" (1931:624).

As Malinowski's writings became better known, especially his vivid descriptions of the Trobriand Islanders, his influence widened and deepened. Soon he had won a large following among young British anthropologists who came under his spell at the University of London, where he taught. Indeed, his teaching had something of a messianic zeal: "At first . . . Malinowski was a small voice," wrote I. C. Jarvie. "Yet with quite startling rapidity it began to be heard in the corridors of British anthropology. Before we know where we are there is a mob of Malinowski followers charging around tearing the place to pieces and rebuilding" (1969:43).

But though he later took some interest in social change, especially in colonial Africa, Malinowski never cast a benevolent eye on evolutionary reconstructions carried out on a large scale. As Kroeber then noted, "Malinowski so far has preferred to travel his dazzling orbit unhampered by even rudimentary historical considerations" (1935:563).

Radcliffe-Brown

A. R. Radcliffe-Brown was a different sort of functionalist. He had studied the works of the French sociologist Émile Durkheim and been much influenced by them. Thus he often called his own work comparative sociology rather than anthropology. Like Malinowski, he argued that a culture is "normally a systemic or integrated unity in which every element has a distinct function" (quoted in Lowie 1937:223).

However, Radcliffe-Brown had read Herbert Spencer as well as Durkheim and declared that "We can give provisional acceptance to Spencer's fundamental theory [of social evolution], while rejecting the various pseudo-historical speculations which he added to it" (1952:8). And this acceptance of a tempered evolutionism, he added, "gives us certain concepts which may be useful as analytical tools" (1952:8).

Thus he believed that within the "systematic comparative study of many diverse societies . . . there is a place for a theory of social evolution" (1947:82). Indeed, at one time he even went so far as to call himself an evolutionist. In an article entitled "Evolution, Social or Cultural?" he actually said, "It has been one of my aims as an evolutionist to try to discover the interconnections between religion and the structure . . . of societies" (1947:81). And he also saw "no reason . . . why the two kinds of study—the historical and the functional—should not be carried on side by side in perfect harmony" (1952:186n.).

In *theory*, then, Radcliffe-Brown was willing to allow space inside his tent to the evolutionist determined to trace the origin and development of institutions. But in *practice* it was rather a different story. The evolutionist was asked to leave the tent as soon as he began to make *inferences* about the general course of human history using means that Radcliffe-Brown characterized as "the method of conjectural history." This method he regarded as "one of the chief obstacles to the development of a scientific theory of human society" (1952:50). Since he conceived of social evolution "as essentially a process of diversification" (1947:80–81), the continual divergence and redivergence of cultures due to the endless changes in local circumstances, he was led to the inescapable conclusion that "any culture, any social system is the end result of a unique series of historical accidents" (1952:185).

Yet any broad evolutionary formulation had to have as a starting point this "unique series of historical accidents." And it had to make inferences, even speculative ones, where hard historical evidence was not immediately available. In a letter to Claude Lévi-Strauss, Radcliffe-Brown made clear his attitude toward such evolutionary inferences: "I regard any genetic hypothesis," he declared, "as being of very little importance, since it cannot be more than a hypothesis or conjecture" (1953:109).

Thus, if there were to be laws of social process—and Radcliffe-Brown was keen on the idea of sociological laws—they had to be *synchronic* rather than *diachronic*. With regard to the possibility of formulating laws of social development—diachronic laws—he was anything but optimistic: "To establish any probability for such conjectures [i.e., well-founded historical reconstructions] we should need to have a knowledge of laws of social development which we certainly do not possess and to which *I do not think we shall ever attain*" (1952:50; emphasis mine).

Nonetheless, Radcliffe-Brown did flirt with the notion of what he took to be synchronic laws governing human social systems. At one point in his monograph "The Social Organization of Australian Tribes" he speaks of "a universal sociological law though it is not yet possible to formulate precisely its scope, namely that in certain specific conditions a society has need to provide itself with a segmentary [clan] organization" (1931a:109).

Such a statement, however, was enough to set Lowie's teeth on edge and he proceeded to pour scorn on Radcliffe-Brown for having made it. "Whoever heard of a universal law," wrote Lowie, "with an as yet undefinable scope, of a law that works in certain specific *but unspecified* conditions? Is it a law that some societies have clans, and others have not? Newton did not tell us that bodies either fall or rise" (1937:225).

Yet, vague as he was in expressing it, Radcliffe-Brown was onto something. Let me venture to suggest what it was. The "unspecified conditions" that Lowie derided may well turn out to be a society's attainment of a certain level of population. If this is so, Radcliffe-Brown's statement becomes a law, an *evolutionary law*, namely, that as societies grow in size, they reach a point at which internal segmentation (principally in the form of clans) begins to occur. And the facts of ethnography seem to bear this out. Thus, one can ask, is there a native village of, say, 500 or more persons anywhere in the world which is *not* internally segmented?

The sad fact is that their respective theoretical positions clouded the vision of both men: Radcliffe-Brown, because his *synchronic* bias failed to let him see more deeply into what was essentially a recurring *diachronic* process; Lowie, because his own brand of anti-evolutionism left him unprepared to appreciate a genuine evolutionary formulation when it came to him partially disguised.

Malinowski and Radcliffe-Brown not only began British social anthropology, they influenced it in a way that was both profound and persistent. To this day, British functionalists (or structural-functionalists, as they now prefer to call themselves) remain at best indifferent, and in some cases downright hostile, to cultural evolution.

Having thus brought "structuralism" into the picture (even if indirectly), it is worth noting that French structural anthropology, best represented by Claude Lévi-Strauss, proved no friendlier to evolutionism than did straight-out functionalism. Moreover, I would argue, a nonevolutionary approach may actually *impede* one's understanding of structural phenomena. Let me illustrate this point with Lévi-Strauss's discussion of moieties.

In *Structural Anthropology* he writes: "almost as many kinds of dual organization are known as peoples possessing it. Where then does it begin and where does it end? Let us immediately rule out evolutionist . . . interpretations" (Lévi-Strauss 1967:10). But let us see how a simple evolutionary perspective might have contributed to a deeper understanding of the origin and function of moieties.

Lévi-Strauss (1967:128–160) makes a distinction between *diametric* moieties and *concentric* moieties. The former divide a village down the middle into equal halves; the latter divide it into an inner and an outer ring. Were he an evolutionist, Lévi-Strauss might have suggested that diametric moieties are characteristic of egalitarian societies, whereas concentric ones are characteristic of more nearly stratified ones, the two rings comprising it dividing a village into a higher-status inner moiety and a lower-status outer moiety.

Concentric moieties might thus represent, not just a structural variant, but a more *evolved* form of dual organization, occurring among societies that were no longer purely egalitarian, but had begun to develop important status differences. This suggestion may prove to be false, of course, but at least it is a *plausible* interpretation of the difference between the two types of moieties, a difference that otherwise remains unexplained. The suggestion might have been pursued to some advantage, instead of being ruled out of court by fiat as "evolutionist."

Anti-Evolutionism in Later British Social Anthropology

Returning to British social anthropology, let us see how the early functionalists put their stamp on the generations to follow.

Anthony Giddens (a sociologist, actually) informs us that "Human history does not have an evolutionary 'shape' and positive harm can be done by attempting to compress it into one" (1984:236). Lucy Mair, in commenting on Fred Eggan's prediction that British social anthropologists will come to make greater use of the "comparative method," concedes that "we have been more and more interested in following . . . changes over time in social institutions," but concludes that "it is unlikely that we shall return to the ethnologists' interest in the source of cultural elements" (1970:46).

But where Mair was polite and tentative in expressing her feelings about cultural evolution, Edmund Leach was blunt and unequivocal. He began by denying its relevance to the sorts of problems British social anthropologists were concerned with, remarking that "whether or not evolutionary doctrine is true, it is certainly quite irrelevant for the understanding of present-day societies" (1957:125). And he also spoke scornfully of "the total inadequacy of all anthropological dabblers in conjectural history" (1982:51). As for himself, he declared that "Anthropologists of my sort are not counterfeit historians who devote their energies to the reconstruction of a past which we cannot possibly know" (1982:49).

This unshakable mind-set against the pursuit of evolutionary studies at times led British social anthropologists to adopt some rather strange positions, even the more acute ones among them. Thus Max Gluckman, writing in 1965 and aware that during the previous decade there had arisen "a new school of anthropologists emphasizing evolutionary development in a much more sophisticated manner" (1965:114), was nevertheless led to utter a series of remarkable statements (1965:114).

At the time he was writing, Gluckman was familiar with Elman Service's proposed sequence of stages of political evolution, which consisted of Band, Tribe, Chiefdom, and State. But despite Service's clear depiction of them as successively higher and more complex stages, Gluckman held that this sequence "does not necessarily mean that . . . states have a more complicated social organization" than societies of a lower stage (1965:113). "Furthermore," he says, "we cannot be sure that one has evolved out of the other in the general sweep of human history" (1965:113). Surely he can't mean, for example, that a state does not have to be preceded by a chiefdom, but can

develop directly from a band. Or can he? Yes, he can! At least he comes perilously close to suggesting this very possibility: "we cannot be sure that if
mankind everywhere was first organized in hunting-bands, no section
could move from that type of polity straight to well-organized statehood
without passing through intervening stages" (1965:113).

Now, Gluckman knew better than that. *No* society ever went from a band
to a state in a single jump, without first passing through the intermediate
stages. Moreover, any good functionalist can offer a dozen structural reasons why such a giant leap would have been impossible. But apparently so
afraid was Gluckman of appearing to be abandoning the functionalist credo
and embracing some kind of invariable evolutionary sequence that he was
ready to give voice to a most absurd proposition.

This deep-seated unwillingness on the part of British social anthropologists to countenance the validity of any historical reconstruction has not,
however, been universal. It has been openly challenged by one of their own.
E. E. Evans-Pritchard began his critique of his colleagues by questioning the
basic premise of functionalism: "I cannot accept, without many qualifications," he wrote, "the functional theory dominant in English anthropology
today" (1969:20).

Not only did he question the article of faith that every trait had a specifi-
able, integrative function, he also rejected the auxiliary notion that societies
could be sufficiently understood by examining their structure and function
at the time they were being studied. "[I]t must be accepted that far from the
history of a society or an institution being irrelevant to a functional study
of it, we only fully understand it when we can view it not only in the present but also retrospectively" (Evans-Pritchard 1969:56). "The claim that
one can understand the functioning of institutions at a certain point of
time without knowing how they have come to be what they are," he
protested, "is to me an absurdity" (1969:21). He likened it to the belief that
"we can understand the anatomy and physiology of a horse without requiring to know anything about its descent from its five-toed ancestor"
(1969:55). And he concluded the argument by stating: "The fact that nineteenth-century anthropologists were uncritical in their reconstructions
ought not to lead to the conclusion that all effort expended in this direction
is [a] waste of time" (1969:21).

The narrow functionalist point of view that made British social anthropologists working in Africa disinclined to account for the emergence of
complex societies on that continent deprived them of the chance to make a
great contribution to the comprehension of the process of political evolution. Native African societies manifested almost every gradation involved in
the process, from nomadic band to autonomous village to the state. Yet this

rich comparative material that British Africanists had at their fingertips and could have used to construct a detailed and convincing sequence of political development was never so employed, and a great opportunity was missed. To be sure, many descriptive monographs of the highest quality were turned out, but the deepening of our understanding of the rise of states from simple beginnings was carried no further.

It was not only the *stages* of political evolution that were missed. The *process* of political development that led to the state was also left unexplored. For example, had British Africanists only asked themselves why it was that a number of states had arisen among those societies wedged in between lakes and mountains in the Interlacustrine region of Africa, while no states had evolved to the east, they might have hit upon the importance of environmental circumscription and resource concentration in state formation. Not surprisingly, of course, they failed to find what they were not looking for.

Remaining Islands of Cultural Evolutionism: James G. Frazer

Though cultural evolution was under attack and in full retreat on both sides of the Atlantic, it had not been completely routed from the field. Islands of resistance to anti-evolutionism still remained. We can, in fact, identify three such "islands" where anti-evolutionism was pretty much disregarded and evolutionary work was being actively pursued. Let us begin with the first of these "islands," represented by James G. Frazer.

In a way, Frazer belongs with the classical evolutionists, and in fact we have already discussed him there, if only sparingly. His "intellectual debut," as his biographer put it, came in 1885 when he was allowed to read a paper at a meeting of the Anthropological Institute (Ackerman 1987:40). Among those present was Herbert Spencer, and in a letter to Francis Galton, chairman of the anthropology section, thanking him for being given the opportunity to speak to the Institute, Frazer wrote: "That Herbert Spencer should be [in the audience] . . . is more gratifying to me than I care to say, for my intellectual debt to his writings is deep and will be life long" (quoted in Ackerman 1987:22).

Frazer's most famous book, *The Golden Bough,* was first published in 1890, but its fame came mainly in the twentieth century. It was revised in 1900 and subsequently expanded to 12 volumes. In this work, which in its one-volume abridgment became immensely popular, Frazer held that "the belief and behavior of classical antiquity could be fully understood only in the light of, and in comparison with, those of 'savages' and 'primitives,' which they closely resembled" (Ackerman 1991:216).

In giving his reasons for turning more and more to the study of primitive peoples, Frazer wrote: "Civilization is extremely complex, savagery is comparatively simple, and moreover it is undoubtedly the source from which all civilization has been ultimately derived by a slow process of evolution. It seemed to me therefore that if we are to understand the complex product we must begin by studying the simple elements out of which it was gradually compounded" (quoted in Kardiner and Preble 1961:73).

The theoretical framework upon which Frazer built a number of his studies was the concept of survivals. In the preface to one of his most important books, *Folk-lore in the Old Testament* (1918), he made explicit the logic behind that concept:

> Modern researches into the early history of man, conducted on different lines, have converged with almost irresistible force on the conclusion that all civilized races have at some period or other emerged from a stage of savagery resembling more or less closely the state in which many backward races have continued to the present time; and that, long after the majority of men in a community have ceased to think and act like savages, not a few traces of the old ruder modes of life and thought survive in the habits and institutions of the people. (quoted in Downie 1940:55)

Then, bringing this general argument down to cases, he went on to say how he proposed to apply the concept:

> Despite the high moral and religious development of the ancient Hebrews, there is no reason to suppose that they formed an exception to this general law. They, too, had probably passed through a stage of barbarism and even of savagery; and this probability, based on the analogy of other races, is confirmed by an examination of their literature, which contains many references to beliefs and practices which can hardly be explained except on the supposition that they are rudimentary survivals from a far lower level of culture. It is to the illustration and explanation of a few such relics of ruder times, as they are preserved like fossils in the Old Testament, that I have addressed myself in the present work. (quoted in Downie 1940:55–56)

It was Frazer's contention, running through several of his books, that in the evolution of human thinking about how the external world could be controlled there had been three major stages: magic, religion, and science. Magic he thought of as the earliest stage since it invoked only automatic, mechanical means involving such things as spells, incantations, and formulas, and did not require the notion of personalized spirits or gods. This view may not be widely accepted today, but at the same time it is difficult to refute. In any case, Frazer, while always ready to formulate theories, was anything but dogmatic in his attachment to them. Thus he wrote: "it is the fate of theories to be washed away . . . and I am not so presumptuous as to expect or desire for mine an exemption from the common lot. I hold them all very lightly, and have used them chiefly as convenient pegs on which to hang my collection of facts" (quoted in Kardiner and Preble 1961:80).

Although associated with Cambridge for much of his life, Frazer never taught there, and thus never built up a cadre of students who might have defended his ideas and carried them further. Moreover, he pursued his studies independently of professional anthropology, and thus never became part of its mainstream. However, his elegant style of writing, his wealth of colorful illustrations, and the universal appeal of the subjects with which he dealt, all served to mark him as one of the outstanding cultural evolutionists of the early twentieth century.

Hobhouse, Wheeler, and Ginsberg

Leonard T. Hobhouse is generally regarded as a sociologist and moral philosopher, yet he made an excursion into anthropology of enough significance to qualify him as an important figure in early twentieth-century evolutionism. In 1915, in collaboration with two of his students, G. C. Wheeler and Morris Ginsberg, he published a study entitled *The Material Culture and Social Institutions of the Simpler Peoples*. His objective in this work was to determine what degree of correlation might exist between a society's mode of subsistence and various aspects of its social and political organization.

Before presenting the results of his evolutionary study, Hobhouse acknowledged that he was aware of the errors committed by—or at least imputed to—the classical evolutionists, and indicated his desire to avoid them. For example, wishing to disassociate himself from what he considered a crude unilinear evolutionism, he wrote: "Anyone with a sense for the facts soon recognises that the course of social evolution is not unitary but that different races and different communities of the same race have, in fact, whether they started from the same point or not, diverged early, rapidly, and in many different directions at once" (1930:1).

And he rejected the notion that "any given institution must take its rise in one form and must pass through a series of graded changes in a uniform direction" (1930:4). In the present study, he affirmed, there were to be no presuppositions. Instead, he sought to formulate "a theory which would really grow out of the facts themselves" (1930:1).

In order to ascertain what these facts were he proposed to use the comparative method and to do so on a large scale. Thus in his sample there were no fewer than 643 societies, the largest cross-cultural sample employed up to that time. The societies in the sample were grouped into several levels or "strata," based on the degree of development of their respective modes of subsistence. Just as "it is in the main from the actual composition and arrangements of existing strata . . . that the geologist infers the history of the earth's crust," he argued, it is by the application of "analogous methods that any scientific theory of social evolution must rely" (1930:2).

Hobhouse first ranked societies according to an objective attribute that was generally agreed to be a determinant of overall culture level, and then looked to see to what extent advances in various other aspects of social organization were associated with advances in this one. "The development which seems best to serve this purpose," he said, was "that of . . . the control of man over nature as reflected in the arts of life" (1930:6), that is, in what we would call the mode of subsistence.

"We seek . . . first to distinguish the advancing grades of . . . [subsistence], and, secondly . . . to determine how far various forms of political and social institutions can be correlated with each grade" (1930:7). These institutions included such things as forms of government, judicial procedure, social stratification, and property ownership.

The 643 societies in the sample were then classified into eight subsistence types: Lower Hunters, Higher Hunters, Dependent Hunters, Incipient Agriculturalists, Pure Agriculturalists, Highest Agriculturalists, Lower Pastoralists, and Higher Pastoralists, and the criteria for inclusion in each category were specified (1930:17–27). These eight types of subsistence were not thought of as representing a single line of development, however, but rather constituted a line that bifurcated after the stage of Higher Hunters was reached, with Lower Pastoralists being regarded as more or less equivalent to Pure Agriculturalists, and Higher Pastoralists as roughly comparable to Highest Agriculturalists (1930:26–27). When diagrammed, the evolutionary "tree" of subsistence practices looked somewhat like a wishbone (1930:29).

The correlations obtained by the authors were presented in a series of tables. We can use as an example the trait "regular system of public justice" (as contrasted with the private redress of injuries). Setting aside the pastoralists for this correlation, a regular system of public justice was present in 1 percent of Lower Hunters, 5 percent of Higher Hunters, 11 percent of Dependent Hunters, 21 percent of Incipient Agriculturalists, 26 percent of Pure Agriculturalists, and 42 percent of Highest Agriculturalists (1930:72).

Overall, the findings of Hobhouse, Wheeler, and Ginsberg revealed an impressive degree of association between modes of subsistence and various features of social and political organization. Beyond that, however, the authors did not choose to go. For example, they made no attempt to arrange the various traits they had investigated into a single line representing the relative order in which societies, by and large, had developed them. Thus their findings might be characterized as safe and solid, rather than bold and venturesome.

The main criticism that can be leveled against this study involves the sample it employed. It was not chosen with an eye toward faithful representation of the primitive peoples of the world. For example, 11 percent of all the 643 societies in the sample, and 34 percent of all hunters, consisted of Australian aborigines. Moreover, the possible effects of diffusion on the correlations obtained—"Galton's problem"—was in no way controlled for. However, in evaluating the work of Hobhouse, Wheeler, and Ginsberg as a whole, we can say that it was a very ambitious undertaking, carried out with prodigious effort, and resulting in the finding of many distinct and demonstrable regularities in the evolution of culture.

Sumner and Keller

In the early 1870s, William Graham Sumner happened to read Herbert Spencer's *The Study of Sociology* and, as he later wrote, "These essays immediately gave me the lead which I wanted to bring into shape the crude notions which had been floating in my head" (1889:265–266). He soon formed a class at Yale for reading and discussing Spencer's book, the first course in sociology ever taught in an American university (Starr 1925:387).

What Sumner found of value in *The Study of Sociology* was that it offered a "conception of society, of social forces, and of the science of society [which] was just the one which I had been groping after, but had not been able to reduce for myself" (Sumner 1889:266). For Sumner, Spencer's book "solved the old difficulties about the relation of social science to history, . . . and offered a definite and magnificent field for work" (1889:266).

Sumner read some of Spencer's other works as well, notably *The Principles of Sociology* and *Descriptive Sociology* (Starr 1925:345), and from them he derived two cardinal ideas for his future work: first, the principle of social evolution, and second, the importance of accumulating a large body of ethnographic data to be used in generating and testing his theories and generalizations. As he read Spencer's *The Principles of Sociology* Sumner reported, "I was constantly getting evidence that sociology, if it borrowed the theory of evolution in the first place, would speedily render it back again enriched by new and independent evidence" (1889:166).

Speaking at the farewell banquet given to Spencer just before he left New York after his only visit to the United States, Sumner unreservedly proclaimed his allegiance to evolution: "I can see no boundaries to the scope of the philosophy of evolution," he declared. "That philosophy is sure to embrace all the interests of man on this earth. It will be one of its crowning triumphs to bring light and order into the social problems which are of universal bearing on all mankind" (Sumner 1918:404–405).

In the preface to his groundbreaking book, *Folkways*, published in 1906, Sumner remarked, "In 1899 I began to write a text-book of sociology from material which I had used in lectures during the previous ten or fifteen years" (1906:iii). However, as he continued to work on it, the book he envisioned grew unmanageably in size. Indeed, when he died, it remained in the form of manuscript fragments and of voluminous notes, and did not see publication—as *The Science of Society*—until fully seventeen years later.

As Sumner worked on his projected textbook on sociology, he tells us, "I wanted to introduce my own treatment of the 'mores' . . . [but found] I could not do justice to it in a chapter of another book. I therefore turned aside [from what was to become *The Science of Society*] to write a treatise on the 'Folkways'"(1906:iii). A principal message of this new book was that "the folkways are habits of the individual and customs of the society which arise from efforts to satisfy needs . . . and so they win traditional authority. . . . Then they become regulations for succeeding generations and take on the character of a social force" (Sumner 1906:iv).

After finishing *Folkways*, Sumner returned to what he hoped would become his magnum opus, but fell far short of completing it. When he died in 1910, in addition to parts of the manuscript, he left behind a vast accumulation of ethnographic data. "Never seeming to feel that he had enough material," his student, Albert G. Keller later wrote, "he still continued to read a great deal" (Sumner and Keller 1927:I, xxiii). Although Sumner never lived to see them published, he was proud of his accumulation of facts and boasted that if Spencer had had "those notes up in my attic," *The Principles of Sociology* "would have been a better book" (Keller 1933:32).

It fell to Sumner's faithful student and collaborator, Albert G. Keller, to continue the project, gathering even more material and arranging the huge collection of ethnographic data finally accumulated—from nearly 3,000 sources—into publishable form. In four massive volumes, this work appeared in 1927–1928 as *The Science of Society*. Today it sits gathering dust on library shelves, an all but unknown and untapped treasure trove of ethnographic data.

In finishing *The Science of Society*, Keller did more than add material and splice together the fragments of manuscript bequeathed to him by Sumner. He gave the whole work more concrete shape and clearer direction. "Professor Sumner enjoined upon me," wrote Keller, "when we were talking over the work I had set out to do upon his collection and manuscripts, that he wanted me to be bound in no degree whatsoever by what he had written" (Sumner and Keller 1927:I, xxiv). And indeed Keller introduced elements of his own into the work. For example, as he wrote in his introduction to it, "I . . . have made explicit and emphatic the conception of evolution in the mores—an idea implicitly recognized in Sumner's writing but explicitly denied by him" (Sumner and Keller 1927:I, xxv).

Thus it is that in the first chapter of the book we read: "In their developed forms institutions are very complex. . . . they reveal at once their evolutionary quality in the very fact that they constitute adjustments to life conditions. This book will substantiate that fact in almost every paragraph" (Sumner and Keller 1927:I, 35). And a few pages later Keller remarks, "Having scanned the process by which societal adjustment is attained, we are in a position to realize that the actual societal forms which result from it must constitute an evolutionary series" (Sumner and Keller 1927:I, 39).

In addition to these repeated allusions to evolution and to an evolutionary sequence, two other threads ran through *The Science of Society* even more strongly. One was *causality* and the other *function*. The "maintenance mores," as Sumner and Keller often called subsistence, were presented as being the motive power of society, and, along with this, examples were continually presented of the numerous and complex interrelations that existed among customs and institutions.

Sumner had at first strongly embraced social evolution, but he appeared to have backed away from it as he worked on what became *The Science of Society*. It was Keller who reinjected it into the book as he continued to expand and revise. In an unpublished paper that apparently was intended for inclusion in *Folkways*, but was ultimately left out, Sumner had written: "as we go upwards from the arts to the mores and from the mores to the philosophies and ethics, we leave behind us the arena on which natural selection produces progressive evolution out of the close competition of forms some of which are more fit to survive than others, and we come into an area which has no boundaries and no effective competition" (quoted in Keller 1931:325).

Remarking on Sumner's disinclination to apply to social evolution the mechanisms that had been so successful in explaining organic evolution, Keller wrote: "As for the systematic application to the folkways of the central idea of Darwinian evolution—adaptation to environment, secured through the operation of variation, selection, and transmission—I do not believe that it occurred to Sumner to undertake it" (Keller 1931:409).

But Keller was not prepared to follow his mentor in this regard. "It is my belief," he affirmed, that before Sumner could have been satisfied that he had rounded out his *Science of Society,* "he would have been obliged to return to the topic of evolution in its relation to the folkways" (Keller 1931:409). And after carefully reflecting on the matter, Keller reached "the conviction that some understanding must be arrived at respecting societal evolution before it would be possible to complete a general book on the science of society" (Keller 1931:410).

In order to provide this "understanding," Keller temporarily set aside work on *The Science of Society* and in 1915, five years after Sumner's death, published his own book, *Societal Evolution*, in which he systematically applied the Darwinian factors of variation, selection, and transmission to the evolution of human society. This book stands as the first attempt ever made to apply, in a rigorous and thoroughgoing fashion, the Darwinian model to the study of social evolution. It was not to be the last.

In 1931, in an enlarged edition of *Societal Evolution*, Keller made a sharp distinction between the Darwinian and Spencerian conceptions of evolution. After quoting Spencer's definition with its emphasis on increasing definiteness, coherence, and heterogeneity as the characteristics of evolution, Keller objected to it: "Who can refute this? Yet who can use it? . . . This formula, in comparison with the Darwinian factors, helps in no way toward scientific discovery; it is not the cloud by day, nor yet the fire by night. Rather it is like the vault of an overcast sky; it covers all things, but nobody can get his direction from it and fare forth" (1931:14).

"Evolution is adjustment to life-conditions, and that is all there is to it," Keller asserted (1931:326). And in the 400-odd pages of the book he proceeded to give many examples of the Darwinian mechanisms at work in the transmutation of societies.

George P. Murdock

The line of evolutionism pursued and kept alive by Sumner and Keller did not entirely end with them. It was continued, if in a qualified and attenuated form, by Keller's most prominent student, George P. Murdock. Murdock's doctoral dissertation had been an edited translation, under the title of *The Evolution of Culture*, of Julius Lippert's *Kulturgeschichte der Menschheit* (Lippert 1931), a work that had been extremely influential on both Sumner and Keller. As Murdock wrote in his introduction to it, "The extent of the debt of Sumner and Keller to Lippert is revealed by the fact that in their monumental work, *The Science of Society*, they refer to him no less than four hundred separate times, far more than to any other one authority" (Lippert 1931:xxvi).

In 1937 Murdock contributed an article entitled "Correlations of Matrilineal and Patrilineal Institutions" to a Festschrift for Keller. The conclusions reached in that article were guardedly sympathetic to a moderate evolutionism. Thus Murdock concluded that "The unilateral evolutionism theory emerges as unsatisfactory, to be sure, but by no means so devoid of a reasonable factual basis as is generally assumed" (Murdock 1937b:469). And summarizing his own views on the subject, which were those of Sumner and Keller as well, Murdock wrote: "The sociological school refuses to accept the dictum that cultures are merely congeries of traits assembled by the historical accidents of invention and diffusion, and it regards the repudiation of general laws or principles in the social sciences as probably unjustified and certainly premature" (1937b:450). Then, reaffirming a position that Sumner had staunchly held to in *Folkways,* Murdock observed that the "[sociological school] prefers to assume that there is operative in culture a tendency toward integration, a strain toward consistency" (1937b:450).

In its scope, *The Science of Society* had been broadly comparative, but had nevertheless failed to employ anything like a systematic sample of societies. The sheer number of societies used was expected to overcome any problems arising out of the charge of unrepresentativeness. However, in a graduate seminar that had served as preparation for writing the article that was to appear in the Keller Festschrift, Murdock had drawn a carefully selected sample of 230 societies that he used to test theories about bilateral versus unilineal descent, rules of post-marital residence, exogamy and endogamy, and the like. This sample proved to be the germ out of which developed the Human Relations Area Files, a large and systematically arranged corpus of data that, by facilitating the application of the comparative method, was to provide future students with a means to test evolutionary hypotheses and propositions.

Murdock, however, pursued only a limited evolutionism. For example, as part of the study just cited, he recorded the presence or absence of the following eleven traits among the 230 societies in his sample: agriculture, domesticated animals, writing, pottery, weaving, metallurgy, full-time specialists, money, social classes, government, and priesthood. He failed to list the names of the societies in his sample, but we know that included in it were an Eskimo group and some higher-level societies, possibly the Maya or the Inca. Had he tallied the presence of these eleven traits among his 230 societies, their occurrence would have ranged from 0 for the Eskimo (and presumably other simple societies) to 11 for a few higher-level societies. Murdock would thus have arrived at a crude but nonetheless objective measure of their relative degrees of cultural development.

This would have been a useful and important achievement, especially coming at a time when anti-evolutionism was at its height in America. But at the time, Murdock was not interested in the cumulative aspect of cultural evolution, and thus missed a chance to present a valid index of it. Not until some three decades later did he finally turn his hand to such an attempt, but by that time others had already done so successfully, and so instead of being in the forefront of this endeavor he had to content himself with being one of the followers.

The Barren Landscape

But these three attempts to keep evolutionism alive—those of Frazer, Hobhouse and associates, and Sumner and Keller—were but flickering candles, unable to resist the strong anti-evolutionary winds that were now blowing over the anthropological landscape. Julian Steward (1956:69) remarked that by the early part of the twentieth century, cultural evolution was "left for dead." And using much the same wording, Alexander Lesser (1985a:78) declared in 1939 that the evolutionism of Morgan, Tylor, and Spencer was "as dead as a doornail." Thus by the mid-1920s, with the virtual extinction of cultural evolutionism—and indeed of any robust form of theorizing—anthropology had fallen deep into a Dark Age.

The credit for dethroning classical evolutionism in anthropology, wrote George P. Murdock (1937a:xiv), "must go in large measure to Franz Boas and his followers." Nor did they themselves hesitate to assume it. Paul Radin (1933:4), for example, one of the most prominent members of the Boas School, affirmed that the successful challenge to the evolutionary point of view had been brought about "notably by Boas," adding that "a good part of his energies and those of his school" had been devoted to that end.

It is true that Lowie (1946:227) once claimed that "Boas and his students attacked not evolution, but [only] Morgan's and other writers' evolutionary schemes." However, this view is hard to sustain in the face of statements by Boas' own students, such as Ruth Benedict's (1931:809) assertion that "the idea of evolution . . . has to be laid aside in the study of culture" or Ruth Bunzel's (1938:578) allusion to "the fallacy inherent in *all* evolutionary arguments." On this matter, Radin (1939:303) specifically contradicted Lowie, affirming that "if Boas and his school rejected the developmental schemes of Tylor and Morgan this must, in no sense, be ascribed to the inadequacies and crudities of these schemes, but rather to the fact that they rejected all developmental schemes." And in fact Lowie himself had declared more than twenty years earlier that "Anthropology . . . is now elaborately backwatering. It is itself rapidly drifting to the anti-evolutionary, historical method" (Lowie 1920:533).

In any case, there is little doubt that evolutionism *was* rejected, and that by the 1930s it was in total eclipse. Radcliffe-Brown (1947:80) offered testimony to this effect: "In 1931, when I spoke of social evolution in my lectures in [the University of] Chicago," he wrote, "one of the students pointed out to me that 'Boas and Lowie have proved that there is no such thing as social evolution.' I found that this was a generally accepted view in the United States."

Theorizing Disavowed

At this point we may ask: On what basis had the theory of cultural evolutionism been rejected by American ethnologists? But before considering this question, it should be pointed out that the reaction by Franz Boas and his school was not confined to evolution alone. It ran deeper than that. It stemmed from a frame of mind in which theorizing of any kind was held suspect and thus avoided. This hostility toward theory was pointed out by several of Boas' own students. Paul Radin (1933:253) for one spoke of "an exaggerated distrust of theories of whatever description" on the part of Boas, and Alexander Goldenweiser (1925a:247), observing that "the critical habit tends to discourage creative contributions," found among Boas and his followers "a certain timidity in the face of broader and more speculative problems," and, accordingly, "a reluctance to indulge in . . . synthesis."

No better epitome of this anti-theoretical attitude of the Boas school can be found than Berthold Laufer's (1930:162) flat admission that "I am in a state of mind where I would no longer give a dime . . . for a new theory, but I am always enthusiastic about new facts."

These statements seemed to justify Murdock's (1954:18) assertion that "The most striking characteristic of American anthropology during the first quarter of the twentieth century, which was dominated by Franz Boas, was its negative attitude toward most theories which had gained a measure of acceptance in the human sciences."

By the late 1930s things had reached such a pass that Clyde Kluckhohn (1939:333) felt justified in declaring that "to suggest that something is 'theoretical' is to suggest that it is slightly indecent." Nor was this assessment of the deadening effect of Boasian particularism anything new. As far back as 1920, A. L. Kroeber (1920:380), in reviewing Lowie's *Primitive Society,* warned his colleagues that "As long as we continue offering the world only reconstructions of specific detail, and constantly show a negative attitude toward broader conclusions, the world will find very little of profit in ethnology."

Writing in the 1930s, Ralph Linton found among his fellow anthropologists the same disinclination to theorize, to seek broader generalizations. Summing it all up in "The Present Status of Anthropology," he wrote that "the main difficulty of ethnology today lies not in the lack of data but in the uncertainty of what to do with the material already in hand. The science has plenty of limited objectives, but is weak in its conceptual framework" (Linton 1938:246).

Historical Particularism

The approach that replaced theorizing in American ethnology was an earth-bound empiricism, manifesting itself in the form of historical particularism. In 1920 in *Primitive Society,* Robert Lowie (1947:436) had already issued the clarion call heralding this approach. "The period has come," he proclaimed, "for eschewing the all-embracing and baseless theories of yore and to settle down to that sober historical research involved in the intensive study of specific regions."

One of the reasons Boas himself gave for his allegiance to historical particularism as early as 1904 was that "the historic view contains a strong aesthetic element, which finds its satisfaction in the clear conception of the individual event" (Boas 1974:26). And on those occasions when Boas sought to go beyond the individual fact and to group various facts together—as for example in his study of the elaboration of the Raven myth on the Northwest Coast—he limited himself to narrow and cautious reconstructions. It was such theoretical restrictions that Boas placed on himself that led Lowie to lament that his "aversion to systematization is the despair of many readers," adding that "Those who crave bold generalizations are certainly doomed to disappointment" (Lowie 1937:152, 155).

Epitomizing Boas' constrained approach to the vast accumulation of data in his field, White (1987:200) later wrote, "Not only did he fail to see the forest for the trees, he could scarcely see the trees for the branches, or the branches for the twigs." Thus it was, Sapir (1927:100) observed, that as a result of Boas' dedicated efforts, "The older schematic evolution . . . relapsed into the proverbial chaos of history."

One of the most incisive critiques made of Boasian historical particularism was that of George P. Murdock (1937a:xiv–xv): "Franz Boas and his followers have lost themselves in a maze of inconsequential details." And as a result, Murdock argued, the Boasians "have lost sight of the primary function of a science, the formulation and testing of generalizations." Instead, he charged, "they have timidly proposed but few cross-cultural hypotheses, and these mostly of a negative tenor." Thus the Boasians had "isolated their discipline from the main current of modern thought and made of it a sort of antiquarian appendage to the social sciences."

6

Early Stages in the Reemergence of Evolutionism

Leslie A. White

The anthropologist who took the first step, and played the main role, in leading the discipline out of the theoretical morass in which it was mired was Leslie White. Though himself not a student of Boas, White had been taught by two of Boas' students, Alexander Goldenweiser and Edward Sapir, and thus had imbibed indirectly from their mentor's cup. "I was trained in the Boasian tradition of anti-evolution," White (1987:12) later wrote. However, a variety of experiences had produced a transformation in White's views. Chief among these influences was perhaps his experience with his students at the University of Buffalo, where he first taught:

> I had some very intelligent and alert students in my course. They had never heard that the theory of evolution—so fundamental in biology—was out of place in ethnology. They challenged me on the issue. I repeated all the reasons the Boasians offered for rejecting the theory of cultural evolution. My teaching may have been acceptable to some of my students, but certainly not to all. They pushed me into a corner. Before long I had realized that I could not defend the doctrines of anti-evolutionism; then I realized that I could no longer hold them; they were untenable. (White 1987:13)

The opening gun in the battle that ultimately led to the reconquest of anthropology for evolutionism was scarcely heard at the time it was fired. It came in 1931 in a review of Bernhard Stern's biography of Lewis H. Morgan. In that volume Stern (1931:135) had written that "cultures . . . are

99

complex and . . . too variable to fit into any definite social evolutionary scheme." To this statement White (1931:483) took exception, saying, "Mr. Stern, like many preceding critics, points out errors of Morgan's procedure, and then throws overboard the concept of evolutionary development of culture. This is quite unwarranted, in the reviewer's opinion. Mr. Morgan's shortcomings in the [eighteen] seventies do not invalidate a concept of cultural evolution in 1931."

Seven years later in an article entitled "Science is Sciencing," White again took note of the anti-evolutionism that had anthropology firmly in its grip. While in the latter half of the nineteenth century, during "the 'boom' days of evolutionism," he wrote, "[a] few giants like Herbert Spencer, E. B. Tylor, and Lewis H. Morgan . . . were able to occupy the cultural field for a time, the anti-evolutionists regained the field and have held it successfully since the turn of the century" (White 1949a:20).

White acknowledged that Morgan and Spencer had "committed errors" in applying evolutionary theory, but argued that in their zeal to expose those errors, twentieth-century anthropologists "have poured the baby out with the bath" (White 1949a:21). However, he confidently predicted that "As social science matures, [evolutionism] . . . will win its way on the cultural level as it has upon the biologic and inanimate levels" (White 1949a:21).

The following year, 1939, in an article entitled "A Problem in Kinship Terminology," White returned to the fray, insisting that the evolutionary approach was a valid and fruitful one, capable of shedding light on specific problems in ethnology. Toward the end of this article he wrote:

The explanation that we have offered [of the Crow and Omaha kinship terminologies] is of course, one inspired by an evolutionary view of culture: institutions, cultures, grow, develop, evolve. The fundamental process in cultural (superorganic) phenomena as well as in organic and even inorganic phenomena is, in the judgment of the present writer, evolutionary. The application of the viewpoint and principles of the philosophy of evolution is as essential to the solution of many problems in culturology as it is in biology or physics. (White 1987:237)

That same year, White presented a paper at the annual meeting of the American Anthropological Association in Chicago entitled "The Evolutionary Approach." For the first time in public, White "spoke out in a forthright manner in support of evolutionist theory in ethnology." Speaking in front of an audience that included Franz Boas himself, this was an exercise in iconoclasm. So strongly against the grain of ethnological orthodoxy did

White's remarks go that his comeuppance quickly followed. "When I had finished," White (1987:14) later wrote, "Ralph Linton, the chairman of the session, remarked that I ought to be given the courtesy extended to suspected horse thieves and shady gamblers in the days of the Wild West, namely, to allow them to get out of town before sundown."

Esther Goldfrank (1978), a student of Boas, was present at that session and has left us an eyewitness account of it. According to her recollection, "White spoke with extreme passion, his tone strident, his language intemperate" (1978:151). In his talk, Goldfrank recalled, White accused Boas of "paying lip service to theory, while actually destroying theory in American anthropology" (1978:153).

"As could be expected," Goldfrank continued, "Boas' friends (and many had been his students) quickly rose to his defense. The eighty-year-old dean of American anthropology alone seemed un-

Leslie A. White

moved. When the session ended he left the room surrounded by those closest to him, his silence louder than any biting retort" (1978:153).

Some time after reading Goldfrank's account of this dramatic incident, I began to wonder if anyone else was left alive who had witnessed it and might have a different recollection of what happened. I therefore submitted a query to that effect to the "Cooperation Column" of the *Anthropology Newsletter*. I received just one reply: from Alexander Lesser. Lesser made no mention of White's paper. In fact, he did not write a letter at all. He merely sent along an old photostatic copy of a story about the meetings that had appeared in the *New York Times*. The story failed to refer to White's paper, but it did report on one Lesser himself had given entitled "Evolution in Social Anthropology."

I never communicated with Lesser about his response, but my surmise was that he wanted it known that while White's presentation may have received all the notoriety, he himself, with much less fanfare, had also dared to give a paper at the Chicago meetings on the forbidden topic of cultural evolution.

But there is more to the story. After he had given his paper in 1939, Lesser mislaid it, and it stayed lost for more than a decade. Eventually, though, he found it, and submitted it to the *Southwestern Journal of Anthropology*, which published it in 1952. The paper was prefaced by a note explaining that it "is offered now, as given in 1939, because of the greatly increased interest in the subject that has developed during the intervening years" (Lesser 1985a:78).

After first reciting a litany of all the alleged errors of the classical evolutionists, which modern evolutionists were admonished not to commit, Lesser presented his arguments in favor of cultural evolution, the most convincing one being how functional prerequisiteness could be used to establish certain evolutionary sequences. He argued, for example, that "The existence of markets implies a prior condition of trade without markets, and also of specialization and social division of labor. Trade for profit is later than trade for use. Credit systems imply prior conditions of barter without a standard medium of exchange" (Lesser 1985a:87). These were all facts well known to, but somehow overlooked by, the preceding generation of anthropologists. So a new evolutionism, Lesser implied, could be built on the lapses and oversights of the old Boas school.

The ensuing struggle to rehabilitate evolutionism in cultural anthropology, in which Leslie White took the lead, was a long and painful one for him. As he later recalled:

> The ethnologist who held to the theory of evolution found neither friend nor refuge on the anthropological landscape. For years I was virtually alone in my advocacy of cultural evolution. To make matters worse, I came to the defense of Lewis H. Morgan; I felt he had been treated very unfairly by Boas and his disciples . . . and labored to restore him to the place of dignity, honor, and great scientific achievement he had enjoyed during his lifetime. . . . I was ridiculed and scoffed at. Everyone knew that evolutionism was dead; my nonconformist behavior was regarded as an aberration. (White 1987:14)

Diffusion versus Evolution

It is time now to examine some of the specific issues over which evolutionism had been rejected, and the manner in which White challenged these objections. In this struggle, he had first to prune away many of the false claims and misrepresentations of the anti-evolutionists before he could put forward his own evolutionary interpretations.

The factor most often advanced by members of the Boas school as presenting an insurmountable obstacle to the postulation of any evolutionary regularities was the existence of diffusion. In this regard, Robert Lowie was the most outspoken. As early as 1917 in his little book *Culture and Ethnology,* Lowie (1917:95) had argued that "the actual development of a given culture does not conform to innate laws necessarily leading to definite results, such hypothetical laws being overridden by contact with foreign peoples," that is, by diffusion. Then again in *Primitive Society* he asserted: "One fact, . . . encountered at every stage and in every phase of society, by itself lays the axe to the root of any theory of historical laws [i.e., of any evolutionary regularities]—the extensive occurrence of diffusion" (Lowie 1920:434).

This view became pervasive in American ethnology to the point that, according to Goldenweiser (1925a:234–235), students "began to think of the study of cultural diffusion as the main preoccupation of ethnology, and some of these began to support the view that most, if not all, instances of cultural similarities should be explained by diffusion through historical contact." This belief in the primacy of diffusion became so ingrained that when Radcliffe-Brown (1947:81) came to teach in the United States in the 1930s, he tells us, "I found many students and anthropologists in America who had been so thoroughly indoctrinated with the idea that the fact of diffusion of culture refutes any theory of social evolution that it was impossible or useless to discuss the subject."

In seeking to counter the arguments of the anti-evolutionists, White maintained that evolution and diffusion were not antagonistic but complementary. He pointed out that the Boasian contention that the classical evolutionists disregarded or dismissed diffusion (as Goldenweiser [1925a:226] had, for example) was untrue. He argued that "far from seeing an antithesis between evolution and diffusion, they saw that these two processes work harmoniously together, the one originating culture traits, the other spreading them far and wide" (White 1987:45).

Speaking more broadly, we can say that diffusion enables a society to acquire a trait that it was not ready to invent for itself, but could put to use once invented elsewhere and made available to it. Thus diffusion fosters and facilitates the overall development of individual societies by adding to their cultural inventories, providing them with a larger culture base from which they, in turn, can proceed to make other inventions of their own.

It should be emphasized that no attempt is being made to deny or belittle the importance of diffusion. All the contrary. Accordingly, I would not dispute Goldenweiser's (1925a:239n.) assertion that diffusion constitutes "the 'yeast' of the historic process." In fact, we can confidently assert that the overwhelming preponderance of traits in the cultural inventories of preliterate as well as modern societies is the result of their having borrowed them over the course of centuries or millennia, rather than having invented them for themselves.

For example, bronze metallurgy did not have to be invented again and again. It is such a useful art that, once invented, its advantages over the use of stone tools were so great and so obvious that the process immediately began to diffuse in every direction from its center of origin. Thus there were probably no more than three separate origins of bronze metallurgy, two in the Old World and one in the New.

It is even possible that the bow and arrow was invented just once—in North Africa, some 15,000 to 20,000 years ago—and from there spread to almost every corner of the globe. However, we must introduce this caveat: Whether the co-occurrence of the same trait in two or more separated areas constitutes a case of diffusion or of independent invention cannot be decided by fiat. Each case must be examined and decided on its own merits.

However, in some ultimate sense, invention must be given priority over diffusion. After all, culture traits have to be invented before they can be diffused. Even Robert Lowie, the leading apostle of diffusionism, was clear on this point. In a chapter on the determinants of culture in *Culture and Ethnology* (1917:73), he cheerfully admitted that "before peoples can communicate their culture to others with whom they come in contact, they must first evolve these cultures," adding that "this insistence on contact of peoples as a condition of cultural evolution does not solve the ultimate problem of the origin of culture" (1917:73).

Perhaps the most balanced assessment of the role of diffusion was made by Ralph Linton (1936a:324): "Diffusion has made a double contribution to the advance of mankind. It has stimulated the growth of culture as a whole and at the same time has enriched the content of individual cultures. . . . It has helped to accelerate the evolution of culture as a whole by removing the necessity for every society to perfect every step in an inventive series for itself."

The Derivation of Evolutionary Formulas

In view of this "symbiotic" relationship between the two processes, White asked (1987:45), "How has it been possible for the Boas school to declare that diffusion negates evolution? The answer is simple: the Boas school has confused the *evolution of culture* with the *culture history of peoples.*" And this he called "a fatal mistake for ethnological theory" (White 1987:139). Again and again he repeated emphatically that "the cultural formulas [of the evolutionists] have nothing to do with peoples" (White 1987:45).

Whence, then, were these "evolutionary formulas" derived? White was not very explicit about this, indicating only that they were not arrived at inductively, but rather by the action of "creative imagination" (White 1987:91–93).

No sooner had White expressed this view than Robert Lowie was on him, saying, "White nowhere explains how he supposes the formulae to have been ultimately derived. Are they empirical inductions? In that case they must rest on observations of the history of specific tribes. Or are they all *a priori* constructs like the precious notion about the uncertainty of fatherhood as the cause of matrilineal reckoning in early times?" (Lowie 1946:231).

David Bidney (1946:293) also jumped into the fray against White, arguing along similar lines: "there can be no evolution of culture in general apart from the cultural histories of given societies." And he went on to say, *"the concept of logical stages of cultural development presupposes the notion of the actual history of the cultural process.* By themselves, and apart from the historical process, the stages of cultural development are but abstractions, useful to the student of culture, but not ultimately intelligible or explanatory of the dynamics of culture."

Lowie and Bidney were right. White had overstated the case. Evolutionary formulas are not pure abstractions with no basis in actual facts. Years ago, in discussing this issue, I summarized my opinion as follows:

> I do not accept the view that a general evolutionary sequence is somehow entirely separate and distinct from the culture history of particular peoples. Such evolutionary sequences as exist do so only by virtue of the fact that many societies have evolved in similar ways during the course of their individual histories. An evolutionary sequence is thus a generalization of the order of development that societies by and large have tended to follow. Individually, societies *exemplify* this sequence; together they *constitute* it. (Carneiro 1970b:835)

However, if we look beneath some of White's more extreme assertions, it is possible to understand, and accept, what he meant by them. The general sequence represented by the succession of stages Paleolithic > Neolithic > Bronze Age > Iron Age was firmly established in the nineteenth century and never seriously questioned thereafter (Lowie 1929:77). White contended that this general evolutionary sequence, however it had been derived, did not have to be followed by *any particular society* during the course of its own history. And he used as an example of this the skipping of a Bronze Stage of metallurgy by a number of tribes in sub-Saharan Africa—a fact often cited by the Boasians as illustrating the failure of a general evolutionary sequence to be followed. White (1987:47) countered the Boasian argument as follows: "Granting that certain African tribes went directly from the stone age to the iron age, would this in any way invalidate the evolutionist's sequence of Stone, Bronze, and Iron? Not in the least. The fact that a tribe gets a complex of traits from a foreign source by diffusion has nothing whatever to do with the series of stages in which this culture complex developed."

In the evolution of culture as a whole, White argued, the sequence Stone > Bronze > Iron was valid as a general evolutionary sequence *regardless* of what had happened in the culture history of any given society.

So far so good. But what he failed to argue—indeed, what he even seemed to deny—was that in the culture history of *some* actual society this sequence *had* to have been followed. Otherwise, how could one say such a sequence existed at all? Lowie and Bidney had accused White of talking as if he had pulled his general evolutionary sequences out of a hat. White could have reasonably defended his position had he simply admitted that there was *some* relationship between a general evolutionary sequence and the culture history of peoples.

White's stance confused more than just Lowie and Bidney. Murdock was also thrown off by it, arguing that "the only cultural processes are historical. . . . I cannot accept the contention of White that evolution is a separate cultural process" (Murdock 1949:116n.; see also p. 131). Years later, he again maintained that "evolution consists of real events, not of abstractions from events, so that evolutionary development is historical in the strictest and most literal sense" (Murdock 1965:134).

But if no evolutionary sequence is *fully* exemplified by the culture history of any particular society, then it must be derived by a process of *abstraction*. "Abstraction" in this sense means by a comparison of the culture histories of many different societies and then by a selection and generalization of that succession of events that *most* societies appear to have undergone. If in a preponderant number of historical instances, corvée labor had preceded markets (let us say), then we would be justified in saying that in the evolution of human society *as a whole,* the corvée had developed before markets. Murdock is right, then, in saying that evolutionary sequences are based on *actual histories.* But at the same time White is right in saying that such a sequence is not based on the history of *any specific* society.

There is, however, a qualification to be made here. Let us begin by quoting White again: "The fact that certain tribes went directly from stone-working to iron-working in no way invalidated the evolutionist claim that *in the process of technological development* a bronze stage preceded a stage of iron" (White 1987:63–64).

Here we are introduced to the fact that in cultural evolution there are certain sequences in which *functional prerequisiteness* plays a determinative role. For example, it is apparently the case that in the evolution of metallurgy it may be necessary to master the techniques underlying bronze metallurgy before a society can advance to the point of smelting iron ore and producing iron artifacts from it. In this case, the sequence bronze metallurgy > iron metallurgy may be asserted to be technologically necessary to have been passed through *somewhere,* despite the fact that many societies in sub-Saharan Africa (and probably elsewhere in the world) went directly from the use of ground stone tools to the manufacture of iron implements.

Now such an eventuality—that is, the skipping of an evolutionary stage—is much more common in technology than in social organization. This is true because technology diffuses much more readily than organization, the latter requiring the existence of a receptive social structure before it can occur. As Murdock (1949:196) once noted, "the forms of social organization seem singularly impervious to diffusion."

Functional prerequisiteness occurs in many fields of culture, thus imparting a necessary direction to, and giving an impetus to, many evolutionary sequences. This is especially true when we are considering the relative order of development of pairs of traits or trait complexes. Linton (1955:53), for example, observed—and no one has ever thought to question the observation—that "The development of agriculture and settled village life everywhere preceded the emergence of the city." Similarly, Leslie White (1987:108) asked, "Would anyone care to maintain that kingship could precede chieftainship, [or] money precede barter . . . ?" And, as we have seen, Alexander Lesser offered a number of instances of functional prerequisiteness, showing that its existence provides the underpinning for evolutionary sequences.

Cultural Relativism and the Rating of Cultures

One of the bases on which the Boasians rejected cultural evolution was the contention that no objective standards existed by which cultures could be rated or evaluated. Therefore, they argued, no culture could be said to be any higher or lower than any other. This doctrine of cultural relativism, elevated to a high principle, became a cornerstone of the Boasian view of culture and of their anti-evolutionism.

Just how ingrained this principle became among members of the Boas school can be shown by examining their own words. In *Primitive Society,* Lowie (1947:438) asserted that "in the sphere of social life there is no objective criterion for grading cultural phenomena." Alexander Goldenweiser (1925a:229) maintained that "a comparative measure of progress [i.e., evolution] implies standards and these are dependent on judgments of value which are of necessity subjective." Appearing to summarize the professional opinion of the day, Melville Herskovits (1973:36) remarked that "we are agreed that objective indices of cultural inferiority and superiority cannot be established."

To continue the litany, Ruth Benedict (1934:1) asserted that "our customs and those of a New Guinea tribe are two possible social schemes for dealing with a common problem, and in so far as he remains an anthropologist he is bound to avoid any weighting of one in favor of the other." Finally, Margaret Mead (1943:193) stated emphatically that, as anthropologists, "Our contribution has been the recognition of the co-equal value of human cultures seen as wholes. . . . We have stood out against any grading of cultures in hierarchical systems."

In combating this monolithic conviction of the Boasians that the rating of culture was subjective, and therefore invalid, Leslie White put forth two arguments. First of all, he argued that the Boasians had confused *arbitrary* and *subjective*. All standards of measurement are arbitrary, he said. We can measure a man's height in inches or centimeters. But they are not necessarily subjective. Two or more observers can measure a person's height and come up with the same figure, within only a slight margin of error. Similarly, if we say that one culture is "better" than another in some unspecified moral sense, that evaluation is subjective. But, said White, there are also *objective* ways of assessing or evaluating cultures. And if we apply these objective standards, all cultures do not come out on the same dead level of equality. Some would be higher, or more advanced, or more complex, or more evolved than others. Can anyone seriously maintain, for example, that the Inca were no more complex or evolved than the Yahgan?

While acknowledging that there were several objective standards of comparison, White had his own preferences: "We can measure cultures by a number of objective and vitally significant indexes: amount of food and other human-need-serving goods produced per unit of human labor, infant mortality, death rates for various diseases; life expectancy, etc. The best single index, however, by which all cultures can be measured, is *amount of energy harnessed per capita per year*" (White 1987:76).

White never actually applied this measure to individual cultures himself. When I once asked him about this, he replied, "That's for *you* to do," meaning not me personally, but his students and followers. It was not long after White earnestly began his campaign to resuscitate evolution that serious attempts were made to rate cultures objectively, and we will deal with these attempts later.

In Spite of Themselves

For the present we will continue with another of White's arguments against the Boasians regarding the rating of cultures as either higher or lower. He demonstrated in exhaustive detail that on this score the Boasians were markedly inconsistent, and that in spite of themselves had repeatedly done so (White 1987:110). When we look at societies around the world, the differences in culture level are so marked and so obvious that they intruded themselves into the consciousness of even the most dedicated Boasian when his theoretical guard was down. As White (1987:80) put it, "Whenever . . . [the Boasians] dealt with matters of theory or principle in ethnology they gave full allegiance to their anti-evolutionist philosophy. But when it came to interpreting cultural phenomena themselves as they observed them, they could not avoid using these concepts. The evolutionist character of culture simply forced itself upon them by sheer weight."

In the first place, the Boasians had to admit that some forms of social structure had followed others in the evolution of society. Thus Lowie (1940a:251) observed that "Clans do not arise in the very earliest stages of society, but on somewhat higher levels . . . ultimately disappearing under a strong centralized government." In the same vein, Goldenweiser (1931:660) noted that "ancestor worship is recognized as a feature of more advanced rather than [of the] most primitive conditions."

When it came to the comparative rating of cultures, White caught Lowie off base. When Lowie remarked that "most ethnographers would place the Pawnee above the Omaha and the Omaha above the Teton" (Lowie 1940b:413), White (1987:79) was quick to say that this "is . . . grading cultures on a fairly fine scale."

In one of his tiffs with White over the issue of evolution versus anti-evolution, Lowie (1946:225) had raised the question: "How could any ethnographer [as Morgan had done] ever put the Polynesians into the same category with [aboriginal] Australians and *below* the Northern Athabascans?" True enough. This was a glaring error on Morgan's part. But implicit in Lowie's criticism—certainly unacknowledged by him—was the belief that there *was* a correct ordering of these societies in terms of their relative complexity, only Morgan had gotten it wrong!

One of the criticisms often leveled at the classical evolutionists by the Boasians—and still repeated by others to this day (e.g., Feinman 2000:7)—was that in their evolutionary sequences, Western societies always appeared at the top. That may well be true. However, one can't help wondering what the Boasians would have said if in one of their evolutionary scales the classical evolutionists had put Victorian England at the bottom and the Australian aborigines on top!

A full-blown, yet in a way surreptitious effort by a Boasian to rank cultures objectively was made by A. L. Kroeber (1939), always the more broad-ranging and farseeing of Boas' students. I refer to Kroeber's attempt in *Cultural and Natural Areas of Native North America* to place all North

American Indian societies into one of seven "levels of cultural intensity," with plusses and minuses being used to make even finer discriminations between them. We will deal with Kroeber's "levels" in more detail when we discuss the more formal efforts later made to rate cultures objectively.

Throughout the 1940s, Leslie White continued to write articles in which he sought to expose what he deemed to be errors of the anti-evolutionists and to establish the validity and utility of a resurgent evolutionism. Chief among these articles were "History, Evolutionism, and Functionalism: Three Types of Interpretation of Culture" (1945a), "Diffusion vs. Evolution: An Anti-Evolutionist Fallacy" (1945b), and "Evolutionary Stages, Progress, and the Evaluation of Cultures" (1947).

The cumulative effect of these trenchant articles was to bring about a gradual yet almost inexorable change in the climate of anthropological opinion about cultural evolution. And White himself saw this change as well-nigh irresistible. Thus he wrote: "It would be curious, indeed—more, it would be incomprehensible—if this theory [evolution], which has been so fundamental in the biological sciences, so fruitful and illuminating in the physical sciences, where it is coming to be used more and more in astronomy, . . . and in many of the social sciences, should not find a place in cultural anthropology" (White 1959:viii–ix).

For all of the 1940s and much of the 1950s, White stood alone among American ethnologists, fighting single-handedly for the cause of evolution. Toward the end of this period, however, an ally appeared on the scene.

Julian H. Steward

During the early years of his career, Julian Steward was known first and foremost as a cultural ecologist who had shown the value of ecological interpretations in deepening anthropology's understanding of the cultures of the Great Basin (Steward 1938). One of the outstanding results of Steward's study of the impact of the environment on the cultures of this region was his substitution of a robust ecological determinism for the reigning flabby "possibilism" favored by members of the Boas school. It was the lessons he had learned in trying to account for the structure of Paiute and Shoshone bands that led Steward away from the trait distribution studies of his teacher, A. L. Kroeber, to a concern with total cultures and what influences had shaped them. And this concern with causes Steward carried over when he later turned his attention to evolution.

Steward's interest in cultural evolution seems to have begun when, while at the Smithsonian Institution, he assumed the editorship of the *Handbook of South American Indians*. In searching for a suitable ground plan for this work, he decided that the best course would be to organize its several volumes according to the differences in complexity of the various societies to be included in them. And the range of culture levels he had to consider was great: from the tiny family bands of the Yahgan to the vast and mighty Inca empire. This broad spectrum of cultures he chose to divide into four types—basically (although not so named) that of bands, tribes, chiefdoms, and states, each type being dealt with in a separate volume.

Parallel to, but independent of, Steward's work on the *Handbook,* a number of archaeologists working in Peru were setting aside traditional chronologies and proposing evolutionary stage sequences for the central Andes. Since the word "evolution" still bore the taint of the generally discredited nineteenth-century efforts along these lines, Andean archaeologists disguised the evolutionary nature of their sequences by calling them "functional-developmental terminologies."

In 1947 a Wenner-Gren Foundation symposium was held in New York City at which several of these archaeologists put forward rather similar developmental sequences for the Andes and also for Mesoamerica. Because of the evolutionary framework he had imparted to the *Handbook,* Steward was invited to participate in the symposium. His assignment was to see if he could synthesize the individual sequences proposed by the archaeologists into a single grand scheme that would faithfully encompass and reflect cultural development in both major regions of the New World. The fruit of his efforts was the following sequence of stages (Steward 1948:104):

1. Pre-Agricultural
2. Basic Agricultural Beginnings
3. Regional Developmental or Formative
4. Regional Florescent
5. Empire and Conquest

Encouraged by the apparent acceptance of his scheme, Steward decided to take a bold step forward and generalize it still further. The article in which he did so ranks as one of the great landmarks of twentieth-century cultural evolutionism. In preparing it, Steward reasoned that if the sequence he had presented earlier had accurately depicted the course of development of New World civilizations, it should be possible, with only minor alterations, to come up with a scheme that applied to the Old World as well. His master synthesis was presented in a now-classic article published in the *American Anthropologist* and entitled "Cultural Causality and Law: A Trial Formulation of the Development of Early Civilizations" (Steward 1949). The sequence Steward now proposed consisted of seven stages:

1. Hunting and Gathering
2. Incipient Agriculture
3. Formative
4. Regional Florescence
5. Initial Conquests
6. Dark Ages
7. Cyclical Conquests

This sequence, Steward believed, faithfully reflected the origin and growth of civilization in Mesopotamia, Egypt, India, and China, as well as in Nuclear America.

As we have seen, when dealing with the cultures of the Great Basin, Steward was strongly inclined to look for causation. Thus it was natural that he should ask himself what it was that accounted for the impressive developmental regularities he had found. He concluded that the factor that had given impetus to the parallel development of these civilizations was irriga-

Julian H. Steward

tion. All six had developed in arid or subarid regions, and thus water had been of paramount concern to them. And here he drew on the "hydraulic hypothesis" put forward by his colleague at Columbia University, Karl Wittfogel (1957). According to this theory, the obvious advantage to be gained by integrating local irrigation systems into larger networks, a process that required the creation of overall managerial controls, brought into existence the elaborate bureaucracy that, in essence, constituted the state.

However, at a special symposium held at the annual meeting of the American Anthropological Association in Tucson in 1953, Steward's developmental scheme and its determinants were put to the test. And the results were mixed. On the one hand, no one contradicted the worldwide applicability of Steward's sequence of stages. However, regional specialists on Mesopotamia and China argued that in those two important areas large-scale irrigation had *followed* the rise of the state, not *preceded* it (see Carneiro 1970a:734, 738n.). That being the case, the causal mechanism

Steward had invoked to account for the parallel developments of these high cultures was shot out from under him.

This apparent refutation of the hydraulic hypothesis he had relied on had a profound impact on Steward. Instead of rejoicing that his sequence of stages had held up, Steward was distressed that his causal mechanism had broken down. And so he recoiled from the unilinear evolutionism that was such a striking—if unacknowledged—feature of "Cultural Causality and Law," and retreated into what he termed "multilinear evolution."

In an article entitled "Evolution and Process," written in 1953, Steward announced his *démarche*. He began by distinguishing three types of cultural evolution, which he called *unilinear, universal,* and *multilinear. Unilinear evolution* was that form of evolution that Boas and his followers had attributed to nineteenth-century scholars such as Morgan, Tylor, and Spencer, according to which (it was alleged) every society, in the course of its evolution, had to proceed through the same sequence of stages. This form of evolution, as the Boasians had before him, Steward summarily dismissed.

Universal evolution was Steward's term for the brand of evolutionism that he said was practiced by Leslie White and V. Gordon Childe in order to avoid the pitfalls of unilinearism: "Aware that empirical research of the twentieth century has invalidated the unilinear historical reconstructions of particular cultures, which constituted the essential feature of nineteenth-century schemes, White and Childe endeavor to keep the evolutionary concept of cultural stages alive by relating these stages to the culture of mankind as a whole," rather than to each individual society (Steward 1955:16).

Steward acknowledged that the universal stages proposed by White and Childe might be valid, but, he said, "are so general that they are neither very arguable nor very useful" (Steward 1955:17). Accordingly, Steward set universal evolution to one side and proposed to follow instead what he preferred to call multilinear evolution.

Now, at the time he wrote "Cultural Causality and Law" Steward (1949:5) argued that "to stress the complexity or multiplicity of the antecedents . . . of any institution makes it impossible to isolate the true causes of the institution." He therefore resisted having recourse to "convergent evolution," feeling that it led too easily to looking for a unique constellation of causes for each development, and thus might become "another means of denying the possibility of isolating cultural regularities." And this he was staunchly opposed to doing, affirming that "It is important that anthropology explicitly recognize that a legitimate and ultimate objective is to see through the differences of cultures to the similarities, to ascertain processes that are duplicated independently in cultural sequences" (1955:180). Arguing along the same lines, he had earlier forcefully declared, "It is obvious that the minutiae of culture history will never be completely known and that there is no need to defer formulations until all archaeologists have laid down their shovels and all ethnologists have put away their notebooks" (Steward 1949:24–25).

By the time he wrote "Evolution and Process," though, Steward was a changed man. He now hastily backed away from the search for robust and far-reaching regularities. Diversity now loomed larger in his mind than uniformity. Thus in characterizing the new approach he was proposing to pursue, he made it clear that although multilinear evolution was "like unilinear evolution in dealing with developmental sequences, . . . it is distinctive in searching for parallels of *limited* occurrence instead of universals" (Steward 1953a:315). And three pages later he reiterated that multilinear evolution "deals only with . . . *limited* parallels of form, function, and sequence" (1953a:318; emphasis mine).

Clearly, a radical change had come over Steward. The bold, intrepid Steward of "Cultural Causality and Law" was no more. He had been replaced by the cautious, timid Steward who confessed that using the very word "evolution" made him nervous since it "still strongly connotes the nineteenth-century view." Thus, he was hesitant to employ it, succumbing only because he could "find no better term" (Steward 1955:5).

And so Steward turned his back on the unilinearism that he had once so successfully pursued. The striking developmental regularities he had once fearlessly exhibited he now disowned. Indeed, he was ready to assert *by fiat* that he was no longer interested in searching for the widest regularities and the greatest uniformities that could be attained.

Steward's change of heart did not go undetected. Some of his colleagues commented on it. A puzzled George P. Murdock (1965:136) was led to observe that "Unless I completely misread him, . . . [Steward] considers all cultural evolution to be basically multilinear and regards cases of parallel development as exceptions demanding special investigation."

And though Leslie White regarded him as almost his only ally in the uneven struggle against anti-evolutionism, he nevertheless chided Steward for his theoretical timidity. Steward, White (1987:126) declared, "wants generalizations but, as he says repeatedly, they must be . . . [of] limited scope." To White, this seemed virtually a contradiction in terms. "Try to imagine," he said, "a law of falling bodies, or of gravitation, of limited scope. Steward resembles one who discovers that this river and that flows down hill but is unwilling to go so far as to assert that 'rivers flow down hill.'"

Still, White was ready to acknowledge Steward's contribution to their joint efforts. Compared to White's more combative, sometimes strident advocacy of cultural evolution, Steward's espousal of it was more modulated and tempered. Thus in the early days of resurgent evolutionism, Steward's version of it, being blander, was therefore more acceptable to those ethnologists and archaeologists who were beginning to be intrigued by the possibility that there might be something valid and useful in the concept after all, and were cautiously groping their way toward it. White (1987:128) readily admitted this, pointing out that "the return of evolutionism may have to be made slowly, a step at a time," adding that "Steward has already done much to remove the stigma placed upon the concept."

The final irony in Steward's professed avowal of multilinear evolution is that he never did any of it. Nor did he even indicate in any of his later papers just how it was to be done. His article "Tappers and Trappers," written jointly with his colleague Robert Murphy (Murphy and Steward 1956), is occasionally cited as an example of multilinear evolution. But interesting as the paper is, it is only a study in the parallel (or convergent) acculturation of Brazilian rubber tappers and the fur trappers of the Canadian Subarctic.

There is no question that Julian Steward had his great moments, but there were times when his writing could be muddled and intellectually perverse. For example, in his article "Cultural Evolution" (1956), he stated unequivocally of the classical evolutionists that "their schemes were erected on such flimsy theoretical foundations and such faulty observations that *the entire structure collapsed* as soon as it was seriously tested" (Steward 1956:70; emphasis mine). Really?

Six lines earlier, Steward had quoted Morgan as saying that "It can now be asserted upon convincing evidence that savagery preceded barbarism in all the tribes of mankind, as barbarism is known to have preceded civilization." How could Steward have maintained that the evolutionary scheme thus encapsulated had "entirely collapsed"? Could he point to a single region of the world where Barbarism had preceded Savagery, or where Civilization had preceded Barbarism?

V. Gordon Childe

The third member of the triumvirate that led the way in resurrecting cultural evolutionism was V. Gordon Childe. Childe, an Australian-born British archaeologist, had in his early days been a strong advocate of diffusion in interpreting European prehistory. Thus, for example, in the opening pages of *New Light on the Most Ancient East*, Childe (1935:1–2) had written: "one thread is clearly discernible running through the dark and tangled tale of these prehistoric Europeans: the westward spread, adoption, and transformation of the inventions of the Orient."

But in the mid-1930s his perspective began to change, largely through his acquaintance with the writings of Karl Marx. Marx placed a heavy emphasis on the dynamics of culture, especially on the importance of economic factors in bringing about social change. In thinking harder about cultural dynamics Childe came to realize more and more that diffusionist explanations merely pushed the origin of traits and institutions to some other region, and that they thus failed to wrestle with the problem of how these traits and institutions had arisen in the first place. And so how a people came to civilize themselves, how institutions had emerged and developed, became, for Childe, a problem of increasing concern.

The first published evidence of this sea change in Childe's thinking came in 1936, with the publication of *Man Makes Himself*. In this work, in which he discussed in rich detail the origins of Mesopotamian and Egyptian civilization, Childe did not altogether turn his back on diffusionary explanations. Thus he wrote that the Neolithic and Urban revolutions "occurred almost simultaneously in Egypt and Sumer. . . . In each case the revolution was based on the same scientific discoveries, and resulted in the addition to the population of the same new classes. It is hard to believe in the independence of these events, especially when the proofs of long-standing intercourse between the areas is recalled. . . . Some sort of diffusion had evidently

been going on" (Childe 1951a:135). "Yet," he added, "no theory of one-sided dependence is compatible with the contrasts revealed by closer scrutiny. Urban civilization was not simply transplanted from one center to another, but was in each an organic growth rooted in local soil" (Childe 1951a:135).

In time, Childe became an outspoken foe of uncritical and indiscriminate diffusionism. Thus, after citing the outlandish claims of Elliot Smith, William J. Perry, and Lord Raglan, he stated: "In this extreme form, as an antidote to evolutionism, diffusion is a reversion in anthropology to something like cata-

V. Gordon Childe

strophism in geology; it is liable to be mystical and anti-empirical. . . . If 'no people can civilize itself' [as Lord Raglan had contended], we would still be savages if some *deus ex machina* had not by a miracle raised one society of savages to civilization" (Childe 1946:246).

Childe's view of cultural development as "an organic growth rooted in local soil" was nothing less than an espousal of *in situ* evolution. And it was one of the main themes of *Man Makes Himself,* and again, of *What Happened in History,* which appeared six years later (1942). Although Childe never concerned himself with New World prehistory, these two books of his were widely read by American archaeologists, and opened their eyes to the great intellectual gains to be made by focusing less on chronology and typology and more on the dynamics of the culture process.

In *Man Makes Himself* and *What Happened in History,* Childe depicted the emergence of an agricultural economy and the development of cities in the Near East as being such momentous transformations as to warrant being called *revolutions.* The former he called the Neolithic Revolution and the latter the Urban Revolution. The use of the term "revolution" for these major changes was most likely suggested to Childe by his reading of Marx and Engels. In any event, the terminology stuck, and archaeologists today speak freely and frequently of the Neolithic and Urban revolutions, not only in connection with the Old World, but sometimes even with the New.

It must be recorded, though, that Childe took a step backward with the publication of his last book, *Social Evolution,* in 1951. Despite its title, the book is a recitation of virtually every Boasian anti-evolutionary allegation, as if the supposed misdeeds of the classical evolutionists were still a menace to sound evolutionary theory at the time Childe was writing. Julian Steward gave the book a harsh review, saying that its "emphasis upon differences, denial of significant parallels, and explanation of similarities through diffusion is essentially historical particularism. . . . Why, then, call this 'social evolution'?" (Steward 1953b:241).

But against the backdrop of his groundbreaking work on Near Eastern prehistory, and his elucidation of the dynamics of the cultural evolutionary process, the sins of Childe's last volume must be regarded as only a minor transgression.

Like Steward's, Childe's brand of evolution was more muted and moderate than White's, and so less challenging of the still-dominating tenets of anti-evolutionism. It was also based more solidly on archaeological evidence. Thus American archaeologists could cite Childe's work safely, whereas citing Leslie White's was only done with trepidation. Accordingly, we must credit Childe with having helped to soften the ground on which the tree of a resurgent evolutionism was to take root and grow tall.

It was in the late 1940s, not long after the publication of the second of Childe's two best-known works, that evolutionary stirrings began to be felt in American archaeology. However, we shall postpone a discussion of this until later. Let us now turn to what was happening in American ethnology following the effects produced by the writings of White and Steward.

Evolutionism in Ethnology in the 1950s

The reemergence of cultural evolutionism in American ethnology was slow in coming. Writing long after the fact, White (1987:14) noted: "My campaign in the 1940s [on behalf of cultural evolutionism] was carried on in the journals. [It] . . . attracted considerable interest, but won very few converts—except, possibly, among graduate students." But he never lost heart. In 1947, during the depth of anti-evolutionism, White (1987:95) wrote, undaunted, "I believe . . . that the era of reaction will come to an end some day, and that cultural anthropology will again become . . . hospitable" to cultural evolution. Indeed, he thought he saw already among some anthropologists "some dissatisfaction with the Boasian point of view and a considerable interest in evolutionism" (White 1987:95).

As an example of this ill-defined feeling that culture change should be put into some sort of evolutionary perspective one can cite Robert Redfield's famous study, *The Folk Culture of Yucatan* (1941). In this work, Redfield introduced the concept of a "folk–urban continuum," the peasant village lying at one end of it and the city at the other. Although this was clearly a *continuum*, Redfield chose to emphasize the *contrast* between the two polar types at either end, rather than the *process* that led from one to the other. This process was, in fact, *evolution*, but anti-evolutionary sentiment still dominated, and Redfield evidently thought it best to tread lightly on what could be construed as dangerous ground.

In an earlier article, which foreshadowed the folk–urban continuum, Redfield had also been careful to disassociate himself from anything that might sound like evolution. Thus, he said, "it is not necessary for us to assume that the life of the village we are studying [in Yucatan] represents an earlier stage in the development of what we now find in the town" (Redfield 1934:63). Yet, in the very next sentence, he declared that "one can go back either in time or in space, one can delve into memory [of townspeople] or retreat into the bush, and reach the same set of facts" (Redfield 1934:63). It would appear, then, that evolutionism was trying to squirm its way through, despite Redfield's best efforts to keep it at bay!

Twenty years later, the genie was again trying to force its way out of the bottle, this time with greater success. In *The Primitive World and Its Transformation*, which appeared in 1953, Redfield was readier to see the change he had witnessed in Yucatan—that from a simple village culture to a more complex urban one—as being a recurrent, well-nigh universal one. In the introduction to that volume he wrote: "In the wide view here to be taken, the several thousands of years during which the first cities rose in half a dozen places become a single happening, the coming of civilization." And boldly taking the world's cultural achievements and binding them together, Redfield (1953:ix) announced that "History is here conceived as the story of a single career, that of the human race." Thus he appeared to be embracing the "universal evolution" that Steward had imputed to V. Gordon Childe. But though Redfield repeatedly cited Childe and his work, he nonetheless still shied away from labeling as "evolution" the process he was vividly portraying.

Redfield, then, provided a prime example of the tropismatic groping for a higher synthesis of the trends manifested in individual culture histories, but still coupled with a certain wariness about allying himself with the more outspoken evolutionists.

Here and there in the 1950s studies appeared that, with considerable caution and numerous reservations, nevertheless espoused the evolutionary point of view. In 1955, for example, Ralph Linton published *The Tree of Culture*, which included a chapter entitled "Cultural Evolution." Even though half the chapter was devoted to arguing against the proposition that there was any true regularity in cultural development, still, the main body of the book—which ran to nearly 700 pages—was devoted to tracing the growth of culture in various parts of the world.

Two years earlier, in 1953, an unusual seminar was held under the auspices of the Society for American Archaeology. The proceedings of this seminar were later published under the title "Functional and Evolutionary Implications of Community Patterning" (Beardsley *et al.* 1956). The members of the seminar, ethnologists and archaeologists, attempted to construct a series of distinctive types of successively more complex cultures, which would be reflected in their settlement patterns, patterns that were archaeologically observable. The resulting typology was meant to provide archaeologists with a means of inferring the occurrence of certain nonmaterial traits among societies about which little more was known than the layout of their settlements. The types of settlements distinguished by the seminar were the following:

1. Restricted Wandering
2. Central-Based Wandering
3. Semi-permanent Sedentary
4. Simple Nuclear Centered
5. Advanced Nuclear Centered
6. Supra-nuclear Integrated

Using ethnographic evidence, the members of the seminar indicated what kinds of subsistence practices and social structure tended to be associated with each type of settlement. One of the conclusions was that "our categories constitute stages or levels of development in an evolutionary sequence. Each clearly grows out of a previous one and into a following one" (Beardsley *et al.* 1956:152).

Years later, in a test of the suitability of these settlement types for archaeological inference, Charles McNett (1970) set about trying to correlate the occurrence of some thirty nonmaterial culture traits with the six types of settlement pattern, using a cross-cultural sample of 48 societies. After a sophisticated statistical analysis, he found that the presence or absence of certain of these traits was closely associated with a particular type of settlement pattern. Therefore, he concluded, an archaeologist could, with reasonable confidence, infer the presence or absence of such nonmaterial traits among prehistoric societies whose settlement pattern alone was known (McNett 1970:882).

At any time between, say, 1920 and 1950, Robert Lowie, with his great interest and knowledge of political organization, could have introduced the concept of "chiefdom" as an evolutionary stage between the autonomous village and the state. All the necessary information was known and accessible to him. But he failed to do so. Evolutionary formulations were simply not part of his intellectual frame of mind. It was left to Kalervo Oberg to devise this category, today so central to any discussion of the earlier stages of political development. In the year 1955 there appeared in the pages of the *American Anthropologist* an article by Oberg in which he distinguished, among the native cultures of South America, seven types of society representing successively higher levels of sociopolitical organization. Here for the first time in ethnology the word *chiefdom* made its appearance as a label for one of these societal types. Moreover, "chiefdom" was given a clear and cogent definition, one that even today (in my opinion) has not been improved upon.

Oberg's article, bursting with implicit evolutionism, was to have a profound influence on American anthropology. Its effect was like that of introducing a magnet among a bunch of dispersed iron filings: It caused vague and unsystematic notions to line up in a distinct pattern. But this systematization of ideas was a two-step process. First, the importance of Oberg's levels of organization had to be recognized by Elman Service, and then transmuted by him from *types* to *stages,* a more overtly evolutionary formulation. However, we shall postpone a fuller discussion of this sequence until Chapter 7.

The year 1958 saw the publication of Marshall Sahlins' *Social Stratification in Polynesia.* This work was essentially Sahlins' dissertation, written under Elman Service at Columbia University, but its evolutionary roots could be traced back to Sahlins' days as a graduate student of Leslie White's at the University of Michigan. Though written before the concept of chiefdom had been formally proposed, the volume carefully examined a number of island cultures of Polynesia that clearly stood at different levels of sociopolitical development. The more advanced of these cultures—Tahiti, Hawaii, and Tonga—would shortly be categorized as chiefdoms. In fact, due principally to Sahlins' work, Polynesia soon became recognized as the region of the world most closely identified with chiefdoms. Sahlins accounted for the cultural differences among these Polynesian societies largely in terms of environmental and economic variables.

Polynesia was also the region of another parallel but competing evolutionary interpretation by Irving Goldman, "Status Rivalry and Cultural Evolution in Polynesia," which appeared in 1955. In this article Goldman (1955:688) found that "the conditions promoting evolution were everywhere active in Polynesia." He noted that: "Polynesian cultures vary in a continuous series from the 'simple' atoll societies of Ontong Java and Pukapuka to the highly organized 'feudal' kingdoms of Hawaii. These variations suggest an evolutionary sequence, which is borne out by the evidence from tribal historical traditions . . . and from other sources" (Goldman 1955:580). By comparing island with island, Goldman (1955:689–694) was able, within the compass of only six pages, to present a thumbnail sketch of cultural evolution in Polynesia that for clarity and conciseness could hardly be improved upon.

Other works organized along evolutionary lines appeared in this decade as well. One such was Walter Goldschmidt's *Man's Way* (1959), which offered a robust, straightforward, and unapologetic evolutionism. Unlike Linton's *The Tree of Culture, Man's Way* made no attempt to trace the actual steps societies had followed in their upward climb. Instead, the volume was devoted to analyzing the processes and determinants that accounted for the ascent. As Goldschmidt (1959:106) explained: "In the theory set forth here, the forces that make for growth lie in the natural tendency for the means of production to develop and improve. Social institutions do not provide the basic dynamic of evolution; in a sense, they do not themselves evolve. Rather, they adjust to meet new circumstances as they arise, either through a change in environment or through a technological growth."

Goldschmidt went on to elaborate his views on the mechanisms involved. He pointed out that in his conception of evolution, functionalism played an important role. Social institutions, he said, "served the continued life of the society," and they changed during the course of evolution because "all parts of the social system . . . form an integrated whole so that changes in one part require adjustments in others" (Goldschmidt 1959:107).

We shall meet this wedding of evolutionary and functional theory again later in these pages.

The fruitfulness of the evolutionary approach was becoming more widely recognized, and evolutionary studies were beginning to be pursued on a broad front. No longer was work in this domain stayed by the dead hand of Franz Boas. White's optimism had been rewarded. As he noted triumphantly in his foreword to Sahlins and Service's *Evolution and Culture*, "The concept of evolution has proved itself to be too fundamental and fruitful to be ignored indefinitely by anything calling itself a science" (White 1960:vii). With evident satisfaction White went on to proclaim that "anti-evolutionism has run its course and once more the theory of evolution is on the march" (White 1960:vii).

The Darwin Centennial

Were one to pick a date when it could be said that evolutionism in American ethnology had once again reestablished itself, it would have to be 1959. In that year White published *The Evolution of Culture*. The volume was a lucid and trenchant recapitulation of much of what White had written on evolution in earlier articles. And it contained as well an elegant and illuminating treatment of cultures as functioning systems, one that could hardly have been improved upon by any British social anthropologist. However, the volume did not break any new theoretical ground. And though it dealt with the general principles and processes of cultural evolution, it failed to propose any theory of the rise of the state or the origin of civilization.

In gentle terms, I tried to express my disappointment in the evolutionary contributions of *The Evolution of Culture* when I reviewed the book at the time it appeared:

> Those who have followed White's writings on cultural evolution, and have looked forward to the publication of this work, may find in it less in the way of evolutionary formulations than they had expected. They may also feel that, while the contrast presented between primitive society on the one hand and early civilization on the other is most enlightening, the process by which the transformation from one to the other took place might have been discussed in more detail. (Carneiro 1960:7)

Despite its failure to live up to expectations, *The Evolution of Culture* was, without question, an important book. However, the main factor contributing to the recognition of 1959 as the turning point marking the reemergence of cultural evolution was its being the year of the Darwin centennial.

In the face of countless celebrations honoring the 100th anniversary of *On the Origin of Species,* and especially of a major symposium held at the University of Chicago, American anthropologists could hardly fail to ask themselves, "How can all the other natural sciences celebrate the hundredth anniversary of this great intellectual achievement, and anthropology be left out?"

Many years later Leslie White (1987:14–15) still remembered the occasion vividly:

> At the Chicago Centennial were gathered distinguished, reputable scientists—biologists, geologists, psychologists, ethnologists—as well as anthropologists from many foreign countries. . . . They were . . . respectable . . . and they were evolutionists. How then could evolutionism be "bad"? Some anthropologists came up to me during the meeting and confided that they "had really been evolutionists at heart all along"; some, I noticed, looked around to see if anyone was within hearing distance before they made this private confession.

About the same time, the Anthropological Society of Washington, at the initiative of Betty Meggers, who had been a student of White's, organized a series of lectures on cultural evolution given by distinguished anthropologists such as George P. Murdock, Clyde Kluckhohn, Robert Braidwood, and White himself. These lectures were later collected and published by the Society under the title *Evolution in Anthropology: A Centennial Appraisal* (1959).

The occurrences of 1959 may be said to have been a prelude to the publication the following year of a slim volume edited by Marshall Sahlins and Elman Service entitled *Evolution and Culture,* a book that was destined to have a powerful impact on the discipline of anthropology. As a testament to its immediate and continuing influence on the profession is the fact that today, more than forty years after its initial publication, the book is still in print. This volume contained essays by Sahlins and Service, but also by David Kaplan and Thomas Harding, students of theirs as well as of Leslie White.

The most widely read and influential of these four essays was that by Sahlins, entitled "Evolution: General and Specific," which will be discussed later. Almost as noteworthy was Service's chapter, "The Law of Evolutionary Potential," which argued that the major steps in cultural evolution were taken, not by the society then in the cultural forefront, but by another, one less wedded to the established ways.

As mentioned above, Leslie White wrote a foreword to this volume in which he praised the bold new advances made by its four contributors. Eyeing their new departures a bit wistfully, White explained, almost apologetically, why he himself had not done more along these lines:

> A few decades ago the opponent of antievolutionism [meaning himself] had to fight a series of propositions designed to refute evolutionist theory such as "the facts of diffusion negate evolutionism." . . . The opponent of these theories had to adapt himself to the propositions advanced by the Boasian antievolutionists and was therefore restricted in his scope and perspective. He had to develop a type of theory in opposition to specific criticisms and attacks. (White 1960:xi)

But for Service, Sahlins, and their students, White declared, the situation had been quite different:

> [T]hese younger anthropologists have been free from such handicaps. They were not reared in an atmosphere of antievolutionism; they accepted cultural evolutionism from the very start and have therefore been relatively free from the restrictions of polemics; they have been free to explore the implications of the theory of evolution as it applies to culture and to develop its many and fruitful possibilities. And they have done so exceedingly well. (White 1960:xi)

By the beginning of the 1960s, largely by dint of Leslie White's unrelenting efforts on its behalf, cultural evolutionism had gradually regained a large measure of anthropological respectability. Often, though, this respect was bestowed only grudgingly. For example, writing to Stanley South in 1957, Stephen Williams noted that "most American anthropologists that I know are in very general agreement with White but would almost rather cut off their tongue than admit it" (quoted in South and Green 2002:6).

The very term "evolution," when applied to culture, had made many anthropologists uneasy, and even raised the hackles of a few. When Melville Jacobs read a paper on cultural evolution at a meeting of the American Anthropological Association in 1947, Melville Herskovits stood up from the audience and urged him to replace the term "evolution" with "development," a term that he felt was "less encumbered with undesirable connotations" (Jacobs 1948:564n.–565n.).

Years before, Alexander Lesser had had the same experience. As he tells it, "In 1939, when I [presented a paper on] "Evolution in Social Anthropology" . . . at [the American Anthropological] Association meetings in Chicago, I had been warned by a social scientist who was by no means extreme in his view that 'evolution' was a dirty, dangerous word, and urged to replace it by the word 'development'" (Lesser 1985b:92).

Even anthropologists less hostile to cultural "evolution" than Herskovits still did not feel entirely comfortable with the word. For example, in *Configurations of Culture Growth*, A. L. Kroeber (1944) avoided "evolution," preferring "growth" instead. And as we have seen, Julian Steward (1955:5) felt compelled to admit his uneasiness with the term: "Since 'evolution' still strongly connotes the nineteenth century view, I hesitate to use it but find no better term." Even today, when the word "evolution" appears unself-consciously in the titles of books by such anthropologists as Patrick Kirch (1984), Bruce Trigger (1998), C. R. Hallpike (1988), and Tim Ingold (1986), some scholars, like Robert Drennan (1991:113), claim that they find themselves "somehow reluctant to use it."

7

Issues in Late
Midcentury Evolutionism

New Steps Forward

Leslie White had pruned away the dry, sterile undergrowth of anti-evolutionism. One by one, he had undercut the arguments put forward by Boas
and his disciples and had shown that evolution was a valid and rewarding
organizing principle, an extremely useful tool with which to practice anthropology. But he had not gone much beyond that. Since his early writings, in which he proposed the harnessing of energy as the measure and
mover of evolution, he had not proposed any new theory. As he indicated in
his foreword to the book by Sahlins and Service, future contributions to
cultural evolutionism were to be made by the next generation of anthropologists. And in that generation, Sahlins and Service were among the leaders. In fact, White (1960:xi) called the essays in their slim volume "the best
treatment of cultural evolutionism that we have seen."

Earlier I noted that there was a reluctance on the part of some anthropologists to use the very word "evolution." This hesitation was in part a holdover
from the days of out-and-out anti-evolutionism. But it also stemmed from the
fact that there was a certain ambiguity and difference of opinion as to what the
term "evolution" meant. To what kind of process was it to apply? On this score,
there was much disagreement. Accordingly, some of the early analysis of the
concept was directed toward a clarification of the concept of evolution.

General and Specific Evolution

One of the first of these serious attempts was made by Marshall Sahlins in
his article "Evolution: Specific and General," the lead essay in *Evolution and*

Culture. Sahlins distinguished two types of evolution, which he labeled *specific* and *general.* With organic evolution in mind, he made this distinction: "specific evolution is the production of diverse species, general evolution the production of higher forms. . . . To recapitulate: specific evolution is 'descent with modification,' the adaptive variation of life 'along its many lines'; general evolution is the progressive emergence of higher life 'stage by stage'" (Sahlins 1960:19, 22).

Moreover, Sahlins felt that this distinction applied to cultural evolution as well: "There are myriads of culture types . . . and an even greater variety of cultures proper. . . . How has this [variety] come about? In a word, through adaptive modification: culture has diversified as it has filled in the variety of opportunities for human existence. . . . Such is the specific aspect of cultural evolution" (Sahlins 1960:23).

But, Sahlins continued, "Specific evolution is not the whole of cultural evolution. Culture not only produces adaptive sequences of forms, but sequences of higher [i.e., more complex] forms; it has not only undergone phylogenetic development, but over-all progress. In brief, culture has evolved in a general respect as well as a specific one. General cultural evolution is the successive emergence of new levels of all-round development" (Sahlins 1960:28).

The distinction made by Sahlins clearly identified the two ways in which one could view the changes that culture had undergone. On that score, there was general agreement. However, one could ask, were both these kinds of changes to be called "evolution"? The characterization made by Sahlins of specific evolution was the same as that embodied in Charles Darwin's view of the history of organic life as "descent with modification." According to this view, *all* changes undergone by animal species were to be considered evolution.

However, there also existed a more restricted notion of what evolution was, one that would limit the term to what Sahlins called "general evolution." It was Herbert Spencer, not Charles Darwin, who had first defined "evolution," and he applied the term not just to *any* change, but only to those changes that embodied increased definiteness, coherence, and heterogeneity—in a word, *increased complexity* (Spencer 1896:391). Thus there was a choice to be made here. In what sense were anthropologists to apply the term evolution, the Darwinian or the Spencerian? Was evolution to refer to *both* types of change indiscriminately, as Sahlins proposed, or was it to be limited to what he called "general evolution"?

Apparently, Leslie White (1987:70)(for whom evolution was simply "a temporal sequence of forms") was perfectly happy to use the term broadly, applying it to both aspects of the process subsumed by Sahlins under "evolution." Thus in his foreword to *Evolution and Culture* White wrote that "specific evolution is just as much evolution as general evolution" (White 1960:ix). Some scholars, however, have chosen to follow Spencer in this regard and to restrict "evolution" to a process of change exhibiting increased complexity, and to regard "specific evolution" as a form of history, manifesting full particularity. Robert Murphy (1971:32), for one, remarked that "Specific evolution is known in less wordy circles as 'history.'" Perhaps "specific evolution" is more than just "history" if it is applied only to adaptive change, but that still does not make it evolution in the Spencerian sense.

(The issue of whether a Darwinian or a Spencerian "model" is more appropriate for the study of cultural evolution is one that has been, and still is being, minutely analyzed and hotly debated in anthropology [e.g., Munro 1963; Freeman 1974]. It will surface again in these pages.)

It can be noted here, though, that to apply the (Darwinian) notion of specific evolution to particular cultures as they change through time presents certain difficulties. For example, if we adopt this view, *all* aspects of the changes undergone by Rome from its founding in 752 BC until the collapse of the empire in AD 410, a span of more than a thousand years, are "evolution." According to this view, then, the decline and fall of the Roman Empire were just as much "evolution" as its growth and development. Now, while everyone would agree that the entire sequence of events in the life of Rome, from beginning to end, constitutes "history," it seems to me that calling *both* phases of this history "evolution" is to apply the same term to what, in fact, were *opposite processes.* One consisted of aggregation and integration, the other of fragmentation and disintegration. To avoid the glaring contradiction of calling both contrasting phases by the same term, I would follow Spencer's usage here and apply "evolution" only to the expansive and florescent phase of Roman history.

Another area of discussion that needs clarification is that of the relationship between unilinear and multilinear evolution on the one hand, and specific and general evolution on the other. In his foreword to *Evolution and Culture,* White (1960:ix) wrote that "evolution in its specific . . . aspect is multilinear; evolution in its general aspect is unilinear." I believe, though, that the matter can be viewed differently.

The historical development of a single society can truly be called evolutionary (in the Spencerian sense) if it has undergone a series of changes that have made it more complex, even if that series of changes is not closely paralleled by that of any other society—is unique, in other words. To decide whether the sequence of historical events undergone by a particular society is evolutionary or not, all we have to do is examine the nature of those events. We need not compare them with those undergone by any other society. If the history of other societies shows similar developmental trends, all well and good. But a particular series of historical events need not display parallels to the development of any other society to qualify as being evolutionary.

Thus, a single historical line of development does not have to be a case of "specific evolution," just because it is restricted to one instance. It can be a case of "general evolution" (in Sahlins' sense) if its discernible direction is toward increasing complexity. One can, therefore, quite properly speak of the development of Minoan or Harappan civilization as manifesting *general* evolution even though each, in its full particulars, was unique. Similarly, one can speak of the general evolution undergone by, say, the Zapotec or the Zulu if we are discussing phases in the history of these societies during which they were on an *ascending trajectory*.

However, I for one would prefer not to speak of the decline and disappearance of Minoan or Harappan civilization as being part of their "evolution." I would rather characterize that phase of their history as being part of their *dissolution* or *devolution*. But if I were *forced* to adopt Darwinian or, rather, "Sahlinsian" terminology with regard to the later, disintegrative phases of Minoan and Harappan history, I suppose I would have no choice but to refer to it as "specific evolution."

History versus Evolution

The issue of history versus evolution, one facet of the debate just discussed, was not a new one in anthropology. It had been joined a decade and a half earlier by Leslie White and A. L. Kroeber in the pages of the *Southwestern Journal of Anthropology*. The roots of this controversy, though, can be said to go back even further, to an article entitled "History and Science in Anthropology," which Kroeber had written in 1935. In this article he charged that Franz Boas, despite being hailed as the leader of the so-called American Historical School, in fact distrusted the historical approach and actually did not *do* history (Kroeber 1935:544, 555). Moreover, he added, Boas and his followers found "historical reconstruction unsound and sterile" (Kroeber 1935:547).

Kroeber himself had big plans for history. He envisioned a *large* history that was "not to cling timorously or mechanically to the thread of narration," but to "understand [the past] in terms of successively larger integrations" (Kroeber 1935:568). Indeed, he declared, "the distinctive feature of the historical approach . . . is not dealing with time sequences . . . but an endeavor at descriptive integration" (Kroeber 1935:545). Clearly, then, Kroeber thought of history as offering a wide canvas on which one was to paint with broad strokes.

In the article just cited, Kroeber divided the approaches of anthropology into just two: "history" and "science." All the work done by anthropologists was made to fit into one or the other of these categories. There was no room for "evolution." Any large-scale study of the past Kroeber was ready to assimilate into "history." So, when Leslie White, in his article "History, Evolutionism, and Functionalism: Three Types of Interpretation of Culture" (1945a), made a clear distinction between "history" and "evolution," Kroeber balked. Replying to White the following year, he proclaimed himself unable to accept White's tripartite classification. He preferred his own dichotomy of "history" and "science," declaring that "if this dichotomous view is sound, there is no apparent room for White's evolutionism" (Kroeber 1946:13). And as for what White called evolution, "Some [of it] . . . seems actually to be history; some of it science" (Kroeber 1946:15).

White, however, was not convinced. He resisted Kroeber's attempt to meld what he considered two distinct approaches into one, and repeated the contrast between them: "History says that one event precedes or succeeds another, evolution says that one form grows out of another" (White 1987:111). And in his review of Kroeber's magnum opus, *Configurations of Culture Growth*, White again took pains to draw the distinction he saw: "An historical account of events . . . is not at all the same as an evolutionist account. The *history* of horses, writing or money is quite a different thing from an account of their respective *evolutions*. The one deals with phenomena as unique events, with reference to specific time and place, the other deals with classes of phenomena without regard to specific time and place. The one particularizes, the other generalizes" (White 1987:203).

The work White was reviewing, *Configurations of Culture Growth* (1944), provided an outstanding example of Kroeber's theoretical ambivalence. It was a halfway house between Boasian particularism on the one hand and the all-out evolutionism of Leslie White on the other.

As far back as 1920, Kroeber had been aware of the scientific shortcomings of anthropology as then practiced. In a review of Robert Lowie's cautious and skeptical volume, *Primitive Society*, he had warned his colleagues that: "As long as we continue offering the world only reconstructions of specific detail, and consistently show a negativistic attitude toward broader conclusions, the world will find very little of profit in ethnology" (Kroeber 1920:380).

Writing fifteen years later, Kroeber (1935:567) felt that anthropology had still failed, "to any considerable degree . . . to integrate [its data] into a larger system of processes." And this, evidently, is what he intended to do in *Configurations*. Reviewing this massive tome of nearly 900 pages, White found much to praise. He noted that the book tried "to bring order out of chaos, to render culture intelligible," adding that it was "a continuation, and the most impressive example, of Kroeber's attempt to find his way out of the Boasian wilderness" (White 1987:200–201).

But, by his own admission, Kroeber's *Configurations of Culture Growth* was not an unqualified success. He confessed to "some lowering of expectations in the course of my work" (Kroeber 1944:762), and concluded that: "I see no evidence of any true law in the phenomena dealt with; nothing cyclical, regularly repetitive, or necessary. There is nothing to show either that every culture must develop patterns within which a florescence of quality is possible, or that, having once flowered, it must wither without chance of revival" (Kroeber 1944:761).

In attempting to explain Kroeber's failure to discover the patterns and trends he was seeking, or to achieve the depth of understanding he had hoped for, White attributed it in part to his failure to fully embrace the evolutionary point of view. And he also thought Kroeber had failed to look at those aspects of culture that more clearly exhibited long-term trends than did music, painting, and literature. In short, he thought Kroeber had failed to lay hold of the material elements of the culture process (White 1987:202–205).

As a whimsical epilogue to the dispute about history and evolution that White and Kroeber had carried on for many years, we may cite an interchange between the two men that occurred in the course of a panel discussion held during the Darwin centennial celebration at the University of Chicago. In his remarks, Kroeber had persisted in contending that "the two words [history and evolution] mean the same thing, namely, long-term change." But White again rejected this contention and stuck to his view that history and evolution "are fundamentally different, in that one is particularizing, the other generalizing." With some weariness, apparently, Kroeber replied that after coming to the conclusion "that White and I have been sleeping in the same bed for thirty years, . . . now he says that they were two beds" (White, Kroeber, *et al.* 1960:212, 206). Actually, White had been saying that all along!

Archaeology and Evolution

As that branch of anthropology that, per force, dealt with long-term culture change, archaeology inevitably became involved in the issue of evolution's proper role in the interpretation of the past. However, if, during the first four decades of the twentieth century, ethnology languished in the theoretical doldrums, so apparently did archaeology. Even Franz Boas, noted for his dedicated disinclination to embrace theory, spoke scornfully of archaeology, once complaining to Alexander Goldenweiser (1925a:247n.–248n.) that "A man who finds one potsherd passes with us as an archaeologist, one who finds two potsherds, as a good archaeologist, one who finds three, as a great archaeologist."

Indeed, during the 1930s and 1940s, there was very little concern in American archaeology with delineating the broad course of culture change, let alone with getting at the dynamics of the process. The reigning interpretive scheme was the so-called Midwestern Taxonomic System, devised by W. C. McKern. The McKern system "organized archaeological materials into categories based on degree of likeness of the assemblages being unearthed" (Caldwell 1959:303), employing such terms as Phase, Focus, Aspect, etc., for these assemblages without making any attempt to propose relationships between cultures through space and time (Brose 1973:99–100). In a word, the McKern system was static and sterile. But in this, it merely reflected the narrowness and shallowness of the archaeological thinking of the day.

A dissatisfaction with the status of archaeology began to emerge in the 1940s, marked especially by the publication in 1948 of Walter W. Taylor's *A Study of Archaeology*. American archaeologists, he said, "have categorized events and items, tagged them, but not investigated them in their dynamic aspects." As a result, he found that his discipline "is not in a healthy state. Its metabolism has gone awry. It is wasting and not assimilating its foodstuffs" (Taylor 1971:94).

As a cure for the malaise that afflicted archaeology Taylor advocated a "conjunctive approach," in which more attention would be paid to spatio-temporal relationships among archaeological assemblages (Brose 1973:104–105). Indeed, much of the discussion in *A Study of Archaeology* was devoted to theory and interpretation. It is noteworthy, however, that there was no real consideration of evolution. The sole discussion of it (p. 19) appears to dismiss it out of hand. Clearly, it was still too early in the day for archaeology to embrace it.

It was not in North America at all but in South America that evolution began to rear its head among archaeologists. In the 1940s a good deal of important archaeological work was being done on the coast of Peru. Convinced that Andean culture history "cannot be merely a subdivision in time, but must, at each stage reflect the state of development of the different cultures," Rafael Larco Hoyle (1966:12), a Peruvian archaeologist, proposed the following sequence of stages for the cultures of the Chicama Valley (Larco Hoyle 1948:10, 1966:11):

1. Preceramic
2. Early Ceramic
3. Formative (*Evolutiva*)
4. Florescent (*Auge*)

5. Fusion
6. Imperial

This evolutionary scheme was, according to Junius Bird (1964:ix–x), designed "as a substitute for and improvement on the use of an ever-increasing and overlapping list of pottery type and cultural horizon designations."

Larco Hoyle's new classification was presented at the Chiclín Conference held in Trujillo, Peru, in 1946. And the time was ripe for it. Most of the archaeologists who attended the conference—including Wendell Bennett, William Duncan Strong, and Gordon Willey—were then working in the neighboring Virú Valley on a program of survey and excavation aimed at revealing the broadest aspects of cultural development in northern Peru (Willey 1953:xvii–xix). Thus they were receptive to any general developmental scheme that would go beyond such period designations as Chancay black-on-white, which focused only on ceramic styles, to something more comprehensive, more synoptic. Indeed, they were more than supportive of such a scheme; they were ready to propose versions of it themselves (Willey 1946:133–134; Bennett 1948:6). But so strong was the taboo against "evolution" among archaeologists that they referred to their series of stages by the clumsy euphemism of "functional-developmental terminologies."

Interest had now been piqued in these evolutionary schemes and (as recounted in Chapter 6) a Viking Fund Conference was held in New York City in 1947 at which several such sequences, somewhat revised and extended so as to cover Mesoamerica, were proposed. It was at this conference, as we have seen, that Julian Steward attempted to subsume these series of stages into one master sequence that encompassed all of Nuclear America.

In disguise and under an assumed name, then, cultural evolution was slowly and tentatively coming out of the closet. There was now a greater interest and willingness among American archaeologists to try out "functional-developmental terminologies" with which to encapsulate and epitomize cultural developments in North America.

To be sure, American archaeologists were still careful to pledge their allegiance to "history," and not allow themselves to be seduced by the demimonde of evolutionism. William Duncan Strong (1953:392), for example, affirmed that he could not see "any clear difference between culture history and cultural evolution other than one of relative abstraction." And in much the same vein, Gordon Willey (1961:443) remarked, "I cannot appreciate the difference between a general universal evolution of culture and a general universal culture history."

True to his word, when Willey and his collaborator, Philip Phillips, in their influential volume *Method and Theory in American Archaeology*, proposed a general series of stages for cultural development in North America—namely, (1) Lithic, (2) Archaic, (3) Formative, (4) Classic, and (5) Post-Classic—they were quick to declare that "ours is not an evolutionary scheme" (Willey and Phillips 1958:70). Commenting on their reasons for shying away from calling their sequence evolutionary, Joseph Caldwell (1959:307) cocked a jaundiced eye and remarked, "I found their arguments unconvincing."

By the mid-1950s there were decided evolutionary stirrings within the discipline of archaeology. Moreover, they were occasionally given open voice. One of the first such expressions came in Stanley South's paper "Evolutionary Theory in Archaeology" (South 1955). Clearly and boldly South announced:

> American archaeology is now in a period of transition. It is breaking out of its Boasian shell of fact gathering and is beginning to emerge as a science based upon a theoretical foundation. Gradually more and more archaeologists will come to realize the importance of a theoretical framework for their profession. And, slowly, they will begin to admit, how deeply the roots of archaeological theory lie within the evolutionary theory outlined by Tylor and Morgan. (South 1955:21–22)

Anticipating Willey and Phillips's demurrer, which was still some three years down the road, South wrote: "The current trend in archaeological theory is to use this evolutionist approach, and then hasten to make reservations and apologies for the resemblance between the developmental sequences 'newly arrived at' and those of Morgan" (South 1955:15). And noting the dread with which the term "evolution" was still regarded, South (1955:18) did not hesitate to chide his colleagues: "If archaeologists are going to use evolutionary stages, and operate under basic evolutionary assumptions, why not say so? If the concept is the same why worry about the word?" South was convinced, and tried to persuade his colleagues, that the reality of evolution is "one of the necessary assumptions upon which archaeology depends if it is to aspire to anything more than merely writing historical description" (South 1955:3).

Though published in a minor journal—*Southern Indian Studies*—South's article gained considerable currency and elicited responses from many ethnologists and archaeologists. One of them was Gordon Willey, who echoed the feelings of many old guard archaeologists when he wrote, "I suppose my own interests are, to a large extent, the particulars of history" (quoted in South and Green 2002:4). Under the influence of Jeremy Sabloff, however, Willey was eventually won over to the evolutionary point of view, and later acknowledged that "[b]y the late 1960s a change had taken place in American archaeology" that saw "a tacit acceptance of cultural evolution" (Willey and Sabloff 1974:181).

But though the discipline as a whole might have undergone something of a conversion, Willey himself continued to regard specific and unique histories as lying closest to his heart. Thus, three years before he died, after acknowledging the importance and widespread manifestations of such things as population concentration and increasing complexity in both technology and political organization, he concluded by admitting that "I don't find these generalizations terribly interesting. The more fascinating thing to me has always been the historical particulars" (quoted in South and Green 2002:5).

Four years after South's seminal paper, during the year of the Darwin centennial, a second young archaeologist, William G. Haag, came forth with another forthright espousal of evolutionism. He pointed a critical finger at Willey and Phillips, whose *Method and Theory in American Archaeology* had recently appeared, and admonished them for "carefully avoid[ing] any contaminating *explanations* of culture change which presumably would take historical developmental descriptions out of the realm of culture history and into the nether land of cultural evolution" (Haag 1959:101). And while Haag lamented that American archaeologists "have largely rejected it by voice vote," he remained optimistic about the prospects of evolutionism. Hard to detect as it might be, he felt that the trend was in the right direction: "Despite slowness of pace," Haag wrote, "the archaeologists' theoretical framework evolves toward increased use of evolutionary premises" (Haag 1959:91, 104). Looking into the future, Haag saw good arising from this trend: "American archaeologists are uniquely enabled to turn to evolutionism as a guiding, unifying concept that would order much of what now appears to be unoriented endeavor" (Haag 1959:104).

One reason, perhaps, why archaeologists failed to embrace Leslie White's evolutionism more readily and apply it more vigorously was that they were uncertain of just how to put it to work. They might agree in general terms that later cultures were more complex than earlier ones, and that the harnessing of energy was indeed the great driving force of civilization. But in interpreting what they were finding in the ground, of what practical use was evolution? Robust and stimulating it might be, but White's evolutionism was still highly abstract and programmatic. It was true that, substituting more modern labels for two of its three terms, White still accepted Morgan's and Tylor's broad evolutionary stages of "Savagery," "Barbarism," and "Civilization." But as far as providing a more fine-grained and useful set of evolutionary stages, White had nothing concrete to offer. Still, archaeologists urgently needed help in this regard. They were looking for some sound and solid framework to assist them in making sense of the succession of particular cultures they were unearthing. It was at this point that ethnology came to the rescue.

Service's Sequence of Stages

In 1955, in the pages of the *American Anthropologist,* the ethnologist Kalervo Oberg proposed a typology of cultural forms based on differences in sociopolitical structure. Although Oberg's typology was proposed specifically for lowland South and Central America, it clearly was also applicable to societies in other parts of the world. The typology was as follows:

1. Homogeneous Tribes
2. Segmented Tribes
3. Politically Organized Chiefdoms
4. Feudal-Type States
5. City States
6. Theocratic Empires

It is important to note that what Oberg was proposing were *types,* not *stages.* At the time he was writing, anti-evolutionism was still so firmly in the saddle that setting forth a sequence of evolutionary stages might be expected to draw heavy fire.

It fell to Elman Service to see clearly that what Oberg presented as *structural types* were also *evolutionary stages.* Of Oberg's six types, Service's eye was drawn particularly to that of *chiefdom,* a sociopolitical form that, prior to Oberg's formulation, had no well-established name. As Oberg (1955:484) defined it, the category of "chiefdom" referred to a form of polity occupying a position intermediate between tribes and states. As such, it labeled a very important form of society that spanned a broad range of political development. It supplied a necessary term, then, in the evolutionary progression from autonomous villages to complex states. As Service saw it, the recognition of this concept focused attention on a stage in the evolution of society that, if not totally unrecognized before, had at least remained essentially anonymous.

In his influential book *Primitive Social Organization* (1962), Service somewhat simplified Oberg's set of types and proposed a fourfold evolutionary sequence of sociopolitical forms that consisted of *Band, Tribe, Chiefdom,* and *State.*

Not long after the appearance of this series of stages, it was criticized by Morton Fried (1966). His principal objection centered on the stage of

"Tribe," which he felt was not a universal stage in sociopolitical evolution. On the contrary, Fried thought it was only a response to the dislocation and disruption undergone by aboriginal societies as a result of European contact. Thus, he concluded, "I do not believe that there is a theoretical need for a tribal stage in the evolution of political organization" (Fried 1966:539).

A few years later, Fried himself proposed an evolutionary sequence of societal development. He of course eliminated Service's "tribe," calling it (after "race"), "the single most egregious case of meaninglessness" in anthropology (Fried 1967:154). Those societies that Service had allocated to the stage of "tribe," Fried lumped, along with Service's "band," into the category of "egalitarian society." Next in Fried's sequence came "rank society," a stage more or less equivalent to Service's "chiefdom." This was followed by "stratified society," which was roughly the same as Service's "state." But Fried also proposed a category of "state," as somehow different from "stratified society," and this was the last stage in his sequence.

The concept of "stratified society" was, of all of Fried's stages, "the most difficult to illustrate," because, he said, "stratified societies lacking political institutions of state level are almost impossible to find" (Fried 1967:185). That is, if a society was stratified, it was, according to Fried's criteria, essentially a state. This meant that a society that was stratified but yet somehow lacked the political institutions of a state was, in effect, a null class, a category without members!

Elman R. Service

It was perhaps because of this anomaly, combined with the peculiar and awkward way in which Fried defined "egalitarian society" (a form of society in which there is "social recognition of as many positions of valued status as there were individuals capable of filling them" [Fried 1967:52]), that Fried's sequence of stages never caught on. At least not in its entirety. It is true that "rank society" is commonly used as equivalent to "chiefdom," and of course "egalitarian society" was already in general use long before Fried made it a formal stage of his evolutionary sequence. Service (1968a:167) readily accepted Fried's strictures with regard to the tribe and recanted, deciding to "abolish" it as a general stage in his typology of sociopolitical development. And he went further, truncating his evolutionary sequence by collapsing it from four stages into three and renaming them: (1) Egalitarian Society, (2) Hierarchical Society, and (3) Archaic Civilization (Service 1968a:167).

(Noting the erratic distribution of "tribes" in the primitive world, I suggested [Carneiro 1987:761], as Joan Townsend [1985:142] had before me, that the stage of "Autonomous Village" replace that of "Tribe".)

But the world did little note nor long remember Service's emendation of his own sequence. In fact, Service himself appeared to have recanted his recantation, because three years later, in the revised edition of *Primitive Social Organization* (1971a), he retained the "Tribe" as a stage in his evolutionary sequence, noting only that "the law and order imposed by colonial powers could have the effect of restricting or even reducing the territories controlled by the tribal kin group without otherwise disturbing the tribe" (1971a:126).

At any rate, *Band, Tribe, Chiefdom,* and *State* was the sequence that survived, and it came to exert an enormous influence on archaeologists, an influence that still endures. In fact, Service's fourfold sequence of stages, says Alice Kehoe (to her evident dismay), remains the "gospel truth" and, she believes, is "still the standard reference among American archaeologists" (Kehoe 1998:165).

Among those American archaeologists Kehoe had in mind, the first ones to seize upon Service's sequence of stages and apply it in a thoroughgoing manner were William Sanders and Barbara Price, who employed it as a framework against which to measure cultural developments in prehistoric Mesoamerica. In the preface to their groundbreaking work *Mesoamerica: The Evolution of a Civilization* (1968), they informed their readers that they proposed to view Mesoamerican archaeology "from the perspective of recent developments in general anthropological theory" (1968:xiii). Moreover, they expressed the view that "ethnological and archaeological data can be encompassed by the same general theory" (1968:xiv). Sanders and Price left the clear impression that Service's sequence of stages, so useful to them, could be used to make illuminating reconstructions of cultural development in other areas of the world as well.

And in fact, looking back over a quarter century of archaeological work, Aram Yengoyan (1991:12) could assert that "Service's evolutionary framework has had a critical and lasting impact on archaeologists who are dealing with chiefdoms, early and archaic states, and the rise of civilizations."

The area of North America to which the Band–Tribe–Chiefdom–State scheme was most readily and fruitfully applied was the Southeast. The most distinctive and intriguing of Service's four stages was the chiefdom, and the Southeast was a region replete with prehistoric chiefdoms, many of which survived into early historic times. Archaeologists have examined southeastern chiefdoms with a vengeance, and nowhere else in the world today has the development of chiefdoms been more thoroughly investigated.

In the process of studying this and other areas, archaeologists developed criteria for ascertaining whether cultures whose material remains were recoverable had passed the autonomous village stages and attained the level of chiefdom. Particularly diagnostic of chiefdoms were differential burials, luxury grave goods, monumental architecture, and a hierarchy of settlement sizes.

Service's sequence, with the chiefdom stage again drawing the most attention, soon began to be applied to the prehistory of other regions outside the Western Hemisphere. For example, Colin Renfrew, in *Before Civilization* (1973, 1976), found it particularly relevant to the interpretation of the Neolithic and Bronze Age cultures of Britain and Malta. Societies with the features Service had attributed to chiefdoms, said Renfrew, had built the great stone temples of prehistoric Malta and the henges of Neolithic Britain. Moreover, he suggested that our understanding of how and why these structures were erected would be enhanced by looking at historically known chiefdom-level societies in other parts of the world, such as the American Southeast, Africa, and, especially, Polynesia, where similarly imposing stone structures had been built (Renfrew 1976:174–181, 256–259). Here, then, was a clear call for ethnography to be brought to the aid of archaeology, a cooperative endeavor that *Mesoamerica: The Evolution of a Civilization* had also exemplified and advocated (Sanders and Price 1968:74–97).

The acceptance of a symbiotic relationship between ethnology and archaeology has been one of the pillars of a resurgent evolutionism. After all, though set apart by the different methods they employ, the two are but complementary ways of studying the same phenomenon. Prehistoric societies and living ones are in no way categorically distinct. They are the same sort of thing. The principal difference between them is that one class of them survived while the other perished. Still, the latter, as long as it was "alive," operated in essentially the same way as ethnographically known societies facing similar sorts of challenges and attempting to meet them in similar ways.

Ethnology and archaeology, then, are simply different research procedures, each adapted in its own way to pursuing the same broad objective—attainment of the fullest possible understanding of how human societies have functioned and how they have evolved.

Like any two cooperating partners, however, ethnologists and archaeologists, in pursuing evolutionary objectives, are at times apt to compete. Having laid out what each considers its proper turf, each is prone to guard against presumed encroachment. Even when fundamentally in harmony, ethnologists and archaeologists like to proclaim the primacy—or at the very least the equality—of their subdiscipline in carrying out evolutionary reconstructions.

Processual Archaeology

The melding of evolutionary ethnology—"neo-evolutionism" as it was often called—with archaeology's continuing concern with understanding change and its causes gave rise in the 1960s to the "New Archaeology," also called, more descriptively, "processual archaeology." There were several elements to this new approach to the study of the past. We can distinguish them as follows: (1) a concern with *process*, not merely with history; (2) a reliance on *evolutionary theory*, derived principally from ethnology; (3) the search for *explanations* rather than just description; (4) the embracing of *determinism*, with the causal factors being drawn chiefly from the philosophy of cultural materialism; (5) focusing more concertedly on *ecology* and *adaptation;* and (6) the formulation of generalizations or laws.

Writing toward the end of the 1960s, Kent Flannery, one of the leaders of the New Archaeology, noted that "one of the current theoretical debates in American archaeology" is "whether archaeology should be the study of culture history or the study of cultural process" (Flannery 1972b:103). At that time he estimated that "Perhaps 60 percent of all current ambulatory American archaeologists are concerned primarily with culture history" and that about "10 percent, both young and old, belong to what might be called the 'process school'" (Flannery 1972b:103).

Much as he aligned himself with the processualists, Flannery was not disposed to turn his back on the historical approach. "By no stretch of the imagination," he wrote, "do all process theorists propose to reject history, because it is only in the unfolding of long sequences that some processes become visible" (Flannery 1972b:106).

The "process" of the processual archaeologists was pretty much evolutionary process. The two were deemed to be largely coterminous. As Lewis Binford (1972:110) put it, "Concern with evolution is concern with the operative processes." And this "evolution" was a conceptual framework Binford had borrowed from the work of White, Steward, Service, Sahlins, and Fried (Trigger 1984:278; Dobres and Robb 2000:6).

To quote Flannery (1972b:104) again, processual archaeologists "hope to explain, rather than merely describe, variations in prehistoric human behavior." And "explanation" meant discovering and marshaling the causal factors that accounted for the operation of the process being described. Just what the causal factors were differed according to the case under study, but especially according to the theorist involved. Though specifically different, they were generically alike. These causal factors were drawn largely from the arsenal of cultural materialism. Surveying the history of American archaeology, David Hurst Thomas (1998:451) remarked that "the processual agenda in archaeology relies heavily on the principles of cultural materialism."

In their own survey of American archaeology, Willey and Sabloff (1993:224) agreed that the "position of most New Archaeologists—although not always overtly formulated—in practice assumes the technical-economic realm of culture to be the primary determinative one in change, with the social and ideational realms changing in secondary reaction to it." Then, after this assertion, Willey readily admits that this concern with the determinants of culture change "marks a distinctive difference from that of the historical-developmental stage approach" that he and Philip Phillips had employed in their earlier work, "where no attempt was made to pinpoint causality" (Willey and Sabloff 1993:224).

Since, whatever the culture being investigated, it was situated in a physical environment to which it had to adapt, ecological considerations generally played a prominent role in the processualist's attempt to account for the factors that had shaped it. Ecology, then, was one of the major pillars of cultural materialist interpretations of the sinews of culture change.

Toward what target was all this powerful intellectual artillery aimed? "The ultimate goal of processual archaeology," says Thomas (1998:75), "is to produce law-like generalizations." And while not so ready to embrace this objective himself, Bruce Trigger (1984:277) nonetheless recognized that "the highest goal of archaeology"—meaning *processual* archaeology—"was not to understand history but to emulate social anthropologists by trying to formulate laws of human behavior."

Lewis Binford and Middle Range Theory

It is generally agreed that the opening salvo in the campaign for a "New Archaeology" was the publication in 1962 of Lewis Binford's paper "Archaeology as Anthropology." Binford had studied under Leslie White at the University of Michigan and had imbibed and absorbed White's evolutionism. And in his earlier writings, he spoke with passion and conviction of archaeology's role in furthering cultural evolution.

Binford was sure that "Archaeologists should be among the best qualified to study and directly test hypotheses concerning the process of evolutionary change" (Binford 1962:224). Yet he believed that archaeology must broaden its horizons and cease being satisfied with narrow reconstructions of individual histories. "Specific 'historical' explanations," he wrote "add nothing to the explanation of the processes of cultural change and evolution" (Binford 1962:218).

Binford took on the mission of prodding his colleagues into contributing to this great objective. Thus he admonished them that: "Archaeology must accept a greater responsibility in the furtherance of the aims of anthropology. Until the tremendous quantities of data which the archaeologist controls are used in the solution of problems dealing with cultural evolution ... we are not only failing to contribute to the furtherance of the aims of anthropology but retarding the accomplishment of these aims" (Binford 1962:224). A great deal of work lay ahead for archaeology if it was to achieve this goal, for "only when we have the entire temporal span of cultural evolution as our 'laboratory' can we make substantial gains in the critical area of social anthropological research" (Binford 1962:219).

Following these broad pronouncements, Binford himself turned to more limited objectives. Specifically, he has concerned himself with the relationship between the behavior of living peoples—primarily hunters and gatherers—and the material remains they leave behind for future archaeologists to unearth and interpret. To study this behavior he decided to turn away from excavation and to begin a specialized kind of ethnographic field work, most notably among the Nunamiut Eskimo of Alaska. "As a neo-evolutionist," David Hurst Thomas summarized (1998:435), "Binford believed that there was a high degree of regularity in human behavior and that ethnographic study would reveal much about aspects of past cultures not directly observable from the archaeological record."

It was Binford's contention, as Bruce Trigger (1989:300) noted, that "archaeologists must be trained as ethnologists. Only by studying living situations in which behaviour and ideas can be observed in conjunction with material culture was it possible to establish correlations that could be used to infer social behaviour and ideology reliably from the archeological record." In other words, this was ethnography in the service of archaeology.

It is noteworthy, though, that while proclaiming his allegiance to cultural evolution, Binford has never really toiled in its vineyards. He has rarely concerned himself with long-term change, but has stuck pretty much to what he called "middle range theory." His "processual" archaeology usually focuses on relatively short segments of change rather than on extended transformations.

But like the evolutionists who influenced him, Binford is interested in general and recurring processes rather than in unique historical events. Indeed, one of his objectives is to turn the latter into exemplifications of the former. In accounting for cultural forms, one might add, Binford generally looks to ecological factors as the primary determinants of beliefs, customs, and institutions. Thus his brand of archaeology, like that of most evolutionists, is firmly rooted in the materialist camp.

Ethnographic Analogy and Parallels

Time was when archaeologists felt that in their reconstruction of extinct cultures they were narrowly restricted to what could be learned directly from material remains. Thus James A. Ford, writing in 1952, argued: "If traces of ancient political ideas, religious practices, or forms of social organization were preserved, and could be sampled and classified, then archaeologists certainly would take advantage of such material. Unfortunately, these are not available to us, and we are forced by circumstances to rely on more durable cultural equipment" (Ford 1952:319).

But the processual archaeologists who began to emerge in the 1960s entertained more ambitious plans for their discipline. And in an effort to expand their horizons they sought the aid of ethnography. As Robert Dunnell (1980:77) observed, "If one thing is clear about the new archaeology it is that it was intended to be explicitly modeled on sociocultural anthropology and to make contributions to anthropology." (Even the grand old "preprocessualist," Gordon Willey, had once declared, "American archaeology is anthropology or it is nothing" [quoted in Flannery 1972b:102].) Moreover, in support of their use of ethnographic analogy, the new archaeologists could cite remarks by their esteemed predecessor, V. Gordon Childe. Childe (1946:250) was firm in his belief that "The ethnographers' picture of a contemporary savage or barbarian society can with due reserve be used to supplement the archaeologists' picture" of extinct societies at the same general level of culture.

Ethnology (in the broad sense) could provide two sorts of assistance to the aspiring young processual archaeologists: (1) evolutionary theory, which up to that time had been generated almost exclusively by ethnologists, and (2) ethnographic analogy, drawn from the rich coffers of countless monographic studies, works that could provide archaeologists with parallels to help flesh out the bare bones of the material remains their spades and trowels were uncovering.

But there was widespread and entrenched opposition among many archaeologists to allowing ethnologists into their domain. And much of this opposition seemed to be based on the feeling that this was an unwarranted and unwelcome trespass that would compromise the autonomy and integrity of archaeology, and thereby diminish the status of its practitioners. Richard Gould (1980:3) feared that archaeology would "run the risk of adopting a kind of client relationship toward social and cultural anthropology," and warned his colleagues that "we cannot allow archaeology to be presented as a kind of imperfect anthropology of the past" (Gould 1980:250).

Norman Yoffee (1993:67) balked strenuously at the idea of trying to interpret political developments in Ancient Mesopotamia "through a series of ethnographic analogies masquerading as social evolutionary theory." William Longacre (1970:136) voiced his apprehension that if archaeologists based their interpretations "on the ethnographic present, then we are saying we have nothing to learn from the past." In short, as Lyman, O'Brien, and Dunnell (1997:213) put it, "archaeologists wanted to be more than the bastard stepchildren of anthropology." Using similar words but without the stigma of illegitimacy, Dobres and Robb (2000:14) declared that "archaeology does not have to be the intellectual poor cousin of anthropology, gratefully and uncritically accepting hand-me-down concepts and theories."

But was all this nothing more than a proprietary reflex on the part of traditional archaeologists, intent on guarding their turf against infiltration by their sister subdiscipline? James Hill (1977b:60) seemed to think so when he advised his colleagues that "The fact that prehistoric data are often quite different from data gathered by ethnographers should not mislead us into thinking that the nature of our explanations must be different."

Two separate issues are involved here: One is, To what extent are archaeologists justified in borrowing *theories* from ethnology? The other is, To what extent are they justified in borrowing *facts*? Discussion of the former will be postponed until later in this volume. The latter, already addressed in preliminary fashion, will now be discussed more fully.

Ethnoarchaeology

In his book *Living Archaeology* (1980), Richard Gould notes that one approach to "the use of ethnographic observations as a way of 'explaining' archaeological findings is the use of analogy." But Gould has no use for ethnographic analogy. "Here," he says, "is an idea whose time has *gone*" (1980:x). Instead, he proposes to rely on "ethnoarchaeology," or as he prefers to call it, "living archaeology."

It seems to me, though, that Gould has dismissed the idea of ethnographic analogy too quickly. It should not be a matter of one or the other. Ethnographic analogy and ethnoarchaeology, while not the same thing, are nevertheless closely allied. They have the same objective, namely, to maximize our knowledge and understanding of extinct cultures. The difference comes in their ways of proceeding.

Ethnoarchaeology is the study of the ways in which living societies leave a material residue of their culture. How a living society disposes of its garbage, for example, will provide clues that may assist the archaeologist in interpreting the remains of a prehistoric culture. Ethnographic analogy, on the other hand, has a rather different focus. It is concerned with those traits of living cultures that do *not* leave a material residue. The presence of such traits in an extinct prehistoric society is thus more difficult to ascertain. However, we cannot say, by fiat, that it is impossible to do so. It is a problem to the solution of which one must apply scientific *inference.* The result will not be irrefutable *proof,* but it may at least provide an answer with a certain degree of probability.

How is ethnographic analogy applied? The procedure is simple and straightforward. The archaeologist examines living cultures that, in various ways, appear to resemble the prehistoric culture he (or she) has excavated and that he is striving to understand to the fullest. If in those presumably similar living cultures a certain trait, *X,* is present in a substantial majority of cases, then it is a *reasonable inference* (nothing more) that it was also present in the extinct culture.

For example, if from the size of an archaeological site it is deemed likely that the population of the settlement it represented exceeded 500, and if among ethnographically known villages of 500 or more persons unilineal descent groups are present in a large proportion of the cases, isn't it more likely than not that the society whose settlement was excavated *also* had unilineal descent groups?

That is the simple essence of ethnographic analogy. The reasoning behind it seems to me sound and compelling. Yet Gould maintains that "the argument by analogy has already fallen into disrepute among many if not most ethnoarchaeologists" (1980:x). To this contention my reply would be: If an archaeologist, of whatever stripe, chooses to deprive himself of this tool, he does so to his own impoverishment.

General Systems Theory

Though it may appear something of a digression, it is nonetheless appropriate here to discuss general systems theory, since it became an important adjunct to the analysis of cultures employed by a significant number of processual archaeologists.

General systems theory can be traced back to the writings of the theoretical biologist Ludwig Bertalanffy. Its great appeal to the newly emerging processual archaeologists was that it was "scientific," at a time when they were turning away from idiographic descriptions and aiming at nomothetic generalizations. General systems theory, it was thought, "brought archaeological research into the mainstream of the social sciences and of the other sciences in general" (Willey and Sabloff 1993:313).

General systems theory dealt with human societies as organized *systems*, subject to perturbations to which they were forced to respond and, if possible, overcome. Key concepts in "GST" were equilibrium and homeostasis. It focused on the deviation of societal variables away from acceptable values or magnitudes, and how, by means of negative feedback mechanisms, a society could reestablish its original condition or a close approximation to it. GST showed, in other words, how a system—in this case, a *social* system—normally operates in order to adapt and endure.

Writing in 1967, Kent Flannery declared, "My prediction for the next decade is that we shall see general systems theory . . . applied successfully to American archaeology in spite of the loudest mutterings of the establishment" (Flannery 1972b:107). And Flannery's prediction appeared to be confirmed when James Hill, writing ten years later, said of himself and of his close colleagues that "our general framework is based on general systems theory" (Hill 1977a:7).

The conceptual structure of general systems theory worked well enough as long as the problem was one of how a society, temporarily disrupted by some external intrusion, was able to revert, more or less, to its previous state. As applied to human societies, general systems theory had as two of its important components the familiar elements of *functionalism* and *ecology*, which came into play as a society sought to reassume an equilibrium after adjusting to alterations in external conditions. It was, in short, a story of "adaptation lost, and adaptation regained."

But, as soon became apparent, general systems theory had its limitations. It had not been designed, nor was it geared, to explain long-term directional change, that is, *evolution*. And its theorists admitted as much. James Hill (1977b:64), for example, one of its leading exponents, remarked that "most systems theorists . . . have not really come to grips with systemic change." And speaking of "equalizing processes," Hill (1977b:63) noted that "this kind of process will not, by itself, account for cultural change." And he added, "In short, homeostatic mechanisms are behavioral responses that serve to *prevent* change" (Hill 1977b:64; emphasis mine).

Summing up the situation, Robert Wenke (1981:99) remarked that "amidst this general acceptance . . . there are those who are convinced that while GST terminology and forms of analysis may profitably be used . . . to reconstruct the operation of extinct systems, nevertheless, it cannot provide truly evolutionary explanations."

That was, perhaps, something of an overstatement. Whereas *negative* feedback mechanisms acted to restore a previous equilibrium and thus prevent change, *positive* feedback mechanisms existed that provided an avenue for state-transforming change—for evolution—to occur. As Flannery (1968:68) noted, "'positive feedback' processes . . . amplify deviations, causing systems to expand and eventually reach stability at higher levels."

And Flannery was right. The amplification of disturbances, causing the overthrow of old equilibria, could lead in some cases to the development of new structural features allowing the society to cope successfully with the altered conditions of existence. And what would one term the incremental accumulation of adaptive structural elements, producing increased complexity, if not evolution?

Respectability Regained

The 1960s found evolutionism once again in the ascendancy, in both ethnology and archaeology. As Willey and Sabloff (1974:182) in their *History of American Archaeology* summed up developments in their field, "the theory of cultural evolution was generally anathema as late as the 1950s," but "[b]y the late 1960s a change had taken place in American archaeology. There had been a tacit acceptance of cultural evolution" (1974:181). This sea change was, in fact, best epitomized by Willey himself. Viewing "evolution" with trepidation in the late 1950s, by 1974 he had declared himself a convert. To be sure, he had not become a zealous advocate of evolutionism, but at least he had come to accept the idea that evolution could be validly and fruitfully pursued in archaeology.

Writing jointly with Jeremy Sabloff, Willey attempted to explain the basis of his (and Phillips's) former discomfort with evolution. First of all, he said, in reference to the labeling of their sequence of steps in North American prehistory, they had been "hesitant to use the word 'evolution' because of what seemed to them to be its deterministic and causal implications." And they had "shied away from anything that seemed to them to be deterministic or that would readily *explain* the series of stages by which they viewed the New World past." To excuse this timidity Willey remarked that their reluctance in this regard "was a hesitancy in keeping with the anti-evolutionary attitude of the times" (Willey and Sabloff 1974:179).

This "elucidation" of the matter, however, strikes me as less than convincing. First of all, it is clear that an *explanation* of Willey and Phillips's sequence was logically independent of the sequence itself; thus it did not commit them to any particular form of determinism. But even if the sequence had somehow carried within it its own determinants, would that not have enhanced it rather than diminished it? It seems ungracious, though, not to accept Willey's conversion at face value and let it go at that.

Among the zealous "New Archaeologists," the acceptance of evolutionism was more than just "tacit," as it might have been for archaeologists as a whole. It was forthright and vigorous. Indeed, wrote Willey and Sabloff, the New Archaeology soon came to have "a predominantly evolutionary point of view" (1974:183).

"Neo-Evolutionism"

When in the 1960s, in the teeth of continued opposition, cultural evolutionism began to establish itself in a reinvigorated form, those who had opposed it all along began calling it "neo-evolutionism." This label was not a new one. Robert Lowie had already used the term in his *History of Ethnological Theory* (1937:226, 289). However, Leslie White bristled at the idea that it was a fitting designation for the brand of evolutionism he was championing. In openly resisting this new epithet he remarked:

> some of the die-hards would not admit that the "new" evolutionism was the same as the "old" evolutionism of Tylor—that evolutionism is evolutionism; they insisted upon calling it "neo-evolutionism," which in my opinion, is a misleading and unjustifiable term. One may properly speak of Neo-Lamarckianism, Neo-Thomism, etc., but not of neo-gravitation, neo-urbanism, neo-militarism—or neo-whiskey, after the repeal of the Volstead Act. (White 1987:15)

Nevertheless, the word gained currency, and is today freely and frequently used, although it is generally avoided by White's former students and followers.

The ascendancy of a resuscitated evolutionism continued into the early 1970s. In 1972, for example, Kent Flannery published an often-cited and very influential article entitled "The Cultural Evolution of Civilizations." Flannery had studied at the University of Chicago and was one of a cohort of Young Turks, including such men as Robert Whallon, James Hill, and William Longacre, who were to become the vanguard of the "New Archaeology." Warmly embracing Service's sequence of Band, Tribe, Chiefdom, and State as accurately reflecting the successive stages in cultural evolution, Flannery described the principal characteristics of each stage in some detail, and went on to present a synoptic chart showing "Types of societies in ascending order of sociopolitical complexity, with ethnographic and archaeological examples of each" (1972a:401–404).

In the next few pages Flannery discussed various "prime movers," such as irrigation, warfare, population pressure, and trade, each of which had been proposed as the principal driving force behind cultural evolution. Critical of them all as single-factor determinants, he went on to construct an elaborate explanatory system in which the interplay of these and other factors would eventually lead, he hoped, to a successful "generative model for the state" (1972a:421).

In ethnology, as in archaeology, cultural evolution was becoming acceptable again—indeed, almost fashionable. Already in 1960 Leslie White had anticipated that this would happen: "We may safely predict that evolutionism in cultural anthropology will become respectable and even popular in the future. As a matter of fact, we may expect to see more than one anthropologist come forward and tell us that he has actually been an evolutionist all along" (White 1960:viii).

Sure enough, a few years later, Margaret Mead (1964:ix) remarked that on rereading Thomas Henry Huxley's *Foundations for Ethics*, "My interest in evolution was *reawakened*" (emphasis mine). Not so with Melville Herskovits, however, who staunchly proclaimed, in defiance of White's prediction: "As far as I am concerned, he need not fear. I shall be one anthropologist who . . . will not come forward and tell us that 'he has actually been an evolutionist all along'" (Herskovits 1960:1051).

8

Features of the
Evolutionary Process

Developmental Stages

We have seen what a great impetus was given to evolutionary studies in anthropology, especially in archaeology, by the formulation of a useful set of developmental stages. The issue of stages had always been a bone of contention between evolutionists and anti-evolutionists, the latter claiming, repeatedly and emphatically, that the very notion of stages was inherently flawed.

Edward Sapir (1927:99), for example, argued that "the doctrine of social stages could not be made to fit the facts laboriously gathered by anthropological research." And in similar words Alexander Goldenweiser (1931:659–660) held that "With the accumulation of adequate anthropological material the concept of uniformity of stages was shaken and then collapsed altogether." Not to be outdone, Melville Herskovits (1952:527–528) asserted, in no uncertain terms, "I am *glad . . . to reaffirm my belief* that the use . . . of such a concept as 'stages of development' implies a belief in a type of social evolution that cannot, on the basis of objectively verifiable data, be established as valid" (emphasis in the original). And finally, Bernhard Stern (1928:353) assured his readers that "culture is too complex and the forms of combination of social institutions too variable to fit into any definite social evolutionary scheme."

This repudiation of the validity of evolutionary stages was, of course, a great exaggeration. The utility and indeed the indispensability of cultural stages as a way of encapsulating and highlighting the general course that culture had followed in its development could hardly be dismissed. It had been clearly understood and forcefully stated by the classical evolutionists. E. B. Tylor (1916:20), for example, had said: "wherever there are found elaborate arts, abstruse knowledge, complex institutions, these are the result of gradual development from an earlier, simpler, and ruder state of life. No stage of civilization comes into existence spontaneously, but grows or is developed out of the stage before it."

And while Morgan's sequence of the development of marriage proved erroneous, his general series of cultural stages, consisting of Savagery, Barbarism, and Civilization, remained perfectly sound. These stages, with their names intact, had been retained by archaeologists of such standing as V. Gordon Childe and Grahame Clark. Childe (1944:8) took pains to specify just what he meant by these labels:

> The terms *savagery, barbarism* and *civilization* . . . technically denote successive stages in social and economic development as defined particularly by the ethnographer Morgan and the economist Engels. . . . A *savage* society here means one that depends for its livelihood exclusively on hunting, fishing and collecting, whereas all *barbarians* augment their food supply by cultivating edible plants, breeding animals for food or combining both activities. The term *civilized* is reserved, in conformity with the word's derivation, for people who dwell in cities.

Clark entitled one of his books *From Savagery to Civilization* (1946), and included in it synoptic charts (pp. 67, 105) showing just which traits were associated with which stages.

Among social anthropologists, one of them, Bronislaw Malinowski, used the word "savage" in the title of one of his books: *The Sexual Lives of Savages in North-Western Melanesia* (1929a). Technically, though, Malinowski used the term incorrectly. The Trobrianders (to whom he applied it), being fully agricultural, were actually "barbarians," not "savages."

Nevertheless, the words "savage" and "barbarian" grew too jarring to the increasingly sensitive anthropological ears. The Berndts (1973:20) stated the case for abandoning these terms as follows: "In serious comparative studies, 'savage' and 'barbarian,' with its 'barbarous' overtones, are no longer acceptable as labels for categories of mankind in this evolutionary type of sequence. There is something altogether too derogatory about them."

So, while their essential meaning was retained, the stages themselves were renamed, "savages" becoming "hunters and gatherers," and "barbarians" becoming "horticulturalists." "Civilization," though, was deemed to sound "civilized" enough not to require rechristening.

To be sure, there were other sequences of stages than Morgan's. There was also the developmental sequence designated by the labels Paleolithic,

Mesolithic, Neolithic, Bronze Age, and Iron Age, first proposed by European archaeologists in the nineteenth century, and never seriously challenged since.

In eastern North America, the cultural sequence of Paleoindian, Archaic, Woodland, and Mississippian, proposed by archaeologists while they were still in their anti-evolutionary phase, showed that no matter how opposed to evolution they might be in principle, in practice they could hardly avoid it in the synoptic presentation of their work.

These two sequences of stages were soon joined by another, which was deemed more suitable for portraying the greater span of cultural development that had occurred in Mesoamerica. This sequence consisted of Preceramic, Incipient Agriculture, Formative, Pre-Classic, Classic, and Post-Classic. And there was also Alex Krieger's (1955:247–250) evolutionary series, which consisted of Early Hunting, Food Gathering, Food Producing, Urban Living—obvious enough and of course irrefutable.

Kent Flannery (1972b:102) surveyed the situation and summed it up well: "When the concept of cultural evolution emerged triumphant after years of suppression, archaeology showed great interest in evolutionary sequences and in the classification of 'stages' in the human career." Despite an occasional dissident voice, there was general agreement that evolutionary stages were part of the enduring conceptual structure of archaeology.

It was not a question, then, of stages or no stages. It was a matter of *which* set of stages to employ and for *what* purpose. Allied to this was the question of what *criteria* were to be used in constructing a series of stages. Were they to be technological, economic, political, or some other? Alternative sequences, moreover, were not necessarily incompatible. They might be complementary, each highlighting different aspects of cultural development. And a society's standing in one sequence need not necessarily be the same in another. Thus, though outranking it politically, a chiefdom might rank no higher than an autonomous village when it came to technology.

Let me return briefly to Gordon Willey's groundless apprehension that calling his developmental sequence "evolutionary" might somehow commit him to some form of determinism. Such a fear, as I indicated above, was quite unfounded. A sequence of stages and the *determinants* of that sequence are two different things. It is curious, in this regard, that another leading anthropologist, A. L. Kroeber, also had a mistaken notion about evolutionary stages and their determinants, but his misapprehensions ran in the *opposite direction* from Willey's. In the opening pages of his famous textbook, *Anthropology*, Kroeber (1948:6) wrote: "It became common practice in the older anthropology to 'explain' any part of human civilization by arranging its several forms in an evolutionary sequence from lower to higher and allowing each successive stage to flow spontaneously, without specific causes, from the preceding one."

Thus, while Willey lived in fear that an unpleasant determinism would somehow exude from the pores of any truly evolutionary sequence, Kroeber was afraid that an evolutionary sequence would present one stage flowing out of another spontaneously and automatically, thus sapping it of the vital ingredient of causation!

What constitutes the *determinants* of an evolutionary sequence is, of course, a matter of the greatest interest, and it will be dealt with in a later section. Here I would like to consider the *refinements* in an evolutionary sequence that become possible as we delve more deeply into the developmental process. And to do so I would like to return to that celebrated evolutionary stage, the chiefdom.

It is obvious on the face of it that the concept of chiefdom spans a very broad range of societal forms. A simple chiefdom may encompass only a dozen or so villages, as did that of northern Kiriwina in the Trobriands. At the other end of the chiefdom scale, though, we find such imposing polities as Hawaii, which might almost be labeled a proto-state. Clearly, there is a lot here to be lumped within an undivided category.

The desirability of distinguishing gradations in the continuum of political development between autonomous villages and the state became evident to archaeologists as they became increasingly familiar with the prehistoric and early historic cultures of the Southeast United States. Accordingly, in 1978, Vincas Steponaitis (1978:420) proposed to divide the chiefdoms of this region into two types, *simple* and *complex*. The basis for this distinction was clear: Simple chiefdoms had *two* levels of organization, complex chiefdoms had *three*.

From the point of view of labeling important transitions in political evolution, dividing the category of "chiefdom" into two certainly represented an advance. And the distinction between simple and complex chiefdoms is now routinely made by Southeastern archaeologists. However, a *further* distinction can be made in the category of chiefdom. Prompted by ethnohistorical accounts of the Coosa chiefdom of northern Georgia (Hudson 1988, 1990) and the Powhatan chiefdom of tidewater Virginia (Rountree 1989), I was led some years ago to propose a *third* stage in the development of chiefdoms. Why did this additional distinction appear warranted?

Among complex chiefdoms (or, as I prefer to call them, *compound* chiefdoms) the usual practice is for a victorious paramount chief in the interminable wars that characterize them to retain in office the political leader of a smaller chiefdom that he has just conquered. However, bridling under the subordinate status imposed upon him, the vanquished chief is always looking for an opportunity to break free. (Such an occurrence was witnessed by the Spaniards among the Coosa [Hudson 1990:102].) However, paramount chief Powhatan had instituted the practice of systematically removing from office the original lesser chiefs of conquered groups and replacing them with his many brothers and sons, men more likely to remain loyal to his cause (Rountree 1989:117–118, 142).

Since this modification introduced a greater degree of integration and cohesion into the structure of a chiefdom, I proposed to call a polity that had achieved this stage of organization a *consolidated chiefdom* (Carneiro 1992b:37). The resulting three-phase developmental sequence for chiefdoms would then be: (1) simple, (2) compound, and (3) consolidated. Not only does this extended typology yield a more fine-grained evolutionary sequence, it also points at the very *process* that gave rise to it.

Here, then, is but one example of the fruitful results to be obtained from a refinement of stages. Terry Rambo (1991:29) is quite right in stating that "[c]onstruction of typologies of stages remains a major preoccupation of cultural evolutionists"—at least with those who concern themselves with the major phases that have marked the evolution of culture.

Process versus Stages

One discordant note may be sounded here to disturb the otherwise happy chorus of voices singing the praises of stage sequences in cultural evolution. It is sometimes objected that the notion of evolutionary stages is now passé, and that the modern-day evolutionist is more concerned with *process* than with *stages*. Thus Herbert Lewis (1968:103) declares that "typologies are static by nature and cannot yield productive insights into matters of process and development." Mark Leone (1972:22) echoes the thought, asserting that "The implicit question in every one of the stage schemes is how does one stage become another. This latent flaw has been understood by most modern anthropologists studying culture change." And Terry Rambo (1991:54) is equally convinced of the inutility of stages: "Reconstruction of evolutionary sequences as an end in itself, however, is scientifically sterile. It leads to scholastic arguments about the correct number of stages. . . . It is by itself incapable of generating important new theoretical questions." So, according to these views, the stage concept has the "latent flaw" that it cannot yield "productive insights," and can lead only to "scholastic arguments." What reply is to be made to such contentions?

Simply this. Stages are descriptive categories. They delineate significant and distinctive "way stations" in a general process. They are not meant to describe that process, but they do *invite* attempts to account for the passage from one stage of this process to another. Thus identifying stages is not at cross-purposes with a concern with process. Not at all. The two are complementary, and enhance and reinforce each other. Stages, as Friedman and Rowlands (1978:269) put it, are "cross-sections of a complex of processes."

In discussing the stages they use to describe the evolution of human society, Johnson and Earle (1987:313–314) tell us: "These labels [of their stages: family, local group, Big Man collectivity, chiefdom, archaic state, and nation state] do not signify perfectly discrete levels or plateaus, to one or another of which all known cultures must be assigned; rather they designate stations along a continuum at which it is convenient to stop and make comparisons with previous stations."

Examined closely, these "stations" are rarely quiescent. They are generally in ferment, frothing and bubbling with anticipation of things to come. As Jacques Cauvin (2000:14) expressed it, "What 'characterises' a period is almost always prefigured in the period that precedes it." Stages thus contain the seeds of their own transcendence, which indeed can often be seen germinating. To the discerning eye, then, process can be seen virtually jumping out of stages!

In discussing Zapotec civilization, Marcus and Flannery have some illuminating things to say in this regard. First of all, they proclaim their allegiance to the concept of stages:

> stages are heuristically useful. Band, autonomous village, and rank society do for the archaeologist what fish, reptile, and mammal do for the paleontologist. They provide shorthand references to widely-agreed-upon categories of societies, each characterized by an interrelated set of social and political institutions. We can recognize those categories both in the anthropological present and in the archaeological past. (Marcus and Flannery 1996:236)

But then, in the last chapter of their book, which they entitle "Evolution Without Stages," they abruptly change gears and concern themselves with what happened *between* stages, that is, processes that led from one stage to another. In this endeavor, they explain, "Transitional periods—those brief phases of rapid evolution during which the system changed . . . —become more crucial to our analysis than the long, stable periods which gave rise to our typology of stages" (Marcus and Flannery 1996:236).

Thus it is that stages and process are made to dovetail almost seamlessly when used to depict and explain the course of cultural evolution. The objection to the use of stages thus turns out to be hollow and without merit.

Scale Analysis and the Refinement of Sequences

Divided and subdivided as they might be, evolutionary stages are nevertheless broad categories. That's what they are *meant* to be. We need to identify and label a few major contrasting phases into which a unitary process like cultural evolution can be divided. Stages mark the big steps in evolution. However, if looked at up close and in detail, evolution actually comes in (so to speak) on little cat's feet. To put it less metaphorically, we can say that cultural evolution takes place by the incremental aggregation of many individual traits. And by ascertaining the *order* in which these traits entered the moving stream of culture we are able to perceive a fuller, richer picture of the precise course of its evolution. We can think of this process as consisting of the small steps that form part of an immense staircase. Albert Spaulding (1960:454) once expressed it very neatly when he said, "there are stair-steps in culture change, and the steps lead consistently upward."

Anthropologists have long been interested in determining where, in an overall evolutionary trajectory, a given culture trait makes its appearance. Robert Lowie (1946:230) once observed that "If clans arise independently the world over out of similar antecedents, the clan may reasonably be put into a definite place in a chronological [=evolutionary] series." And what we can do for one trait, like clans, we can do (at least in theory) for an entire suite of traits. During the course of evolution, each trait in a sequence entered that sequence, not haphazardly, but at some more or less definite point in relation to other traits in the sequence. This is essentially what Leslie White (1987:67) was saying when he wrote, "Certainly few would admit that banking may precede barter, or that parliaments . . . might precede tribal councils. Who is willing to concede that hereditary kings might have preceded elected chiefs in the course of human history?"

Now, if there is a reasonable presumption that culture traits entered the overall evolutionary progression in a regular order, what was that order? And how is it to be ascertained? Until relatively recently, the tools were not available to facilitate making such a determination. But with the invention of a technique called Guttman scale analysis, a means became available for doing just that.

Guttman scale analysis provides a way of taking a collection of traits and a sample of societies and determining if those particular traits appear to have originated in a regular order among those societies (see Carneiro 1970b:835–838). Applying scale analysis with this objective is an example of the comparative method put to work in the service of cultural evolution. Such an analysis takes a body of traits inventoried *synchronically* from a number of societies around the world and derives from it a *diachronic*

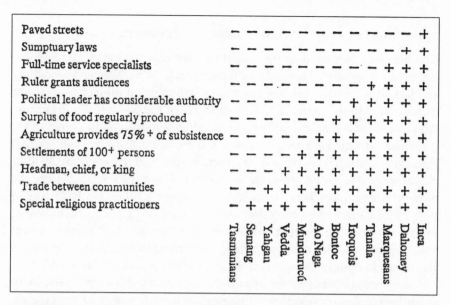

	Tasmanians	Semang	Yahgan	Vedda	Munduruci	Ao Naga	Bontoc	Iroquois	Tanala	Marquesans	Dahomey	Inca
Paved streets	−	−	−	−	−	−	−	−	−	−	−	+
Sumptuary laws	−	−	−	−	−	−	−	−	−	−	+	+
Full-time service specialists	−	−	−	−	−	−	−	−	−	+	+	+
Ruler grants audiences	−	−	−	−	−	−	−	−	+	+	+	+
Political leader has considerable authority	−	−	−	−	−	−	−	+	+	+	+	+
Surplus of food regularly produced	−	−	−	−	−	−	+	+	+	+	+	+
Agriculture provides 75% + of subsistence	−	−	−	−	−	+	+	+	+	+	+	+
Settlements of 100+ persons	−	−	−	−	+	+	+	+	+	+	+	+
Headman, chief, or king	−	−	−	+	+	+	+	+	+	+	+	+
Trade between communities	−	−	+	+	+	+	+	+	+	+	+	+
Special religious practitioners	−	+	+	+	+	+	+	+	+	+	+	+

FIGURE 8.1   Scalogram showing the apparent order of development, from bottom to top, of eleven selected traits among a sample of twelve societies that are arranged in order of increasing complexity (or degree of evolution) from the Tasmanians (at the extreme left) to the Inca (at the extreme right).

(evolutionary) sequence. In essence, it is a way of inferring the past from the present.

Scale analysis takes advantage of the fact that, to a large extent, as anthropologists have affirmed many times over, *culture is cumulative.* Over the course of evolution, new traits are successively added to a society's cultural inventory at the same time that old traits are being retained. (To be sure, this is not all there is to evolution; besides cumulation, there is also the *replacement* of traits [Carneiro 1974:105]. But cumulation is the lion's share of evolution.)

Speaking more specifically, scale analysis starts with a matrix in which traits and societies are plotted against each other, and rearranges this matrix according to certain rules. The rearrangement does two things: It arranges the *traits,* from bottom to top, in the order in which the societies appear to have developed them, and it arranges the *societies,* from left to right, according to their respective degrees of evolution. Thus, for example, from Fig. 8.1 we can infer that "sumptuary laws" developed after "trade between communities," and that Dahomey was more highly evolved than the Semang.

The scalogram was prepared using only a limited number of traits and societies. Although the information contained in it is correct, this scalogram was prepared primarily to help demonstrate how the technique works. The objective of the study was to apply the procedure to a large body of traits and a large sample of societies. When this was done, the results showed that there was indeed a readily discernible regularity to the order in which certain culture traits have been evolved (see Carneiro 1970b:844–845).

Thus the technique of scale analysis permits one to go behind broad cultural stages and to get at the fine gradations in the evolutionary process. In a sense, what scale analysis enables us to do is to reveal *microevolution*, that is, the small steps by which cultural evolution has actually proceeded. However, the term "microevolution" is generally used with a different meaning. It commonly refers to culture change as observed under even higher magnification, so that one is dealing with the behavior and influence of actual individuals and following their role in the unfolding of events. This is the kind of "evolution" Margaret Mead (1964) had in mind in her study *Continuities in Cultural Evolution,* and that we will discuss below in connection with what is now called "agency theory."

Verifying Inferred Sequences of Development

The use of scale analysis permitted us to show that for at least 50 selected traits (and actually, a good many more) it was possible to say that these traits had evolved in roughly the same order among a worldwide sample of 100 societies (Carneiro 1970b:840–841). Of course, as stated above, the order of development thus arrived at was an *inference*. It was based on an examination of purely *synchronic* data. The obvious next step was to try to verify this order historically, that is, to try to ascertain if it had actually been followed by a society whose culture history could be traced over the course of several centuries.

The search for such a society led to Anglo-Saxon England, for which there is a rich body of readily accessible historical information. From the available sources it was possible to determine the approximate dates, and therefore the relative order of appearance, of a large number of traits that were also part of the scale analysis study. The results of this test showed that indeed the order of development of traits arrived at through scale analysis had been substantially followed by a particular society—Anglo-Saxon England—during the course of its historical evolution (Carneiro 1968:355–359).

Directionality in Evolution

We are now in a position to take up the matter of *directionality* in cultural evolution. Half a century ago Ralph Linton (1955:50) remarked that culture change "can be regarded as evolutionary only insofar as the changes which have gone on in culture show some definite, fairly consistent direction." Archaeologists too generally agreed that, by and large, long-range culture change had revealed such directionality. We have already quoted Albert Spaulding to the effect that the steps in culture change "lead consistently upward." And before him, V. Gordon Childe (1942:7) affirmed that "Archaeology does disclose general trends, cumulative changes proceeding in one main direction."

More recently, Robert Murphy (1979:196) maintained that "The term cultural evolution, if it means anything at all, must refer to historic processes that are orderly and have a direction." Attempting to summarize prevailing anthropological opinion on the subject, Kaplan and Manners (1972:49) declared that "Despite the endless definitional disputes, all anthropologists would agree that minimally the concept of evolution implies directional change."

This, however, proved to be an illusion. No sooner does someone proclaim the existence of a solid consensus in anthropology than dissident voices spring up in dispute. And so it was with directionality. Those who seek to apply a strictly Darwinian model to cultural evolution are quick to deny any perceptible direction to it. For example, Robert Dunnell (1980:39), a bred-in-the-bone selectionist, speaks of "the lack of internal direction characteristic of evolutionary change." And his colleague Robert Wenke holds that "The essence of Darwinian evolution is nondirectional variability on which natural selection operates," and that "natural selection is adaptive and wholly opportunistic in character" (Wenke 1981:86, 112).

Writing jointly, Dunnell and Wenke (1980:9) expressed the view that "environment acts through selection on nondirectional variation to produce the *apparent* direction of change at the higher scales." But why "apparent"? Introducing this qualification strikes me as a false note. Natural selection produces *real* directional change. Appearance in this case *is* reality. By the accumulation of a series of adaptive changes, each of which represents a structural advance, natural selection gives rise to an evolutionary trajectory with a clear direction. And that direction is toward increased complexity.

Leslie White stated without equivocation that "evolutionist theory maintains that cultures proceed from the simple to the complex, from the primitive to the highly developed" (White 1947:54). And Elman Service (1968b:222) echoed his remark: "we think of evolution as directional: generally from small to large, from simple to complex organization." The scale analysis study just cited likewise depicts cultural evolution as directional— the direction being that toward the accumulation of more and more traits, an unmistakable manifestation of increased complexity.

Some anthropologists who continue to be entrenched in their opposition to increased complexity as the direction of evolution claim, as we have seen, that it plays no role in organic evolution. They might be surprised, therefore, to learn what their master, Charles Darwin, had to say on the subject. Speaking of the heightened adaptation in organisms brought about by natural selection, Darwin wrote in *On the Origin of Species*: "This improvement inevitably leads to the gradual advancement of the organisation of the greater number of living beings throughout the world" (1872:97). And what was to be the measure of this advancement? On the very next page Darwin tells us: "If we take as the standard of high organisation the amount of differentiation and specialisation of the several organs in each being, . . . natural selection clearly leads toward this standard [i.e., increased complexity]" (1872:98). The defense rests.

Complexity as the Hallmark of Evolution

An increase in complexity, coming about through successive differentiations and integrations, was for Herbert Spencer (1863:216) the very hallmark of evolution. But then, with the coming of the age of Boas, the use of complexity as a standard of development fell on hard times. As Garry Chick (1997:278) has observed, "the notion of cultural complexity . . . was run out of the anthropological community in the early 20th century and was held at bay until its utility became too obvious to ignore."

The career of Robert Lowie illustrates this change in attitude toward the use of increased complexity as the yardstick of cultural evolution. In 1920 in *Primitive Society*, speaking of "social features" in an evolutionary context, Lowie stated that "they can be graded only on subjective grounds and must scientifically be treated as incommensurable. . . . In the sphere of social life there is no objective criterion for grading cultural phenomena" (Lowie 1920:438, 439).

By 1948, however, Lowie had apparently undergone a change of heart. At least slightly. Writing that year in his book *Social Organization,* he was willing to accept "increasing complexity and differentiation" as characterizing cultural evolution, but only with the "serious qualification" that while "frequent," these characteristics were "not indispensable accompaniments of the evolutionary process" (Lowie 1948:33).

Yet the acceptance of increased complexity as the touchstone of evolutionary advance, even by acknowledged evolutionists, was not always a simple and straightforward affair.

Thus, in his treatment of cultural evolution, Julian Steward had some contradictory things to say about complexity. In one breath he asserted that "complexity as such is not distinctive of the evolutionary concept" (Steward 1953a:314). But then, on the same page, he turned around and argued that what really betokened evolution was "increased levels of sociocultural integration." It was this, he said, that distinguished cultural evolution from mere culture history, which might show change, all right, but change that did not involve any kind of structural transformation. For Steward (1953a:314), then, it was the introduction of new "developmental levels . . . marked by the appearance of qualitatively distinctive patterns or types of organization" that constituted evolution.

Yet, what were these "developmental levels" and "qualitatively distinct patterns" if not manifestations of increased complexity? Growth in complexity takes two forms. First, there is *differentiation,* as in the proliferation within a society of the number of its occupations and professions. The culture of New York City thus can be said to be more complex than that of an Amazonian Indian village by virtue of the fact that the Manhattan Yellow Pages lists more than 1,000 occupational specialties, not one of which is to be found in a tribal village in the Amazon.

The other aspect of increasing complexity is the formation of *hierarchies* in the institutional structure of a society. Every organization of any size—a corporation, an orchestra, the Catholic Church, the army, the government—has successive structural levels, each of which encompasses more units, and exercises a greater degree of control than the level below it.

Those anthropologists who keep their gaze fixed on the adjustment of societies to surrounding conditions tend to enthrone adaptation as king of the evolutionary process. They generally point to the biologist's emphasis on adaptation to justify their own belittling of increased complexity as the major element of evolution. But a biologist's narrow focus on adaptation should not be allowed to obscure the broader picture, which reveals, in the organic realm, a striking increase in complexity over geologic time. After all, once there were only unicellular organisms, whereas today multicellular animals of great size and complexity inhabit the earth in vast numbers. Some biologists, of course, see this when they look up and cast their eyes on the broad sweep of evolution. Julian Huxley (1962:163), for one, sought to emphasize it when he wrote, succinctly: "It is obvious to common sense that some organisms are *higher* than others—that a dog is higher than his fleas, or a fish higher than a jellyfish." And we have just seen that Charles Darwin was well aware of the increased complexity that animal species had shown over time, and even suggested how it could be gauged.

Disgruntled voices can still be heard, though, resisting the idea that evolution is a movement toward increased complexity. And in venting their objection they sometimes raise false arguments. Alice Kehoe (1998:220), for example, maintains that, "Contra Spencer and his partisans, complexity is not the evolutionary goal state." The simple answer to this objection is that a process can have a *direction* without having a *goal.* No one doubts that the direction of the Second Law of Thermodynamics is toward a state of maximum entropy, but would anyone dream of suggesting that that was its *goal?*

Is Evolution Irreversible?

Biologists are forever telling us that "organic evolution is irreversible." Is the same thing true of cultural evolution? Several anthropologists seem to think so. Or at least they *say* so. For example, Leslie White (1959:30) maintained that "The evolutionist process is irreversible." Betty Meggers (1991:191) agreed, saying that "The position I will advocate accepts evolution as a universal process of irreversible change." And for James Hill (1977b:64), "the term evolution, refers primarily to irreversible change." Are they right?

Before we can resolve this dilemma it is necessary to engage in a bit of semantic analysis. If evolution is *defined* as change in the direction of increasing complexity, then the opposite change—change in the direction of simplification—cannot be evolution. It must be something else. Spencer called it *dissolution.* Today we usually refer to it as *devolution.* Only if we adopt the biologist's definition of evolution as *any* sort of change—including change that brings about simplification—can we say that evolution is irreversible. Why? For the simple reason that time cannot flow backward. And since time cannot be reversed, any change that has occurred has proceeded *in the direction of time,* and thus must be irreversible, whatever form it takes.

But, as I have argued before, the biologist's definition of evolution is a very unsuitable one for the cultural anthropologist. Clearly there is something distinctly different between the process of growth and development that produced the Roman Empire at its height, and the one that marked its decline and fall. This difference strikes me as being so fundamental and distinct—since, after all, it reflects *opposite movements*—that it deserves terminological recognition. And, following Spencer, I would reserve the word "evolution" for the former, "anabolic," process, and for the latter, "catabolic," process I would employ some other word, such as "dissolution," "devolution," or "retrogression."

Whatever terms we use, though, there is unanimous agreement among anthropologists that not every change undergone by a society has raised it from simplicity to complexity. Regression may not be the prevailing direction in which societies have traveled in their individual histories, but there is nothing impossible about structural breakdown and simplification. It is only too well known. Matthew Johnson (1999:130) put it simply and effectively when he wrote:

> Spencer's view of evolution . . . specified a definite direction from simple to complex. In many versions of evolutionary theory, however, there is no *a priori* reason why social forms cannot move in the other direction in certain circumstances, that is from complex to simple. This is what is proposed with the collapse of cultural systems and their "return" to "simpler" forms of society, like the Ancient Maya after the Classic Maya Collapse or the ancestral pueblos of Chaco Canyon.

It is clear, then, that the path traveled by a culture during its period of growth and florescence is indeed reversible. From the peak it may once have attained a culture can turn around and proceed in the opposite direction. That does not mean, of course, that the path followed by a society in declining from relative complexity to relative simplicity has to be the *mirror image* of the way it evolved. Reversibility does not require reverse symmetry. If a society developed a series of traits, *a, b, c, d,* and *e* in that order, it is not necessary—nor indeed likely—that in regressing it should discard them in exactly the reverse order. A society's decline, to say nothing of its collapse, might well be so abrupt that one could scarcely determine in *which* order it had lost these traits.

A related point to be made here is that there is nothing *inevitable* about evolution in the way Spencer (or his followers) conceived of it. Not that the opposite hasn't been alleged. For example, Alexander Alland (1967:173) once said that, for Spencer, evolution "does not depend upon conditions," when in fact Spencer (1896:588) affirmed just the reverse: "Evolution is not necessary, but depends on conditions."

Spencer did not see evolution as proceeding automatically, as unfolding according to some inherent principle. "Evolution," he wrote, "is commonly conceived to imply in everything an *intrinsic* tendency to become something higher. This is an erroneous conception of it. In all cases it is determined by the co-operation of inner and outer factors" (Spencer 1890:93). (What these factors are we shall see when we examine the determinants of cultural evolution in Chapter 9.)

Present-day anthropologists working along evolutionary lines have no trouble at all accepting the fact that cultural development is neither foreordained nor inescapable. Thus, speaking of those who study the process of state formation, Marcus and Feinman (1998:6) remark that "such scholars do not believe in inevitability; they know that not every autonomous village society gave rise to a chiefdom, nor did every group of chiefdoms give rise to a state." Charles Spencer (1987:378) concurs: "I . . . see nothing inevitable about this development [that is, of chiefdoms and states]. Chiefdoms do not necessarily evolve into states." But Spencer then goes on to examine political evolution retrospectively, and here he *does* find an element of necessity: "*if* a cultural system evolves from an egalitarian form to the state," he says, "I think the developmental trajectory must proceed through the chiefdom."

The Objective Rating of Cultures

Given the fact that cultural evolution can be defined as a movement in the direction of increased complexity, there is still a lot more to be said on the subject. For one thing, the general advance in complexity that has characterized the progression of culture as a whole has not been partaken of equally by all societies. Some have evolved further than others. Indeed, some have evolved *much* further, despite the fact that all existing societies, simple or complex, have culture *histories* that extend back over exactly the same length of time.

Tacitly if not explicitly, many anthropologists have been ready to equate *degree of evolution* with *level of complexity*. And that being the case, it has seemed to them that some objective measure might be devised to ascertain the relative complexity—and thus the degree of evolution—of individual societies.

As one might expect, Leslie White was quite ready to accept the idea of rating culture objectively, and proposed a yardstick for doing so. "The best single index . . . by which all cultures can be measured," he wrote, "is *amount of energy harnessed per capita per year*" (White 1987:76). However, he never actually attempted to make this determination for any society.

Energy utilization is one way of numerically rating cultures. There are other ways as well. At least as early as Alfred Tozzer (1925:9) anthropologists have been quick to affirm that "culture is cumulative." A quarter of a century after Tozzer, Kroeber (1948:297) noted that "the process of cultural development is an additive and therefore accumulative one." Implicit in this assertion is the belief that a society's position on an evolutionary scale could be gauged by its inventory of certain selected traits. In the first edition of his textbook *Anthropology*, Kroeber constructed a "stepped pyramid" showing that the greatest accumulation of high-level culture traits was found in Nuclear America among the Aztec, the Maya, and the Inca, and that the inventory of these traits tailed off as one proceeded away from this region in either direction (Kroeber 1923:facing p. 340).

The idea of comparing societies, especially North American tribes, and at the same time ranking them on a more or less objective basis, continued to intrigue Kroeber. He returned to the matter in *Cultural and Natural Areas of Native North America* (1939). In this work, based on his vast and detailed knowledge of the Indian cultures of the continent, he assigned a numerical score to each of the 24 subareas into which he divided North America. Representative cultures from each area could then be given a grade on a scale of 1 to 7. For example, the Washo graded 1, the Blackfoot 3+, Acoma Pueblo 5, and the Aztec 7 (Kroeber 1939:map facing 222).

In 1948, Carleton Coon (1948:612), one of the few anthropologists sympathetic to cultural evolution in those early days, also tried his hand at rating cultures. He assigned the various societies included in his *Reader in General Anthropology* to one of six levels of complexity. The levels were based on four criteria: "(*a*) The specialization of individuals, (*b*) Amount of consumer goods obtained by trade, (*c*) Number of institutions to which an individual may belong, (*d*) Complexity of institutions" (Coon 1948:612). To give some idea of how Coon ranked the societies included in his study, on Level 1, the lowest level, were the Yahgan, on Level 2 were the Arunta, on Level 3 the Trobriand Islanders, on Level 4 the Ruwalla, on Level 5 the Aztecs, and on Level 6 the Romans.

Attempts along similar lines, but with more formal and explicit categories of evaluation, began to be made in the 1950s. Most notable among them was Raoul Naroll's "Index of Social Development." The basis of Naroll's scheme was not unlike Coon's. His index was a combination of three factors: the size of the society's largest settlement, the number of craft specialties, and the number of "team types," that is, organizational units such as clans and age grades. The numerical values for these three factors were ascertained and then weighted and manipulated mathematically in a complicated way. The result was a numerical score for each of the thirty societies in Naroll's sample. At the bottom of his scale were the Yahgan with a score of 12, somewhere in the middle were the Flathead with 27, and at the top were the Aztec with 58 (Naroll 1956:705).

The next anthropologist to try his hand at rating cultures objectively was Munro Edmonson in his slim volume *Status Terminology and the Social Structure of North American Indians,* which appeared in 1958. Counting the number of terms in the language of each society that labeled achieved statuses and associational groups, Edmonson produced a ranking of several dozen North American tribes. For example, the Chipewyan had a score of 16, the Sioux 33, and the Zuni 67 (Edmonson 1958).

In the mid-1960s, stimulated by Naroll's pioneer efforts, I too became interested in trying to rate cultures objectively. To do so, I proposed a method that was an offshoot of the scale analysis project described above. An extensive list of traits had been prepared for this study: 354 for the first version,

618 for the final one. These were all traits that seemed to have a good initial probability of showing cumulation. That is, they were the sorts of traits that, once developed by a society, tended to be retained indefinitely rather than being discarded somewhere along the line. The sum total of such traits a society possessed seemed to me to provide a good rough-and-ready index of its level of complexity, and thus of its degree of evolution. I decided to call this the Index of Cultural Accumulation (Carneiro 1970b:845–849). As just indicated, the final version of this list contained 618 traits, and the rankings of a few of the 72 societies included in the sample, based on how many of these traits they possessed, are presented below:

Roman Empire	572
Tahiti	254
Bavenda	170
Ao Naga	125
Mandan	77
Yanomamö	23
Alacaluf	3

Note that between the highest- and the lowest-ranking societies there was a spread of 569 traits. This compares with a spread in scores of only 46 between the highest-ranking society (Aztec) and the lowest-ranking one (Yahgan) in Naroll's study. Thus it seemed to me that the Index of Cultural Accumulation provided a more realistic and refined measure of the range in cultural evolution among pre-industrial societies than did Naroll's Index of Social Development.

Earlier we saw that back in the mid-1930s George P. Murdock, a lukewarm evolutionist at best, missed an opportunity to provide anthropology with an early and simple, yet objective and useful, index of culture level. At that time, and for a long time thereafter, Murdock thought of cultural evolution as being little more than adaptation to surrounding conditions. Eventually, though, he came to see that increasing complexity was also an important component of evolution, if not its most salient feature. And in 1973, he too finally got on board, proposing a scale for gauging a society's cultural complexity. In doing so, Murdock made use of ten categories, including Agriculture, Urbanization, Money, Density of Population, and Social Stratification. Within each category he applied a 5-point scale ranging from 0 to 4. For example, for the category of "Money," he assigned a score of 0 to a society that lacked any kind of medium of exchange, and gave a score of 4 to a society if it had coined money. This scale, which might well be called the Index of Cultural Complexity (although he left it unnamed),

Murdock applied to a worldwide sample of 186 societies. The scale scores obtained by these societies ranged from 1 for the Yahgan to 39 for the Babylonians (Murdock and Provost 1973).

Other indexes of cultural complexity (or degree of evolution) have been proposed by social scientists outside the field of anthropology, notably by the sociologists Linton Freeman and Robert Winch (1957) and Robert Marsh (1967), and by the economist Edgar Bowden (1969). Bowden's index, though ostensibly based on sophisticated statistics, has the shortcoming of failing to give anything like a realistic spread in culture level between the simplest and the most advanced societies in his sample. Thus his simplest, the Polar Eskimo, has a score of 0.28, while his most complex, the Aztecs, score only 1.73 (Bowden 1969:866). In this regard, Marsh's Index of Societal Differentiation must be regarded as superior: His scale scores range from 0 for the Yahgan to 109.4 for the contemporary United States (Marsh 1967:366–374).

However, whatever limitations these indexes may have, one feature about them is striking: the high degree of intercorrelation there is among them. When the index of rank order correlation is used to compare one ranking with another, the coefficient is uniformly high. For example, the coefficient of rank correlation between Naroll's Index of Social Development and Freeman and Winch's Index of Societal Complexity is +.865, while that between Kroeber's supposedly "subjective" Index of Cultural Intensity and Carneiro's Index of Cultural Accumulation is +.903. And between the Index of Cultural Accumulation and Murdock's unnamed index of societal complexity the coefficient of rank correlation is +.944.

The significance of these high correlations is clear: A society's cultural complexity (=degree of evolution) is something concrete and objective. It can be assessed and expressed in numerical terms. And it is very similar regardless of which index is used. These findings, of course, run counter to the contention by members of the Boas school that societies are "incommensurable," and that any attempt to rate them is purely subjective and therefore invalid. The objective assessment of cultures is not only possible, but useful. It has applications that ramify throughout the domain of culture, as we shall soon see.

However, setting aside for the moment numerical measures of cultural complexity, it is worth noting that there is a mounting recognition on the part of many anthropologists, especially archaeologists, that growing complexity is a striking feature of the development of human societies. Take, for example, two recent expressions of this view. Robert McC. Adams (2001:345) has observed that "Two interrelated trends, toward increased hierarchical differentiation and toward complexity, have characterized . . . social evolution since the end of the Pleistocene." And Brian Fagan (1999:234) had no hesitancy in asserting: "If there is a general trend over time, it is to-ward increasing social and political complexity."

Rates of Cultural Evolution

One of the immediate benefits of an objective numerical index of culture level is that it permits us to ascertain rates of cultural development. Anthropologists of all stripes have long been interested in rates of evolution. Repeatedly they have commented on the marked acceleration in the speed of development in culture that has occurred over more recent millennia. In *Anthropology and Modern Life*, for example, Franz Boas expressed himself unequivocally on the matter. "In the very earliest times of mankind," he wrote, "culture must have changed almost imperceptibly" (1962:132). But, he noted, "Since the earliest times, the rapidity of change has grown at an ever-increasing rate," so that "[c]hanges which in the beginning required tens of thousands of years, later thousands of years, occurred now in centuries and brought about constantly increasing multiplicity of forms" (Boas 1962:134).

But increased acceleration is only part of the story as far as rates of evolution are concerned. Another aspect of the matter has to do with the pace, the "tempo and mode," of evolution. The great stir that the theory of punctuated equilibria created in the field of organic evolution in the 1970s was not matched in cultural evolution. Why not? Because anthropologists, on their own, had long recognized the "punctuated" nature of culture change. They had observed that cultures tended to evolve in fits and starts rather than in a uniformly smooth and gradual manner, and that periods of stagnation and regression have alternated with those of advance.

As just noted, this was no recent discovery. The Boasians, as anti-evolutionist as they might have been in principle, were well aware of cultural evolution in practice, and of the unevenness of its course, and gave this realization frequent expression. As early as 1917 Lowie noted that "Culture . . . is a matter of exceedingly slow growth until a certain 'threshold' is passed, when it darts forward, gathering momentum at an unexpected rate" (1929:78).

In 1925 Alexander Goldenweiser, in one of his disputes with the classical evolutionists, claimed that they had espoused "The evolutionary concept of gradual change" (1925a:227), as against the idea that change came in surges, interspersed with periods of quiescence. He favored the notion that "relatively sudden change is at least as characteristic of the developmental process as is gradual transformation" (1925a:228). He held that "every change in culture is preceded by a period of delay during which there is an accumulation of those factors which prompt the impending change. When . . . the resistance is overcome, the change comes—with a spurt" (1927:74).

Boas himself observed that "The rate of change in culture is by no means uniform. We may observe in many instances periods of comparative stability followed by others of rapid modifications" (Boas 1962:134).

It was all well and good to talk freely about rates of cultural evolution, and to agree that they were variable at different times and in different places. But the assertions made about these varying rates were largely impressionistic. How were rates of evolution to be determined in a concrete and quantitative way? Obviously, in order to do so, two things were required. First, an objective numerical assessment had to be made of a society's level of complexity at some base point. And second, a similar assessment needed to be made of the same society at successive points in time. The first requirement could be met by any one of the various indexes of culture growth that had been proposed and applied to ethnographically known societies. The second, though, was much harder to fulfill. It required going back in the history of a given society and ascertaining its level of complexity at various dates. In that way numbers could be obtained that could then be plotted on a graph against time, and a curve, and an equation, fitted to the pattern of growth thus obtained.

The only instance of such an exercise that I am aware of was one involving a study of Anglo-Saxon cultural development (Carneiro 1969). In carrying out this study, the presence or absence of the 618 traits on the scale analysis trait list (discussed earlier) was ascertained at 50-year intervals over the course of Anglo-Saxon history, from AD 450 until 1087, shortly after the Norman conquest. The number of traits present at each half-century mark was then plotted on a graph. Inspecting the growth curve thus exhibited, Anglo-Saxon cultural development seemed to divide into two segments. The first, from 450 to 650, was marked by a rapid but nonetheless regular increase. The second phase was marked by an equally regular but distinctly slower rate of increase (Carneiro 1969:1019).

The interpretation made of this was the following: The first half of Anglo-Saxon history was a period marked by relatively rapid innovation, manifested by a sharp increase in the number of culture traits present. The second was characterized by a slower rate of innovation, but at the same time by a *proliferation* of those traits already invented. For example, during the latter period there was an increase in the number of royal estates from 1 to 1,442, and in the number of water mills from 1 to 5,600. (For a fuller explanation of this contrast see Carneiro 1969:1020–1021.)

The measurement of rates of cultural evolution is a field currently lying fallow. Many of the regularities and interpretations revealed or suggested by the Anglo-Saxon study remain to be explored and tested by similar studies of the historical development of other societies.

Before leaving the subject of varying forms and rates of cultural evolution and how they might be portrayed, it is instructive to examine a suggestion first made by Robert Braidwood and Gordon Willey (1962:351) and later elaborated by Robert McC. Adams. Adams (2001:356) suggested that "we could think of the emergence of complexity in terms of two contrastive metaphors, a 'ramp' or a 'step.' As an ideal type, a ramp implies a steady course and pace of development, a smoothly unfolding series of complementary trends following a seemingly linear path without abrupt transformations or temporary reversals. A step emphasizes more sudden and disjointed changes, an abrupt 'step' upward to a new plateau of complexity." He found these two "metaphors," the step and the ramp, not just of theoretical interest, but of practical use to "characterize the course of development in Mesopotamia and Mesoamerica respectively" (1966:17).

At one point in discussing cultural evolution of the "ramp" type, Adams (1966:170) spoke of it as "following a seemingly 'orthogenetic' pathway without abrupt transformation or temporary reversals." Of course, one must be careful not to speak casually of evolution as being rectilinear. A more circumspect way of describing it would be to say that, while clearly moving in the direction of increased complexity most of the time, the evolution of culture has not followed a straight line. Or, to put it more precisely, in the course of their individual histories, societies have often paused in their development, and sometimes even retrogressed (Carneiro 1996:273).

The Mechanisms of Cultural Evolution

The vast domain of cultural evolution, or, more precisely, its study, can be divided into three major sectors: the *course* of evolution, the *mechanisms* of evolution, and the *determinants* of evolution. We have just finished dealing with the first of these, but before we go on to consider the second, we must examine briefly how the anthropological study of cultural evolution began.

As Leslie White pointed out, "the theory of evolution was introduced into cultural anthropology independently of the work of Darwin and indeed, of biology in general" (1987:129). And White was right. If we look at the writings of Morgan, Tylor, and Spencer we will not find any attempt to cast cultural evolution in a Darwinian mold. The bulk of their writings on the subject dealt with the *course* of evolution, and more specifically with the *direction* of the evolutionary process. Thus, for example, we have Morgan laying out the stages of Savagery and Barbarism, which led up to the stage of Civilization. And, as we have seen, Spencer formally defined the direction of evolution as a movement toward increased complexity.

At the same time that Morgan and Spencer were writing, the scientific world was also becoming increasingly aware of Darwin's work. In this endeavor, Darwin made the *mechanism* of organic evolution the central feature of his theory. Other than the fact that organic evolution proceeded by successive adaptations to immediate local conditions, Darwin was not much concerned with the overarching direction of evolution. We see, then, that this dichotomous treatment of evolution—one stressing the general *direction* of the process, and the other focusing on its *mechanisms*—existed from the very start.

But it is important to keep in mind that these elements were complementary rather than contradictory. Morgan and Tylor, and above all, Spencer, were interested in *how* culture evolved, not just the course it had followed, although they did focus primarily on the latter. In recent decades, though, anthropologists have tended to pledge their allegiance to one side or the other, rather than trying to encompass them both. This is particularly true of the partisans of mechanism, who have often belittled or even rejected the other approach.

As far back as the mid-1930s, George P. Murdock had proclaimed his distaste for the Spencerian mode of cultural evolution, with its emphasis on an essentially linear progression toward increased complexity. If anthropologists were to be allowed in the halls of cultural evolution at all, he thought, they should model their approach on that of biologists. And in doing so they should keep in mind that "in organic evolution, the sequence of forms is branching [as organisms seek to adapt to diverse local conditions] rather than unilateral or ladder-like" (Murdock 1937b:446).

With the reembracing of cultural evolution in the 1960s and 1970s, the focus of its practitioners turned largely to *processes,* that is, toward the mechanisms of evolution, rather than to its general course over an extended period of time. That had been amply demonstrated and was more or less taken for granted. So it is to the question of *how* culture evolved—by what *means* it changed—that we now turn our attention.

First though, we need to distinguish clearly between the *mechanisms* of cultural evolution and its *determinants.* Simply put, the mechanisms are the *means* through which determinants—whatever they may be—operate. The two things are logically separate and distinct. One can espouse the operation of a certain mechanism, such as natural selection, without thereby committing oneself to any particular theory of cultural determinism. Thus we saw when discussing the classical evolutionists that James G. Frazer, an idealist rather than a materialist, felt perfectly comfortable arguing that correct ideas won out over false ones by a process of natural selection. Here, then, was a mechanism open to one and all.

I have said that mechanisms and determinants are logically distinguishable. In practice, though, they are intimately bound together. Mechanisms serve as the vehicles through which determinants operate, and determinants must have mechanisms through which to express their effect.

The Darwinian Model

When the *fact* of cultural evolution had become pretty well accepted in the 1960s, anthropologists began turning their attention to the mechanisms that brought it about. And in doing so, many of them found in the Darwinian factors a ready-made model to embrace and apply. As far back as 1915, Albert G. Keller applied to an explanation of social evolution the same factors that Darwin had employed in accounting for organic evolution. Thus he discussed societal evolution in terms of innovation (mutation), transmission (heredity), variation, adaptation, and natural selection.

After a long hiatus during which no one was thinking of cultural evolution in terms of a Darwinian model or much of anything else, one of the first scholars to invoke the Darwinian factors again in studying cultural evolution was Donald T. Campbell, a psychologist. Campbell's article "Variation and Selective Retention in Socio-Cultural Evolution," published in 1965, became something of a landmark. After its publication, it was frequently cited by anthropologists who, casting about for a way to explain cultural development, found in it a plausible set of mechanisms.

Campbell made it quite clear from the start where he stood in the Darwinian/Spencerian divide on the nature of cultural evolution: "In reviewing the current relevance of the concept of socio-cultural evolution," he wrote, "the analogy to the variation-and-selective-survival mechanism is regarded [by Campbell himself] as more valid and more valuable than the analogy of a progressive direction of increased size and complexity of integration" (Campbell 1965:46).

Campbell then discussed several other theories, finding them inadequate to account for the dynamics of cultural evolution. "The above theories," he noted, referring to these, "all focus on describing the *course* of such evolution, rather than describing the *processes* which produce it" (Campbell 1965:22, emphasis mine). It was these processes, as embodied in the "variation-and-selective-retention" model, "appropriately borrowed from biological evolution," that he thought would best account for the course that cultural evolution had actually taken (Campbell 1965:22).

However, the acceptance of natural selection as the mechanism of choice in accounting for cultural evolution, Campbell observed, resulted in the denial of this evolution having had any clear Spencerian direction, for, he stoutly maintained, "natural selection is a meandering process almost entirely shaped by environmental contingencies" (Campbell 1965:22). The inescapable conclusion was, as biologists generally asserted, that *any* sort of change was to be regarded as evolution.

The application of the Darwinian factors to an understanding of cultural evolution started slowly. As late as 1978, Boyd and Richerson could affirm (with perhaps a touch of exaggeration) that "although there is an enormous literature in anthropology . . . which examines cultural evolution, very little of it is properly within the Darwinian tradition" (1978:130). Since Campbell's day, the number of anthropologists espousing a Darwinian approach to the study of cultural evolution has dramatically increased. It is instructive to examine some of their work.

As was to be expected, physical (biological) anthropologists are the ones who have been in the forefront of this endeavor. They were, after all, the ones most familiar with the Darwinian factors, and thus most likely to invoke and apply them. Moreover, they seem not to have been conversant with what ethnologists and archaeologists had done along evolutionary lines. So, assuming that there was no sound and illuminating theory of cultural evolution "out there," they felt it was up to them to provide it.

The best known of these efforts is Robert Boyd and Peter Richerson's *Culture and the Evolutionary Process* (1985). When they began their work, they tell us, "we could find no systematic theoretical argument for cultural behavior that paralleled the Darwinian theory of biologists" (1985:vii). And until quite recently, they say, "theorists of cultural evolution showed little interest in underlying mechanisms of evolution" (1985:290). Indeed, they speak of "The rejection of a central role for Darwinism by the mainstream of twentieth century social science" (1985:1), presumably having Franz Boas and his students in mind, but ignoring Leslie White and his "neo-evolutionist" followers.

Differing from some of their sociobiological colleagues, Boyd and Richerson do not regard culture as just another form of behavior, but see it as something categorically distinct. Consequently, they hold that "the existence of culture causes human evolution to be fundamentally different from that of noncultural organisms" (1985:99). Still, they regard natural selection as an overarching process—a "force"—that operates in two domains, having "essentially the same character in both cultural and genetic systems" (1985:4).

But what Boyd and Richerson are primarily concerned with is not natural selection as such, but rather how natural selection is provided with the raw material on which to work. And so their focus is much more on the *transmission of differences* in behavior, from individual to individual and generation to generation, than it is on the grand sweep of human history that is generally thought of as "cultural evolution." Indeed, cultural evolution in this sense is not really dealt with by them.

It is clear that Boyd and Richerson's concern is with the fine-grained behavioral details of *micro*-evolution. Thus, what they present to us is "a micro-level theory" (1985:296). And in a later work they repeat that "To understand culture change we must account for the microevolutionary processes that increase the numbers of some cultural variants and reduce the number of others" (1992:179).

Operating at this level, it is inescapably on individuals and their immediate behavior that their microscope is trained. "As in the case of genetic evolution," they say, "individuals are the primary locus of the evolutionary forces that cause cultural evolution, and in modeling cultural evolution we will focus on observable events in the lives of individuals" (1985:7). True to their word, in accounting for culture change, the tools they use are drawn heavily from individual psychology and learning theory. Thus one frequently encounters in *Culture and the Evolutionary Processes* such statements as, "The nature of the cultural variants favored by guided variation depends on the psychological criteria that determine how culturally acquired behavior is modified by learning" (1985:12). And great emphasis is placed on which behavioral traits make an individual an "attractive model" (1985:287) for others to follow, thereby helping to propagate the innovations attributable to him or her.

Many of the mechanisms employed by Boyd and Richerson are the familiar ones of organic evolution. For example, they state that "individuals characterized by some cultural variants will be more likely to survive or attain social positions that cause them to be imitated than individuals characterized by other variants" (1985:285). And again they say that "To demonstrate that natural selection is a force in cultural evolution, we must still show that individuals characterized by alternative cultural variants differ in their probability of surviving and becoming effective models" (1985:173).

There is little doubt that *some* social change—indeed, a large amount of it—occurs in this way. For culture to change, behavior must change. But it seems to me that too great an emphasis in Boyd and Richerson's work is placed on individual psychology and learning, too many innovations are seen as resulting from "errors in social learning" (1985:283). By and large, the imitation of persons of high prestige by lesser folk is the way Boyd and Richerson account for the adoption and spread of culture traits. They fail to seriously consider the adaptive advantages *of the traits themselves* as being a major factor in the evolutionary process. Did the American Indian who first abandoned the spear in favor of the bow and arrow do so because of the greater *prestige* of the man he saw using the bow, or did he do so because he recognized the bow's *inherent superiority* as a hunting weapon? Did Boyd and Richerson exchange their slide rule for a pocket calculator because they were emulating an esteemed professor, or because they found the pocket calculator to be a vastly more accurate and efficient mathematical tool?

To sum up my argument, I would say that there are certain problems of long-term cultural evolution—indeed, of even short-term, fine-grained cultural change—that are much more amenable to solution if attacked on a *cultural* level than on a *psychological* or *biological* one. Superficially all cultural change can be said to involve personal *choice*, but it is often more realistic and enlightening to think of individuals as merely *ratifying* an outcome that has been largely determined beforehand by the relative advantage of one competing cultural trait over another.

Furthermore, this understanding of the workings of natural selection in the field of culture has an additional, and rarely noted, advantage. It conforms much more closely to the original Darwinian conception of natural selection than the one embraced by Boyd and Richerson (as well as William Durham [1992:343–345]), since it makes *nature*—that is, surrounding conditions, the external world—the impersonal and decisive selecting agent, rather than assigning that function to the often idiosyncratic and capricious choices of individuals.

I want to make it clear, however, that I am not questioning the operation and efficacy of natural selection in the realm of culture. There is no question that natural selection operates on culture, and that it does so in a pervasive, rigorous, and thoroughgoing way. Moreover, natural selection works on several levels at once: on individual traits, on social institutions, and on entire societies. It is the combined action of natural selection on all of these levels that, over countless millennia, has produced cultures in the variety of forms in which we find them today. (See Carneiro 1992c.)

Biologists and biological anthropologists have made a number of other attempts to depict cultural evolution as proceeding along Darwinian lines. Foremost among these are those of L. L. Cavalli-Sforza (1971; Cavalli-Sforza and Feldman 1981) and William Durham (1979, 1991, 1992). They differ in certain respects from the approach of Boyd and Richerson, but no attempt will be made to discuss them here. I would, however, like to examine one more effort to recast cultural evolution along Darwinian lines, namely, that made by David Rindos (1985).

I cite this attempt because it illustrates the lengths to which some biological anthropologists have gone in slavishly applying the Darwinian model to culture. To begin with, Rindos is at pains to disassociate himself from Spencerian evolution. This disavowal is, of course, nothing new. Many of his predecessors began in just the same way. In good Darwinian fashion, Rindos asserts that "the ultimate determinant [read: "mechanism"] in cultural evolution is selection" (Rindos 1985:74). In this assertion—although he is unaware of it—he is not really at odds with Spencer. But now comes a parting of the ways. Rindos states that as raw material to work on, "Darwinian selectionism requires *undirected, heritable* variations" (1985:65). Now, in organic evolution, these "undirected, heritable variations" are the result of mutations, and mutations, everyone knows, occur randomly as far as the adaptive needs of the organism are concerned.

So in order to stick to a strictly Darwinian view of evolution, Rindos argues that the cultural counterpart of mutations—inventions—must also be random and undirected. And here he is stepping hip deep into quicksand. He would have us believe, against overwhelming evidence to the contrary, that inventions are essentially random. To be sure, some inventions are, in part at least, serendipitous. But to a large extent invention is a *directed* process, with well-recognized objectives being consciously pursued.

To dispel any doubts on this score one need only think of the process that led up to the invention of the steam engine by James Watt. Watt's achievement was the culmination of a long series of advances that took place over the course of a century. Edward Somerset, Thomas Savery, Thomas Newcomen, and John Smeaton had all previously produced inventions aimed at the same objective—finding an efficient mechanical means of using steam to drive a pump that would remove water from flooded coal mines in northern England. Watt's crowning invention was thus anything but random and undirected. It was the capstone of the rigorous pursuit of a definite goal.

Rindos is on an equally slippery slope when he contends that it is only the "undirected generation of new traits" that "permits an authentic Darwinian cultural evolutionism." Really? Are we to believe, then, that if a particular cultural variation did *not* originate randomly but was, from the start, directed toward a specific objective, that natural selection could not operate on it? How can a trait be declared immune from natural selection purely on the basis of its origin?

Such, then, are the pitfalls into which an excessively Darwinian approach to cultural evolution can lead one.

Despite the criticisms offered above of the efforts of biological anthropologists to invade the domain of cultural evolution, there is also something positive to be said for it. Their entry into this field, which began in the late 1970s, coincided with a decrease of interest in cultural evolution on the part of ethnologists. Thus a vacuum of sorts had been created that biological anthropologists were quick to try to fill. And by so doing they provided an infusion of new life into an arena of anthropology where it was sorely needed. Even though there were shortcomings in their perspectives and analyses, their work did point up the fact that here was an important field of study lying fallow, which needed cultivation.

And indeed, so assiduously did biological/physical anthropologists apply the Darwinian model to cultural evolution that Susan Cachel was led to proclaim, after noting the blind alley into which an excessive cultural relativism had led ethnologists, that "At the present time, . . . physical anthropology alone retains the original emphasis on evolution which once created and organized all of anthropology. Evolutionary anthropology now is equivalent to physical anthropology" (Cachel 1989:188).

To be sure, this was an overstatement, uttered in apparent ignorance of what those few ethnologists, still toiling in the vineyards, had done and were doing in the way of cultural evolution. And of course, as we have seen, archaeologists too were becoming more and more explicitly evolutionary in their outlook and formulations. Even among archaeologists, though, a now familiar argument was being heard. The Spencerian view of evolution was being denounced and rejected by some, while the Darwinian model was put forward as the only proper way to proceed.

One of the most insistent voices raised in this regard was that of Robert C. Dunnell. According to Dunnell, cultural evolutionism, as commonly understood, "is a direct descendant of the Spencerian philosophical position and not the scientific paradigm associated with Darwin" (1980:40). For him, only the Darwinian approach was valid (1980:50), yet he insisted that "Darwinian evolution has yet to be applied systematically as an explanatory framework in sociocultural anthropology or archaeology" (Dunnell 1980:50).

In asserting that the kind of evolutionary approach he called for had never actually been followed, and certainly formed no part of the "neo-evolutionism" of Leslie White and his disciples, Dunnell was rather wide of the mark. The concept of natural selection played a significant role in the way evolutionary ethnologists and processual archaeologists, beginning at midcentury, envisioned the workings of cultural evolution.

The matter can be thought of in the following way. To begin with, natural selection is intimately bound up with adaptation. Indeed, the result of natural selection *is* adaptation: Less well adapted forms fall by the wayside, while better-adapted ones survive and proliferate. And both concepts—natural selection and adaptation—were implicitly if not explicitly part of cultural evolutionism as envisioned and effected during its resurrection. Julian Steward, the father of cultural ecology and one of the three great midcentury evolutionists, made adaptation to environment the primary focus of his studies of societies in the Great Basin and the Southwest (Steward 1937, 1938). And Leslie White was nothing if not an adaptationist when he asserted that "Culture is a specific and concrete mechanism employed by a particular animal organism in adjusting to its environment" (1949b:360).

Even before Steward and White, George P. Murdock had proclaimed the central role of adaptation in evolution, affirming that "The term 'evolution,' of course, means *merely* a process of adaptive change" (1937a:xvi; emphasis mine). And he clung staunchly to this belief. Thus, nearly thirty years later, he wrote: "If the term evolution is to have a legitimate place in the technical vocabulary of anthropology, it must designate, like its biological prototype, not some nebulous abstraction, but a very concrete process of orderly adaptive change" (Murdock 1965:142).

Still, making adaptation coextensive—even coterminous—with evolution has its problems. It implies, for example, that the better adapted a society, the more evolved it is. By this logic, if the Paiute can be shown to have been better adapted to their environment than the Aztecs were to theirs— and the Paiute survived while the Aztecs succumbed!—then one would have to conclude that the Paiute were more *evolved* than the Aztecs, a dubious proposition to say the least.

It seems to me that the only way out of this dilemma for the strict cultural Darwinist is to grit his teeth and adopt the very same view of cultural evolution that biologists have of organic evolution, namely, that evolution consists of *any* change undergone by a society. If one is thus prepared to accept the conclusion that the Paiute might indeed have been more evolved than the Aztecs, then let him bear the albatross of that anomaly.

Richard Blanton, for one, appears to be ready to do just that. He tells us that "cultural evolution, like biological evolution, probably moves opportunistically, solving only today's problems, proceeding rather blindly, without predetermined course, into the future. . . . we know that neither biological nor cultural evolution proceeds *necessarily* from the simple to the complex" (Blanton *et al.* 1981:13). If that is how he sees the matter, then the only problem Blanton has to face is finding a *label* for those overwhelmingly directional changes that, in many parts of the world—including Mesoamerica, where Blanton himself works—gave rise to civilizations of impressive complexity.

To the Spencerian evolutionist, however, having *defined* evolution as change in the direction of increasing complexity, what to call those great parallel cultural developments Blanton has described poses no problem at all.

Adaptation Considered Further

Perhaps a few more words should be said about adaptation in relation to evolution. In the narrowest sense, adaptation may be thought of as a tracking device by means of which a society continues to seek adjustments to its environment, since no environment remains static indefinitely. As the environment changes, a society may be expected to adjust and readjust to these changes in its external conditions. To be sure, some of these adaptive changes may not entail any large structural changes in the society. However, sometimes these modifications do bring about new structural features designed to carry out new functions, or to perform old functions more efficiently. Since the addition of new structural elements to a society, almost by definition, entails an increase in the society's complexity, adaptation can often be said to be an *agent* of evolution in the Spencerian sense. Indeed, one way to look at cultural evolution is to regard it as a succession of adaptive changes undergone by a society as it seeks to adjust to changes in its physical and social surroundings, in the process of which it increases its complexity.

The major adaptive changes that a society is called upon to make are usually those involved with the material conditions of existence. As Murdock phrased it more than half a century ago, "On the whole, changes occur most readily and frequently, and with the most far-reaching consequences, in the realm of material culture, the food quest, and economic organization, and readjustment in the other parts of culture usually have their origin here" (Murdock 1937b:451).

It is these readjustments that constitute the internal transformations undergone by a society as it seeks to accommodate its internal structure to changes induced by external circumstances. The nature of these internal readjustments has long interested social scientists. A century ago, William Graham Sumner wrote that the "folkways," that is, the customs and institutions of a society, "are . . . subject to a strain of consistency with each other, because they all answer their several purposes with less friction and antagonism when they coöperate and support each other" (Sumner 1906:5–6).

Expressing much the same thought in different words, Murdock, Sumner's intellectual heir, wrote: "a culture is a system in the process of achieving equilibrium by the integration of its elements. Any change disturbs the balance and initiates a process of readjustment throughout the system" (Murdock 1937b:451).

Perfect integration, though, is not to be expected. As Murdock went on to say, "The readjustments initiated by economic and other changes often require years or even generations for their accomplishment—an interval for which Ogburn has coined the apt term 'cultural lag.' Long before an equilibrium has been attained, other changes have occurred and set in motion new processes of readjustment. . . . Hence cultures appear forever in a state of flux, always approaching but never achieving integration" (Murdock 1937b:452).

Functionalist anthropologists have often distanced themselves from cultural evolutionism, as if the two approaches were incompatible. But there is no inherent reason why the two should be thought of as antagonistic. On the contrary, as Alexander Spoehr succinctly stated, "the very meaning of functional dependence is that change in one variable results in change in a dependent variable" (quoted in Evans-Pritchard 1969:47). And evolution is a succession and accumulation of certain types of change, many of them adaptive readjustments to altered conditions of existence.

That there is no necessary contradiction between functionalism and evolutionism is recognized and accepted by modern-day evolutionists. For example, Elman Service, one of evolutionism's leading spokesmen, quite calmly affirmed that "modern evolutionism can embrace structural-functionalist conceptions" (Service 1971b:vi).

Typological versus Populational Concepts

The adaptive transformations just alluded to as occurring during the course of cultural evolution bring up another issue in which biological anthropologists and their cultural counterparts can be said to have opposing views. This is the question of whether the outlook best suited to the study of cultural evolution is typological or populational. The great apostle of populational thinking in organic evolution—a biologist whose ideas on the subject have influenced a good many anthropologists—is Ernst Mayr. And in this connection it is worth quoting Mayr's remarks at some length:

> The assumptions of population thinking are diametrically opposed to those of the typologist. The populationist stresses the uniqueness of everything in the organic world. . . . All organisms and organic phenomena are composed of unique features and can be described collectively only in statistical terms. . . . The ultimate conclusions of the population thinker and of the typologist are precisely the opposite. For the typologist, the type (*eidos*) is real and the variations an illusion, while for the populationist the type (average) is an abstraction and only the variation is real. No two ways of looking at nature could be more different. (Mayr 1959:2)

Mayr left little doubt that in this conceptual dichotomy he himself stood foursquare with the populationists. And because of the prestige of his pronouncements, he has succeeded in making converts among a number of cultural anthropologists. Murdock, for example, remarked that "As Mayr has so aptly expressed it, the biologist since Darwin views evolution from the point of view of population, not of types" (Murdock 1965:132). Moreover, it is clear that he felt anthropologists should follow suit. And indeed others—many others—have expressed similar feelings. Let us listen to a bit of this recitation.

David Rindos (1984:75) announced that "Cultural selectionism . . . repudiates . . . typological classifications of culture and culture change." Robert J. Wenke (1981:87) complained that "cultural evolutionism has focused on creating typologies rather than examining empirical variation." And Garth Bawden (1989:330) was convinced that "it is time for us to reject typological [that is, stage] theory in favor of a perspective that more closely conforms to observable evolutionary reality." "One of the errors of evolutionism," declared Robert Murphy (1979:190), "was to attribute a solid and concrete reality to what were at best handy typological pigeonholes." And finally, Terry Rambo (1991:71), with evident regret, notes that "The social sciences have been slow to adopt population thinking."

But in advocating populational instead of typological thinking are anthropologists following a pied piper who has strayed beyond the limits of his professional bailiwick? While not questioning the validity of Mayr's pronouncement in his own field of biology, there are powerful reasons for questioning his implied rejection of typological thinking in cultural anthropology.

A key element in this discussion, one that distinguishes human behavior from that of all other animals, is *culture.* And the existence of culture makes all the difference in the world. One of the differences can be expressed as follows: Subhuman animals live in relatively amorphous *aggregates,* whereas human beings live in highly delineated *structures.* The emergence of culture transformed human behavior; it led to the formation of a series of *types* of social units for the understanding of which *typological* thinking is essential.

These structural units—these types—cannot be understood simply by taking account of the *number* of individuals they contain, as populational thinkers would appear to advocate. Instead, they find their significance and explanation in the criteria that define and delimit them. Lineages, clans, moieties, phratries, age grades, classes, guilds, dioceses, regiments, ministries, corporations, institutions, etc. are all typological units, with boundaries, rules, rites, emblems, initiations, charters, and the like. They are the sorts of features that define their membership and set one group of individuals apart from another. These structural units are the very means by which much of human social life is organized and carried on.

Once they come into existence, however, the characteristics of these units are not set for all time. They change. Furthermore, new structural forms arise as circumstances demand. In effect, it is in the increase in number of these structural units, and in their elaboration, that we see evolution manifested. And it is investigating the origin, structure, function, and change in these kinds of structural units that anthropologists, especially evolutionary anthropologists, are engaged in.

Now, how could a strictly populational approach deal with the origin and evolution of such units? They simply cannot be described, let alone explained, by treating them as mere aggregates of discrete individuals. Being discernible and distinct structural units of a society, *labels* must be assigned to them. And these labels designate *types*.

Is it really true that, as Mayr would have it, biology can turn its back on typology? Kent Flannery, in effect, answered this question in the negative when he wrote that in making evolutionary studies, the anthropologist "needs terms like 'autonomous village,' 'chiefdom,' and 'archaic state,' for the same reason that paleontology needs terms like 'reptile,' 'bird,' and 'mammal.' . . . Such short labels provide us with shorthand references to some very common types" (Flannery 1995:22).

Earlier we saw the enormous and beneficial impact that the introduction of the concept—the *type*—"chiefdom" had on both ethnologists and archaeologists as they sought to reconstruct the past. Now, if culture evolves by creating new *types* of structure, then our understanding of this process is furthered by creating more refined typologies that reflect, not only the gross movements of this process, but also its fine details.

For example, let us take the chiefdom again. Standing by itself, the chiefdom is a broad category representing the general form of political organization that bridged the gap between the autonomous village and the state. But how much richer our understanding of the actual process of political development becomes when we recognize that there was not just a single undifferentiated "chiefdom" but various *types* of chiefdoms—simple, compound, and consolidated—which represented substages in the political progression leading to the formation of the state.

There is one way, though, in which "populational" and "typological" thinking come together and mutually enrich each other. It occurs when we are dealing with the transition from quantity to quality. It has long been noted that there are processes in nature in which a *quantitative* buildup in some entity, once it reaches a critical point, leads to an abrupt *qualitative* transformation. The example of this process most often cited is the conversion of water into steam by the continued application of heat.

The importance of this relationship for understanding change was discussed by Marx, and especially Engels (Carneiro 2000:12926–12927). Contemporary Marxist anthropologists, though, have all but ignored it, focusing instead on the "dialectic" in their efforts to explain the dynamics of social change. Nonetheless, a few anthropologists have seen the importance of this relationship and applied it. Leslie White was probably the first one to suggest this mechanism as the most plausible way to explain the origin of the human capacity for culture:

> Now in many situations we know that quantitative changes give rise of qualitative differences. Water is transformed into steam by additional quantities of heat. Additional power and speed lift the taxiing airplane from the ground and transform terrestrial locomotion into flight. The difference between wood alcohol and grain alcohol is a qualitative expression of a quantitative difference in the proportion of carbon and hydrogen. Thus a marked growth in the size of the brain in man may have brought forth a new kind of function. (White 1949a:32–33)

This relationship, invoked here by White to account for a major step in organic evolution, can be fruitfully applied to cultural evolution as well. One can, for example, see the origin of social segments such as lineages, clans, moieties, age grades, and similar structural divisions, which are found in many primitive societies, as a response to a growing population. Faced with an increase in the number of residents, villages must deal with the possibility of fissioning. And while they often do split after becoming larger, many villages have successfully resisted such divisive tendencies by developing social segments. The argument that social segments serve to inhibit village fissioning can be phrased as follows:

> With social units like clans and moieties in existence, village residents no longer form part of an undifferentiated mass, but are assigned to one (or more) segments of the society. Instead of leaving it an amorphous aggregate, then, clans and moieties impart to a society a kind of cellular structure that makes it more resistant to the shearing forces which steadily increase as a village grows larger, and which threaten its existence. (Carneiro 2000:12928)

An elaboration in structure initiated by a growth in population is the most common manifestation of quantitative-to-qualitative changes in social evolution. An increase in the sheer number of persons—a process familiar and congenial to the dedicated populationist—results in time in new structural features. *Numbers* have thus given rise to *types*, and so the twain has met.

9

What Drives the
Evolution of Culture?

Elman Service versus Marvin Harris

Deep down, no one can really deny that there has been a tremendous amount of cultural evolution from the Paleolithic to the present. The more controversial question is, *How* or *why* did this evolution take place? That is to say, what have been the *determinants* of this evolution? That question continues to be the most important and most debated issue in evolutionary theory today. A revealing way to introduce this whole discussion is by quoting from a series of articles and letters to the editor exchanged between Marvin Harris and Elman Service more than thirty years ago.

The year 1968 saw the publication of Harris's landmark volume *The Rise of Anthropological Theory*. In reviewing this book in *Natural History* magazine, Service stated that Harris's treatment of evolutionism, both classical and modern, was, "much to my surprise, unsympathetic and inept" (Service 1968c:74). In fact, Service added, "With respect to the evolutionist authors I am most familiar with—L. H. Morgan, L. A. White, M. D. Sahlins—I found Harris' scholarship shockingly bad" (1968c:74).

Service went on to say that in Harris's critique of much of the anthropological theory propounded in the twentieth century, "The basis for the criticism of these attempts finally becomes apparent: they are varyingly bad depending on how far they depart from Harris' version of what he calls cultural materialism" (1968c:75).

Service then noted that in Harris's cultural materialism "causal primacy in cultural change is to be found in the technoenvironmental and technoeconomic sectors of culture, with social and ideological aspects to be regarded as dependent variables" (1968c:75). Service regarded this as an exaggeration, remarking that "Few anthropologists will be convinced that important evolutionary changes must originate in the above order" (1968c:75). And then, in a plea for theoretical impartiality, he added, "should not causality be sought by the scientist wherever it occurs?" (1968c:75).

In the very next issue of *Natural History*, Harris replied that Service should not have been "surprised" by anything in *The Rise of Anthropological Theory*, having previously read the book in manuscript at the request of the publisher. Moreover, not only had Service read it, he had "strongly recommended it for publication!" (Harris 1969a:72). In fact, in a personal letter to him from which Harris proceeded to quote, Service had spoken of it as an "excellent . . . manuscript," adding that he was "enthusiastic about it and full of admiration for the great amount of work" it represented (Harris 1969a:72).

Wherein, then, Harris asked, did Service's criticism of the book lie? And Harris answered the question himself by saying: "the principal substance of that letter concerned Service's objection to my treatment of Sahlins, Service, White and Morgan" (1969a:72), concluding that "What Service is now surprised about is my refusal to make the changes he recommended" (1969a:72).

A parallel dispute between the two men was taking place about the same time in the pages of the *Southwestern Journal of Anthropology*, in which the evolutionary issues dividing the two were pointedly explored. In "The Prime-Mover of Cultural Evolution" (1968d), Service noted that the main burden of his article was "to argue against the widespread notion that a theory of cultural evolution necessarily involves a monistic determinism, a 'prime-mover' of some sort" (1968d:396). However, Service made it clear at the outset that his article was not meant to be "an expression of indeterminism, . . . but only a statement that the acceptance of one prime-mover to the exclusion of others inhibits what should be an empirical study of the locus of causality" (1968d:396). His article concluded with this strong statement:

> *Down with prime-movers!* There is no single magical formula that will predict the evolution of every society. The actual evolution of the culture of particular societies is an adaptive process whereby the society solves problems with respect to the natural and to the human-competitive environment. These environments are so diverse, the problems so numerous, and the solutions potentially so various that no single determinant can be equally powerful for all cases. (1968d:406)

Therefore, Service held, "the question of what is prime-mover in any case of specific evolutionary change is an empirical question, the answer not to be found in advance of research by commitment to a specific theory of prime-movers" (1968d:407).

In his rejoinder, Harris remarked that he found Service's "discussion of monistic determinism" to be "regressive and obscurantist" (1969b:198). He argued that his own cultural materialism, while it "assigns priority to the study of the material conditions of sociocultural life" (1969b:198), was nonetheless not "monistic." Indeed, to characterize it fully, he had referred to it in his book as "techno-environmental" and "techno-economic," and in fact, in order to indicate its full ecological breadth, he included within it population, as well as technology, environment, and economics. In fact he noted that he would have called it by the "literary atrocity" of techno-econo-environmental determinism, "but my editor would not permit it" (1969b:199)!

Thus Harris rejected Service's (1968d:406) contention that his cultural materialist principle was a "single magical formula which will predict the evolution of every society," and in refuting Service, he quoted his own statement in *The Rise of Anthropological Theory* that "Each application of the principle . . . results in a separate theory, the confirmation or rejection of which is dependent upon logical and empirical operations whose specific terms and instruments cannot be deduced from the general statement" (1969b:199).

Still, Harris argued against the attitude that one should be completely "open minded, completely eclectic" when casting about for the determinants of a cultural phenomenon: "The practical consequences of the eclectic option with respect to research and theory building is the multiplication of fragmented middle-range, contradictory, indeterministic, and idiographic observations" (1969b:203).

With this illuminating if acerbic debate as a background to the issue of how best to account for the variety of forms that have arisen in the course of cultural evolution, let us examine the major factors that have been proposed as determinants.

Cultural Causality Examined

We have previously drawn the distinction between the *mechanisms* of cultural evolution and its *determinants,* and have spent some time discussing the former. Now it is time to turn to the latter.

Ethnologists, and especially archaeologists, did much during the latter half of the twentieth century to establish the *fact* of cultural evolution, and to lay out its general course. "Amid a good deal of tumult and shouting," declared Alexander Lesser (1985b:92), "social and cultural evolution have taken their place in anthropology alongside biological evolution as facts of human history. . . . Present debate concerns *how* the evolutionary process took place." Concurring in this view, James Hill (1977a:3) remarked that "Describing the course of evolution does not explain it." Accordingly, attention became increasingly focused on identifying the various factors deemed to be determinants of cultural evolution, and on assessing their relative contributions to the process.

Despite Service's cry of "*No prime-movers!*" it is hard to sustain the view that *all* determinants are equal, that there are not *some* factors whose effect is more powerful and pervasive than others. It is only reasonable, therefore, to suppose that there is a *hierarchy* of causes. To be sure, in any historical instance the determinants at work may be all intertwined, and the task of the evolutionist is to disentangle them, sort them out, and distinguish the important from the trivial ones.

Nevertheless, talk of "determinism" and "causality" in the realm of culture has not always sat well with anthropologists. Needless to say, this is a particular sore point with "post-processualists," as we shall see in a moment, but even before them there was often a certain lack of boldness, not to say timidity, when it came to finding causes for the patterns that were coming to light.

For example, Gordon Willey readily admitted that he and Philip Phillips had "shied away from anything that seemed to them to be deterministic or that would readily *explain* the series of stages by which they viewed the New World" (Willey and Sabloff 1993:216). Thus "no attempt was made [by them] to pinpoint causality" (Willey and Sabloff 1974:183).

However, long before Willey and Phillips, the followers of Franz Boas had already been skittish about matters of cultural causation. Lowie, for example, would often retreat into historical particularism when facing such a question. Thus he proclaimed that "we must abandon the quest for general formulae of cultural evolution and recognize as the determinant of a phenomenon the unique course of its past history"—thereby avoiding having to identify and weigh the various factors at work in bringing about some end result (Lowie 1929:96).

And A. L. Kroeber seems to have been in the dark about the motive forces that spurred on cultural evolution. Groping his way along in his search for these forces he wrote: "The entire complex process of forward movement may have been actually initiated by any one of its interwoven components, for all we know—by urbanization, or by metallurgy, writing, the divinity ascribed to rulers, or by some other factor" (Kroeber 1948:273). Unable or unwilling to assign causal primacy to anything, Kroeber found refuge in a comfortable neutrality.

What to an earlier generation may have been an inability to sort out the complex of determinants at work in an evolutionary process, became for some in a post-processual age a badge of philosophical conviction. According to Kristian Kristiansen and Michael Rowlands (1998:2), who are in a position to know, "Shanks and Tilley . . . have advocated historical indeterminacy in relating present to past." And this was part and parcel of what Ian Hodder (1999:130) pointed to as "contingency," a view of the world "which is so much in vogue at present."

In the more moderate words of Bruce Trigger (1984:294), "The gradual rejection of the neoevolutionary views that played such an important role in the development of the New Archaeology is leading . . . to a more complex and less deterministic view of human behavior."

But contingency and indeterminacy were not solely creatures of postmodernism. There were some traditional, or even processual, archaeologists who were baffled, or at least cautious, in dealing with causal analysis while picking their way through the intricacies of culture history. It was about them that Trigger (1984:289) wrote, "For many archaeologists the complexity of early civilizations, or of any human society, renders the concept of causality meaningless for discussing their origins."

Even such a clear-eyed and tough-minded archaeologist as Kent Flannery (1998:xviii) has at times uttered statements like "Social evolution is stochastic, not deterministic." Now, if I may put Terry Rambo's words into Flannery's mouth, I think it would give us a fuller notion of his position: "the course followed by cultural evolution, like that of biological evolution, is indeterminate. The outcome we observe is the result of a multiplicity of stochastic events. It happened only because all of these events occurred as they did. It would have happened differently if they had not" (Rambo 1991:91).

"Stochastic," then, really means "unpredictable," rather than "undetermined." The *actual course* of a society's culture history may be affected by so many factors, large and small, that a *general knowledge* of the evolutionary processes involved will be insufficient to fully account for it. But the *principle* of determinism has not been overridden thereby. The determinants are there, hard at work, but their *multiplicity* and *intricacy* may be such as to obscure their mode of operation, and thus lead to the false conclusion that they were missing.

The very nature of cultural causation has come in for considerable scrutiny. One of the questions raised in this connection is whether or not causation is "linear." Another is whether, in accounting for cultural evolution, there is a single factor that far outweighs all the others ("monocausalism"), or whether there are multiple causes, each exerting a more or less equal effect. The two questions are logically distinct and should be kept apart.

In speaking of Robert McC. Adams's theory of the rise of early Mesopotamian and Mexican civilizations, a theory that postulates no "prime movers," "but rather a whole series of important variables with complex interrelations," Kent Flannery remarks that "This model does not satisfy those who . . . feel that simple explanations are more elegant than complex ones, but it appeals to those of us who like circular rather than linear causality" (Flannery 1972a:408).

Causality, however, is *necessarily* linear, since the flow of time is linear. Events follow each other in a strict linear progression. Thus in any well-known temporal sequence there is never a question of which event came first and which followed. Causes always precede their effects. But granting that, it is possible that in any given instance of change, causation is not *unitary* but *composite*. Several factors may contribute simultaneously to produce a given effect. Still, to reiterate what has already been said, this does not mean that each of the several causes involved contributed to the effect in equal proportion. Some may have exerted a greater influence than others.

There is yet another way in which causation in cultural evolution can be analyzed. Causation may be said to be *spiral* in the sense that factors may react in such a way that something that may be a *cause* at one stage of the process may in turn become an *effect* at a later stage. And then this effect may once more play a causal role in a later stage, and so on. Schematically, the process may be represented as follows: A > B > A' > B' > A" > B". Factor A is successively cause and effect. But since it is unlikely to appear in the same form at every stage of the sequence, we label its successive manifestations A, A', and A".

It seems to me that the word *spiral* is more appropriate here than the word *circular*, because circular suggests a return to the very same condition at which the process began, whereas spiral suggests that, while A may recur in its causal role, it will not be the very same A, but A in a somewhat different form. Having taken a noticeable twist, the evolutionary process can be said to have brought about a discernible change of state.

We may illustrate this with a concrete example, one used earlier in a different context, namely, the invention of the steam engine. Considerable pressure existed in English society for more coal to be produced. This economic pressure led to experiments that culminated in an important technical advance—the steam engine—an invention that permitted English coal mines to be pumped dry, and thus able to produce the needed coal. This technological innovation led in turn to a great transformation in English society. Thus we see the spiraling of cause and effect: society > technology > society.

Now, in examining any long evolutionary sequence and asking which of various factors came first in the chain of related events, the answer may not be at all clear. It may depend on just where in the causal chain we choose to begin our analysis. Technology and society are so interactive that at any given point it may well be that one or the other appears as *the* factor that initiated subsequent change. Indeed, if we try to seek out the "ultimate" determinant of some evolutionary sequence, we may find ourselves looking up the barrel of an infinite regress of events whose beginning point can no longer be discerned!

But in analyzing cultural evolution it is still a valid and important question whether or not, as a general rule, certain factors can be singled out as exerting a preponderant influence on the course of events. In simple terms, as we look over the course of history, do we find a "prime mover" or a "democracy of causes"?

Impressed with the diversity of factors operating in the cultural evolutionary process, most anthropologists have argued for a plurality of causes in accounting for a particular evolutionary step. "Nor does it appear," says the archaeologist Bruce Trigger (1989:403), "that any one part of the cultural system plays an overwhelmingly predominant role in shaping the whole." And with undisguised vehemence, Elman Service (1971b:25), as we have seen, declared, "*Down with prime-movers!* There is no single magical formula that will predict the evolution of every society." James Hill (1977a:14), though acknowledging that he and many of his archaeological cohorts were drawn to population pressure as the preponderant cause of social evolution, nevertheless concluded that "most of us would admit, I think, that systematic explanations do not necessarily (or even often) involve prime movers."

Hill (1977a:14) went on to say what most anthropologists would agree is true, namely, that "The determination of the relative importance of specific kinds of variables in an explanation is a matter for empirical demonstration in the cases at hand."

Determinants: White and Steward Considered Separately

Nevertheless, the lure of the single cause as an explanatory mechanism is great. In accounting for the general course of cultural evolution, Leslie White subscribed to what Service (1971b:15) called "a simple monistic causality." Seeing culture as distinguishable into a technological, a sociological, and an ideological component, White (1987:117) remarked that "the roles played by these three classes of traits in the life of the human species are not equal by any means. The technological aspect is the most important by far; the sociological and ideological aspects are dependent upon the technological and are to a large extent given form and content by it." He continued, "Cultural evolution as a whole, therefore, is a function of technological evolution in particular" (White 1987:118).

The centerpiece of White's technological determinism was the utilization of energy. In what is often referred to as "White's Law," he declared that *"culture evolves as the amount of energy harnessed per capita per year is increased"* (White 1949a:368). But this is not a complete statement of his views in the matter. To the above, White (1949a:363) adds, *"or as the efficiency of the instrumental means of putting the energy to work is increased."*

Thus White did not downplay the role of tools and machines in this process. Indeed, he wrote that cultural evolution "is a matter of tools as well as energy. There must be means of harnessing energy and means of putting it to work. . . . If the energy factor is constant, culture can advance as the means of harnessing energy and putting it to work are improved" (White 1987:119).

Although a major truth underlies White's formulation of the relation of energy to cultural advance, it is not the whole story. The fact is that great sociopolitical advances were achieved without any major technological advances having preceded them. Consider, for example, the Uto-Aztecan linguistic group of western North America. At one time, every representative of this group was a simple hunting-and-gathering band society, as the nineteenth-century Paiute continued to be. Yet one of their number, the Aztecs, developed a large and complex empire, and accomplished this with no significant increase in the amount of energy harnessed per capita per year. It was the reorganization and redirection of human labor on a large scale, not the tapping of new energy sources, that was responsible for the Aztecs' achievement.

Elman Service, a former student and erstwhile follower of Leslie White, made much the same point: "[H]as the material, technoeconomic aspect always been the prime mover? The change from primitive chiefdoms to early states and then to empires in Mesoamerica, Peru, and probably elsewhere seems to have been first in the political sector" (Service 1968b:226).

In propounding his well-known "hydraulic hypothesis," Karl Wittfogel thought he had found the key to the rise of the world's early civilizations. His argument ran as follows. In certain arid areas of the world, where autonomous villages had survived by constructing small-scale, local irrigation works, there came a time when they realized it would be to their mutual benefit to set aside their individual sovereignties and join forces, creating a large political unit capable of integrating their various local irrigation systems into a single network of canals. The body of officials they created and empowered to manage this enterprise brought the core institutions of the state into existence. From here on, it was simply a matter of elaborating this core into a full-fledged system of government (Wittfogel 1957:18).

At first, Julian Steward adopted the hydraulic hypothesis as the mechanism *par excellence* by means of which he hoped to explain the rise of early civilizations. Though there is little explicit acknowledgment of the fact in

"Cultural Causality and Law," Wittfogel's hydraulic hypothesis is indeed the theory Steward relied on to account for the parallel and independent developments he pointed out. But Steward abandoned this theory when specialists in some of the arid areas of the world where civilization first arose, such as Mesopotamia and North China, pointed out that in these areas the state had *preceded* large-scale irrigation instead of following it (Adams 1960:281; Gernet 1968:92). It was the state, then, that had made these extensive irrigation networks possible, not the other way around.

What Wittfogel had found, and seized upon, was a false correlation. Or rather, a correlation that he mistakenly thought implied *causation*. Although it was true that most of the areas where civilizations had arisen autochthonously were arid or semiarid, the important common element, the underlying causal factor that held the key to the rise of states there, was that they were areas of environmentally circumscribed arable land (Carneiro 1970a).

Though deprived of what he once considered to be *the* specific determinant of the development of high cultures, Steward nevertheless continued to look to cultural ecology as providing the most satisfactory means for explaining the evolution of culture generally. Cultural ecology had two principal components: environment and technology. Environment was external to human societies and essentially independent of them. It was something that existed "out there," and to which all societies had to adapt. Technology was the means by which they did so.

Boas and his followers had regarded environment as essentially static, and as a limiting factor rather than an enabler as far as cultural development was concerned. Steward, however, saw the environment in a more favorable light. It posed challenges to be met and provided opportunities to be taken advantage of. To be sure, he took pains to see that his cultural ecology not be labeled "environmental determinism" because the effect of the environment on a society was not direct and unmediated. It always had to pass through the "lens" of the society's technology, and be "refracted" by it. Yet Steward did not regard the environment as simply a neutral factor. He did not shy away from assigning it a positive role, a causal role, in shaping culture. Moreover, he saw that in earlier periods of human history, and among surviving hunters and gatherers, where technology was rudimentary, the role of environment had proved greater. "The simpler cultures are more directly conditioned by the environment than advanced ones," he said (Steward 1955:40). "In advanced societies," on the other hand, "the nature of the culture core would be determined by a complex technology and by productive arrangements" (Steward 1955:39).

The concept of a "culture core" was central to Steward's thinking about the dynamics of evolution. He defined this core as consisting of "the constellation of features which are most closely related to subsistence activities and economic arrangements" (Steward 1955:37). So it was this element of culture that was most closely geared to the material conditions of existence with which a society had to cope.

However, in addition to technological and economic factors, this cultural core included some associated social and political structures (Steward 1955:37). Moreover, the more societies found themselves in similar ecological circumstances, the more their cultural cores were likely to resemble each other. Thus Steward held that "In the irrigation areas of early civilizations the sequence of socio-political forms of cultural cores seems to have been very similar despite variations in many outward details or secondary features of their cultures" (Steward 1955:41). These "secondary features" of society, being further removed from primary concerns with subsistence and survival, became more and more variable. They developed around that cultural core, but did not directly reflect it.

The processual archaeologists emerging in the 1960s and 1970s were drawn to Steward's brand of evolutionism—largely because it grew out of his cultural ecology. Unlike White's, Steward's evolutionism was concerned with *particular* adaptations to *particular* environments. And archaeologists, after all, were perforce excavating particular sites located in particular habitats. So in forging their explanations of what they were discovering in the ground, archaeologists found adaptations to changing local conditions— that is, ecological explanations—the most congenial means to account for the changes they observed in their sequences.

All this was clearly seen and summarized by William Sanders and David Webster (1978:278), who wrote of Steward's contributions: "The most significant value of Steward's work is, of course, his accommodation of ecological and evolutionary theory. The inclusion of the natural environment as a variable provides his approach with the expanded potential to explain cultural *variety*—in other words, specific rather than general cultural evolution."

Steward and White Compared

Although both Steward and White looked to the material conditions of existence to find the major determinants of culture and to account for its evolution, they emphasized different aspects of them: White, the technology, and Steward, the environment. In discussing the determinants of culture, White (1949a:368n.) had written: "The functioning of any particular culture will of course be conditioned by local environmental conditions. But in a consideration of culture as a whole, we may average all environments together to form a constant which may be excluded from our formula of cultural development."

Steward, however, found this way of stating the issue unacceptable. In reviewing *The Science of Culture* he wrote:

> Cultural differences are in part a function of the environmental variables, which White will not admit into the formula of causality. He disposes of environment in one short paragraph (p. 339), which declares it to be a constant, and in a brief footnote (p. 368) which admits its local importance but states that culturological "laws" are concerned with culture as a whole, *all* environments being averaged to form a constant factor! . . . Evidently shunning the stigma of "environmental determinism," he refuses to see that any given cultural heritage would have to be adapted to local habitats and that the processes of adaptation, the cultural ecology, would be creative ones. (Steward 1950:209)

Here, I think, Steward had the better of the argument. It is true that in accounting for what Steward called "secondary features" (traits like the couvade, teknonymy, or mother-in-law avoidance), White was right in believing that specific environmental features played no role in bringing them about. But when we try to account for the "cultural core" of a society, including much of its sociopolitical structure, we cannot dispense with the environment, we cannot eliminate environmental features from the equation.

Elsewhere (Carneiro 1970a) I have argued that it was in certain specific types of environment—areas of circumscribed agricultural land—that the state first arose, and that this specific environmental feature greatly facilitated its rise. One can argue, of course, that a few early states arose in areas of *non*-circumscribed agricultural land. But in these cases they did so later and more slowly. There is no question, then, that environmental circumscription was an important *catalyst* in the process of state formation. Thus it cannot readily be canceled out of the equation as long as we are interested in determining where and when states first arose. And everyone would agree that this question is of no small importance.

It would be a mistake, though, on the basis of this passage at arms between White and Steward, to classify White and his followers as antagonistic to cultural ecology. Consequently, June Helm greatly overstated the case when she wrote, in an article entitled "The Ecological Approach in Anthropology," that "the Whitean school . . . is antipathetic, in its sweeping universalism, to the empirical tradition that has fostered the ecological approach in anthropology" (Helm 1962:638n.–639n.). A more correct assessment of the matter is that of Gordon Willey and Jeremy Sabloff (1974:219n.), who noted: "the 1960s have shown [that] White's students have been in the forefront of the development of a systematic, ecological approach to Archaeology."

Ecological Approaches: Limitations and Pitfalls

One of the distinguishing features of those post-Boasian anthropologists who have concerned themselves with theory is that they were not content to merely scratch their heads or shrug their shoulders when confronted with a seemingly irrational practice, as was the case in an earlier day. To give an example of the once-prevailing view—that of anthropology's traditional readiness to accept a strange cultural form as unfathomable or indecipherable—consider the following explanation offered by A. L. Kroeber. Faced with the intricate social structure of the Ge-speaking groups of central Brazil, Kroeber concluded that this intricacy was a manifestation of "the play-derived, though unconscious activity of culture" (1948:395–396). Not content with this modest obfuscation, Kroeber went further. After describing Ge social segments, including moieties, in some detail, he was led to conclude that "Many of the institutions [of primitive society] are true luxury products. They almost certainly serve some function; but it may be a minor one. . . . A great deal of the picture suggests the play of earnest children or the inventive vagaries of fashion" (Kroeber 1948:398).

It is only fair to note, however, that Kroeber's own colleague, Robert Lowie, who had a greater familiarity with Ge social structure than Kroeber, saw more deeply into the matter. To him, Ge moieties were not a source of puzzlement at all: "A moiety system," he wrote, "is not an abstruse intellectual creation, but a form of organization that naturally and, in some cases, inevitably arises from demographic conditions" (Lowie 1948:247).

Lowie's interpretation may be taken as an adumbration of things to come. Latter-day cultural ecologists have made a dedicated effort to ascertain, or at least to propose, an adaptive function for such seemingly aberrant cultural practices as the potlatch (Piddocke 1965) and scapulimancy (Moore 1957). They have argued, and presented evidence, for the view that the potlatch and scapulimancy play some ascertainable role in the survival, security, and cohesion of the societies that practice them. As David Hurst Thomas (1979:136) has correctly observed, "Cultural materialism, cultural ecology, and cultural evolution are all mainstreams within this general adaptive strategy of research." And Bruce Trigger (1989:337) recognized this, although he hardly embraced the approach wholeheartedly, when he spoke of "neo-evolutionary anthropology with its almost exclusive preoccupation with ecological explanations."

It is quite true that cultural evolutionists are virtually all cultural ecologists. The *converse*, however, is not necessarily true. All cultural ecologists are *not* evolutionists. And here we must hark back to the argument made earlier that adaptation and evolution are not coterminous. The cultural ecology of,

say, Andrew Vayda (1967, 1969) or Roy Rappaport (1967a, 1967b) views societies as functioning systems that are normally in a state of equilibrium or
near-equilibrium. And when this equilibrium is disturbed, and the system
falls out of balance, a homeostatic device comes into play that brings the society back to something approaching its previous condition.

The Tsembaga Maring, for instance, provide a fine example of how peri-
odic pig feasts serve as a homeostatic mechanism among Highland New
Guinea societies. As described by Rappaport (1967a:28–29), "the operation
of ritual among the Tsembaga . . . helps to maintain an undegraded environment, limits fighting to frequencies which do not endanger the existence
of the regional population, adjusts man–land ratios, facilitates trade, dis-
tributes local surpluses of pig throughout the regional population in the
form of pork, and assures people of high quality protein when they are
most in need of it." An equilibrating mechanism indeed!

Many societies, especially the simpler ones, can no doubt be seen and
studied as well-integrated, smoothly running systems, essentially in a state
of equilibrium. But it is not these societies that offer us the best clues toward unraveling the process of evolution. Nor is it ecological anthropologists devoted to studying such well-equilibrated societies in minute detail
who are likely to discover and lay bare the determinants of cultural evolution. As James Hill (1977a:6) observed of this type of cultural ecology, "the
approach suffers from being nonevolutionary; it will not, by itself, explain
change. It is, for the most part, focused on describing societies as they are
[i.e., how they function], rather than on discovering the processes through
which they arrived at their current states."

Indeed, a close ecological study of a given society often predisposes one
toward an earth-bound particularism, in which the society is seen as completely unique. The intricate features of each ecological mosaic stand out in
sharp relief, making the student guarded, not to say skeptical, about offering any statement regarding the society's evolution. Thus it was that Robert
Netting (1977:6), who represented this type of cultural ecology, found
broad evolutionary interpretations "premature," concluding that cultural
ecology is still "too busy dealing with the details of specific subsistence, instances of micro-evolution" to undertake a broad synthesis of its findings.

The conclusion to which we are irresistibly drawn is that societies in flux,
in a state of *dis*-equilibrium, are the ones we must turn to in order to find
the incipient stages of evolutionary change. And though adaptation and
reequilibration play a role in this process, it is a more complex one, differing from that observed when, say, a Tsembaga village, thrown temporarily
out of kilter, returns to its previous condition following a successful pig
feast. The distinction here is that between *state-restoring* changes and *state-*

transforming changes. In the terms previously used, the causal process involved in evolutionary change is not *circular,* but *spiral.*

Functionalism and Evolutionism Join Forces

There is a related question here that we now need to address. It is simply this: When it comes to accounting for change, what is the relation between functionalism and cultural evolution? We have already seen that those anthropologists who styled themselves functionalist were strongly disinclined to attempt to reconstruct the course of evolution. However, this disinclination did not sit well with those for whom broad historical synthesis was the primary objective.

V. Gordon Childe, who likened functionalism to observing "the cyclical movement of the clock hands around the dial," conceded that "as a method" it was "beyond reproach." Nonetheless he asked the question, "must the science of man stop there? Is the task of anthropology exhausted in giving a series of distinct pictures of individual cultures . . . ? (Childe 1946:247). More reproachfully, Alexander Lesser (1985b:94) chided "The early functionalists who made a fetish of exclusively synchronic study" and thus "left diachronic phenomena, history, out."

However, an interesting thing happened when cultural evolutionism reemerged in the 1950s and 1960s. It took functionalism captive, so to speak, and put it to work in the service of evolution. The result was an amalgam that might be termed, clumsily perhaps, *adaptive ecological functionalism.* It was an approach to the study of change that had one eye on state-*restoring* changes, and the other eye firmly fixed on state-*transforming* changes.

This composite theoretical approach met with a hostile reception in several quarters. Its critics accused it of being a kind of deplorable functionalism-in-disguise. Norman Yoffee (1979:6) complained that evolutionism had "performed the feat of metamorphosing social evolution into neofunctionalism." And Robert Wenke (1999:369) admonished his colleagues that "the formulation of a powerful evolutionary theory will require that we avoid the naive 'functionalism' of early versions of cultural evolutionism: i.e., evolutionary theory must supply some explanation for cultural change other than that a given cultural characteristic made a positive contribution to a culture's efficiency of adaptation."

Wenke's complaint harks back to the old debate between functionalists and nonfunctionalists in which the point was frequently made that the *function* of a trait and its *origin* were two different things; that you couldn't account for how a trait arose by specifying what function it now served.

Superficially, that argument is correct. You cannot say, for example, that you have accounted for the four-chambered heart by explaining how the auricles and ventricles operate in concert to pump blood to the rest of the body. The analysis cannot be allowed to stop there. Let us try to carry it further.

In summarizing Rappaport's work among the Tsembaga, Andrew Vayda (1967:x) made the following observation: "the object of [functional] analysis is a demonstration of how things work rather than an explanation of why they exist or how they have come to be. In Rappaport's study, the presence of a certain ritual in the cultural repertoire of the [Tsembaga] Maring people [that is, pig feasts] is simply accepted as given, and the problem is to show how these rituals operate in relation to various environmental processes and in relation to land use, warfare, food distribution, and other Maring activities."

All this is true, of course, but let us probe deeper. There was a time when pigs existed among the Tsembaga but not pig feasts. In the natural course of things, the pigs proliferated and began to ravage the yam fields, causing disruption and turmoil in Tsembaga society. Presumably, various ways were tried to cope with the problem of too many pigs. Some probably failed, but finally the mechanism of the pig feast was hit upon, tried, and proved effective. Accordingly, a cultural element came into existence that not only performed a useful function, but also introduced a distinctive new structural element into the society. Its adoption thus constituted an *evolutionary* step.

Here we have, in microcosm, the way evolution operates, with ecological adaptation working in tandem with increasing complexity. But this is only the simplest form of an evolutionary change. Often, the introduction of some modification in a society, especially if it is an important one, has a tendency to ramify and reverberate throughout the entire society. As Robert Murphy (1979:200) put it, "Societies and their cultures form systems, and any disturbance in a part of a system may affect the others." This is certainly true for, as Alexander Spoehr (1950:11) wrote many years ago, "the very meaning of functional dependence is that change in one variable results in change in a dependent variable."

Cultural evolution, then, when looked at in broad perspective, can be seen as consisting of a series of adaptive readjustments, each adding to the structural complexity of the society and often initiating a series of other internal changes that further contribute to its evolution. In this manner, functionalism and evolutionism may be harmoniously reconciled and be seen as cooperating partners in the enterprise of producing long-term societal transformation.

But what we have just been discussing are still just *mechanisms*—the ways in which the various factors and forces involved in a process operate and interact in bringing about change. Just *what* these factors and forces are is another matter, as is assessing their relative magnitudes in determining the general course of evolution. We are brought, then, to the point of identifying some of these factors and forces and adjudging their effects. And it should not be a surprise that the first sorts of determinants we turn to should be ecological ones.

Population Pressure as a Determinant of Evolution

When the term "cultural ecology" is used, the elements that first come to mind are likely to be environment and subsistence. And to be sure, in these elements reside major causal factors in propelling cultures on their evolutionary courses. However, ecological determinants may begin with environment and subsistence, but they do not end there. In fact, among the ecological determinants most often cited as paramount in accounting for the rise of chiefdoms and states, population pressure stands first and foremost.

The nature and magnitude of the effect of population pressure on political evolution, though, are still issues of controversy. Those who argued on its behalf have met vigorous opposition. So central has this issue become in any serious discussion of cultural dynamics that it is worth quoting, in some detail, the arguments raised by advocates on both sides.

Champions of the primacy of population pressure insist that many of the structural changes that arose in human societies were in response to new situations brought about by a significant increase in human numbers. Already in the writings of Herbert Spencer we can find a clear recognition of this: "as population augments, divisions and subdivisions become more numerous and more decided" (Spencer 1897:449–450). And Albert G. Keller (1931:26) held a similar view: "Culture is developed when the pressure of numbers on land reaches a degree at which life exerts stress on man."

Though not known for his search for the determinants of social structure, Franz Boas (1930:100) nevertheless wrote: "In general, a correlation between density of population and diversity of cultural traits may be observed. Political organization depends upon the size of social units and upon density of population."

Not long after, another ethnologist, Ralph Linton, was also impressed with the causal relationship between population pressure and cultural evolution. "It is generally recognized," he wrote, "that complex technology and elaborate political organization can only develop or survive in the presence of fairly dense populations" (Linton 1940:32).

Shortly thereafter, Walter Goldschmidt (1948:454–455), during a discussion of primitive social structure in general, expressed the same view: "clan organization is a response to the developed institutional needs of a society under increased population."

Echoing the sentiment, Fred Eggan (1950:288) held that, in general, "Phratry groupings are integrative devices for larger populations." Then, bringing the argument down to cases, Eggan declared that "with the growth of population . . . the development of multi-lineage clans was almost inevitable in the western Pueblos" (Eggan 1950:300).

When they deal with cultural evolution at all, most ethnologists are likely to discuss it in terms of the origin and elaboration of small-scale social segments, such as clans, moieties, and phratries. Archaeologists, on the other hand, are usually concerned with the broad sweep of cultural evolution, encompassing the emergence and development of major social, political, and economic institutions. And, like their ethnological colleagues, many of them have found in population pressure the motive force spearheading such developments.

In their influential book *Mesoamerica: The Evolution of a Civilization,* for example, William Sanders and Barbara Price (1968:74) affirmed forthrightly that "Population growth may be considered as a primary process in the cause-and-effect network" of cultural evolution.

This statement, moreover, can be taken as more than just a statement of general principles. Archaeologists have found population pressure to be a causal mechanism in the evolution of cultures in various parts of the world where they have excavated. One of the most notable examples of this was provided by Philip Smith and Cuyler Young. Influenced by the assertion of the Danish economist Ester Boserup in her very influential book *The Conditions of Agricultural Growth* (1965) that increasing population has been the principal force underlying technological and social change, Smith and Young (1972) wrote a long paper seeking to substantiate this proposition. In order to do so they marshaled evidence from Greater Mesopotamia spanning a period from the end of the Pleistocene to the beginning of the third millennium BC. Their paper was the centerpiece of a colloquium held at the University of Pennsylvania in 1970, with some dozen scholars exploring the relation between population growth and cultural evolution in areas of the world where they had worked (Spooner 1972).

Smith and Young saw their work as an exemplification of Julian Steward's cultural ecology, since it was "a study of the adaptive reactions of a society to its natural and social environments," conditions that "create internal processes of change" (Smith and Young 1972:2). The conclusion they expected on theoretical grounds, one that they also reached on the basis of empirical evidence, was that although population pressure in Mesopotamia was not "the sole *deus ex machina* or prime mover responsible for all cultural and technological change," it was nonetheless the most powerful single force at work. "[W]e are prepared to argue," they wrote, "that, while of

course population growth and technological development are mutually re-
inforcing, population growth is more of an independent variable than technology since it can occur in the absence of technological innovation, but it
is unlikely that the latter will take place in the absence of population pressure" (Smith and Young 1972:53).

In another part of the world, and speaking more narrowly of the Yang-
shao period of the Chinese Neolithic, Kwang-chih Chang (1968:102–103)
observed that "toward the end of this stage . . . population pressure had
caused the fission of residential villages, which probably has important bear-
ings upon the further development of the North China Neolithic culture
into the next—Lung-shan—stage."

Halfway around the world, among the prehistoric Maya, Kenneth L.
Brown (1982:45) affirmed that "cultural development . . . appears to have
been the result of population growth within the environmental conditions
of the central Quiché area."

And while no great friends of population pressure theory, Gary Feinman
and Jill Neitzel (1984:69, 71), writing about sociopolitical evolution generally, nevertheless felt constrained to point out the close association between
size of population and political structure: "As population increases," they
said, "so does the number of tiers in the decision-making hierarchy. No
large populations are found that have fewer than two political levels; and no
small groups are present that have three administrative tiers. These results
support the general expectation that organizational differentiation should
correlate with greater population size." Correlation and causation are, of
course, not necessarily the same, but that population growth and increased
complexity of institutions should almost invariably go hand in hand points
strongly to the causal effect of the former on the latter.

This is one side of the argument. The opposite side has its proponents as
well, and they have argued their case with vigor and tenacity. Among the
most outspoken critics of population pressure as a prime mover is George
Cowgill (1975:505), who is ready to question almost every argument put
forward by population theorists. For example, he challenges the idea "that a
pervasive and powerful factor in human history has been the strong tendency of human populations to increase up to the point where serious
shortages of important resources are in the offing." And he denies that the
"experience or anticipation of such shortages has been a major factor," let
alone "the dominant factor, in stimulating intensification of agricultural
production and other technical and social innovations."

William Macdonald (1978:181), annoyed that Robert Lawless "would reduce human existence and evolutionary process to the effects of uncon-
trolled copulation," declared flatly, "I deny population pressure the status of

prime mover of cultural evolution." In more modulated tones, Fekri Hassan (1978:50), an archaeologist interested in demography, appeared to concur: "I believe that demographic variables play a critical role in cultural systems, but I do not go so far as to claim that they are invariably the prime movers of cultural evolution."

In similarly guarded terms, Jeremy Sabloff, after citing half a dozen factors commonly proposed as a driving force in cultural advance, went on to say: "Some variables—such as population increase—always seem to be present, but they are not, on their own, sufficient to explain the development of complex societies" (Sabloff 1989:150).

With regard to specific areas of the world where high cultures emerged, the same skepticism about the determining role of population pressure has been expressed by a number of other archaeologists. Speaking of ancient Mesopotamia, Robert McC. Adams (1966:44) remarked: "Possibly the attainment of some minimal population level was necessary to set the process [of urbanization] in motion. But such evidence as there is suggests that appreciable population increases generally followed, rather than preceded, the core processes of the Urban Revolution." And similar arguments against the determinative role of population pressure can be found in Wright and Johnson (1975), Blanton (1975), and Brumfiel (1976).

In his typically colorful way, Kent Flannery has lampooned what he takes to be the excessive claims of some unnamed Mesoamerican archaeologists who attribute to population pressure a whole panoply of cultural developments:

> The origins of agriculture? Population pressure on wild plant resources brought it about. The origins of irrigation? Population pressure on early dry farming brought it about. Ranked society? Population pressure on strategic resources brought it about. Urban civilization? Population pressure on "the human ecosystem" of the Late Formative brought it about. The collapse of urban civilization? Population pressure on the same ecosystem, 1000 years later, brought it about. No question about it: Planned Parenthood could have nipped Mesoamerican civilization in the bud. (Flannery 1976:225)

And Flannery has a point. In undiscriminating hands, population pressure becomes a facile "open sesame" to everything, much as "redistribution" became so during early discussions of the origin of chiefdoms. The existence and operation of population pressure cannot be blithely posited without some evidence of its existence.

Now, population pressure is not an all-or-none phenomenon. There are *degrees* of it. In its early stages, it may not be evident at all. Thus, among a group of swidden cultivators who customarily fallow an abandoned garden plot for twenty years, having to clear it again after only fifteen years because their numbers have grown constitutes *incipient* population pressure. The group can no longer continue a form of gardening it was accustomed to practice because an altered man–land ratio has forced it to change its ways.

Yet a casual observer, walking through the group's territory and seeing that most of its land is still under forest, may readily conclude—erroneously—that the group is free from any kind of population pressure. And, we may remark, if population pressure is not immediately evident *ethnographically,* imagine how much harder it is to detect *archaeologically!*

It is easy to see, then, why those who, on ideological grounds, are opposed to population pressure as a driving force in cultural development are quick to deny its existence when it is not readily apparent. The truth is that at its onset, population pressure may be a subtle and elusive thing. It may be likened to gas building up inside a container: Its presence may hardly be noticeable at first, but eventually, as it presses harder and harder against the sides of the vessel, it produces an unmistakable effect.

The first sign of population pressure is evident in the treatment of arable land. An early indication (as just noted) is a shortening of the fallow period. This may be followed by more intensive cultivation of the land already available, as by more thorough weeding, fencing, irrigation, and the like. Then an effort may be made to bring new land—once considered marginal—under cultivation. Finally, neighboring groups might be dispossessed of their land, as occurred, for example, among the Mae Enga of New Guinea. "When the Mae say that they fight over land," Mervyn Meggitt (1977:14) tells us, "they not only mean it, they are also correct." And according to Raymond Firth (1929:371), the same was true of the Maori: "warfare . . . not infrequently arose among them from disputes about land."

Indeed, this last step, the forceful acquisition of land, may occur simultaneously with, or even *precede,* intensive cultivation, in anticipation of an expected land shortage—this being an instance of "events casting their shadow before them."

Moreover, once this step has been taken, once force has been resorted to for the acquisition of arable land, the way has been opened for categorically new and transforming events to occur. Though dimly at first, the rise of chiefdoms and states may be discerned on the horizon.

To those still unconvinced of the propulsive evolutionary force of population pressure, we may ask, did a chiefdom or a state ever arise in a region of *sparse* population? As Lawrence Keeley (1988:395) once cogently remarked, "The strong association between demographic and socioeconomic complexity also suggests that any claims for the prehistoric development of complexity *unaccompanied* by increases in population pressure are to be treated with extreme skepticism."

To be sure, population pressure does not act in a vacuum or in isolation. It always operates in conjunction with other factors. Thus, when George Cowgill (quoted in Macdonald 1978:175) describes the process that gave rise to civilization in ancient Mexico as "a complex reciprocal interaction occurring simultaneously among many relevant variables," he is right. But while this formulation of the matter has an undeniable appeal to many, it is nonetheless somewhat misleading. Just because the effect of interacting variables in a process is *reciprocal* does not mean that all the variables are *equal* in the magnitude of their effect. There is no virtue in advocating a *democracy* of causes when it comes to accounting for, say, the rise of the state. All causal factors that took part in this process were by no means equal. Or, in the well-worn words of George Orwell, some causal factors were more equal than others!

Before concluding this discussion of population pressure as a determinant of cultural evolution, I would like to cite a pair of important studies dealing with two rather different manifestations of it, one by Michael J. Harner and the other by Robert B. Graber.

Harner reported on a cross-cultural study he undertook based on samples ranging in size from 400 to 1,170 agricultural societies. "[T]he time seems overdue," he wrote in 1970, "for anthropology to consider more seriously the role of population growth and consequent resource scarcity in socio-cultural structure and change" (Harner 1970:68). And he set out to test the proposition that "Growth of population pressure is . . . a major determinant of human social evolution through the mechanism of competition for increasingly scarce subsistence resources" (Harner 1970:67). His underlying premise, and the means by which it was to be tested, Harner set forth as follows:

> [T]aking the pattern of subsistence dependence of the population as a whole, the proportion of the diet deriving from wild food land resources will decline. This building up of pressure on the land subsistence resources should be reflected in a diminishing dependence on hunting and gathering. Using this model, it is therefore proposed that an inverse correlation exists between the degree of population pressure in societies having any agriculture, and the total degree of dependence on hunting and gathering in such societies. (Harner 1970:71)

He further elaborated his theory, stating that "eventually the process engendered by increasing resource scarcity will result in competitive strains sufficient to give rise to hereditary class stratification based upon unequal inheritance of subsistence resources. In its inter-group form such competition will lead to increasing emphasis on the development of centralized military-political organization." And then, "As competition grows further, class stratification and political integration will develop into increasingly complex forms" (Harner 1970:69).

Harner's correlations between population pressure and the developmental level of a society were presented in a series of statistical tables. He was well aware that "Any tables, no matter how impressive the correlations presented, cannot prove the validity of an evolutionary theory . . . but the results in every test here are clearly supportive rather than contradictory, and it is difficult to conceive of a legitimate statistical test which could controvert the results" (Harner 1970:80).

The conclusion that Harner reached was that the competition between societies engendered by shrinking food resources was a major factor in leading to their continuing development. In his words, "the natural resource scarcity model is a representation of a process which has been extremely powerful in human history, and . . . provides an excellent basis for understanding and predicting social evolution" (Harner 1970:85). Resource scarcity, then, was a *middle term* between population pressure and the structural developments brought about by the resulting competition over land.

Though he saw an increase in human numbers as the prime mover in cultural development, Harner did not claim the moon for this factor. "Population pressure," he said, "is regarded here as a major determinant of social evolution. But population pressure cannot account for the entire course of history, since it must be assumed that other processes are also at work in any given case" (Harner 1970:68).

I wholeheartedly agree with Harner that among the multiplicity of factors that worked together to give rise to chiefdoms and states, population pressure outstripped the rest. It is a major determinant that, starting slowly, increases relentlessly in its effects until a certain level is reached that prompts decisive action. In the *absence* of concentrations of population, few if any chiefdoms or states ever arose. In its *presence*, many sprang up, responding to the demands that the increasing pressure of human numbers began exerting on existing political structures.

Robert Graber's approach to population pressure and sociocultural evolution is a rather technical mathematical one, and can be given only a brief and simplified summary here. It is Graber's aim to take *qualitative* propositions about sociocultural evolution and reformulate them in *quantitative* terms. In abbreviated qualitative form, here's how Graber sees the interplay between population increase and cultural evolution.

To begin with, population *growth* has to be specified more precisely. The natural tendency of human societies, especially simple, village-level societies, is to grow. But this growth characterizes only the total population of the region. The *density* of this population will remain the same. However, for the population density of a region to remain the same, the average *size* of villages, and the average *distance* between them, must also remain the same. Thus, when villages grow in size beyond a certain point (not greatly in excess of their average size), they will *fission*. Thus there will then be two villages where before there was one. The result is a *proliferation* of villages. The *size* of villages has remained essentially the same, but their *number* has increased substantially.

This process will continue unhindered, says Graber, as long as there is enough land available into which the growing population can expand. Sooner or later, though, the geographic limits of this expansion are reached. How soon this happens depends in part on the size of the area in question and on how sharply bounded—how *circumscribed*—it is.

When the limit of arable land is reached, the existing villages, now finding themselves crowded, begin to compete for the restricted amount of land available. This competition results, first, in an increase in the size of villages, since fissioning is no longer an easy option. Furthermore, large village size bestows a competitive edge during intervillage conflicts. And with warfare thus intensified, the process begins of aggregating once-autonomous villages into multivillage polities, thereby giving rise to *chiefdoms,* which in turn, if the process continues, eventually evolve into *states.*

The evolutionary scenario just described was not unknown before. Graber's contribution has been to specify the variables involved more precisely, to suggest ways of quantifying them, and to perform rigorous mathematical operations on them. The results seem to justify his conviction that "population growth is the 'prime mover,' literally and quantitatively, of political evolution" (Graber 1995:6). Buoyed by the results of his analysis, he looks forward to even greater triumphs, and he is ready to proclaim that "Cultural evolutionism, fortified by population pressure theory, finally has reached the maturity needed to travel this new path; the journey ahead promises to be an exciting one" (Graber 1997:281).

The qualification needs to be made, however, that population *pressure* is not the same thing as population *density.* The former can be said to exist only when the press of human numbers grows so great that it leads a society to take drastic action in an effort to solve a problem that cannot be solved by conventional means. Thus, a shortage of arable land may become so acute that the resident population can no longer be fed even by the intensification of agriculture. At this point, a society may resort to warfare in order to acquire new land at the expense of its neighbors or enemies. To be successful, warfare of this sort may require the organized aggregation of a number of previously autonomous villages, giving rise thereby to a chiefdom.

Having introduced warfare as an ancillary condition, let us now examine its role as a full-fledged determinant of political evolution.

Warfare as a Determinant

Even its staunchest proponents, as we have seen, do not envision population pressure operating alone and unaided. Most see it acting in conjunction with other factors in driving sociopolitical development. Chief among these other factors is warfare. When population pressure becomes severe enough, it impels people to fight. And the warfare that ensues provides the means by which some societies conquer others and incorporate them into themselves, leading to the formation of larger and more complex political units.

Anthropologists were slow to recognize the important role warfare has played in political development, and at times have even stoutly denied its significance. The story of this stubborn refusal, especially by archaeologists, to accept its conspicuous role has been told by Lawrence Keeley in his book *War Before Civilization* (1996). In this volume Keeley accuses his colleagues of "pacifying the past," and of having "a pervasive bias against the possibility of prehistoric warfare" (1996:vii).

In this regard, though, Keeley was ready to indict ethnologists along with his fellow archaeologists: "Relying perhaps on the time-honored archaeological method of ethnographic analogy, archaeologists have increasingly ignored the phenomenon of prehistoric warfare (inasmuch as it has been declared by ethnologists to be weightless and unimportant). They have written warfare out of prehistory by omitting any mention of evidence of prehistoric violence when they synthesize or summarize the raw data produced by excavation" (Keeley 1996:23).

Keeley's book is studded with instances of these oversights. For example, the fortifications—ditches and palisades—that he himself excavated in Early Neolithic sites in Belgium were dismissed by his fellow Neolithic archaeologists as being merely "enclosures" (1996:viii). Indeed, he tells us, at first he was ready to deny his own data: "I was as guilty as anyone of pacifying the past by ignoring or dismissing evidence of prehistoric warfare— even evidence I had seen with my own eyes" (1996:viii). Keeley ruefully admits that he was "so inculcated with the assumptions that warfare and prehistory did not mix that I was willing to dismiss unambiguous *physical* evidence to the contrary" (1996:ix).

But irresistibly the picture changed. "By the beginning of this decade [the 1990s], few Early Neolithic specialists would deny that war existed in what had previously been regarded as a peaceful golden age" (1996:x).

Keeley's book has performed a very useful service in marshaling overwhelming evidence for the occurrence of warfare in prehistoric times. Yet his book stops short of pointing out the full impact of warfare on society, and the great role it played in giving rise to chiefdoms and states. He does not *deny* this effect, he simply fails to *affirm* it.

It was not, of course, only archaeologists working in the European Neolithic who dismissed the existence of warfare in prehistoric times. Mesoamerican archaeologists, for example, did so too, speaking confidently of the "peaceful Maya." It was not until the Bonampak murals were discovered in 1946, with their graphic and gruesome depictions of the treatment of war captives, that Mayanists began to have second thoughts on the matter. And over the ensuing decades mounting evidence has come to light testifying to the Maya's remorseless militarism.

That this evidence has become overwhelming is attested to by the writings of leading Mayanists. For example, in his article "Warfare and the Evolution of Maya Civilization," written in 1977, David Webster (1977:337) declared, "It seems to me that we must now seriously consider whether warfare might not have been an important process in the evolution of Maya society from its very beginnings, and not merely a symptom of its dissolution in the latter part of the Late Classic."

Convinced that warfare was present early in Maya prehistory, Webster (1977:355) wrote: "The position of war leader has a respectable antiquity in Maya society. . . . Artistic representations of bound or downtrodden enemies or armed warriors at Tikal, Calakmul, Bonampak, and other sites push this pattern back into the Classic. . . . military functions were not late acquisitions of the Maya elite, but rather helped to generate this class in the first place."

Webster felt that warfare was instrumental in the rise not only of Maya states, but also at earlier, pre-state phases of political development. The mechanism at work he described as follows: "conflict stimulates organization as an adaptive response; an organized group is a more competitive group, and the pressure to organize for warfare may have evolutionary potential at many political levels. Here I would take issue with Fried (1967), who . . . would restrict . . . [warfare's] evolutionary significance to the process of state formation" (Webster 1977:349). Instead, Webster (1977:344) was ready to sustain the view that "Warfare . . . may have been partially responsible for the evolution of the earliest chiefdoms in the Maya Lowlands as well as the more complex organizational forms."

Joyce Marcus, writing of the radical shift that had occurred in the interpretation of Mesoamerican prehistory, noted that "warfare . . . long viewed as a destroyer of Mesoamerican states, was also a creator of states. Numerous anthropologists . . . have argued that warfare was a critical variable among pre-state societies and early states around the world. Past archaeologists, however, often idealized early Mesoamerican states as 'peaceful theocracies,' devoid of the militarism of later peoples like the Aztec. Today, thanks to the work of several archaeologists, . . . we are beginning to see that armed conflict was important from the very beginning" (Marcus 1992:392).

But old beliefs proved difficult to eradicate, and Marcus (1992:406) noted that "Despite this mounting evidence, the peaceful-theory model has proved slow to die. Even today, some Mayanists argued that the battles were only 'ritual,' between small groups of nobles 'just to get captives for sacrifice.' The many kilometers of defensive works at Tikal, Becán, and other sites tell a different story."

Impressed by the role warfare seemed to have played in political evolution, in 1970 I proposed a theory in which warfare, acting jointly with population pressure and environmental circumscription, was assigned the major role in promoting the rise to the state. Since then, a number of anthropologists have devoted considerable attention to the way in which warfare contributed to the development of chiefdoms and states.

Many anthropologists, though, have resisted assigning to warfare any constructive role in this regard. They have seen war primarily as promoting turbulence and disruption in the history of human society. This reluctance to acknowledge the importance of war becomes particularly noticeable when considering the first crucial steps required in transcending village autonomy and establishing the first chiefdoms. In his book *The Evolution of Political Society*, Morton Fried (1967) granted prominence to warfare in human history once states had emerged, but refused to accord it any significant role in the chain of events leading to the rise of chiefdoms. Nor was he alone in this judgment. When Kent Flannery (1972a:402–403) itemized the various functions of the paramount chief of a chiefdom, his role as war leader was not among them.

The minimizing of war's significance at the chiefdom level was common in earlier discussions of that form of polity. For example, Elman Service (1962:143–152) and Marshall Sahlins (1972:132–148), probably the two most widely quoted writers on chiefdoms, presented that form of society in essentially economic terms, with redistribution and the like being cited as the paramount chief's major role, with little regard paid to his preeminence in political and military matters.

More recently, however, social anthropologists have begun to see the role of warfare in its true light. Thus, for example, C. R. Hallpike (1988:255) remarked: "There seems no doubt that warfare is by far the commonest means by which political authority is extended to new communities, and warfare will operate in conjunction with circumscription to extend the range of existing authority and consolidate its power." Later in the same work he concluded simply that "warfare . . . has been an essential component of the evolutionary process" (Hallpike 1988:372).

And Julian Steward, who at one time had been convinced that irrigation held the key to political development, conceded in his later years that "Warfare may lead to empires without irrigation" (quoted in South and Green 2002:8).

Mention should be made here of a modest volume by Keith Otterbein published in 1970 with the title *The Evolution of War*. The book is a statistical study of war based on a cross-cultural sample of fifty societies. The volume "tests a series of hypotheses which relate level of political centralization to various aspects of warfare" (1970:2). Among the specific conclusions reached in the study is this one: "The more evolved the manner of waging war, the more likely that the political communities of a cultural unit [that is, a society] will be militarily successful" (1970:106). Although the conclusion that success in war is the driving force behind political expansion is not explicitly stated by Otterbein, it nevertheless exudes from every pore of the book.

Trade as a Determinant

The last "materialist" determinant of cultural evolution to be considered here is that of trade, especially long-distance trade, whose principal advocate is William Rathje. It should be noted, though, that Rathje did not propose his theory as a general explanation for the rise of chiefdoms and states everywhere; rather, he limited it to their emergence among the Lowland Maya.

Rathje's theory is an intricate one, but its principal elements can be outlined as follows. The Maya lowlands were essentially uniform environmentally, so that although some trade took place between villages within that area, it was not very extensive trade. Nor did it involve such items as *manos* and *metates,* needed for grinding corn. Moreover, autonomous villages of the lowlands were "not always capable of independently obtaining the basic commodities needed to maintain their subsistence level" (Rathje 1972:371). To do so, it was necessary for them to "give up some of their autonomy to organizations for centralized procurement" of these materials (1972:371).

To solve this problem, they turned to "[t]hose people who could key into long-distance trade" (1972:371). "Such individuals would become integrative nuclei to scattered household populations" (1972:371). And this economic dependence of the autonomous villages of the lowlands on expeditions that periodically made their way to the highlands provided "a road to political, economic, and social power for those who could control long-distance trade" (1972:372).

As this trade matured, giving rise to the "complex organization" needed to carry it out more effectively, strong leaders arose who came to require "luxury paraphernalia" in order to "maintain stratification and organization" (1972:373). Side by side with this sociopolitical development there developed "a specific ceremonial configuration" that enabled people to have "access to the supernatural by means of temples, altars, ritual and astronomical knowledge." And this "ceremonial paraphernalia," while serving the religious needs of the general populace, provided the leaders with "status reinforcement" (1972:373).

Rathje encapsulates his theory as follows: "I hypothesize that complex sociopolitical organization in the lowland rainforests of Mesoamerica developed originally in response to the demand for consistent procurement and distribution of nonlocal basic resources" (1972:373).

Rathje's theory of chiefdom and state formation is clearly a voluntaristic rather than a coercive one. Warfare and conquest play no role in it. But it is hard to see that independent communities would actually have surrendered their sovereignty to the leader of a trading expedition. Moreover, the theory seems to ignore the accumulating evidence, already touched upon, of the prevalence of warfare at the earliest levels of Maya political development. Furthermore, Rathje does not seem to have persuaded his Mayanist colleagues of the correctness of his theory. David Webster, for instance, vigorously dissented from it:

Rathje . . . has maintained that the florescence of Maya centers and the high-status personnel associated with them grew out of long-distance trade in certain "necessary" commodities (such as salt, igneous rock, and obsidian). Like many other archaeologists, I remain unconvinced that these commodities were necessities in any absolute sense, and consequently [that] their acquisition provided a stimulus for hierarchical development. . . . [I]n my opinion long-distance bulk trade such as he envisions was a comparatively late development and was an *acquired* function of already-existing high-status groups, rather than a factor in their initial appearance. (Webster 1977:348–349)

10

Other Perspectives on Cultural Evolution

Ideology and Evolution

Most evolutionary theory has remained grounded in cultural materialism because, to quote that most pragmatic of materialists, Willy Sutton, "that's where the money is." That is to say, as far as providing the greatest intellectual payoff, materialist explanations have, on the whole, been the most robust and rewarding.

Another reason why materialist interpretations have ruled the roost in evolutionary studies is that most of these studies—certainly those conducted during the last thirty years—have been carried out by archaeologists. And dealing largely with material remains, as they necessarily do, has inclined them to look to material factors and conditions as providing the most solid and secure determinants of the cultural changes they study. Thus, as Michael Schiffer (1983:191) observed, "The principle of infrastructural determinism . . . underlies modern archaeology, at least in North America."

At the same time, cognitive and symbolic anthropologists, predisposed as they are to look with favor on the ideological determinants of things, have tended to stay clear of major evolutionary problems, such as the origin of states and civilizations.

Nevertheless, a few social anthropologists who have taken up the challenge of depicting and interpreting cultural evolution have done so under the banner of ideological determinism. Robert Redfield, for example, in his book *The Little Community*, asserted that "The world of man is made up in [the] first place of ideas and ideals. If one studies the rise of urban communities out of more primitive communities, it is the change in the mental life, in norms and aspirations, in personal character, too, that becomes the most significant aspect of the transformation" (1955:30). And in an earlier work, *The Primitive World and Its Transformation*, Redfield (1953:5) stated that "changes in the human mind . . . are the subject of these pages." Later in its pages he stated that his theme was "the transformation of the folk society into civilization through the appearance and development of the idea of re-form, . . . including the alteration of man himself, by deliberate intention and design" (Redfield 1953:113).

Redfield, however, was not content to address himself solely to his ethno-logical colleagues. He had a few admonishing words to say to archaeologists as well: "An archaeologist," he wrote, "should make a little effort to lean de-liberately away from a materialist view of human life and a conception of history in simple terms of economic determinism" (Redfield 1953:3). While not necessarily responding to Redfield's call, a number of archaeologists have in fact been drawn toward a more favorable look at ideas as causal agents in cultural advance.

Faced with the necessity of dealing with developmental change, archaeol-ogists have always had to face the question of how such change is to be ex-plained. Though they have "usually followed the lead of materialist thinkers" in this regard (Demarest 1992:5), and such views have dominated evolutionary explanations, some archaeologists have always looked with favor on interpretations that placed the major emphasis on ideology. For example, a quarter of a century ago Gordon Willey (1976:205) wrote: "If thinking human beings are the generators, as well as the carriers, of culture it seems highly probable that, from very early on, ideas provided the con-trols for and gave distinctive forms to the materialist base and to culture, and that these ideas then took on a kind of existence of their own."

A student of Gordon Willey, archaeologist Michael Coe, wrote along sim-ilar lines: "The precipitous ascent from an early Formative village life to the Olmec civilization is an example of a quantum evolution for which the valid explanation may well lie more in the realm of ideas and institutions rather than in modes of production" (Coe 1968:65).

In the same vein, Kent Flannery sought to distance himself from those ecologically inclined colleagues who minimized the role of ideology in de-termining the course of culture. "Archaeologists," he wrote, "must cease to regard art, religion, and ideology as mere 'epiphenomena' without causal significance" (1972a:400).

Beginning in the late 1970s and increasingly so in the 1980s, archaeolo-gists have been more open to the role of ideas as causal forces. Thus Richard Blanton (1983:204), a Mesoamericanist, pointed hopefully to what he called "the tendency of American cultural evolutionism to turn away from the strongly materialist explanatory schemes and toward explanatory paradigms that include a stronger component of ideological factors in the calculus of causation."

This trend has been widely commented on. For example, in the latest edition of his textbook *Archaeology*, David Hurst Thomas (1998:451) observed that "Within the past decade or so, archaeologists have increasingly turned to the ideas that lay behind the materials of prehistory. Some are now reversing the causal arrow to suggest that *ideology* may have provided the major stimulus driving cultural change." It was the "post-processualists" (whom we will meet again) who were most drawn to the use of ideology as a determinant. Archaeologists of this stripe, Charles Redman (1991:298) noted, were determined to show the world "how nonmaterial domains of societies, downgraded by many New Archaeologists, were crucial in deciphering the past."

Geoffrey Conrad and Arthur Demarest, both archaeologists, are no friends of materialist explanations. In fact, in their joint work *Religion and Empire* (1984) they speak of "the mystical philosophy of cultural materialism," calling it "a doctrine that, unfortunately, has dominated archaeological interpretation for the last two decades" (Conrad and Demarest 1984:195). But they are intent on seeing that domination end. Accordingly, in this volume they set out to show that "ideology, however difficult it may be to deal with archaeologically, must be included as a principal variable in analyses of culture change" (1984:205).

Religion and Empire deals with the great states of the Aztec and Inca, and in this volume Conrad and Demarest make a determined effort to show that *ecological* adaptations are insufficient to account for the rise of such states. They speak readily enough of "adaptations," but what they mean by this are adjustments to *internal* stresses and strains within those societies, rather than to external, "ecological," conditions. And the argument they make is that changes in ideology, specifically, modifications of religious beliefs and practices (which they regard as causal elements), were indeed also adaptive. They were adaptive "in that they . . . fulfilled the needs of interest groups (in both cases military elites) powerful enough to institute them. They were also adaptive in that they assured the . . . success of the Inca and Aztec societies in their military struggles with the peoples around them" (Conrad and Demarest 1984:198–199). Now, while military victories against surrounding enemies might, at first blush, be regarded as an external and therefore an ecological triumph, Conrad and Demarest put a different spin on it:

> Yet even on this society-wide level, military success itself can be explained only in terms of the "internal" (non-ecological) workings of the societies. The fanatical militarism of the Mexica and Inca resulted from class, small-group,

and economic and political interests, combined with the unique advantage in battle given by ideological necessity: without victory in combat the Aztec sun would perish and the Inca ruler/gods, living and dead, could not be maintained. (1984:199)

This analysis purports to establish the primacy of ideology in the rise of two mighty empires. But does it? Admittedly, ideology may be said to have acted as an *immediate* spur or goad to successful military action. If Aztec and Inca warriors were not highly motivated to fight and fight well, success might have eluded them. But doesn't this military ideology require an explanation? Surely it didn't cause itself. It had *antecedents*. And wouldn't it provide a fuller and more satisfying understanding of the rise of martial states like the Aztec and Inca if we could identify such antecedents?

Could not military action itself, brought on by the insistent and repeated demands of warding off enemy attacks—or conquering their territory!— have *engendered* an ideology that provided the religious underpinnings that impelled men to fight so effectively? Could not *ecological* necessity, then— as surely defense or offense against enemies must be said to be—have given rise to the *ideology* involved?

Let us put the matter this way. The cultural materialist does not proclaim the independent action of material conditions. That would be absurd. These conditions must somehow be translated into ideas, and these ideas must be funneled into individuals so as to galvanize them into action. The idealist likes to begin the causal analysis with the unquestioned motivating power of ideas. The materialist prefers to begin the analysis one step further back, going *behind* ideas to see how they arose in the first place and came to enter people's heads.

In 1992, Demarest and Conrad were at it again. That year they edited a volume entitled *Ideology and Pre-Columbian Civilizations*, several chapters of which were written by archaeologists working with various high cultures of Nuclear America. These archaeologists, who were known *not* to be firmly in the camp of cultural materialism, "were asked to address the evidence from their period and region of experience to try to ascertain the role of ideology in cultural evolution" (Demarest 1992:10). While varying in the degree of support each gave to ideological determinants, the archaeologists included in the volume marshaled what arguments they could in favor of the causal role of ideas in the rise of New World civilizations. How successfully they had done so was examined in a summary chapter near the end of the book (Carneiro 1992a).

One of the primary manifestations of ideology is, as we have seen, religion. And a few more words need to be said about the role of religion in the development of chiefdoms and states. Morton Fried was pretty firmly in the materialist camp when it came to accounting for cultural evolution. Nonetheless, he took a very jaundiced view of warfare as a factor in the rise of chiefdoms. Instead, he turned to religion (in the broadest sense) to carry out this function. Accordingly, in discussing the source of power that enabled a village chief to transform himself into the paramount chief of a chiefdom, he wrote: "chiefly figures bring little in the way of power to their priestly roles." (That is, he thought of village chiefs as, first and foremost, religious practitioners.) "Instead, it seems more accurate to believe that such small power as they control is likely to stem from their ritual status" (Fried 1967:141).

At first, not many anthropologists followed him in this belief. But more recently, as we have seen, ideology, especially religion, has been increasingly invoked as a causal factor in political development. Some Mayanists, for example, have begun to talk of "shaman kings." But Joyce Marcus (2002:409) will have none of it:

> When scholars call rulers "shaman-kings" and discuss their "mystical powers," they draw on . . . [an] inappropriate assumption: that the power of kings is based on contacting the spirits and on mediating between the supernatural and human worlds. Nonsense. Although Caesar may occasionally have consulted diviners, his *power* came from the Roman legions and the support of the Senate. "Power" is the ability to get people to do what they do not want to do, and it emanates not from a trance but from the military, economic, judicial, and legal arms of the government.

Finally, in a small footnote to the enduring conflict between materialist and idealist interpretations of cultural evolution, it may not be out of place to point out Marvin Harris's curious attempt to consign Leslie White to the camp of the idealists. In his book *Cultural Materialism,* Harris (1979:236) wrote as follows: "an effective response to [cultural] relativism and idealism . . . requires a reformulation of the entire set of epistemological assumptions, including those employed in the name of materialism (like Leslie White's insistence that culture is a realm of symbols)."

Writing thirty years earlier, but as if to answer Harris's allegation, White declared:

> it was the ability to use symbols . . . that made the origin and subsequent growth of culture possible. *But symbols did not provide the motive power for cultural advance.* This could only come from energy. . . . All life is a matter of energy transformations. Organisms enable themselves to live by capturing free energy from

non-living systems and by incorporating it into their own living systems. Culture is man's peculiar means of harnessing energy and of putting it to work in order to make human life secure. (White 1949a:240–241; emphasis mine)

Marvin Harris may have coined the term "cultural materialism," but it was Leslie White who first expounded and applied this approach in an effort to explain how culture evolves. And in *The Rise of Anthropological Theory*, Harris (1968:651) did acknowledge this fact, if only briefly and grudgingly. Here he conceded that "We may credit White . . . with the formulation of this strategy [cultural materialism] (under the pseudonym of evolutionism)."

Marxist Anthropology and Cultural Evolution

At this juncture, having just discussed materialist versus idealist interpretations of the causes of cultural evolution, we might do well to consider the curious case of current Marxist views on the subject. It is "curious" because Marxist interpretations of the evolution of society have themselves undergone a striking transformation.

Everyone knows, of course, that Karl Marx's philosophy of history was based on the premise that the material conditions of existence exert a powerful determining influence on the shape of social institutions. And several decades ago those few anthropologists who then identified themselves as Marxists clung firmly to that premise. Eleanor Leacock (1972:16), for one, was both an outspoken materialist and a staunch evolutionist. "Historical events can be recounted," she said, "but they cannot be *understood* without recourse to a broader theory such as that supplied by 'evolutionism.'"

On another occasion Leacock (1961:412) wrote that "Evolutionary theory is based on the primacy of technology and of economic structure in determining the nature of cultural integration in a society at any given point in time, and in causing a change, to use Steward's terminology, from one 'level of sociocultural integration' to another." And at about the same time she spoke optimistically of "the maturing of a specifically materialistic orientation towards human history on the part of a growing body of scholars" (Leacock 1964:110).

But things took a very different turn from what Leacock had evidently anticipated. A strange bifurcation occurred. In large part, Marxism in anthropology turned its back on its orthodox roots and divided itself into two branches, which may be labeled "humanistic Marxism" and "structural Marxism."

The origins of "humanistic Marxism" can perhaps be traced to Stanley Diamond. In Diamond's writings, we see "the trajectory of Marxist anthro-

pology, veering away from the positivist path" that had previously characterized it (Gailey 1992:7). Diamond and his followers have tended to enthrone "humanism," and turn their backs on "positivist premises about the
possibility of a value-free social science and the neutrality of data" (Gailey
and Patterson 1987:17).

Marxist humanism clearly pits People against Institutions, with its sympathies lying squarely on the side of the people. As in much of modern evolutionism, Diamond's work "focuses in one way or another on the dynamics of state formation," a process he saw as "fundamentally oppressive and
ethnocidal" (Gailey 1992:8). Diamond's writings and those of like-minded
Marxist anthropologists are laced with such value-laden epithets as "oppression," "subjection," "subordination," "enslavement," "exploitation," and
the like—not exactly the vocabulary of a "value-free social science." In this
regard, of course, Diamond and his followers did not fall far from the original Marxist tree.

Nor did they endear themselves to those anthropologists who considered
their discipline an objective science and whose teeth were set on edge by the
Marxists' continued "obsession . . . with the purely exploitative and oppressive aspects of the state" (Hallpike 1988:18).

Another way in which Diamond showed his Marxist orthodoxy was in
his insistence that the "dialectic" be considered the touchstone of true
Marxist materialism. Thus, he debarred Leslie White from the pantheon of
Marxist materialism because in his work White eschewed the dialectic, leaving him no better than "a mechanical or mechanistic, as opposed to a dialectical materialist" (Diamond 1974:341).

Those Marxist anthropologists who have followed Stanley Diamond have
generally taken pains to distance themselves from White's brand of evolutionism. For example, they are critical of White (and Julian Steward as well)
because those theorists "saw societies developing through a linear progression
of stages" (Gailey and Patterson 1987:3), and "linear models of development,
whether or not they purported to be 'multilinear,' could not account for the
internal destruction or dismantling of state institutions" (Gailey and Patterson 1987:4). As if some unspoken necessity required them to do so!

Gailey and Patterson (1987:18) are ready to accept V. Gordon Childe
within their ranks because, although Childe "saw the state as fundamentally
progressive, he recognized that the resulting society was oppressive to the
manual producers." On the other hand, they say, White ignored this oppression and, indeed, "was explicitly sympathetic with controlling the manual workers" (Gailey and Patterson 1987:18). Their evidence for this assertion is a passage in *The Evolution of Culture* in which White writes as
follows:

If the new type of civil society that was being produced by the developing technologies of agriculture and animal husbandry *were to be able to maintain and perpetuate itself,* it would have to achieve and maintain integrity, and this would mean . . . (1) coordinating, correlating, and integrating the various *parts and functions* of which the new sociocultural system was composed . . . and . . . coordinating and integrating the various *social structures* that comprise the system as a whole, namely, the occupational groups—industrial, ecclesiastical, and military. [And it] would have to reconcile the two basic classes of society, the dominant ruling class and the subordinate class, whose interests were not only different but opposite and conflicting at many points, and prevent the subordinate class from disrupting society and reducing it to anarchy and chaos through insurrection and civil war. (White 1959:300–301; emphasis mine)

Upon such evidence is Leslie White indicted as an enemy of the working man!

Closely related to the Marxist anthropologists' fixation on exploitation and oppression is their disinclination to countenance any theory of the origin of chiefdoms or states that has a "functional" basis. That is to say, they discount theories that see newly emerging political leaders as playing any kind of positive or constructive "managerial" role. They stoutly deny what they consider the false assumption that "state societies are functional, stable, and necessary for the maintenance of social order" (Gailey and Patterson 1987:16). An advocacy of such a theory, they declare, betrays "an implicit sympathy with the perspective of the ruling class" (Gailey and Patterson 1987:5), and thus ignores the primarily exploitive nature of this relationship.

Let us turn now to the other branch of modern Marxist anthropology, namely, "structural Marxism." What happened here, in a nutshell, is that Karl Marx was unceremoniously stood on his head by his own disciples. What Marx claimed to have done to Hegel, the new breed of "structural Marxists" did to him.

As we have seen, Marx always regarded the material conditions of existence as primary and basic, and ideology as secondary and derived. But then along came structural Marxism, which, in the words of two of its praçtitioners, "represented one of the first serious attempts to criticise and reform classical Marxism," an approach that they say was "characterised by evolutionary stage theories and simplistic notions of economic determination such as the base/superstructure model" (Kristiansen and Rowlands 1998:5). Structural Marxists turned their backs on this approach and focused instead on "the role of ideology . . . in the determination of social structure" (1998:5).

In fact, they *reversed* the arrow of causation. Ideology became the horse, and economic conditions the cart. Thus, according to Jérôme Rousseau (1985:36), "Inequality starts at the ideological level, to be followed by political and then economic inequality." And, more generally, Rousseau spoke of "the evolutionary sequence of ideology, politics, and economy," in that order, as being the normal succession of phases in societal change (1985:43).

A little more guarded, perhaps, and less heterodox in his interpretation of social causation, Maurice Godelier (1978:8) maintained that "religious ideology is not merely the superficial, phantasmic reflection of social relations. It is an element internal to the social relations of production." And as an example of this, he argued that among the Inca, the belief in the ruler's divine power "was not merely a legitimating ideology, after the fact, for the [existing] relations of production; *it was part of the internal armature of these relations*" (Godelier 1978:10).

But it is not the social anthropologist alone who has been drawn to "structural Marxism." This perspective has held "a seductive appeal to the archaeologist" as well, who finds the idealist bent of the new Marxism particularly congenial (Lillios 2001:240). Indeed, Arthur Demarest (1992:7) tells us, "Marxist approaches to archeology have been the most aggressive in their recent attempts to incorporate ideology as a force in prehistory."

Marxist anthropologists in general have often appeared to be uncomfortable with evolution, expressing this discomfort in a variety of ways. An extreme example is provided by the assertion of the Marxist feminist Michèle Barrett (1985:16) that "evolutionist arguments have little credibility nowadays as explanations of social change." Even more arresting is Bridget O'Laughlin's (1975:359) pronouncement that "We do not have to explain historical development, for that is constant; what we do have to explain are its structural regularities."

Another tactic of contemporary Marxists in dismissing "neo-evolutionism" is to equate it with the alleged sins of classical evolutionism, thereby discrediting both. Thus we find the suggestion that "the current popularity of evolutionary theory in archaeology seems to be indicative of the discipline being unable to break free from the shackles of its nineteenth-century origins" (Shanks and Tilley 1987:144). Similarly, Kristiansen and Rowlands (1998:23) speak dismissively of social evolution as "a hangover of nineteenth-century dogmas of development."

Nevertheless, modern Marxists, if they remain Marxists at all, must be concerned with the major changes undergone by societies and with the dynamics of that process. In doing so, however, they often choose to speak of "transformation" rather than "evolution." But regardless of the label they apply to it, the process they are dealing with is evolution.

When it comes to the sorts of determinants they employ, the choice widens a bit. We have seen that structural Marxists make ready use of ideology as a motive force. But there are still Marxists who fall back on such traditional and familiar determinants as the class struggle. Use of this mechanism may be all well and good once social classes are in existence, but what about evolutionary changes that take place *prior* to the existence of such classes? What about those changes that bring about the very social classes that later become the source of struggle and thus constitute, for orthodox Marxists, the key to social change?

Another word may be said here about "struggle." Marxists are in their element when discussing struggles *within* societies, but what about struggles *between* societies? As we shall see below, they appear loath to assign to such intersocietal struggles any significant role in political development.

As noted before, there is free and easy recourse among Marxists to the dialectical process. At best, however, "the dialectic" does not tell us *which* factors are the major determinants of social change, but only *how* those determinants interact and play themselves out in such a way as to bring about this change. That still leaves the determinant-of-choice to be selected.

Finally, there is one determinant—material as it may be—that Marxist anthropologists are disinclined to invoke in accounting for the rise of chiefdoms and states. This determinant is *warfare*. I will offer here one example of this reluctance. In his archaeological survey of Bronze Age sites in northern Albacete province, Spain, Antonio Gilman sought to account for the social inequality reflected in the "progressively greater wealth differentiation" he found in grave goods (Gilman 1995:249). He rejected managerial, trade, and population pressure theories out of hand. As a Marxist, he was drawn to some form of economic interpretation, but found it difficult to reconcile such a theory with the facts. For one thing, he found no evidence that the class struggle brought the Bronze Age chiefdoms of Albacete into being, since there *were* no social classes there at the beginning of this stage.

The most salient archaeological feature of Bronze Age Albacete that Gilman found was the large number of fortifications. Indeed, his survey revealed no fewer than 270 of them. This, he says, reflected a "clear concern for defense" (Gilman 1995:244). Undoubtedly, then, these extensive fortifications pointed to the prevalence of warfare. Moreover, "That the rich were buried with their weapons," says Gilman (1995:249), "suggests that their part in that strife helped them obtain their relatively privileged positions."

Here is persuasive evidence, then, that in Bronze Age Albacete warfare, leading to the accumulation of power and wealth by successful military leaders, was responsible for the emergence of chiefdoms. Thus the opportunity existed for Gilman to have boldly embraced a warfare-and-conquest theory of chiefdom formation. And, as the quotations above show, he came perilously close to doing so. But in the end, Gilman clung to traditional Marxist causal mechanisms, and talked of the economic exploitation of followers by their leaders, failing to account—as his own data would have allowed him to do—for *how* these leaders acquired the power to exploit their followers in the first place.

Microevolution and Agency Theory

Up to this point we have dealt with sociocultural evolution as the grand sweep of events and cultural forces in an ongoing general process. But this broad trajectory, when examined close up, assumes a different look. The general flow of events begins to reveal the actions of discrete, identifiable human beings. Studied at this level, the overall course of evolution turns out to consist of a series of small steps, of tiny changes, with little apparent direction.

In studying culture change, anthropologists face a choice. As Fred Eggan (1966:164) noted, "those who concern themselves with social and cultural evolution make a distinction between macroevolution and microevolution." Most who have studied evolution have preferred to deal with it in broad scope, that is, at the *macroevolutionary* level. However, a good many anthropologists have chosen to study culture change at the *microevolutionary* level, examining the fine-grained texture of its movements.

In her book *Continuities in Cultural Evolution*, Margaret Mead (1964:152) proposed to work at the microevolutionary level, which she defined as "the level at which the particular individual, or a group of particular individuals, is significant." At this level, she said, "the study of microevolution takes up the task in the attempt to specify the crucial significance of particular individuals in determining where, when and, ultimately, if any of the large-scale changes—changes which, retrospectively, will be seen as evolutionarily directional—will occur" (1964:153).

While having no quarrel with macroevolutionary studies, Mead made it clear that her own preference was for the study of small societies over a short span of time and at a very concrete level. She characterized the differences in the various levels at which change could be studied in the following way:

> Cultural macro-evolution may be defined as evolution that occurs in human cultures at a level at which the specification of individual actors is irrelevant. But a continuum might be constructed on which, at different points, we could

distinguish various levels of specificity: a level at which the character of a particular society, but not any given individual within that society, is crucial; a
level at which a group of individuals is crucial; and a level at which the single
individual is crucial. (Mead 1964:152)

Those who, like Mead, focus steadfastly on culture change at the microevolutionary level are always impressed—unavoidably so—with the importance of the decisions of particular persons and the actions that flow
from them. Accordingly, there is a tendency for them to think of individual
actions as the *driving force* of history. Correspondingly, these same anthropologists may bridle at what strikes them as the indifference, if not the outright denial, of the determining role of individuals assigned to them by
those who work at the macroevolutionary level. Reflecting this point of
view, Mead (1964:23) declared that "one must regard as untenable Leslie
White's contention that the individual, as such, is of no importance." A
decade earlier, her colleague William Duncan Strong (1953:392) had expressed much the same view, calling White "an uncompromising theorist
believing in the evolutionary cultural forces which tend to reduce the
human individual to complete insignificance."

Though this flat-out repudiation of White's point of view strikes me as
somewhat excessive, it does provide us with an opportunity to reopen the
old debate of the individual versus the culture process. This debate, which
never really died, has resurfaced recently in the guise of "neo-evolutionism"
versus *agency theory.* Uncomfortable with the notion of "impersonal forces"
driving evolution forward, some anthropologists have sought refuge in
agency theory. Indeed, some of its proponents have presented it as a new
breakthrough, a novel solution to an old conundrum, one never envisioned
by old-line cultural evolutionists. Let us see just what agency theorists
maintain, and what evolutionists can counter in reply.

The last few decades have witnessed a veritable Greek chorus of opposition to the study of cultural evolution as a succession of cultural forms, divorced from flesh-and-blood human beings. Bruce Trigger (1989:354), for
example, complained that "the mechanistic structure of neo-evolutionary
theory . . . treats human beings as passive instruments rather than makers
of history." Christine Gailey and Thomas Patterson (1987:5) lamented that
in general systems theory (which they regard as a parallel cousin to "neo-
evolutionism") individuals "are conceived not as actors, but as components
of a system, interchangeable with each other."

The chorus continues. In the view of Ian Hodder (1986:25), for processual archaeologists, "individuals play little part" in their theories of how
cultures evolve; "they only appear as predictable automata, driven by cover-

ing laws." More soberly, George Cowgill (1975:506) put the matter this way: "I believe that explanatory formulations in terms of general processes are extremely important. But these explanations remain unsatisfactory if we cannot suggest any plausible individual actions which would give rise to the postulated processes."

Such objections, of course, are nothing new. They were given voice almost a century ago with a plea that it's *people*, not cultures, who do things. Thus Alexander Goldenweiser (1933:59) asserted that "If we had the knowledge and the patience to analyze a culture retrospectively, every element of it would be found to have had its beginning in the creative act of an individual mind." And according to Ruth Benedict (1934:253), "No civilization has in it any element which in the last analysis is not the contribution of an individual. Where else could any trait come from . . . ?" Where else indeed!

Here we have two expressions of what might be called *naive realism. Of course* it's people who do things! Only a deranged metaphysician could argue otherwise. Even Leslie White (1987:285) cheerfully admitted as much: "We grant, of course, that culture emanates from the organisms of the human species; without human beings there would be no culture." And to Margaret Mead's contention that for him the individual is of no importance, one could juxtapose White's statement that "The individual is not irrelevant to the culture process. On the contrary, he is an integral . . . and fundamental part of it" (White 1987:286).

To Gailey and Patterson's suggestion that general systems theorists and evolutionists view individuals as "interchangeable parts," White would again demur. Even though human organisms are "the instrument by means of which the culture process effects its changes," nevertheless, since "no two human organisms are alike in neurological, glandular, muscular, sensory, et cetera, structure and organization, the behavior of the culture process is conditioned by biological variation" (White 1987:308). Variation in individuals, then, *can* make a difference. Human beings, therefore, are not merely interchangeable parts. They differ in ways that, if looked at on the microevolutionary level, are not insignificant. Not everyone could have invented the calculus or formulated the law of universal gravitation. It took an exceptionally gifted individual—a Newton—to do so.

But it didn't take a Newton to give rise to a chiefdom. Ordinary men could—and did—do so, hundreds of times. And if not exactly *ordinary* men, then at least not *exceptional* men, not men with the intellectual endowment of a Newton. Men who were only a cut or two above their fellows in energy and ambition could accomplish it. After all, no categorically superior intelligence was needed in order to unify a collection of autonomous villages into a multivillage polity.

In echoing the oft-heard charge that "neo-evolutionists" deal with individuals "as pawns locked into an inexorable evolutionary process over which they have no control" (Johnson 1999:142), Paul Roscoe (1993:113) argues that, on the contrary, human agents, "rather than responding mechanically" to the "rules and resources" of their culture, "use them creatively to perform activities and achieve ends."

Again, White's remarks dispel, or rather, accommodate, this criticism: "We do not say that the individual organism receives cultural material in a purely passive way. . . . Human organisms are dynamic systems. They not only receive elements of culture from the outside, they act upon them" (White 1987:292). Nevertheless, White contends that in *understanding* how culture evolves, it is more illuminating to view the individual as "an organization of cultural forces and elements that have impinged upon him from the outside and which find overt expression through him" (White 1987:287). Or, to put it slightly differently, the individual may be regarded as "a catalytic agent" in the culture process, "as well as the locus of its occurrence" (White 1987:291).

The matter can be stated in still another way. If we look at the broad sweep of cultural evolution, the actions of individuals are submerged or dissolved away. What we observe, then, is an ongoing process in which what come to the fore and take shape are cultural trends, patterns, and processes, quite divorced from their human carriers. From this perspective, individuals, regardless of their contributions, are indistinguishable. It is important to keep in mind, however, that by adopting this perspective we are not compelled to deny the fact that it was *people,* flesh-and-blood individuals, who won battles, formed chiefdoms, founded dynasties, or built pyramids. We can *ignore* without having to *deny.* And of course, at this lower level of analysis, individuals are not "interchangeable parts." A lesser man than William the Conqueror might have lost the Battle of Hastings, and Britain might have remained Saxon for centuries more.

Finally, let us take as an example the history of pre-Columbian Peru to illustrate how political developments can be perceived and explained at both the microevolutionary and the macroevolutionary levels. In doing so we will quote from the writings of two Inca specialists, John Rowe and Geoffrey Conrad. To begin with, as Conrad tells us, "The Incas were just one of many historically known peoples who emerged in the south-central Andean highlands in the aftermath of the breakdown of Tiwanaku civilization. In the power vacuum produced by this collapse, petty states and chiefdoms fought to establish themselves as the rightful heirs of Tiwanaku and to reap the benefits this domination would bring" (Conrad 1992:160).

There then ensued a period of military competition among these many polities that led to "a chronic state of petty warfare that lasted from roughly A.D. 1200 to around 1450" (Conrad 1992:161). Conrad continues:

> The Incas rose to imperial power by prevailing in these conflicts, at first locally and eventually across some 4300 kilometers of the Andean world. They began their course of imperialism by emerging victorious from local power struggles after more than two centuries of constant war. To do so, they must have developed an advantage over their neighbors, something that made Inca militarism more successful than that of their competitors. (Conrad 1992:161)

No doubt a number of different factors were involved in this outcome. Might one of them have been superior generalship? Apparently so. Listen next to John Rowe (1946:203): "In early times, neither the *Incas* nor any of their neighbors thought of organizing their conquests as a permanent domain. A defeated village was looted, and perhaps tribute was imposed on it, but otherwise it was left alone until it recovered sufficient strength to be a menace again."

And so things remained for perhaps a century or two: "Down to the reign of Pachacuti, towns very near to Cuzco preserved complete freedom of action and raided one another's territory whenever there seemed to be a good opportunity for plunder" (Rowe 1946:203). But then a categorical change took place in the aftermath of a successful military campaign: "Yahuar Huacac and Viracocha, Pachacuti's immediate predecessors, enjoyed the services of two very able generals, Vicaquirao and Apo Mayta, cousins and Incas by blood. They were probably responsible for the first attempts to organize conquered territory, at least around the capital itself, and their successful campaigns gave the *Inca* state a political importance it had entirely lacked in earlier times" (Rowe 1946:203).

With other able rulers, Topa Inca Yupanqui and Huayna Capac, and no doubt their able generals to lead them, the Incas continued to capitalize on these initial successes, gaining increased momentum and pushing the boundaries of their polity further and further until they encompassed a huge territory organized into a great empire.

Now, had Vicaquirao and Apo Mayta not been the capable generals they were, the Inca might well have failed to achieve such great military triumphs, with their concomitant territorial expansion. *Some other* polity might have done so instead. Thus *some other* empire might have been in place in Peru when Pizarro and his men landed in 1525. So it is to the contributions of *specific individuals* that we owe the *specific facts* of Andean political history.

This, then, is the picture we see when we look at events on a *microevolutionary* level. At the *macroevolutionary* level, however, Vicaquirao and Apo Mayta, Pachacuti and Huayna Capac, fade from view. What we see, then, are the cultural forces that gave impetus to state formation, forces so prevalent and so strong that they were at work all over the Andes, pushing in the same direction—toward larger and larger political units. Such was the nature and magnitude of these forces that we can confidently predict that, given sufficient time, *some* small polity—headed by capable military and political leaders, to be sure—would have emerged triumphant from its many battles, and would eventually have established a large and powerful state over the Andes, roughly on the order of the Inca empire.

Here we see inexorable cultural processes at work, playing themselves out, selecting those individuals best suited to serve as "agents" in carrying out the great evolutionary design. Nor is this mere metaphysical fatalism. What we see at work is not blind fate, but a recurring, determinate set of existing realities, operating in the Andes as they had in other parts of the world, and giving rise to similar results.

Now, which one of these perspectives, which level of analysis, we adopt in our study of changing cultures depends on our aims and objectives. If we are dealing with the broad, overall trajectory of cultural development, then the action of particular individuals is *assumed*, but not *invoked*. However, if we are dealing with a short segment of known history, then the abilities and failings of particular "agents"—the military genius of a Napoleon or the ineptitude of a Louis XVI—will be taken into account. There is no logical opposition between the two points of view.

Kent Flannery (1999:18) has summarized the situation rather neatly: "Agent based perspectives are not destined to make studies of process obsolete. Process and agency have a relationship like that of mutation and natural selection in biological evolution, and in fact, most processes are just long-term patterns of behaviour by multiple agents."

Thus it is fair to conclude that the battle waged between the proponents of the two approaches—cultural determinism and agency theory—may be declared a draw, and each side may retire from the fray, if not triumphant, at least in good order and with mutual respect.

11

Elements of Evolutionary Formulations

Evolution: Unilinear or Multilinear?

There is little doubt that one of the most vexing issues in cultural evolutionary theory is that of unilinear versus multilinear evolution. Two aspects of the problem are, first, how the distinction between "unilinear" and "multilinear" is to be made and, second, which of the two forms best characterizes the course that cultural evolution has actually followed.

It has long been claimed by anti-evolutionists—indeed, it is their chief reason for rejecting evolutionism—that, to a man, the classical evolutionists maintained that all cultures had to go through the same stages, and that cultural evolution was, ipso facto, *unilinear*. Ralph Linton (1936b), for example, said of the nineteenth-century evolutionists that "Coupled with this arrangement of stages went a belief in the unilinear evolution of all institutions and cultures, that is, that all cultures had passed or were passing through exactly the same stages in their upward climb." John Gillin (1948:600) was even more emphatic in making the same assertion: "[I]n its classical form," he wrote, "evolutionary theory held that *all* cultures inevitably must pass through the *same* stages of development" (emphasis Gillin's). Even Julian Steward, whom we might have expected to be better acquainted with the writings of Morgan and Tylor and Spencer, nonetheless was guilty of the same misconception: "The historical reconstructions of the nineteenth-century unilinear evolutionists," he said, "are distinctive for the assumption that *all* cultures pass through parallel . . . sequences" (Steward 1955:27; emphasis Steward's).

However, as we have seen earlier in this volume, the classical evolutionists were by no means entirely devoted to an indiscriminate unilinearism, nor were they unaware of the diverging paths societies had taken in their actual histories. (See also White 1987:112–114.)

Underlying the allegations of the anti-evolutionists that the classical evolutionists were mistaken was the belief that no substantial uniformity in the way cultures had evolved could be sustained. Thus to Franz Boas (1982:254), it seemed "impossible . . . to bring cultures into any kind of continuous series." Goldenweiser (1925b:19) agreed, saying that "No anthropologist today believes in an orderly and fixed procession of cultural development." In the colorful way he often phrased his criticisms, Robert Lowie (1947:435) pointed his finger at diffusion as the factor that vitiated any chance there might have been of establishing a main sequence of cultural development. Accordingly, he wrote that "Any conceivable tendency of human society to pursue a fixed sequence of stages must be completely veiled by the incessant tendency to borrowing and thus becomes an unknowable noumenon that is scientifically worthless."

In short, there was widespread agreement among earlier American anthropologists on the subject of unilinearity. They would all have nodded in agreement with George P. Murdock (1949:xiv) when he spoke simply of "the fallacy of unilinear evolution."

Those who were dyed-in-the-wool anti-evolutionists let it go at that and troubled themselves no further about the matter. But those who, like Julian Steward, thought there was an undeniable and important core of truth in cultural evolutionism, a core that needed to be preserved, defended, and expanded, looked for ways of doing so.

Steward first lightly rapped the knuckles of White and Childe for their apparent unilinearism: "Such modern-day unilinear evolutionists as Leslie White and V. Gordon Childe," he argued, "evade the awkward facts of cultural divergence and local variation by purporting to deal with culture as a whole rather than with particular cultures" (Steward 1955:12). However, he then attempted to rescue them from their untenable position outside the evolutionary pale by erecting a new category, "universal evolution," and assigning them a place in it. As Steward (1955:16) put it: "Aware that the empirical research of the twentieth century has invalidated the unilinear historical reconstruction of particular cultures, which constituted the essential feature of nineteenth-century schemes, White and Childe endeavored to keep the evolutionary concept of cultural stages by relating these stages to the culture of mankind as a whole."

One of the factors militating against the possibility of unilinearity, Steward held, was environmental diversity. White's way around the difficulty posed by the great variety of environments in which societies had evolved was, as we have seen, to say that "in a consideration of culture as a whole, we may average all environments together to form a constant factor which may be excluded from our formula of cultural development" (White 1949a:368n.). This solution, of course, was not to Steward's liking. In fact, he considered it an intellectual evasion, if not actual sleight-of-hand. For Steward, local ecological conditions had always been, since his work in the Great Basin, the prime determinants of a culture, and thus could not be left out of any equation purporting to account for cultural development, whether of individual societies or of all societies taken together.

Childe, Steward thought, had adopted a similar tack. Childe had readily agreed that "As societies have lived in different historical environments and have passed through different vicissitudes, their traditions have diverged, and so ethnography reveals a multiplicity of cultures, just as does archaeology" (Childe 1951b:32). However, he (1951b:35) also noted that a fixation on the particular was "a serious handicap if our object be to establish general stages in the evolution of cultures." Consequently, in order "to discover general laws descriptive of the evolution of all societies we abstract in the first instance the peculiarities due to differences of habitat" (Childe 1951b:35).

Regarding the "abstractions" from ethnographic and archaeological particulars that White and Childe called for, Steward (1955:17) found them not only uncongenial but unrewarding, objecting that their "postulated cultural sequences are so general that they are neither very arguable nor very useful." Moreover, he continued, "If one examines universal evolution with a view to finding laws or processes of development rather than examining it merely in terms of a sequential reconstruction of culture, it is also difficult to recognize anything strikingly new or controversial" (Steward 1955:17–18).

What was Steward's proposed way out of this predicament? How were robust and significant evolutionary formulations to be arrived at? Steward (1955:18) concluded that while "We may deduce from the data of . . . cultural evolution that new organizational forms will appear in succession, . . . the specific nature of these forms can be considered only by tracing the history of each in great detail." Thus we are led irresistibly, Steward contended, to what he called *multilinear evolution.*

Before discussing Steward's characterization of this form of evolution, it is well to recognize that at one time he himself had flirted—and quite successfully—with unilinear evolution. In his landmark article "Cultural Causality and Law," he had proposed a series of stages through which the early civilizations had passed. Operating with Wittfogel's hydraulic hypothesis as the underlying causal mechanism in accounting for these parallel developments, Steward (1949:17) qualified his generalization by stating that "the formulation here offered excludes all areas except the arid and semiarid centers of ancient civilization." However, he never stated that his sequence of stages could *not* apply to those humid areas where civilization had also arisen. And he soon discovered that Yucatan, a region of low tropical rain forest, "appears to fit the formulation made for the more arid areas to the extent that its sequences were very similar to those of Mesoamerica generally" (Steward 1949:17). And there were also indications that his sequence of stages might apply to other areas of high cultural development as well.

Furthermore, in addition to his having found archaeological evidence of the parallel development of most if not all of the early civilizations, it was clear that despite the entrenched opposition to it at the time (1949), unilinear evolution had a decided appeal for Julian Steward. Thus he admonished his anti-evolutionist colleagues that "to stress the complexity or multiplicity of the antecedents or functional correlates of any institution makes it impossible to isolate the true causes of the institution" (Steward 1949:5). He therefore opposed a reliance on "convergent [multilinear?] evolution rather than parallel evolution" in accounting for developmental uniformities, suspecting that recourse to the former might be "another means of denying the possibility of isolating cultural regularities" (Steward 1949:5).

What led to Steward's *démarche* and his retreat from unilinear to multilinear evolution is an interesting story in itself, which I have tried to piece together elsewhere (Carneiro 1974:95–96), but it is unnecessary to recount it here. The fact remains that not long afterward, in his article "Evolution and Process" (1953a), Steward introduced his conception of multilinear evolution and indicated how it was to be pursued.

Now, in doing so, Steward used some unfortunate phraseology, referring to multilinear evolution as a "*methodology* based on the *assumption* that significant regularities in cultural change occur" (Steward 1955:18; emphasis mine). Of course, whatever its nature, multilinear evolution is not a "methodology," but a *characteristic* of the historical phenomena themselves. And its existence is not an "assumption," but supposedly a *fact*, to be arrived at empirically. However, it seems uncharitable to dwell any further on Steward's *lapsus linguae*.

In laying out what one is to do in studying multilinear evolution, Steward says certain things that, on the face of it, appear contradictory or at least inconsistent. Thus he tells us that one of his objectives is the determination of "whether any genuine or meaningful similarities between cultures exist" (Steward 1955:19). And again, he states that multilinear evolution has a great "interest in determining recurrent forms, processes, and functions" (1955:19). However, one gets the impression that these regularities should not be *too* recurrent or *too* parallel, for he makes it clear that he is after only *limited* regularities, "rather than world-embracing and universal laws" (1955:19). More than once he states that multilinear evolution "deals only with . . . limited parallels of form, function, and sequence" (Steward 1953a:318). And in an article entitled "Cultural Evolution," written in 1956, Steward reaffirmed his allegiance to multilinear evolution: "The facts now accumulated indicate that human culture evolved along a number of different lines; we must think of cultural evolution not as unilinear but as multilinear. That is the new basis upon which evolutionists today are seeking to build an understanding of the development of human cultures" (Steward 1956:73–74).

It would appear, then, that the discovery of a regularity, or the formulation of a generalization, of truly wide applicability is something that Steward would find disquieting or disconcerting. Steward, then, is on the horns of an ambivalence: Limited regularities are good, but one must be wary of broader ones. On this score, White gently chided him, saying, as pointed out in an earlier chapter, that "Steward resembles one who discovers that this river and that flow down hill but is unwilling to go so far as to assert that 'rivers flow down hill'" (White 1957:541).

To be sure, the evolutionary lines that led to the rise of Egyptian, Babylonian, Inca, and Maya civilizations, though generally parallel, were by no means identical in every respect. Nor did it require the acuity of a Franz Boas or a Robert Lowie to recognize this. The classical evolutionists were well aware of it themselves, as were those few evolutionists who carried on their tradition into the twentieth century. For example, in their famous work *The Material Culture and Social Institutions of the Simpler Peoples,* Hobhouse, Wheeler, and Ginsberg (1930:26) declared that "the course of social evolution is not unitary . . . [the] different races and different communities of the same race have, in fact, whether they started from the same point or no, diverged early, rapidly, and in many directions at once."

However, as one of these authors later observed, "The multilinear character of development does not exclude an underlying unity and continuity" (Ginsberg 1953:59). Here, though, we are faced, not with a theoretical question, but with an empirical one: When we examine the evolutionary trajectories of those human societies that traveled far in their development, how much recurrence, how much regularity, how much parallelism do we find? Clearly, the search cannot be left to what Eleanor Leacock (1972:18) described as a "theoretically flabby . . . 'multilinear' evolution," whose objectives, by Steward's own avowal, are strictly limited. Instead, the search should be placed in the hands of an evolutionism with broader horizons and more ambitious objectives. Furthermore, one needs to spell out in considerable detail just what traits and events are to be used in comparing developmental sequences.

The fact is that unilinear and multilinear evolution may be, and in fact are, manifested in the development of actual societies. The trick is to recognize this from the start, and to extract one from the other. For example, when dealing with political evolution, we encounter an undeniable unilinearity. Ancestrally, all human societies were once nomadic bands that later, after the invention of agriculture, evolved, for the most part, into autonomous villages. Some of these villages developed into multivillage chiefdoms, and a limited number of chiefdoms in turn went on to become states. Consequently, the common line in the evolution of all states has been one of band > autonomous village > chiefdom > state. No known case exists of a number of autonomous villages having evolved directly into states without first having been chiefdoms. Sub-Saharan Africa may have gone directly from a Stone Age to an Iron Age, skipping a Bronze Age, as the Boasians loved to point out, but every African state was once something that we could readily identify as a chiefdom. The skipping of stages thus has its limits.

It may be interjected here that a chiefdom may, for a time, *relapse* back into autonomous villages, and a state may likewise break down into the chiefdoms out of which it first arose, without thereby violating any evolutionary premise. *Unilinear* does not mean *rectilinear.* Advanced forms of political organization may temporarily revert to simpler ones, before advancing again to even higher forms. Or indeed, following a breakdown, a complex polity may never advance again. Historical developments, then, are saw-toothed rather than straight-lined.

In view of this argument, I believe Lowie (1927:112) was in error when he stated: "Modern ethnology rejects the notion of unilinear evolution; it does not, in other words, believe that some mystic *vis politica* urges all societies alike to traverse the same stages towards a strongly centralized state." But the force that produced this development, wherever it occurred, was of course no "mystic *vis politica.*" Some very commonplace organizational considerations were at work. They involved the practical necessity of compounding and recompounding, as larger political units were being built up out of smaller ones. One might invoke here the principle of limited possibilities, first given formal expression by Alexander Goldenweiser, a leading member of the Boas school.

Another way in which Lowie fails to face the issue squarely is this: The unilinear evolutionist does not say that every society *must* evolve in the same way, since he does not assert that every society *must* evolve! The existence of hunting and gathering bands even today—to say nothing of hundreds of autonomous villages—proves that societies do not *automatically* evolve. In the absence of the appropriate conditions that foster their evolution, they will tarry at a lower level, without thereby violating any principle of cultural evolution. What the unilinear evolutionist *does* say is that *if* a so-

ciety evolves to a certain level, then it will have gone through certain identifiable forms or stages in the process.

Nor does the unilinear evolutionist contend that the evolution of states
will be identical, or even closely alike, in every detail. What he does assert is
that the major steps in the evolutionary progression, the way in which political building blocks were successively assembled, were essentially the
same. So again, Lowie (1927:112) was wrong in affirming that "It is not possible to grade peoples according to the degree in which they approach that
goal [i.e., the formation of a state]; if several distinct paths are conceivable,
progress along any two of them becomes incommensurable." Of course, if
one insists on looking at each minute detail in the evolution of every
state—at the particular *history* of each state—then one is bound to find elements that will distinguish its development from that of every other state.
Yet, only intellectual perversity would lead one to deny that *some common
thread* runs through the evolution of states generally.

In passing, it is interesting to note how, in the field of political evolution,
where a broad unilinearity is so clearly evident, there is still a certain timidity on the part of nonevolutionists to embrace the obvious. Thus, Lucy Mair
(1962:107–108), in summing up her observations on African political systems, writes: "in the minimal governments which have been described, we
can see some of the prerequisites for the establishment of a hereditary
monarchy." But, she quickly adds, "I do not assert that those people which
now have hereditary monarchs must once have had a political organization
like that of the Nuer [that is, stateless]." Then, summoning up all her
courage, she declares: "Nevertheless, it is reasonable to suppose that they
have not had a state form of government ever since the dawn of their existence as human beings."

Returning to the main theme, we can say that there is an interplay between *general trends,* partaken of by most evolved societies, and *particular
developmental tracks,* which only a limited number of evolved societies have
followed. We can illustrate this counterpoint between unilinear and multilinear evolution in the schematic diagram shown in Fig. 11.1.

Here the traits numbered 1, 2, 8, 9, 12, and 13 have all evolved in the same
order—that is, *unilinearly*—by the hypothetical societies represented in the
diagram. On the other hand, the rest of the traits, numbered 3, 4, 5, 6, 7, 10,
and 11, were evolved in a somewhat different order by the societies represented. With respect to the latter traits, these societies have evolved *multilin-
early.* Thus, evolution can be *both* unilinear and multilinear at the same time.

Just because we used numbers in Fig. 11.1 does not mean that there aren't
actual culture traits that behaved that way in actual evolutionary sequences.
Traits can be found that correspond to certain numbers on the "evolution-

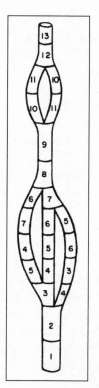

FIGURE 11.1
Evolutionary tree showing schematically
the relationship between unilinear and
multilinear evolution by means of branching
out from and back to a central trunk. The
numbers within the sections represent
successively developed traits.

ary tree" in that they follow each other in a fixed order. The unilinearism thus depicted—and it is substantial—can most readily be shown by examining *pairs* of traits.

Thus, we can assert with complete confidence that in every instance of autochthonous development, barter preceded money, shamans preceded priests, chieftainship preceded monarchy, chiefly redistribution preceded taxation, dirt trails preceded paved roads, tribal councils preceded parliaments, towns preceded cities, pole-and-thatch construction preceded stone architecture, chiefly adjudication of offenses preceded law courts, bush spirits preceded high gods, etc. And one could cite a host of other such pairs of traits that invariably followed each other in fixed chronological order.

Furthermore, such an invariant temporal linkage is not limited to *pairs* of traits. One can come up with successively longer chains of traits that can be said to form a single—unilinear—evolutionary sequence. For example, a unilinear sequence of eleven traits was presented in Carneiro (1970b:836). And this set does not begin to exhaust the number of traits that can be so arranged.

This is not to say, of course, that there aren't also a great many traits—especially those between which there is little "evolutionary distance"—that

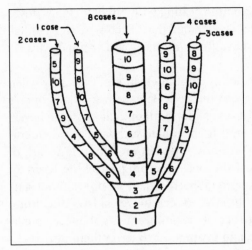

FIGURE 11.2
Evolutionary tree showing multilinear evolution as a divergence of branches away from a central trunk. The thickness of the trunk and of the branches is proportional to the number of societies contained in each. The numbers in the sections of the trunk and the branches represent traits in the order they were developed.

were not developed in the same order by all societies. This kind of occurrence is shown schematically in Fig. 11.2, which, making use of ten unidentified numbered traits, shows five different orders in which several sets of societies might have evolved them.

The great issue of whether unilinearity and multilinearity are antagonistic and irreconcilable forms of the evolutionary process or whether they could be harmoniously conjoined was answered by Leslie White (1987:114) in the following words: "Unilinear interpretations of cultural development are as relevant and as valid as multilinear interpretations; they are merely two different but complementary aspects of one and the same process." And again, White (1953:72) declared that "there is no conflict between unilinear and multilinear evolution. They are simply complementary aspects of the same phenomenon, two different points of view from which processes can be observed."

The similarities between various early state-level societies have been pointed out countless times. Speaking of the Maya and Ancient Egypt, for example, Ralph Linton (1955:59) noted that the two cultures "show striking parallels which, it would seem, can only be explained on the basis of some general trend in cultural development which we can describe as evolutionary."

After a detailed comparative study of two pre-industrial civilizations in his well-known book *The Evolution of Urban Society,* Robert McC. Adams (1966:174–175) felt assured in asserting that "the parallels in the Mesopotamian and Mexican 'careers to statehood' . . . in the forms that institutions ultimately assumed as well as in the processes leading to them, suggest that both instances are most significantly characterized by a common core of regularly occurring features."

And in their introduction to a volume dealing with "archaic states," Joyce Marcus and Gary Feinman (1998:7) concluded that "Each state is . . . different in some respects from other states, but early states as a group do display similarities."

The existence of broad regularities in cultural evolution, especially when looked at unilinearly, strongly suggests the possible existence of laws of culture. Even those anthropologists who were doubtful of their existence nevertheless sometimes pointed to attempts to formulate such laws as a desideratum. Thus Franz Boas (1940:634) once wrote that an "important task of ethnology, [is] the investigation of the laws governing social life." And an avowed evolutionist like Julian Steward (1955:18) made no bones about stating that "It is certainly a worthy objective to seek universal laws of cultural change." Accordingly, let us turn to actual pronouncements about the possibility of discovering cultural laws, and to attempts to ferret them out.

Laws of Cultural Development

The formulation of laws of culture has been a goal of anthropology from its inception. Underlying this aim was the belief that cultural phenomena were no different from other phenomena of nature, and existed within a framework of cause and effect. This being the case, they were fully susceptible to scientific investigation that could lead to the ascertaining of laws no different in kind from those of physics or chemistry. As E. B. Tylor put it, "If law is anywhere, it is everywhere" (quoted in White 1949a:107).

In the early decades of the twentieth century this optimistic view continued to be expressed. Thus in *Psyche's Task*, published in 1913, James B. Frazer proclaimed:

> The aims of this, as of every other science, is to discover the general laws to which the particular facts may be supposed to conform. I say, may be supposed to conform because research in all departments has rendered it antecedently probable that everywhere law and order will be found to prevail if we search for them diligently, and that accordingly the affairs of man, however complex and incalculable they may seem to be, are no exception to the uniformity of nature. Anthropology, therefore, in the widest sense of the word, aims at discovering the general laws which have regulated human history. (Frazer 1913a:159–160)

But as the discipline moved into the era of Boasian particularism, this expectation began to fade. It gave way to a conviction that the facts of social life were so convoluted and so discrepant that finding any clear and concrete cultural laws among them was all but hopeless. Thus by the mid-1930s Murdock (1937b:447) could write that "The historical school" proceeded from the "basic assumption . . . that culture change follows no general laws or principles, . . . but is the product of 'historical accident.'"

Curiously enough, though, Franz Boas himself, on more than one occasion, spoke favorably of "laws." But they were *psychological* laws, not cultural ones. Thus he wrote that "We wish to discover the laws governing the development of the mind" (Boas 1949:638), and that "the object of anthropological research . . . [is] to elucidate psychological laws" (Boas 1896a:742).

More fully—if not more clearly—Boas laid down his reasons for espousing psychological laws while rejecting cultural ones:

> In my opinion a system of social anthropology and "laws" of cultural development as rigid as those of physics are supposed to be, are unattainable in the present state of our knowledge, and more important than this: on account of the uniqueness of cultural phenomena and their complexity nothing will ever be found that deserves the name of a law excepting those psychological, biologically determined characteristics which are common to all cultures and appear in a multitude of forms according to the particular culture in which they manifest themselves. (Boas 1982:311)

How interesting! These would appear to be elusive psychological laws indeed since they failed to show themselves openly, but would be found only in a variety of cultural disguises that would first have to be penetrated before their underlying identities could be discerned.

If Boasian anthropologists did not declare outright that the formulation of cultural laws was unattainable, they at least put it off into the distant future. This uncertainty on the subject can be perceived in the writings of Robert Lowie. In one of Lowie's early works, *Culture and Ethnology,* published in 1917, he says: "The field of culture . . . is not a region of complete lawlessness. Like causes produce like effects, here as elsewhere" (Lowie 1929:88). But then, just seven pages later, he casts serious doubt on the possibility of finding such laws. "The extraordinary extent to which . . . diffusion has taken place," he says, "proves that the actual development of a given culture does not conform to innate laws necessarily leading to definite results, such hypothetical laws being overridden by contact with foreign peoples" (Lowie 1929:95).

By 1920, when *Primitive Society* appeared, Lowie was ready to repudiate any previous stand he might have taken in favor of parallel and recurrent evolutionary sequences. In this, his best-known work, he stated that "a belief in laws regulating the independent reproduction of the same *series* of stages," which he tacitly admitted once having entertained, "I now at the close of my investigation formally abjure" (Lowie 1920:432).

And nearly thirty years later, he contemptuously dismissed the quest for cultural laws, writing that "the use of the term 'law' in any of the social sciences should be discountenanced as pretentiously boastful" (Lowie 1948:50). So intent, in fact, were anthropologists in refuting purported laws of culture and other broad generalizations that among social scientists generally they gained the reputation of being, in Murdock's (1957:251) words, "a detestable bunch of bubble-prickers."

In the midst of this anti-evolutionist desert an occasional lone voice cried out in seeming protest. Clark Wissler's (1923:247) was such a voice, venturing to affirm in 1923 that "all cultures but follow out their careers according to discernible laws." This lone voice, however, soon died without an echo.

Always much more inclined to look for regularities in culture than was Lowie, A. L. Kroeber wistfully looked forward to the day when cultural laws might be discovered, but he was far from optimistic that such a day would ever come. "It will be a great and intensely stimulating day in the course of human understanding," he wrote, "when we determine definable and measurable processes operating under precise laws in history and culture. But a realistic attitude compels us to admit that that millennium is not yet here" (Kroeber 1935:568).

At the time, Kroeber was not actively seeking "historical laws," regarding them as will-o'-the-wisps—worthy of pursuing, no doubt, but hardly about to be caught (Kroeber 1935:568). And when a few years later he did set out to find such laws—in his mammoth study *Configurations of Culture Growth*—he was forced to confess at the end of the book his considerable disappointment: "I see no evidence of any true law in the phenomena dealt with; nothing cyclical, regularly repetitive, or necessary" (Kroeber 1944:761).

In their joint monograph *Culture*, Kroeber teamed up with Clyde Kluckhohn in an encyclopedic survey of definitions of culture. In a concluding chapter to the volume in which they examined the whole field of anthropology, they were forced to conclude reluctantly that "we are still far from being able to state 'the laws of cultural development'" (Kroeber and Kluckhohn 1952:182).

Nevertheless, they held out some hope for the formulation of laws, but only of limited scope: "Culture may well yet reveal 'laws' similar to the 'laws' which the linguist calls sound shifts; only they will presumably be, like these, primarily relations of forms (synchronic or sequential), not laws of efficient causality" (Kroeber and Kluckhohn 1952:188–189). This all but echoed what they had said earlier in the book: "we do not anticipate the discovery of cultural laws that will conform to the type of those of classical mechanics" (Kroeber and Kluckhohn 1952:167).

What sorts of laws, then, might they be? In an afterthought, probably due more to Kluckhohn than to Kroeber, they stated: "So far as these laws are determinable for culture, the prospect seems to be that they will continue to reside largely if not wholly in the psychic or psychoanalytical level" (Kroeber and Kluckhohn 1952:189). So the ghost of Franz Boas had not really been laid to rest, but was still abroad in the land!

Although Boas, were he to entertain the thought of laws at all, preferred them on the psychological level, there were times, nonetheless, when he toyed with the notion of *cultural* laws. However, his statements on the subject were marked by a curious inconsistency. In 1896, in an article that marked the onset of anti-evolutionism in anthropology, Boas was still ready to concede that "laws exist which govern the development of society, [and] that they are applicable to our society as well as those of past time and of distant lands" (Boas 1896b:901). But there were to be twists and turns in the way he regarded this possibility.

In tracing the history of Boas' attitudes toward laws of culture, Lowie (1940c:598) noted that "As for laws, the supposed physicist masquerading in ethnographer's clothing has progressively turned his back upon them." After citing passages from Boas' earlier writings, such as the one quoted above, Lowie stated that "by 1920 the uniqueness of the several cultures is a dominant idea . . . ; and in 1932 culture appears so complex that any generalizations about it are either truisms or spurious" (Lowie 1940c:599). And then by 1936 Boas was convinced that "The data of ethnology are not of such character that they can be expressed by mathematical formulas" (Boas 1936:140).

But Boas was capable of surprises. Thus, in one remarkable passage that virtually takes one's breath away, we find him saying:

> the history of mankind shows us the grand spectacle of the grouping of man in units of ever increasing size. . . . Notwithstanding all temporary revolutions and the shattering of large units for the time being, the progress in the direction of unification has been so regular and so marked that we must needs conclude that the tendencies which have swayed this development in the past will govern our history in the future. . . . The practical difficulties that seem to stand in the way of the formation of still larger units *count for naught before the inexorable laws of history.* (Boas 1945:100; emphasis mine)

What are we to conclude from this extraordinary passage? I would say that with his theoretical guard down, the force of great evolutionary trends was so strong that they could bear in even on a Franz Boas.

British Social Anthropology and Cultural Laws

The founders of British social anthropology, or at least of *functionalism*—Radcliffe-Brown and Malinowski—each had something to say about cultural laws. Years before they came on the scene, Herbert Spencer had drawn a distinction between two types of scientific laws: those of *coexistence* and those of *sequence*. It was laws of the former type that the two British functionalists seemed to envision.

Radcliffe-Brown (1937:23) gave a clear indication of this when he cited as "a very typical natural law: Every male lion has a mane." (One may ask, of course, if this is not part of the descriptive definition of lions rather than a law about them.) In his own field, social anthropology, Radcliffe-Brown proposed two laws. First, in 1929, he wrote that he "was led to formulate the following law: 'Any object or event which has important effects upon the well-being (material or spiritual) of a society or any thing which stands for or represents any such object or event, tends to become an object of the ritual attitude" (Radcliffe-Brown 1929:9). Then, two years later, on the basis of his fieldwork among the Australian aborigines, he formulated "an important principle" that he was ready to call "a universal sociological law," namely, that "in certain specific conditions a society has need to provide itself with a segmentary organization" (Radcliffe-Brown 1931a:441).

These proposed laws (if laws they be) were essentially laws of *coexistence*. As for laws of *sequence*, Radcliffe-Brown was highly skeptical that there were any to be found. Thus, in discussing attempts to make historical reconstructions, he remarked that "to establish any probability for such conjectures we should need to have a knowledge of the laws of social development which we certainly do not possess and . . . which I do not think we shall ever attain" (Radcliffe-Brown 1941:1).

Malinowski was perhaps a bit more receptive to the concept of cultural laws. For example, in 1937 he wrote that he was "still convinced that the search for general laws of cultural process . . . will remain the scientific task of anthropology" (Malinowski 1937:xxi). But, like Radcliffe-Brown, he believed that such laws were likely to be laws of coexistence. Accordingly, he wrote that any "laws of cultural process" would be "valid generalizations as to the mutual dependence of the various aspects of culture" (Malinowski 1937:xxxiii). And again, he remarked that "functional anthropology . . . holds that the cultural process is subject to laws and that the laws are to be found in the function of the real elements of culture" (Malinowski 1931:625).

Years later, E. E. Evans-Pritchard (1969:47) summed up the matter of cultural laws and how they stood in the eyes of British functionalists: "The search for diachronic laws was . . . to be abandoned in a search for synchronic laws." It was clear, then, that if laws of cultural *evolution* were to be found, it would not be by British anthropologists. Even the formulation of laws of coexistence, that is, of synchronic laws, systematically relating one aspect of culture to another, seemed, to Evans-Pritchard, a chimera. "I do not think," he wrote, "that there is any anthropologist anywhere who would seriously maintain that up to the present time any sociological laws have been discovered" (Evans-Pritchard 1951:117).

S. F. Nadel found the concept of cultural evolution too distant and too encompassing to be of much practical use. His sentiments on this score were probably shared by most of his British colleagues:

> The truth of the matter is that evolution belongs to those all-embracing concepts which, though inescapable, are too remote from the concrete problems of empirical inquiry to be of much use in solving them. We need the concept of evolution, as it were, to satisfy our philosophical conscience; but the 'laws' of evolution are of too huge a scale to help us in understanding the behaviour of the Toms, Dicks, and Harrys among societies and cultures, which after all is our main concern. (Nadel 1951:106)

And in his final assessment of the matter, Nadel (1951:106) concluded that "Perhaps, indeed, there are no particular 'laws' of evolution but only one 'law'—or postulate, if you like—that there *is* evolution."

American Anthropologists and Cultural Laws

On this side of the Atlantic, a similar skepticism, if not outright disbelief, continued to reign regarding laws of culture. David Bidney seemed to attribute the impossibility of formulating such laws to the stubborn intractability of historical evidence. Anthropologists "who are seeking for a universal natural history of society and culture subject to natural law," he wrote, "simply are not reckoning with the empirical facts of history" (Bidney 1953:263).

Whatever modest laws of culture had been tentatively proposed were generally derided as obvious and trivial. In this vein, the archaeologist Robert Wauchope (1966:33) was merely echoing a common lament when he wrote that "for a science which considers itself as mature as anthropology does nowadays, this discipline has produced precious few laws—and these chiefly on so broad a level as to be practically useless."

Even among those archaeologists who would style themselves "processualists" there was a certain skepticism regarding the existence of cultural laws. As far as Robert Wenke (1981:87) was concerned, "cultural evolutionism . . . has produced no laws or principles of consequence." And Kent Flannery (1999:19), although generally sympathetic to the cause of cultural evolutionism, nevertheless resisted the notion that any evolutionary generalizations could be phrased as cultural laws:

> Only archaeologists committed to logical positivism, for which physics and chemistry provide the model for science, seek explanation [of cultural phenomena] in 'covering laws.' . . . Archaeologists using 'systems' or 'ecosystems' approaches [instead,] do so precisely because they do not believe in covering laws of human behaviour. . . . Evolutionary archaeology, like palaeontology, leads to 'historical narrative explanation' rather than covering laws.

Still, the hope remained. Walter Goldschmidt (1966:4), for example, who might be considered a member of the wave of "neo-evolutionists" that followed in the wake of Leslie White, while admitting that "social anthropologists have not established any laws of social behavior, as they boldly set out to do," nevertheless felt that the pursuit of such laws should be a "continuing ambition of all scientific endeavor."

This goal was very much in front of Julian Steward when, in 1949, he wrote his landmark article "Cultural Causality and Law," whose very title bore the magic word. He ruefully admitted, though, that in the intellectual climate of the day "it is considered somewhat rash to mention causality, let alone 'law'" (Steward 1949:1). Although Steward proposed no specific laws in that article, he nonetheless argued that the occurrence of parallel, independent developments among the world's earliest civilizations argued for the existence of some underlying lawlike processes. Thus he continued to insist that "It is certainly a worthy objective to seek universal laws of culture change" (Steward 1955:18).

To the familiar objections that "historical reconstructions" were problematical, and even perilous, Steward's (1937:88) reply was that "it is difficult to see how historical reconstructions can be eschewed if one of the objectives of anthropology be the discovery of cultural laws, for a law states a sequence of cause and effect, which obviously requires time for operation."

Six years before the publication of Steward's benchmark article, Leslie White had proposed what came to be called White's Law, namely, a proposition relating cultural development to energy utilization. As we previously noted, the law states that "culture evolves as the amount of energy harnessed per capita per year is increased, or as the efficiency of the instrumental means of putting the energy to work is increased" (White 1949b:368–369). Significant parts of White's writings were devoted to advancing and defending this proposition (e.g., 1943, 1949b:363–369, 1959:39–57, 285–289, 1987:215–221).

An important issue raised in connection to this was: To what extent do general laws apply to individual cases? In one of his articles, Steward (1953a:318) insisted that "White's law of energy . . . can tell us nothing about the development . . . of individual cultures." And White (1945b:346) himself seemed to agree, affirming that "the evolutionist's formulas . . . are not applicable to the culture history of tribes and were not intended for this purpose."

But can this position really be sustained? If a law is a law, does it not apply, in some manner at least, to all particular cases, or to a large proportion of them? Can any case be said to be *immune* from the operation of a general law? If the law is an inductive generalization, is it not made up of its combined manifestations in a whole host of cases?

In 1960, Betty Meggers, a former student of White's, argued precisely this in an article entitled "The Law of Cultural Evolution as a Practical Research Tool": "It will be the purpose of this paper," she wrote, "to dissent from the view that evolutionary theory has only limited and generalized applicability and to suggest how it can be used as a guide in understanding the dynamics of individual cultures" (Meggers 1960:302). And she proceeded to show, for example, how the greater energy yield of wet rice cultivation over that of wild rice gathering had led to a marked elaboration in the culture of the Tanala of Madagascar once they had made the transition from one to the other in their mode of subsistence (Meggers 1960:308–310).

Marvin Harris also argued that any general law, such as White's energy law purported to be, should manifest itself in particular cases. "Does the law of gravitation," he asked, "tell us nothing about particulars? When one predicts a particular eclipse on a particular planet of a particular sun by a particular moon, has this no relation to the general law?" (Harris 1968:649). And he went on to suggest a rephrasing of White's "alleged" law that he thought would raise it to "genuine nomothetic status": "When the ratio of technological efficiency in food production (calorie output per calorie input per total man-hours of production) exceeds 20:1, the probability that stratified endogamous descent groups will be found is greater than chance" (Harris 1968:650). Somehow, it is hard to escape the feeling here that a parody was intended. Or if not a parody, a *reductio ad absurdum*.

(In passing, it may be of some interest to point out that while White's Law appears to be true, its *converse* is not. That is to say, while cultures *do* evolve as they come to harness greater amounts of energy per capita per year, they may also do so *without* harnessing more energy per capita. The Aztecs, for example, had evolved a far more complex culture than the Kuikuru, inhabitants of a typical Amazonian village, even though the Aztecs' per-capita harnessing of energy was no greater than that of the Kuikuru. Lacking draft animals, both societies had only the energy of the human body and that of fire to draw on, but no other. It was through the massing of far larger numbers of people, and organizing and directing their labor toward activities above and beyond subsistence needs—toward culture building, in other words—that permitted the Aztecs to erect and maintain an imposing empire, while the Kuikuru remained a simple autonomous village.)

Leslie White formulated another law that has remained far less well known than his "energy law." This was a law that he proposed to account for the order in which the sciences had evolved. This law was the most significant contribution to the problem of the "filiation of the sciences" since the days of Auguste Comte and Herbert Spencer. The law, which remained unnamed, was set forth by White (1949a:69) in the following words: "Science emerges first and matures fastest in fields where the determinants of human behavior are weakest and most remote; conversely, science appears latest and matures slowest in those portions of our experience where the most intimate and powerful determinants of our behavior are found." In support of this principle White noted that astronomy was the first science to appear, while culturology (his term for the science of culture) was the last.

The notion that the development of culture exhibited such regularities that it should be possible to ferret out and formulate them remained prominently in the minds of White's students. Thus in that small classic *Evolution and Culture* (1960), two of the four contributors proposed laws of culture. Best known of these is Elman Service's Law of Evolutionary Potential. As Service (1960:97) stated it, "The more specialized and adapted a form in a given evolutionary stage, the smaller is its potential for passing to the next stage." Service proceeded to point out that the corollary to this law is that the next major new development in culture is most likely to be made by a society other than the one currently in the cultural vanguard. Thorstein Veblen, who had anticipated Service in propounding this law, had labeled the first element of it "the penalty of taking the lead," whereas Leon Trotsky, who had also preceded Service in formulating it, had referred to the second part of it as "the privilege of historic backwardness" (Service 1960:99).

The second law proposed in *Evolution and Culture* is what David Kaplan, its author, called The Law of Cultural Dominance. Kaplan noted that biologists had made use of the concept of "dominant types." In the organic realm, first came the Age of Reptiles, during which reptiles were the dominant form of land animal. They were followed by mammals, which "represented a more progressive step in evolution and were able to supplant the reptiles as the dominant land group" (Kaplan 1960:71). In the realm of culture, Kaplan argued, the same concept of dominance could profitably be applied. Various types or forms of culture could be distinguished, such as agriculture-based Neolithic, the pre-industrial state, industrially based Western culture, and, Kaplan (1960:73) noted, "Each successive higher culture type has tended to spread farther and faster than previous types."

The actual Law of Cultural Dominance he formulated goes as follows: "that cultural system which more effectively exploits the energy resources of a given environment will tend to spread in that environment at the expense of less effective systems" (Kaplan 1960:75). Clearly, then, Kaplan's law dovetailed nicely with White's law of energy utilization.

Kaplan pointed out an interesting corollary of his law: a seemingly contradictory trend toward heterogeneity on the one hand and a corresponding trend toward global homogeneity on the other. He explained it in these words:

> The contradiction, however, is more apparent than real. Certainly it is true that each successive culture type exhibiting general dominance has become increasingly heterogeneous; it is organizationally more complex, with more parts and subparts, and with a greater functional differentiation between them. At the same time the potential range of dominance of each successive culture type has been correspondingly increased. In its spread, the higher type has been able to dominate and reduce the variety of cultural systems by transforming them into copies, more or less exact, of itself. Thus, cultural evolution has moved simultaneously in two directions: on the one hand there is increasing heterogeneity of the higher cultural type; and on the other hand there is an increasing homogeneity of culture as the diversity of culture types is reduced. (Kaplan 1960:74)

For almost half a century most American anthropologists dismissed the quest for laws of culture, often denying the possibility of their existence. It should be no surprise, then, that only a handful of them should have been proposed. But, to quote E. B. Tylor again, "if law is anywhere, it is everywhere," and thus there is a reasonable probability that more will be found if diligently searched for. Nor need they be "laws" so general and obvious as to be nothing more than trivial truisms.

A law of considerable subtlety came to light as an offshoot of a study of cultural evolution by means of scale analysis (Carneiro 1968). This study yielded a sequence that arranged certain culture traits in their relative order of appearance among societies generally. For example, it was found that the corvée had developed after chieftainship, and that a code of laws had developed after the corvée. These were, however, traits between which there was

a good deal of "evolutionary distance." (The "evolutionary distance" between traits is measured not in terms of time, but by the number of "intervening" traits that arose in the interval between the development of the
lower trait and the higher one.)

Of course the order of appearance of certain traits between which there
is considerable evolutionary distance is obvious enough so that it might
have been surmised without the need of any formal method of discovery.
But the study referred to here was not limited to such traits. It included a
number of traits *close* enough in evolutionary distance so that their relative
order of appearance was neither uniform nor immediately obvious. And indeed, some of these traits, such as the corvée and full-time craft specialists,
were so close together in their evolutionary appearance that, in some cases,
they appeared to have arisen in the *reverse* order of the more common one.
The degree of regularity in the development of traits in this sequence could
be ascertained and expressed in a quasi-mathematical way (Carneiro
1968:366–367). Indeed, it became apparent that the relationship involved
was so distinct and consistent that it could be stated as a law of cultural evolution: "The degree of regularity in the relative order of development of any
two traits in a sequence is directly proportional to the evolutionary distance
between them; the greater the evolutionary distance, the greater the regularity" (Carneiro 2000:251; see also 1968:363).

Thus, for example, for the two traits being close together in evolutionary
distance, it appears that while most societies seem to have developed full-
time craft specialists *before* the corvée, a certain number of them developed
these two traits in the reverse order. On the other hand, if we take two traits
between which there is a great deal of evolutionary distance—say, special
religious practitioners and the presence of an empire—the former developed before the latter with absolute regularity.

The laws cited above are *diachronic* ones, laws of cultural *evolution*. But
some of the generalizations proposed as cultural laws are *synchronic,* or laws
of co-occurrence. As we have seen, the possibility of synchronic laws was
much more congenial to British social anthropologists than was the possible existence of diachronic ones. For example, Sol Tax, a former student of
Radcliffe-Brown, was ready to countenance one. Thus, in speaking of certain California tribes, he wrote: "If there were no natural laws governing
culture, how could the fact that kinship terms *do* go together with certain
social structures in a given number of these [California] tribes, and also in
tribes three thousand miles away, be explained?" (Tax 1955a:11).

The anthropologist most closely associated with attempts to relate types
of kinship nomenclature to particular features of social organization was
George P. Murdock. Near the end of his volume *Social Structure,* Murdock

(1949:259) declared that "cultural forms in the field of social organization reveal a degree of regularity and of conformity to scientific law not significantly inferior to that found in the so-called natural sciences."

In the preceding pages of his book, after presenting repeated instances, in tabular form, of correlations between types of kinship systems and forms of social structures, Murdock remarked that: "Although the above results are perhaps unprecedented in social science, they by no means do justice to the actual possibilities. It must be remembered that multiple factors are operative in every instance, but that in most of our theorems we have isolated only a single factor for analysis. If several factors are taken into consideration at the same time, the magnitude of the coefficients rises appreciably, and usually also their reliability" (Murdock 1949:178–179). And he proceeded to demonstrate this contention with a specific example.

Earlier (on page 153), Murdock had found a correlation of +.68 between neolocal residence and the use of lineal kinship terms for the trio of relatives: mother, mother's sister, and father's sister, as well as a correlation of +.56 between the presence of the isolated nuclear family and the use of lineal terminology for the same set of kin. (In kinship terminology of the lineal type, such as our own, mother is called by a distinct term, not applied to any other relative, whereas mother's sister and father's sister are classed together and called by a term equivalent to "aunt.")

Murdock continued: "If we combine these two factors [neolocal residence and the isolated nuclear family] and add two other characteristic features of our own social structure—strict monogamy and the absence of exogamous unilinear kin groups—we arrive at the results shown in Table 54" (1949:179).

Table 54 shows that the correlation of lineal kinship terminology for mother, mother's sister, and father's sister with the combination of monogamy, isolated nuclear families, neolocal residence, and the absence of exogamous lineages or sibs is an impressive +.91. Murdock concludes by saying: "Similar results are obtainable from an exceedingly large number of similar combinations" (Murdock 1949:179).

It is not possible to say *a priori* just how high coefficients of this sort can be raised if still other relevant factors are included in the correlation. Even with the most repeated and painstaking refinements it may never be possible to achieve correlations of +1.00. Continued ignorance of some of the relevant variables (despite our best efforts to discover them) and, especially, the existence of a time lag between cause and effect may preclude the formulation of statements of association that hold without any exceptions. Perhaps many of the generalizations about cultural phenomena in which we will come to have the greatest confidence may never be verified to a degree higher than that represented by a coefficient of, say, +.95.

Such propositions, though not laws in the sense of being statements of absolutely invariant relations, might nevertheless be considered "statistical laws." Nor would this necessarily diminish their status, for as the philosopher of science Hans Reichenbach (1951:122) pointed out, "statistical laws are not 'less dignified' than causal laws—they are more general forms, among which the causal law represents the special form of statistical correlations holding for 100 percent of the cases."

"Moreover," Reichenbach (1951:122) adds, "causal laws, at least in quantitative form, are never found to hold strictly in observational terms. We do not observe a 100 percent validity: we notice exceptions. Causal laws are introduced by a process of schematization; we assume them to hold for ideal conditions, knowing that the inevitable 'errors of observation' will lead to deviations from the ideal." And in addition to 'errors of observation,' the 'interference' of a second law may prevent the full expression of the first one. This occurs, for example, when centrifugal force keeps a person riding in a loop-the-loop at a county fair from falling out of a gondola car despite being suspended upside down. The law of gravity has not ceased to operate; it has merely been temporarily overridden.

The Comparative Method and Its Application

Like any other scientific law, a "law of culture" is meant to apply to cultures generally, or at least to a significant proportion of them. Thus we would not be ready to accept as a law a proposition that applied to only one group, say, the Kwakiutl, or even to all Northwest Coast tribes, but did not hold outside of them.

To be regarded as a general law of culture, a proposition needs to apply to most societies, if not all. Or, to put it more precisely, it must apply to all those societies existing under the conditions specified by the law. This means of course that, being an inductive proposition, a cultural law would have to be based on an examination of a substantial number of societies. Or at least—since the universe of cultures is so vast—to a representative sample of them. It was a recognition of this fact that led the early evolutionists, intent as they were on generalizing about cultures, to make use of the *comparative method*. Thus for the purpose of writing *The Principles of Sociology*, Herbert Spencer compiled such a large corpus of ethnographic and historical material that he had it published separately in the eight volumes of *Descriptive Sociology*.

Although there are various ways of applying the method, its common feature is the study of a broad range of societies whose cultural similarities and differences, along with the conditions of their existence, can be used to

test, and hopefully verify, general propositions. As we have seen, the nineteenth-century evolutionists, especially Tylor and Spencer, made extensive
use of the comparative method. But as the tide of anti-evolutionism began
to rise around the turn of the century, the method came under direct attack. In 1896, Franz Boas wrote that "The comparative method, notwith-
standing all that has been said and written in its praise, has been remarkably
barren of definite results, and I believe it will not become fruitful until we
renounce the vain endeavor to construct a uniform systematic history of
the evolution of culture" (Boas 1896b:908).

And the followers of Boas were not long in joining the chorus. Alexander
Goldenweiser (1933:76), for example, was critical of it because he felt that
the method "consists of tearing beliefs and customs from their historical
setting." And he further derided the method because, he alleged, it "consisted in the utilization of customs and ideas gathered from many places
and periods, to substantiate genetic [i.e., evolutionary] schemes arrived at
by speculation" (Goldenweiser 1933:125–126).

Well into the twentieth century the same criticism of the method continued to be voiced. Morris Opler (1963:160), for one, characterized "the old
comparative method" as "simply a busy search for plausible examples that
seem to favor a doctrine accepted in advance." Thus, according to Elman
Service (1968b:227), during the period of Boasian ascendancy "both evolutionary theory and the comparative method nearly perished from inatten-
tion." Robin Fox (2000:xxvi) concurred, saying that "The idea of 'reading
off' the past from the primitive present—the essential tool of the comparative method—has been . . . rejected for most of this century." And Alan
Dundes (1986:130) was led to conclude that "despite a series of essays paying lip service" to it, "the comparative method was essentially abandoned by
the majority of anthropologists by the middle of the twentieth century."

Among those essays paying "lip service" to the comparative method,
Dundes might have included those of Radcliffe-Brown, who repeatedly
sounded the same note: "if there is to be a natural science of human societies, its method will be the method of comparing, one with another, social
systems of different kinds" (Radcliffe-Brown 1957:38). And again, he asserted that "by comparing a sufficient number of diverse types we discover
uniformities that are still more general, and thus may reach to the discovery
of principles or laws that are universal in human society" (Radcliffe-Brown
1931b:162). And finally, "it is the wider application and the refinement of
the method of comparative sociology . . . that hold out the promise of a really scientific understanding of human society" (Radcliffe-Brown 1971:vii).

But Radcliffe-Brown's "lip service" went no further. Other than comparing the kinship systems of a few Australian aborigines, he never applied the

comparative method on a broad scale. One might even conjecture that in his repeated championing of the method he was subtly casting aspersions on his rival, Bronislaw Malinowski. Malinowski was known on occasion to try to generalize from his profound knowledge of Trobriand society to the rest of the primitive world. Without naming him directly, Radcliffe-Brown may nevertheless have had Malinowski in mind when he wrote: "One cannot make generalizations from one human society, no matter how well one knows that society. One cannot make valid generalizations about anything which is unique in the universe, about a class which has only one member" (Radcliffe-Brown 1957:38).

Despite Radcliffe-Brown's pronouncements, British social anthropology remained, for the most part, noncomparativist. To be sure, several African societies might be compared by different authors within the pages of a single book, as in Meyer Fortes and E. E. Evans-Pritchard's *African Political Systems* (1940). Nevertheless, British social anthropologists never attempted comparisons on a worldwide scale. Evans-Pritchard (1969:62) even tried to scotch the very idea of broad cross-cultural comparisons, at least those that had an evolutionary objective: "It must be said also that in recent decades even less has been attempted in the way of comparative developmental studies aiming at reaching general statements true of all, or most, societies; and one may be justifiably sceptical about whether they can be reached or, if they can, they will not prove to be so general as to be of little value."

The old familiar refrain! More vehement in his rejection of global comparisons was Edmund Leach, described by André Köbben (1970:585) as "A belligerent non comparativist." Said Leach (1965:299): "If I write a monograph on the Kachin (as I have done) and Murdock chooses (as he has done) to have that book treated as [if] it were a taxonomic description [for inclusion in his World Ethnographic Sample], he is acting within his rights, but from my point of view he is producing tabulated nonsense."

Although it was in the United States that the comparative method, after a long period of inanition, was finally resuscitated and started on its new career, voices from the Old World, other than Radcliffe-Brown's, had been calling for it from earlier in the twentieth century. Thus Edward Westermarck (1901:4), in the opening pages of his *History of Human Marriage*, wrote: "If, then, historical researches based on ethnography are to be crowned with success, the first condition is that there shall be a rich material. It is only by comparing a large number of facts that we may hope to find the cause or causes on which a social phenomenon is dependent."

And half a century later, the archaeologist V. Gordon Childe (1946:251) put it in fewer words: "the comparative method offers the brightest prospect for reaching general laws of the direction of historic progress." More recently, C. R. Hallpike (1988:14) has asserted even more simply, "Social anthropology is nothing if not comparative."

As employed by nineteenth-century anthropologists, the comparative method was used largely for evolutionary reconstructions. And the basis for its application toward that end was stated succinctly by Sir James Frazer (1913a:172): "as savage races are not all on the same plane, but have stopped or tarried at different points of the upward path, we can to a certain extent, by comparing them with each other, construct a scale of social progression and mark out roughly some of the stages on the long road that leads from savagery to civilization."

But as the comparative method began to be used again in midcentury, its proponents felt the need to justify and defend it. Thus in an article entitled "Anthropology as a Comparative Science," George P. Murdock (1957:249) assured his readers that "Whatever other method of investigation may be employed [by anthropologists] . . . the comparative method is indispensable." Alexander Alland argued that its use in anthropology was as valid and fruitful as in biology: "Just as biologists fill in their sketch of sequential development through the examination of living forms, anthropologists utilize material from less technologically developed living peoples." And speaking of his mentor, Radcliffe-Brown, and of his oft-repeated aim of establishing "a natural science of human societies," Fred Eggan (1957:ix) remarked that "Its development depends on the systematic comparison of societies."

To one of the objections often raised by opponents of the comparative method, such as Ruth Benedict with her insistence that societies were unique and therefore incommensurable, John W. M. Whiting (1970:293–294) was ready to supply an answer:

It is, of course, true that any individual case, be it a person or a society, is unique and, as a whole, incomparable with any other individual case. Scientific investigation, however, is based on the assumption that attributes of the whole can be abstracted and compared. Thus it is said that no two snowflakes are identical, and yet it is also a valid statement that snowflakes are hexagonal, white, and will melt in temperature above 32 Fahrenheit. Some investigators may be concerned with the beauty and intricacy of the crystalline pattern of each individual snowflake; others with discovering the general truths about snowflakes. Both are legitimate enterprises. . . .

To those who spoke of alleged misuses of the comparative method by the classical evolutionists, Marvin Harris (1968:155) replied: "there is no specific abuse of the comparative method which could justify the denial of the relevance of our ethnographic knowledge of contemporary pre-state societies to the task of unraveling the course of sociocultural evolution."

The Problem of Sampling

If the essence of the comparative method is to examine and compare the cultures of a large body of societies, the immediate practical question is, what constitutes an adequate sample of them, and how is it to be drawn? After all, if there are some 4,000 known human societies, that number is much too large to encompass in any single investigation. Some manageable portion of it has to be selected.

Both Herbert Spencer and E. B. Tylor used extensive samples of societies in their work. We get some notion of the societies in Spencer's sample by consulting the bibliography at the end of his *Principles of Sociology*. But in Tylor's case, we do not even know the names of the 200-odd societies he used in his famous article "On a Method of Investigating the Development of Institutions" (1889). In either Spencer's or Tylor's case, though, we know it was more likely to have been a "grab sample" than one selected according to specified principles.

The validity of the evolutionary conclusions Tylor drew from his study were immediately questioned by Francis Galton, who was in the audience when Tylor delivered his paper. Tylor's conclusions, Galton argued, could be accepted unequivocally only if the societies used in his study were *independent cases.* If Society B had borrowed Trait x from Society A, then the correlations Tylor had calculated were not firmly supported by the facts. In other words, if *diffusion* rather than *internal development* accounted for the presence of a certain trait among several societies, then those cases, taken by Tylor as verifying his hypothesis, could not truly be considered as having done so. This contamination of supposedly independent cases by the operation of diffusion was later christened "Galton's Problem" by Raoul Naroll.

So the adequacy of ethnographic sampling carried out for the purpose of making cross-cultural generalizations had been questioned from the very start.

A similar but much more stringent and valid concern was raised by Edward Westermarck when he objected to the excessive reliance placed by Émile Durkheim (1954) and his followers on a study of Australian aborigines when generalizing about the religious beliefs of primitive peoples as a whole. Westermarck's remarks are worth quoting at some length:

> As for the French method, I cannot help saying that there are disquieting signs of a tendency to expansion beyond its legitimate limits. Its followers have not

always been satisfied with restricting their conclusions to social phenomena belonging to the same area, but have regarded their method as a direct means of arriving at results of a much wider scope.

Thus Professor Durkheim, in his book on the totemic system in Australia with the significant title "Les formes élémentaires de la vie religieuse," confidently asserts that this system contains "all the great ideas and all the principal ritual attitudes which are at the bottom even of the most advanced religions"; and he then proceeds to a discussion of religion in general, in the belief that if you have carefully studied the religion of one people only, you are better able to lay down the main principles of the religious life than if you follow the comparative method of a Tylor or Frazer. It almost seems as though some kind of sociological intuition were to take the place of comparative induction. (Westermarck 1921:I, 21)

In their classic study, Hobhouse, Wheeler, and Ginsberg (1930) made use of a much larger and more diverse sample than that employed by Durkheim. Still, it greatly oversampled the Australian aborigines. Nevertheless, this did not necessarily vitiate the conclusions reached on the basis of that large and unrepresentative sample. So keen and critical a student of statistical methods in cross-cultural research as Harold Driver (1973:329–330) observed that "Although the sample [of some 600 societies] has been criticized on the grounds that almost all the lower hunters are located in Australia and the highest hunters in North America, most of its generalizations about evolutionary trends are accepted today and have been confirmed by later research."

Perhaps the most striking feature of comparative ethnology from about midcentury on has been the development of a sample of societies that would allow the soundest possible inferences to be made about whatever theories were being tested. Now, it is worth pausing and taking note of the fact that the two principal worldwide samples available today—the Human Relations Area Files and the Standard Cross Cultural Sample—have an almost unbroken pedigree, stretching back to Herbert Spencer.

In preparing to write his magnum opus, *The Principles of Sociology*, Spencer began gathering cultural information from many societies. As he explained in his autobiography, "this compilation of materials was entered upon solely to facilitate my own work" (Spencer 1926:II, 261). Over the years, however, Spencer began to regard this collection of data rather differently: "when some of the tables [into which he had apportioned his data] had been filled up and it became possible to appreciate the effect of thus having presented at one view the whole of the essential phenomena presented by each society, the fact dawned upon me that the materials as prepared were of too much value to let them lie idle after having been used by myself only. I therefore decided upon publishing them for general use" (quoted in Duncan 1904:I, 186–187). Thus was born Spencer's multivolume work, *Descriptive Sociology.*

Eight volumes of *Descriptive Sociology* were published during Spencer's lifetime and another seven after his death. But, as comparative work in anthropology languished during the first decades of the twentieth century, so did the large quarto volumes of *Descriptive Sociology,* which remained unused and virtually unknown. So much so that the Dutch sociologist S. R. Steinmetz (1898–1899:43n.) was led to lament: "The little use which has been made of this immense collection of well established and conveniently arranged facts is a grave reproach to our science."

However, *Descriptive Sociology* did not disappear into total oblivion. Some recollection and appreciation of it remained. Thus George P. Murdock (1954:16) wrote of it: "This work, so little known among sociologists that the author has encountered few who have even heard of it, inaugurated a commendable effort to organize and classify systematically the cultural data of all the peoples of the world for the advancement of cross-cultural research, and thus clearly foreshadowed the development of the present Human Relations Area Files."

There were, however, some intermediate links between *Descriptive Sociology* and the Human Relations Area Files. As we have seen, William Graham Sumner was so impressed by Spencer's work that he began his own mammoth compilation of cultural data from societies around the world. And his faithful student and follower, Albert G. Keller, published in the four volumes of *The Science of Society,* if not a complete list of the societies in Sumner's sample, at least the fruits of their joint cross-cultural research based on it.

As a student of Keller's at Yale, George P. Murdock was, naturally enough, brought up on a heavy diet of cross-cultural research. In fact, his contribution to the Keller *Festschrift* was a cross-cultural study of matrilineal and patrilineal institutions employing a sample of approximately 230 societies (Murdock 1937b:460). This sample, said Murdock, was "selected by the author to represent as adequately as possible the whole range of known civilizations" (Murdock 1937b:460). Nevertheless, Murdock, like Sumner, neither listed all the societies in his sample, nor indicated the method by which he had chosen them. Still, he was well launched on his career of cross-cultural comparisons. A few years earlier he had published *Our Primitive Contemporaries* (1934), an introductory textbook containing accounts of some two dozen societies selected from around the world and running the gamut of cultural complexity from the Tasmanians to the Incas.

Then in 1937, with his sample of 230 societies most likely serving as the nucleus, Murdock began the Cross-Cultural Survey. In the preface to his book *Social Structure,* he (1949:vii) explained:

> The research technique upon which the volume depends, and without which it would not have been undertaken, is that of the Cross-Cultural Survey. Initiated in 1937 as part of the integrated program of research in the social sciences conducted by the Institute of Human Relations at Yale University, the Cross-Cultural Survey has built up a complete file of geographical, social, and cultural information, extracted in full from the sources and classified by subject, on some 150 human societies, historical and contemporary as well as primitive. From these files it is possible to secure practically all the existing information on particular topics in any of the societies covered in an insignificant fraction of the time required for comparable library research.

The Cross-Cultural Survey later changed its name to the Human Relations Area Files (HRAF). Murdock continued to expand the number of societies in the HRAF sample up to some 250. But what seemed to him at the time to be a representative sample of world cultures grew less so the more he studied the matter of representativeness. Indeed, he later wrote that this sample of 250 societies, "when judged by current standards, was so obviously defective in several important respects that it can be excused only as a pioneer effort" (Murdock and White 1969:332).

Years later, under the leadership of Clellan S. Ford, Raoul Naroll, and Melvin Ember, the HRAF came to encompass additional cultures; as of 1990 it totaled 335 (Ember 1991:493).

In 1960 Murdock moved from Yale to the University of Pittsburgh, where, in collaboration with Douglas White, he continued to pursue cross-cultural sampling. There, he instituted a new "World Ethnographic Sample," later rechristened the "Standard Cross-Cultural Sample," which began with a sample of 565 societies (Whiting 1986:684) but came to include more than 1,250. These societies, Murdock wrote, constituted "a very high proportion of all those whose cultures have been adequately described," every effort having been expended "to make certain that no major cultural variant has been overlooked" (Murdock and White 1969:331). This led to the establishment of the Cross-Cultural Cumulative Coding Center (CCCCC) at Pittsburgh in 1968 (Murdock and White 1969:329).

It should be noted that the HRAF and the CCCCC differ in a significant way. The HRAF consists of complete and original unsummarized text files, derived from primary ethnographic sources, and apportioned in the files according to a set of standardized categories covering all aspects of culture.

In the CCCCC, on the other hand, "the coding was not of subject matter, as in HRAF, but of specific culture traits. Results of this work were published in final form as *Atlas of World Cultures*. . . . Its purpose was to allow for quick comparative studies on a large number of precoded topics" (Goodenough 1996:278).

Originally, the 565 societies in Murdock's World Ethnographic Sample were coded for thirty variables, but by the time the sample had grown to more than 1,200 societies, the number of coded variables had increased to more than 100 (Whiting 1986:684). All this material was published as installments of the "Ethnographic Atlas" and appeared in successive issues of the journal *Ethnology*, which Murdock had started at Pittsburgh.

After years of studying the problem, Murdock concluded that the best sampling procedure was to divide the world into "cultural types." Writing jointly with Douglas White, he noted that "Our own research indicates that a carefully drawn sample of around 200 cases essentially exhausts the universe of known and adequately described culture types" (Murdock and White 1969:337). These types were contained within specified geographic regions. Murdock (1966:99) explained the justification for this procedure as follows:

> the universe from which a cross-cultural sample should be properly drawn is not that of all known cultures [that is, societies] but that of all known cultural types. A random sample of all known cultures would result in a heavy overrepresentation of such regions as the Great Basin of North America where numerous local variants of essentially similar cultures have been systematically recorded. What is needed is the kind of sample which will reflect the distribution of cultural variations over the surface of the earth. . . . Each major variant of culture, whether it includes one or many adequately described individual cultures, should have an equal chance of being represented in any sample. This can best be accomplished . . . by classifying the known cultures of the world into types, i.e., clusters of similar and related cultures.

The result was "a representative sample of the world's known and well-described cultures, 186 in number, each 'pinpointed' to the smallest identifiable subgroup of the society in question at a specific point in time" (Murdock and White 1969:329).

One of the "vexing problems" Murdock had to deal with in selecting his cross-cultural sample was to be sure to include "a number of societies that will adequately represent the entire range of known cultural variation," but at the same time to "eliminate as far as possible the number of cases where similarities are presumably due to the historical influence of diffusion or common derivation" (Murdock and White 1969:331). And as a way out of the difficulty, Murdock referred to several methods proposed by others for coping with "Galton's Problem."

Together, the HRAF and the CCCCC constitute a tremendous corpus of highly distilled and organized cultural information about the distinctive cultures of the world. But, we may ask, what has been done with this material? A great deal of cross-cultural research has been carried out using these two reservoirs as sources of data—nearly 1,000 of them, in fact (Ember and Ember 2001:10)—but precious few of these studies have been along evolutionary lines. John Whiting (1970:287) was right when he wrote that most cross-cultural research "has drawn upon the theory of general behavior science rather than that of cultural evolution." Carol Ember and David Levinson (1991:80) confirmed this, stating that "Cross-culturalists do not generally assume that synchronic associations can lead to inferences about specific evolutionary developments."

Indeed, many of the doubters appear to agree with Norman Yoffee (1993:63) that "No processes of long-term changes in the past can be adequately modeled on the basis of short-term observations in the present." Bruce Trigger (1984:294) appeared to agree when he declared that "The duty of evolutionary theory is to explain what has really happened in the past, not to construct hypothetical schemes of development using ethnographic data, which are clearly insufficient for the task."

Michael Shanks and Christopher Tilley (1987:95), for their part, railed against the "sledge hammer of cross-cultural generalizations," fearing that, in Robert Wenke's (1999:334) words, the "traditional methods of cross-cultural comparisons [would] pulverize meaning and significance in history."

Even Kent Flannery (1972a:404), in an early article, was disinclined to accept evolutionary reconstructions based on a synchronic study of a sample of ethnographically known societies, calling such reconstructions "just-so stories."

Still, a few determined souls, unintimidated by such criticisms, have tried to tease diachronic conclusions out of synchronic data. The first and best-known attempt to do so in anthropology's modern era was that of Raoul Naroll (1956), and the essence of it has already been described. While Naroll's study focused on the differences in complexity of the essentially contemporaneous societies in his sample, its diachronic implications were clear: These societies could be thought of as lying along an evolutionary continuum. The complexity of the various societies in the sample was not something fixed and enduring, but had been acquired by them, to different degrees, over the course of their evolution.

In another study, Melvin Ember (1963), using a cross-cultural sample of twenty-five societies, attempted to find what correlation there was between a society's economic system and its political system. Plotting on a graph the number of different types of political officials (his "governmental" measure) against the size of the largest community in the society (his "economic" measure), he came to the following conclusion:

> The above curve [on the graph] supports Naroll's (1956) hypothesis that the evolution of human social systems follows the same allometric type of growth pattern as the evolution of biological systems. The development of one part of the system relative to another is such that the line of their combined growth is a curve which slopes increasingly toward the vertical. Or, in other words, the complexity of social systems, like the complexity of biological systems, seems to increase geometrically. (Ember 1963:244)

The study just cited is actually more in the nature of a virtuoso performance in the statistical manipulation of cross-cultural data than it is an example of an evolutionary study. Or at least one can say that the discussion of evolutionary processes in this study is limited in scope and greatly subordinated to an exposition of the statistical techniques by means of which the results were obtained.

Another attempt using synchronic cross-cultural data, but aimed more fully and directly at extracting and interpreting evolutionary regularities, was one referred to earlier involving the use of Guttman scale analysis (Carneiro 1968, 1970b). This study employed a worldwide sample of 100 societies that was not drawn from either the HRAF or the CCCCC. No attempt was made to select a random sample of societies because in this type of evolutionary study randomness is not a prime consideration. What did matter was that the societies in the sample should span a wide range of cultural evolution, from simple bands to complex states and empires, with the emphasis on higher cultures. This was desirable, indeed essential, so that the relative order of development of the more advanced traits used in the study could be determined. Thus it was deemed advisable to "oversample" the more complex cultures, since only by having a relatively large number of them in the sample would it be possible to determine the relative order of appearance of traits such as taxation and the corvée, or markets and full-time craft specialists.

The number of other attempts that have been made to apply Guttman scale analysis to a sample of societies with the intent of discovering underlying evolutionary patterns has been minimal. Among these few we can cite a study by Brent Berlin and Paul Kay (1969), whose results surprised even the most persuaded evolutionist. Berlin and Kay showed that there was a surprising degree of regularity in the way in which societies, by and large, have developed basic color terms (see also Carneiro 1974:103).

In 1947, Radcliffe-Brown (1947:81) made the reasonable forecast that "By comparing societies of different kinds, and societies in different stages," one might be able to "ascertain what traits of size, structure, function, etc., are habitually associated." Years later, his former student Fred Eggan (1965:368) made an effort to put his mentor's prediction into practice. Having applied to the social organization of the Western Pueblos what he called the "method of controlled comparison," in which he compared societies "on a smaller scale and with a greater control over the frame of comparison" than in some of the global comparative studies then being attempted, Eggan (1965:368) remarked that "The present writer . . . has attempted a comparative analysis of social and cultural systems on the model provided by Radcliffe-Brown, but with a greater concern for change over time" than his mentor had had in mind.

Eggan's findings were diachronic rather than merely synchronic. Still, these changes had only a modest time depth. What he was presenting, then, was really more history than evolution. Or, if it was evolution at all, it was micro- rather than macro-evolution.

The theoretical climate in anthropology over the last decade or two has been such that the number of bold and ambitious evolutionary studies attempted has been limited. But all is not denial or retrenchment. There are some promising signs as well. It seems appropriate, therefore, to turn at this point to a survey of the evolutionary landscape in anthropology at the close of the twentieth century and to see just where the study of cultural evolution can be said to stand.

12

Current Issues and Attitudes in the Study of Cultural Evolution

New and Lingering Opposition to Cultural Evolutionism

It is not a simple matter to characterize the present condition of evolutionary studies. There are too many crosscurrents and back eddies in present-day theory to allow this to be done with a few strokes. The fact is that attitudes toward, and applications of, evolutionary theory in cultural anthropology cover the entire spectrum of opinion—from outright hostility and rejection ("neo-anti-evolutionism") to warm acceptance and fruitful application.

It may be best to begin our survey by considering that body of thought in the discipline that is most opposed to—or perhaps least concerned with—evolutionism, and to proceed from there toward the opposite end of the spectrum, where evolutionism is most ardently embraced.

After wandering in the arid wastelands of particularism, relativism, and anti-evolutionism for many decades, it was ethnology ("social anthropology" to some) that, in the 1950s, resuscitated and reanimated cultural evolutionary theory. But then in the 1970s, as Kent Flannery (1994:113) has remarked, there was a sharp turn in the road: "social anthropology went its own way again—everything became hermeneutics and humanistic, and evolutionists were considered vulgar materialists." More and more ethnologists began turning their backs on cultural evolutionism and busying themselves with narrower, more subjective fields of inquiry, such as "values" and "meaning." But the dark cloud that brought with it hermeneutics and humanistics foreshadowed an even darker sky out of which came the cloudburst of postmodernism.

One of the principal pillars on which the old Boasian anti-evolutionism had rested was cultural relativism. Then, with the reemergence of evolutionism, relativism was trimmed down to its proper size. However, with the advent of postmodernism, cultural relativism has roared back with a vengeance. Indeed, Boasian cultural relativism, compared to its new postmodern apparition, was as the chicken pox to the Black Death.

More traditional anthropologists have bridled at the language of the postmodernists, who not only make free and easy use of words like *alterity, reflexivity,* and *personhood,* but see no reason to stop short of *paratactic, apoplanesis,* and *hypotyposis* (see Carneiro 1995:8). Discourse of this sort Robert Murphy labeled "egg-head rap-talk" (Murphy 1994), and Marvin Harris called its practitioners "untrained would-be novelists and ego-tripping narcissists afflicted with congenital logo-diarrhea" (Harris 1994).

But though profligate with terminology, postmodernists are niggardly when it comes to scientific concepts. For them, there are no classes, no types, no categories. These are all "Western hegemonic concepts" and are to be spurned. And since societies cannot be validly compared, since no society can be said to be more advanced or complex, more heterogeneous or differentiated, than any other, how can they possibly be considered to represent way stations in an orderly evolutionary sequence?

All of this led Lewis Binford to lament: "Anthropology today is in worse shape than it was when I was a student. . . . It has gone more and more into the relativistic camp and more and more into . . . weird humanism—'We're just appreciating the glories of mankind in its variability'—and nobody's trying to explain anything" (quoted in Renfrew 1987:689).

In more measured tones, Kent Flannery (1998:xvii) observed that a number of his colleagues "have fallen prey to archaeology's latest messianic cult, that anti-science, anti-materialist, anti-comparativist movement calling itself 'post-processualism.' For hard cord post-processualists . . . the past is merely a 'text' with no objective reality, to be interpreted intuitively." Perhaps in this number Flannery meant to include the archaeologist Mark Leone, for whom "Scientific methods of study tend to demean the culture of others, as well as the others themselves, by measuring, comparing, objectifying, and denaturing them" (quoted in Thomas 1998:83).

Wrong-headed as it was, at least this critique was intelligible. But what was one to make of Shanks and Tilley's (1992:116) assertion that the past, what archaeologists study, "is a field of polysemy, is informed by values, is constituted in practice. We have," they continued, "emphasized archaeology as being indelibly hermeneutically informed, as dialectic, and as itself embedded in historicity."

Certain it is that postmodernism led its practitioners into strange new territory. For example, in their recent book *Social and Cultural Anthropology: The Key Concepts* (2000), Nigel Rapport and Joanna Overing failed to include "evolution" among the fifty-eight "key concepts" of the discipline, but did find room for "gossip," "irony," "non-places," "the rural idyll," and "tourism."

There is little question that today those anthropologists by whom evolutionism is most conspicuously ignored, if not derided, are those who are in the passionate embrace of postmodernism. Though postmodernism did not create neo-anti-evolutionism, it has, without question, magnified and intensified it.

Still, it can be argued that postmodernism in anthropology should perhaps not really be designated as "anti-evolutionary," as if that were its most distinctive badge. The fact is that, speaking more broadly, postmodernism is anti-science. It recognizes no such thing as objective reality, disdains speaking of truth (Carneiro 1995:5–6, 11). And so anti-evolutionism can be subsumed under anti-science, as a species can within a genus. It is thus not a separate genus by itself. On the other hand, some might say that this assessment is too charitable, that a more accurate characterization of postmodern anti-evolutionism would be that it is one "head" of a hydra-headed monster.

It is curious how biological analogies spring readily to mind when those who see only perversity in postmodernism seek to express their distaste for it. Thus Michael Schiffer remarks that "The frustrating thing about post-processual archaeology"—the archaeological manifestation of postmodernism—is that "it's reptilian. You try to get a handle on it and it's like a snake—it slithers away or changes in color" (quoted in Thomas 1998:86). Altering the metaphor from zoological to botanical, Stanley South and Halcott Green (2002:19) maintain pessimistically that postmodern anthropology, "With pervasive tentacles reaching into all endeavors and a growth rate to put kudzu to shame, . . . is not likely to go away soon."

There is another aspect of postmodernism that also strikes at the root of cultural evolutionism. So fixated have postmodernists become on *ethnography* that they have virtually abandoned *ethnology*. Ethnology has always been that branch of cultural anthropology where theories were born and generalizations crafted. And it was ethnography's task to unearth, record, and transmit to ethnology the raw material upon which to build its theories.

Postmodernism, however, no longer considered it possible for ethnography to fulfill this function. No longer was it to serve as the handmaiden of ethnology. It was decreed to be invalid for ethnography to concern itself with collecting and assembling hard, cultural data. It was the extraction of "meaning" that was important, the hard outer covering of fact being discarded once the soft, blubbery innards had been sucked out.

There was a time when broad questions were a proper subject for debate in anthropology. What was the origin of clans? How did agriculture come about? What function did cross-cousin marriage serve? What factors gave rise to age grades? How did chiefdoms emerge? How did states develop? But important as these questions were once considered, postmodern anthropology would simply set them aside as no longer of any interest or significance. Thus, has anyone even *heard* of a postmodernist theory of the origin of the state? As far as evolutionary interpretations are concerned, then, with the arrival of postmodernism we have reached absolute zero.

Still, anti-evolutionism is probably more tacitly *assumed* in postmodern anthropology than it is directly expressed. For outright denial of evolutionism we perhaps have to go back to the old-fashioned Boasian kind, of which there are still lingering examples. For instance, we have the forthright statement of Herbert Lewis and Sidney Greenfield (1983:12) that they write about state formation from "our anti-developmental, anti-evolutionist, anti-uniformitarian perspective." Similarly, John W. Bennett (1998:387), no friend of cultural evolutionism, paints modern-day followers of this approach as bemused, misguided, and hopelessly over their heads:

> of course the [modern-day] evolutionists continually stumbled over the persistent disorder and variability of the historical record. Their search for *invariant* processes was doomed to ambiguity and few of them had a clear conception of statistical probability, stochastic progression, or chaotic regularity, where recurrent or mutually influential phenomena are so hidden with long-cyclical or permutational multiple factors that only computerized analysis can crack the pattern.

The Attitude of British Social Anthropologists

For the most part, British social anthropologists have continued to remain aloof from cultural evolutionism, when not downright hostile toward it. Moreover, they have succeeded in convincing their sociological colleagues of the wrong-headedness of evolutionism and the futility of attempting to pursue it. Thus, Anthony Giddens (1984:236) was sure that "Human history does not have an evolutionary 'shape,' and positive harm can be done by attempting to compress it into one." J. D. Y. Peel (1969:183) spoke of "the intellectual weakness of all theories of social evolution." And Michèle Barrett

(1985:16) affirmed that "evolutionist arguments have little credibility nowadays as explanations of social change."

Among social anthropologists themselves, however, one could detect a slight change in attitude, a certain softening of the stand against evolutionism. Jack Goody (1971:20) came to the conclusion that "despite the many and often justified criticisms of the application of evolutionary doctrine to social facts, only a real flat-earther would now regard the overall history of political systems as static, cyclical, regressive, indeed as anything other than a process of elaboration." And there was a greater inclination not only to countenance cultural evolutionism in general, but to reexamine its various manifestations, even if cautiously and tentatively. Max Gluckman (1965:83), for one, even dared to dance with the enticing siren, but still held her gingerly and at arm's length. Let us watch him in his guarded minuet.

He begins promisingly enough:

> It is possible to range the political systems of tribes along a scale of morphological development, beginning with the small hunting-band, all of whose members are related to one another by blood or marriage and who accept the leadership of one or more of their senior members. There are larger bands composed of more people. Then we find fairly large tribes organized in an elaborate framework of "kinship" groups, or sets of age-mates, before we come to chiefdoms with some instituted authority and governmental organization, and finally to quite large-scale kingdoms.

However, Gluckman then begins to hedge: "But we shall see that this does not necessarily mean that the states have a more complicated social organization." Then, apparently feeling he may already have conceded too much, he concludes warily by saying, "if we make some arrangement of morphological development in these terms, we cannot be sure that one has evolved out of the other in the general sweep of human history."

At least, though, Gluckman was prepared to dance. Adam Kuper and Edmund Leach would not even step on the dance floor. In his book *The Invention of Primitive Society* (1988), Kuper launches a spirited attack on the notion of "primitive society," declaring that the theory about such a form of society "is about something which does not and never has existed. One of my reasons for writing this book is to remove the constitution of primitive society from the agenda of anthropology . . . once and for all" (Kuper 1988:8).

Kuper is prepared to argue that "there never was such a thing as 'primitive society.' Certainly, no such thing can be reconstructed now." And he goes on to say, "There is not even a sensible way in which one can specify what a 'primitive society' is. The term implies some historical point of reference. It presumably defines a type of society ancestral to more advanced forms, on the analogy of an evolutionary history of some natural species. But . . . there is no way of reconstituting prehistoric social forms, classifying them, and aligning them in a time series. There are no fossils of social organization" (Kuper 1988:7).

But if Adam Kuper is staunchly opposed to the idea of social evolution, Edmund Leach was even more implacably and unswervingly antagonistic toward it. His last published book, *Social Anthropology* (1982), is not only anti-evolutionary, but ranks as probably the most negative treatment of anthropological theory since Paul Radin's *Method and Theory of Ethnology* in 1933. Leach is at pains to disassociate himself from any attempt to infer what social life was like in prehistoric times: "Anthropologists of my sort," he says, "are not counterfeit historians who devote their energies to the reconstruction of a past which we cannot possibly know" (Leach 1982:49). And he adds that "No matter what we do 99.9 percent of prehistory is irretrievably lost and we must put up with that fact, but interestingly enough, the remaining 0.1 percent of the past which remains accessible through [the work of archaeology] . . . is usually quite sufficient to show up the total inadequacy of all anthropological dabblers in conjectural history" (Leach 1982:50–51).

Happily, though, that is not the end of the story. Despite such thundering pronouncements, cracks were beginning to appear in the once-solid wall of British anti-evolutionism. The most explicit and plainspoken among the small new band of British-trained anthropologists ready to accept, and even embrace, cultural evolutionism is C. R. Hallpike, whose book *The Principles of Social Evolution* (1988) marked a significant step in that direction.

To begin with, Hallpike wanted to dispose of what he considered to be an old misconception. There was no inherent opposition, he argued, between cultural evolutionism and British functionalism. The basic antagonism, he declared, lay elsewhere: "Relativism, not functionalism, is the enemy of evolutionism" (Hallpike 1988:7). Turning to more substantive issues, Hallpike made it clear that he would have no truck with the anti-evolutionist views of the likes of Adam Kuper, finding them crippling to the scientific study of society: "This denial of social evolution, and even of the very concept of 'primitive society,' must in the end deprive social anthropology of any distinctive subject of study" (Hallpike 1988:13). But in the face of this stultifying prospect he still remained optimistic, affirming that "Fortunately . . . social evolution is much too important a subject just to disappear because it is unfashionable" (Hallpike 1988:13).

Hallpike's *The Principles of Social Evolution* not only accepted cultural evolutionism as a valid approach to the changes undergone by human societies, it was an exercise in how to carry it out. It included extended and incisive discussions of adaptation, the determinants and direction of evolution, the rise of the state, and the like. In short, Hallpike was not just *talking* about cultural evolution, he was actually *doing* it.

A different sort of book was *Evolution and Social Life* (1986), in which Tim Ingold carried out a painstakingly detailed analysis of a number of ideas involved in cultural evolutionism, from Tylor and Spencer, through Boas and Lowie, to Kroeber and White. Ingold parses these ideas with infinite subtlety, demanding of the reader considerable mental acuity and discipline. Still, it is clear that he regards cultural evolutionism as an approach deserving serious consideration, not one to be merely criticized and then thrown aside, in favor of some other way of dealing with the past. Unlike Hallpike's though, this is a book *about* evolutionism, not *of* it.

Though a Canadian, the archaeologist Bruce Trigger can be counted in the British school since, as he tells us, as a student at the University of Toronto, "I was influenced strongly by the tenets of British social anthropology" (Trigger 1978:vii). In his earlier writings, Trigger gave off the vibrations of someone not especially attuned to cultural evolution. For example, citing Service and Sahlins in particular, he held that "American anthropologists . . . increasingly have used ethnological data to construct speculative and highly abstract sequences of unilinear development. The most popular of these have as levels: band, tribe, chiefdom, and state" (Trigger 1978:71).

Such formulations were uncongenial to Trigger, who was led to "agree with Murdock . . . that the course of evolution . . . must be identified with what actually had happened in the past, not with highly abstract generalizations about what is believed to have taken place" (Trigger 1978:xi). Ethnological analogy was to be distrusted, Trigger (1978:74) said, contending that "archaeology . . . alone can provide accurate information about what has happened in prehistory."

However, in his most recent book, *Sociocultural Evolution* (1998), Trigger has done an almost complete about-face. In the opening sentence of the book he says, "If anyone had told me thirty years ago that in the late 1990s I would be publishing a defence of sociocultural evolution, I would have laughed" (Trigger 1998:xi). But so he has. Though at one point he seems to adopt the rhetoric of postmodernism when he says that "Neo-evolutionism initially represented yet another effort by middle-class intellectuals to rationalize their increasingly privileged position by demonstrating it to be the inevitable result of evolutionary processes" (1998:124), Trigger goes on to call postmodernism "the late twentieth-century incarnation of romanticism" (1998:153). And while allowing that it "has much to say that is of value," he nevertheless makes it clear that "its extremism threatens to recreate rather than transcend the problems of the culture-historical approach.

In particular, postmodernism makes it impossible to gain insight into the origin, structure, and change of social systems" (1998:154).

It is this change, moreover, that Trigger is interested in. Since he takes seriously the argument that surviving primitive peoples may not be pristine representatives of prehistoric cultures, "Social anthropology may turn out to be only a study of acculturation, and archaeology may provide the only reliable information about early stages in the development of human societies" (Trigger 1998:163). What, then, does archaeology have to show in this regard? That there is *directionality* to cultural evolution and that "at least one aspect of [this] directionality is a trend toward greater complexity" (1998:1). And this is important enough for Trigger to be worth emphasizing: "What appears most clearly to characterize changes in societies and cultures in general, and in many specific instances, is a tendency towards increasing complexity" (1998:167).

In accounting for such directional change in cultures, Trigger feels that something is needed beyond the familiar Darwinian model. Thus he states that while the "cultural equivalent of descent with modification may explain the development of cultural diversity," it "does not . . . explain the linear tendencies that prevail in human history" (Trigger 1998:26).

A striking feature of Trigger's latest book is his recognition of an underlying common thread—indeed, a form of *unilinearity*—running through the development of the early civilizations. He begins the discussion of this point by admitting that "Wide differences are . . . apparent in the social values of early civilizations, especially as these relate to elite male roles. Different civilizations viewed the ideal life for a man very differently. The Egyptians admired the well-trained and emotionally self-disciplined bureaucrat; the Aztecs the courageous and valiant warrior; and the ancient Mesopotamians the wealthy landowner" (Trigger 1998:180). Yet marked similarities went along with the differences:

> early civilizations shared important general features. All of them exhibited well-developed social hierarchies and economic inequality. In each civilization a very large portion of the agricultural surplus fell into the hands of a small privileged group. The ways in which this surplus was extracted from its producers were highly variable. . . . But the result was always the same. The surpluses ultimately supported an upper class whose interests were defended by the power of the state. (Trigger 1998:180–181)

Moreover, Trigger is ready to go further, and to find common elements in the supernatural beliefs of the early civilizations: "There was also surprising cross-cultural uniformity in religious concepts. Despite a vast diversity in specific religious beliefs, those who lived in the early civilizations appear to have agreed that the supernatural forces provided the energy that kept the universe functioning" (Trigger 1998:181). And as to these common elements he says:

> The early civilizations were societies in which religion had replaced kinship as a medium of political debate. The similarities in the fundamental structure of religious beliefs in the early civilizations and the constitutional role they played suggest that they were not simply random ruminations or haphazard refinements of earlier belief systems, but a projection of the key features of early class societies into the realm of the supernatural. (Trigger 1998:182)

We find in Trigger's most mature work, then, an understanding of the interweaving of the unilinear and the multilinear in the evolution of culture. The unilinear element may not always be immediately discernible, obscured as it often is by the surface variety, but it can be searched out and laid bare. Thus, from a skeptical and (at best) grudging evolutionist, Bruce Trigger has evolved into a full-fledged, outspoken, and unapologetic exponent of this perspective.

It would not be fitting to conclude this quick survey of the way cultural evolutionism has been treated by British or British-trained anthropologists and archaeologists without mentioning the work of Colin Renfrew. His little book *Before Civilization* (1976) signaled a significant shift in the way in which European prehistorians understood and represented the culture history of their continent.

At the outset, Renfrew gives the impression of being something of an anti-evolutionist, but the import of this work is just the opposite. Before this point can be explained, though, some background is required.

For many decades, European prehistorians had believed that the relatively high cultural development of western Europe during the later Neolithic (the appearance of chiefdoms, essentially) was due to the diffusion of this form of culture from the Balkans, since it appeared to exist earlier there than in western Europe. But then, with the recalibration of radiocarbon dates, it became evident that chiefdom-level culture in western Europe actually predated that in the Balkans. A stark reality suddenly had to be faced by the diffusion-minded archaeologists who had dominated European prehistory: The higher Neolithic culture of western Europe was no longer to be interpreted as having diffused from the east. It had arisen, in fact, autochthonously and had evolved *in situ*.

Once this realization had set in, the *deus ex machina* of diffusion had to be abandoned and some sort of developmental framework—an *evolution-*

ary framework—had to take its place. Initially, this seemed like something Renfrew was reluctant to do, clothed as he appeared to be in anti-evolutionary raiment. "At first sight," he said, "the sudden collapse of the diffusionist framework for Europe might tempt us to revert to an evolutionist viewpoint. But this is no longer adequate." Why not? Because, according to Renfrew, "to ascribe all progress everywhere to innate properties of the mind of man is to give an explanation so general as to be meaningless" (Renfrew 1976:18–19). But this was, of course, a gross and erroneous caricature of how evolutionists explained cultural development, a survival in the mind of Colin Renfrew of an old ingrained prejudice. But when he actually came to grapple with the problem of the rise of chiefdoms in western Europe, it was an evolutionary framework that he embraced and applied, and did so most effectively.

Renfrew had read Elman Service's *Primitive Social Organization* and had found within its pages the evolutionary scheme of Band, Tribe, Chiefdom, and State. Furthermore, he learned how this framework had been successfully applied to cultural development in the New World and in Polynesia. Immersed in what Service and Sahlins had said about chiefdoms, Renfrew found in this form of political organization the key to explaining cultural developments in prehistoric Europe. Speaking of the monumental architecture of prehistoric Malta, for example, he observed that "The temples are so large, and involved so much labour, that they cannot have been the work of small local groups . . . as we have [also] argued for the megalithic tombs of Atlantic Europe" and the cyclopean masonry in Mycenaean Greece (Renfrew 1976:166, 227–232). Rather, these impressive remains were the work of *chiefdoms*, the next evolutionary stage above that of autonomous villages.

Renfrew invoked the same line of reasoning in explaining the great henges of Neolithic England. After quoting an estimate "that the digging of the ditch, and the construction of the bank, of these large henges may have taken something like a million man hours," he goes on to say:

> These considerable investments of labour pose a problem not unlike that set by the temples of Malta. And I believe we can answer it in the same way, by postulating the emergence of chiefdoms in the late neolithic period of Wessex, around 2500 B.C. . . . The causewayed camps of the early neolithic already hint at some inter-community collaboration, and this may have developed in the late neolithic into a hierarchically ordered chiefdom society. (Renfrew 1976:253)

Thus, in the evolutionary framework first proposed by an American ethnologist, Renfrew had found a powerful interpretive tool with which to give a clearer and truer interpretation of the development of Neolithic cultures in Europe than the one it superseded.

American Archaeologists Resist "Neo-Evolutionism"

While most American archaeologists seem to live comfortably enough with "neo-evolutionism," a few have vociferously denounced it. Two who have been in the forefront of this denunciation are Norman Yoffee and Robert Dunnell. In the guise of promoting their own brand of cultural evolutionism, Yoffee and Dunnell have set about to lay waste to all others.

Make no mistake about it, Norman Yoffee has declared war on "neo-evolutionism." What particularly rankles him is that prevailing evolutionary thought, he says, is the offspring of ethnologists rather than archaeologists. Up to now, he feels that archaeologists, to a large extent, have been merely "adaptors or low-brow acolytes of their fellow social scientists," the ethnologists (1993:74). This dependence, he believes, has been highly detrimental to archaeology. Thus, he argues, the time has come for archaeologists to "become unshackled from the bonds of inappropriate theory borrowed from other fields" (1993:74). Accordingly, he issues a clarion call for "new social evolutionary theorists to unite" (1993:74), and foresees "The heady possibility . . . that archaeologists will become important contributors to social evolutionary theory" (1993:74).

Yoffee's principal discontent with "neoevolutionism" stems from its having as a mainstay the familiar evolutionary sequence of Band, Tribe, Chiefdom, and State. This sequence was, of course, first proposed by an ethnologist, Elman Service, on the basis of a prior formulation by another ethnologist, Kalervo Oberg. But what really annoys Yoffee is that this sequence has been widely accepted and applied by archaeologists, in a misguided attempt, he feels, "to flesh out the fragmentary material record of an extinct social organization by means of an [in]appropriate ethnographic analogy" (1993:60). Yoffee is convinced that "the stage-level model used by archaeological neoevolutionists constitutes a 'paradigmatic' dead-end" (1993:60), which he considers a hindrance to the proper analysis of the origin and development of early states.

It is Yoffee's contention that while archaeologists "originally embraced the neoevolutionary model . . . because it strongly allied ethnology to archaeology in one big happy family" (1993:63), the era of familial bliss has passed, and that "many archaeologists who once accepted the model now seem ready to jettison it" (1993:60).

The very concept of evolutionary stages seems fundamentally flawed to Yoffee. "Stages," he writes, "are only failed intellectual exercises at identifying sets of diagnostic features. . . . There is no invariable 'Bauplan' that links institutions in discrete stages" (1993:64). Of Service's four stages the one that most troubles Yoffee, and draws his heaviest fire, is that of the chiefdom. He attempts to undermine its utility as a concept by claiming—erroneously, in my opinion—"that the subject of 'chiefdoms' is light-years away from anything that modern anthropologists [i.e., ethnologists] study" (1993:64). And he compounds his error by stating that "the typological effort to identify a chiefdom was and is useless" (1993:64).

But it seems to me that Yoffee makes some strange and unnatural demands on the concept of chiefdom. For example, drawing on the archaeology of Mesopotamia, the region he is most familiar with, he argues that "none of the supposed characteristics of ethnographic chiefdoms can 'predict' the form of Mesopotamian historic states" (1993:67). But of course, they weren't meant to. A chiefdom describes what *preceded* a state, not what is to *follow* it.

Yoffee goes further, however, stating categorically that "from just about any kind of chiefdom to a Mesopotamian state you cannot get" (1993:67), sounding much like the Vermont farmer who, when asked for directions by the lost tourist, replied, "You can't get there from here."

Of course, even Yoffee would not claim that Mesopotamian states were created full-blown, in complete organizational complexity. *Something* had to precede them. And that "something" could hardly have failed to have many of the features conventionally attributed to a chiefdom, such as being a multivillage polity, having a strong chief, exhibiting social ranking, accumulating luxury goods, having differential burials, engaging in recurring warfare, and the like.

The fact is that the chiefdom stage of culture, which underlay Mesopotamian states, was traversed and superseded before the more evolved stage Yoffee keeps referring to was reached. And just because he appears unfamiliar with it is no proper reason for denying its existence. To be sure, Yoffee knows that something came before the Mesopotamian city-states. He knows that at one time bands roamed freely between the Tigris and Euphrates. Then autonomous villages came to occupy the landscape. Some of these villages in turn gave rise to larger, more complex political units. But what these larger political units were like Yoffee is unable or unwilling to tell us.

Like all other states, those of Mesopotamia must have been built up by the compounding and recompounding of preexisting political units, and by the accompanying elaboration of the structure of these units as they grew in size. The steps marking different phases of this process can be labeled *stages,* which are nothing more than successive, distinctive forms identifiable at various points in a continuum.

But despite their demonstrated utility in designating significant and contrasting periods of cultural development, stages are something to which

Yoffee is unalterably opposed. In one of his diagrams (p. 61) he depicts the sequence of Band, Tribe, Chiefdom, and State as a stepladder, with each stage being a rung in the ladder. To him, this represents a single invariant evolutionary trajectory that he rejects outright. Instead, he offers his own diagram showing four parallel and independent lines evolving separately, each culminating in one of the four familiar categories—Band, Tribe, Chiefdom, and State—and each arising from a common base that he christens with the happy neologism "bandishness."

Now, Yoffee does not make clear the precise meaning of this diagram. However, he appears to entertain the possibility that some states may have arisen directly out of this basal condition of "bandishness," without having passed through the intermediate stage of chiefdom.

This extraordinary possibility has evoked derision from some of Yoffee's colleagues, who have likened his proposed unlikely development, in which "states arise directly from primordial 'bandishness,'" to "Evolution on Mars," since, as Kent Flannery (1998:xx) notes, this truncation of the normal evolutionary sequence "applies only to those parts of our galaxy where mammals arose directly from primordial 'fishiness.'"

Be that as it may, Yoffee is convinced that "The logical outcome of [pursuing currently accepted] evolutionary trajectories may be an abandonment of the taxonomic quest to 'type' societies" (1993:72), something he regards as devoutly to be hoped for. He feels strongly that neo-evolutionist ethnologists have led archaeologists down the primrose path, inducing them to adopt Service's infamous series of stages in the mistaken belief that "such a categorization might elevate their empirical research into the realm of higher evolutionary thought" (1993:72).

Another archaeologist who, while promoting his own version of cultural evolution, would make short shrift of everyone else's is Robert Dunnell. It must be acknowledged at the outset that Dunnell has performed a useful service in stressing the importance of natural selection (or its cultural counterpart) in accounting for the series of changes that cultures have undergone, as I have tried to do myself (Carneiro 1992c). However, his espousal of "selectionism" comes at the expense of every other mode of evolutionary interpretation. Thus he speaks of "The general failure of evolutionary explanations of complex societies" (Dunnell 1980:65). And he denies that there is any clear directional trend in cultural evolution, declaring that "Because of natural selection, evolution cannot be 'progressive'; it is adaptive and wholly opportunistic" (Dunnell 1980:42).

If, as Dunnell insists, there is no discernible direction to cultural evolution, only opportunistic changes, then clearly the notion of stages is all but worthless. Indeed, Dunnell calls stages "a concept without analog in scientific [by which he means biological] evolutionary theory" (1980:45). The set of stages that has become such a staple of historical reconstructions is therefore out of place, because, Dunnell (1988:177) claims, among other things, it "lacked any connection to the existing archaeological evidence of cultural development." Furthermore, "Even if one grants the observational validity of 'bands,' 'tribes,' 'chiefdoms,' etc., in some statistical sense, this 'reality' does not establish their significance in evolutionary or any other explanatory framework" (Dunnell 1980:45).

Dunnell would thus summarily dismiss the work of most evolutionists. "Counterfeit historians," "dabblers in conjectural history," he might have called them, following Edmund Leach. "It is clear," he says in no uncertain terms, "that cultural evolution is neither science, nor theory, nor evolution, if evolution is taken to mean what it does in the sciences. As such, it is inappropriate as an explanatory framework in an archaeology committed to a scientific approach" (Dunnell 1980:50). Again, Dunnell presumptuously takes biology to be the sole touchstone, the only genuine expositor of science.

But it hardly seems worthwhile for Dunnell to fulminate against present-day cultural evolutionism since he considers it, if not dead in the water already, at least dying on the vine. "If anything," he assures us, "the new Cultural Evolution is even less a force in anthropology today than it was in 1974. . . . Were it not for the fact American archaeologists adopted elements of the new Cultural Evolution, . . . [it] would not be of further concern" (Dunnell 1988:182).

And there we might leave Robert Dunnell but for the fact that his message seems to have found a sympathetic echo with at least one ethnologist, Alice Kehoe (1998:216). Kehoe believes that Dunnell's adaptationist "brand of cultural evolution has the virtue, not to be scoffed at, of leveling the playing field for human societies, recognizing that evolutionary biology requires acknowledging that all societies that are contemporary are equally evolved."

But there is an important distinction here that Kehoe fails to make. It is perfectly true that the *histories* of all existing societies are equally long. But this does not mean that all societies are equally *evolved*, if by evolved we mean—as I believe most anthropologists do—advanced along a trajectory of increasing complexity.

Archaeologists Accept and Apply Evolutionism

Not all American archaeologists have such reservations about cultural evolutionism, however, even in its "neo-evolutionary" garb. A number of them, especially those who consider themselves "processualists," openly espouse it.

Archaeologists have, in fact, been in the forefront of those embracing evolutionary theory, putting it to work, and achieving significant results. Indeed, one can go further and say that the task of advancing the study of cultural evolution is today largely in the hands of archaeologists. Ethnologists have, for the most part, abdicated from this endeavor, or, at best, quietly retired from the scene.

One of the most dedicated and unflinching advocates of evolutionary theory in archaeology is Charles Spencer. To the oft-repeated allegation that neo-evolutionism is moribund, Spencer has replied: "The neoevolutionist perspective in anthropology . . . is neither dead nor seriously ailing; with appropriate modifications it can continue to enhance our understanding of the development of complex human societies" (Spencer 1990:23).

Another leading archaeologist, David Hurst Thomas, in his well-known textbook *Archaeology*, in which he offers an even-handed appraisal of the various approaches to the field, nevertheless makes it clear in several passages that cultural evolution is where his sympathies lie:

> Evolutionary thinking has been a major factor in archaeology for decades. (Thomas 1979:135)

> cultural evolution . . . in many ways . . . is the most important anthropological mainstream for practicing archaeologists. (Thomas 1979:126)

> it is virtually impossible to pursue archaeology's ultimate processual goals without a thorough grounding in cultural evolutionary theory. (Thomas 1979:135)

Gary Feinman (2000:4) speaks of the "vibrancy of current discussion" of evolutionary theory, and attributes to it evolutionism's "predominant role in contemporary archaeological practice."

And speaking of practice, one of the archaeologists who has most explicitly employed evolutionary concepts in the interpretation of his field excavations is Robert Drennan, who has written that "cultural evolutionary theory has provided us with a concrete and productive program for empirical research on sociocultural change, especially as concerns the origins of complex societies" (Drennan 1991:115). And he adds his conviction that "it is still the tradition of cultural evolution that offers the greatest promise for building toward more successful models of general principles" (Drennan 1991:116).

In the first edition of their *History of American Archaeology*, Gordon Willey and Jeremy Sabloff advised their colleagues that "As to a systemic view of culture, it is our opinion that unless such a view is informed by an evolutionary outlook it is severely limited as a means of observing and understanding culture change" (Willey and Sabloff 1974:185). By the time the third edition of their *History* had appeared, however, two decades later, they felt their warning had been sufficiently heeded that they could now declare: "Archaeology stands poised for a great stride forward. For the first time, archaeologists can now not only speculate but can verify their speculations (or hypotheses) on the nature and causes of culture change" (Willey and Sabloff 1993:313–314).

Still, as we shall see, not all archaeologists have accepted and applied evolutionism with the same enthusiasm or to the same degree.

Robert J. Wenke's *Patterns in Prehistory* (1999) is one of the leading textbooks in the field. In an earlier article, dealing with the evolution of complexity, Wenke expressed his general allegiance to evolutionism, stating that "the ideas of cultural evolution have remained important parts of most contemporary attempts to explain cultural complexity" (Wenke 1981:84).

Wenke, however, was a colleague and sometime collaborator of Robert Dunnell, and we can detect Dunnell's influence on Wenke when he says that "cultural evolutionism has focused on creating typologies rather than examining empirical variation" and that it has "neglected the concept of natural selection" (1981:87). Wenke also protests that neo-evolutionists have "assumed a direction in the evolutionary record" (1981:87), whereas "the essence of Darwinian evolution," which he and Dunnell take as the one true standard of validity for *all* evolution, "is nondirectional variability" (1981:112).

But that was 1981. By the time Wenke came to write the third edition of his textbook, eighteen years later, one can detect a greater readiness on his part to see a direction in cultural evolution.

Patterns in Prehistory is built on a strong and clearly visible evolutionary scaffolding. Though the book covers three million years of human prehistory, its emphasis is on the last ten thousand, during which cultural evolution has accelerated enormously. The concepts of "evolution" and "complexity" are very conspicuous elements of this book, the words themselves appearing in the title of several of its later chapters. Thus, following a general chapter entitled "The Evolution of Complex Societies," we encounter chapters on "The Evolution of Complex Societies in the Indus Valley," "The Evolution of Complex Societies in China," and "The Evolution of Complex Societies in Mesoamerica." In these chapters Wenke shows with crystal clarity that the degree of cultural development in each of these regions during the several thousand years over which he traces it was so great that presenting and interpreting it as an *evolution* was all but inescapable. And he further shows that the movement of this grand cavalcade had an unmistakable direction, namely, toward increased complexity.

Patrick V. Kirch, one of the leading archaeologists of Polynesia, is well known for his study of the prehistory of that vast island chain, presented in a volume entitled *The Evolution of Polynesian Chiefdoms* (1984). As indicated by its title, the book is an account of how chiefdoms developed on a number of these islands. As Kirch (1984:36) points out, "Polynesia offers fertile terrain for the investigation of political evolution, with the most stratified of Polynesian societies bordering on the true 'state.'"

Since at contact time it exhibited a large number of societies at various stages of political development, Polynesia was an evolutionist's paradise. A synchronic comparative study of these societies, if judiciously carried out, could thus be made to yield a developmental sequence of Polynesian prehistory. But Kirch is unusually guarded when it comes to discussing the matter of evolutionary stages: "The reader should . . . be forewarned that although I use the term 'chiefdom' to characterize the socio-political organization of [certain] Polynesian societies at the contact era end-points, this does not mean that I regard them as exemplars of some evolutionary 'stage,' or that I subscribe to the 'neo-evolutionary' schemes popular in American anthropology during the 1960s and 70s" (Kirch 1984:2). And then, his caution almost turning to defiance, he adds, "I believe that a stadial . . . approach to evolution in Polynesia is something of a 'dead horse,' entirely inadequate as an explanatory framework" (1984:2).

Kirch first set forth his ideas on cultural evolution in Polynesia in 1980 in an article that focused on local adaptations to environmental conditions. However, he informs us that "In more recent years, my collaboration with Marshall Sahlins has influenced my approach to prehistory, tempering a long-standing commitment to ecology with the perspective of a strongly cultural [cognitive? symbolic?] orientation" (Kirch 1984:xii).

One effect of Sahlins' influence on Kirch seems to be that he is wary of being "pigeon-holed with some particular school of anthropology"— meaning, no doubt, "neo-evolutionism." Although at one time Sahlins was a leader of this "school" of evolutionism, he has since found greener pastures elsewhere. Be that as it may, Kirch feels constrained to tell his readers just what he means, and does not mean, by the word *evolution.* "I intend the term to apply simply to technological and social change in the most general sense" (1984:2). And he explains that while his book does not deal with biological evolution, "Darwin's classic phrase, 'descent with modification,' is probably closest to a definition of evolution in the present context" (1984:2).

It would appear, then, that Kirch would ally himself with Sahlins' category of *specific* evolution, while avoiding that of *general* evolution. Yet the facts in the case compel him to paint the evolution of culture in Polynesia on a broad canvas, one on which a pattern of increasing complexity, repeating itself from island to island, is clearly visible. Although Kirch is careful to describe differences in subsistence patterns, political organization, warfare, etc., on each island separately, this detailed itemization does not prevent general evolutionary similarities from showing through. This he readily acknowledges, noting that "it is reasonable to suppose that the evolutionary processes operating on Polynesian societies were parallel in many island groups" (1984:13).

Again and again Kirch points to similar evolutionary trajectories on the various islands. In speaking of warfare, for example, while pointing to features "developed *locally,* in distinctive patterns peculiar to each society," he nevertheless adds that "despite such variation, it is still possible to isolate several dominant factors closely related to the escalation or intensification of Polynesian warfare everywhere" (1984:216). And again, with regard to subsistence economies, he notes that "The intensification of production systems characterizes all Polynesian developmental sequences, even though particular forms and emphases vary from place to place" (Kirch 1984:152).

Near the beginning of this volume, Kirch lists nine "dominant trends" that he says characterized the development of Polynesian societies generally. Then, after listing them all, he concludes:

> The nine major trends summarized above constitute a catalogue of sorts for the technological and social changes that transformed Ancestral Polynesian Society into the chiefdoms witnessed at European contact. Such a catalogue . . . is a necessary starting-point for understanding evolution in Polynesia. To move beyond description and achieve some understanding of the processes of change leading to these trends is the primary aim of the analysis to follow. (Kirch 1984:15)

And these "processes of change" are laid bare clearly, convincingly, and unabashedly. Thus, despite his early disclaimers, Kirch's book is a study in unalloyed cultural evolution. And though he pays heed to the peculiarities of developmental sequences on each island, he makes the *parallels* among them conspicuous and convincing. We can assert, therefore, that Kirch's book is a study in general *as well as* specific evolution. In it one can find unilinear evolution interwoven with multilinear evolution. In sum, it is a study that any "neo-evolutionist," if invited to do so, would have no difficulty embracing as his own.

A freer and fuller application of cultural evolutionism marks the work of Joyce Marcus and Kent Flannery. Like most other archaeologists, Marcus and Flannery shy away from high-flown evolutionary theory when divorced from actual, tangible exemplifications of it. What commands their respect is evolutionary theory grounded in fact, theory that is directly useful in reconstructing and explaining actual sequences of cultural development. And, like many present-day archaeologists, Marcus and Flannery are less concerned with ceramic sequences and architectural styles than they are with the development of sociopolitical organization.

An outstanding example of this perspective can be found in Joyce Marcus's 1993 study of Lowland Maya political organization, in which she paints a vivid picture of early state formation and dissolution. She shows that political development during the transition from chiefdom to state in the Maya area was no simple, rectilinear, irreversible process. Rather, it was marked by recurring ups and downs. In Maya history, states rose but they also fell. Small polities, autonomous at certain points in time, subsequently became incorporated into a larger political unit, only to lapse back into autonomy when the overarching governmental structure loosened its hold on its constituent units.

As early as 1989 Marcus had called attention to this phenomenon: "Because of its repetitive cycles of consolidation, expansion, and dissolution, I referred to this framework as the Dynamic Model." But she notes that "Shortly after I first presented this Dynamic Model, colleagues from other parts of Mesoamerica began to tell me that the model fit their regions as well" (1998:60).

Heartened by this apparent regularity, Marcus began looking elsewhere to see if the same pattern could be identified in the development of other early civilizations. And sure enough, she found ample evidence that it was by no means unique to the Maya. As she reports, "We have now looked at seven series of archaic states—the Maya, Zapotec, Central Mexican, Andean, Mesopotamian, Egyptian, and Aegean. A number of common patterns emerge, one of which is the cyclic unification and dissolution predicted by the Dynamic Model" (Marcus 1998:91).

Marcus's careful analysis is a significant contribution to the understanding of the actual development of archaic states. She depicts not only the general upward movement from chiefdom to state involved in the process, but also the reversals of this movement. She demonstrates unequivocally that in the life histories of archaic states there are alternating phases of integration and disintegration, of consolidation and fragmentation, of *evolution* and *devolution*. The general advance of culture that we call evolution is thus something *extracted* from the specific historical details. And though this trajectory is predominantly upward, it is seldom smoothly rectilinear. Advances are intermingled with retreats, peaks alternate with troughs.

In her study of Maya political development, Marcus dealt with a relatively limited segment of time, no more than a couple of millennia. But in a later work, *Zapotec Civilization* (1996), she and Kent Flannery traced the growth of culture in the Valley of Oaxaca over the course of some 10,000 years. This was not, however, just a narrow study of culture history. Oaxaca, with its long and uninterrupted cultural sequence, provided "a laboratory for the study of social evolution" (1996:23). Marcus and Flannery's work traces this evolution from the simple nomadic bands of Archaic hunter-gatherers all the way to the flourishing Zapotec empire.

Along the way in this evolution there were conspicuous stages. Following the adoption of agriculture, settled villages replaced nomadic bands, and were in turn replaced by rank societies of warring chiefdoms, the strongest one among them gradually subduing and incorporating neighboring chiefdoms until the entire valley had been politically unified into one great state. Directed from its capital city of Monte Albán, Zapotec armies went out to conquer several adjoining valleys until the Zapotec polity had grown large enough to warrant being called an empire.

Without losing sight of the historical specifics, Marcus and Flannery throughout the volume keep a discerning eye on the evolutionary process that culminated in one of the most distinctive and enduring polities of native America. And in its development, the Zapotec exemplified the Dynamic Model that Marcus had first identified among the Maya. It thus provided "one more case of a state that (1) formed when one chiefdom succeeded in subduing its rivals; (2) took advantage of its superior political and military organization to expand against less-developed neighbors; (3) reached its maximal territorial size early in its history; and (4) later lost its outer provinces and began to contract" (Marcus 1998:71).

Zapotec Civilization tells another story as well. It points to the shift in emphasis that has occurred in the history of Oaxacan archaeology, from its earlier focus on "ethnogenesis" and its interest in unraveling the origins of the Mixtec and the Zapotec as a people, "toward the study of social evolution," with its concern with general developmental processes (Marcus and Flannery 1996:29).

Turning to related matters, Marcus and Flannery argue for a reciprocal relation between evolutionary theory and archaeological practice. On the one hand, they say, evolutionary theory provides a way "to account for the archaeological evidence" (1996:29). On the other, "archaeologists have worked steadily to improve their [evolutionary] framework—keeping what seems to work, rejecting or modifying what does not" (1996:30).

Yet, in this dual mission of applying and assessing evolutionary theory, archaeologists do not work alone. They have a collaborator. As Marcus and Flannery (1996:30) explain:

> Most theorists of social evolution come from anthropology [that is, ethnology], and it is easy to explain why. Anthropologists had studied living bands of hunters and gatherers, autonomous village societies, chiefly societies, and states of various types. They control rich and intimate details about living groups, details that no archaeologist could know about the extinct societies he or she studies. On the other hand, archaeologists can study changes over thousands of years, long-term processes difficult to document in living societies. In a way, therefore, archaeology can serve as a kind of "proving ground" for anthropological theory.

Marcus and Flannery see clearly that cultural evolution is a unitary process, manifested alike by living and extinct societies. And to study this process most effectively requires the united efforts of ethnologists and archaeologists. The two are properly colleagues, not competitors. Between them there is, or should be, a harmonious division of labor. The tools of their trade may be different, but they share the same aims and objectives: laying bare the course human societies have followed in their upward climb through history, and in ascertaining the factors that have shaped and powered this movement.

As Flannery (1983:361) observed elsewhere regarding the parallel relation between zoology and paleontology, "The two fields are thus complementary, one providing a wealth of data on modern species and the other documenting the history of evolutionary changes which led up to those species." And though he admits to "a nagging inferiority complex that characterizes many . . . archaeologists," he calls for a bridge between ethnology and archaeology "so they may one day display the symbiosis and mutual respect that zoology and paleontology have displayed for years" (Flannery 1983:362).

Then, as a parting shot, lest ethnologists be tempted to think of themselves as the senior partner in this association, Flannery (1983:362) reminds them that "there are some kinds of anthropology that archaeologists can do better than anyone else. Fellows: if evolution is what you are interested in, then anthropology includes archaeology or it is nothing."

An outstanding example of the collaboration called for by Marcus and Flannery is *The Evolution of Human Societies* (1987), written jointly by an ethnologist, Allen Johnson, and an archaeologist, Timothy Earle. Initially, they tell us, "We had no intention . . . of writing a book on social or cultural evolution," seemingly because "Theories of sociocultural evolution are not popular at the moment" (1987:vii). But the authors could not accept the anti-evolutionism they saw around them in their discipline: "we feel that this turning away from evolutionism, after a period of creativity a generation ago, is not warranted by the evidence. In fact, most researchers on problems of ecology and economy in other cultures work within an implicit evolutionary typology" (1987:vii).

At an early stage of the work, Johnson and Earle organized their book along nonevolutionary lines. But "the point arrived . . . when we could no longer deceive ourselves: in order to present an orderly and synthetic treatment of our subject matter, we had to acknowledge that it could only be done using evolutionary theory and an evolutionary typology" (1987:viii).

Once they decided their book must have an evolutionary framework and that evolutionary theory must be interwoven into its fabric, Johnson and Earle did so diligently and unstintingly. "Our purpose in this book," they say, "is to describe and explain the evolution of human societies from earliest times to roughly the present. Our emphasis is on the causes, mechanisms, and patterns of this evolution, which, despite taking many divergent paths, is explainable in terms of a single coherent theory" (1987:1).

The evolutionary typology that Johnson and Earle employ bears a strong resemblance to Service's Band, Tribe, Chiefdom, and State. They observe that social evolution (as Herbert Spencer noted more than a century ago) involves the compounding and recompounding of sociopolitical units. As they put it, "at each evolutionary stage existing organizational units are embedded within new, higher-order unifying structures. Hamlets are made up of families, local groups of hamlets, regional chiefdoms of local groups, and states of regional chiefdoms" (1987:322).

The volume is organized according to these levels—family, hamlet, chiefdom, and state—and numerous examples are presented of each. For instance, for the family level, the Shoshone and the !Kung San are described; for the hamlet level, the Yanomamö and the Tsembaga; for the chiefdom level, the Trobrianders and the Hawaiians; and for the state level, feudal Japan and the Inca.

Emerging prominently from this book is the notion that to be convincing, an evolutionary study must be studded with actual examples of societies representing different stages of the process, and it must also describe the forces and mechanisms moving it forward. But beyond that, an even broader truth emerges: that if the facts of ethnography and prehistory are marshaled in an orderly and systematic way, cultural evolution cannot be denied. Indeed, it all but jumps out at one.

While it is ideal to have an archaeologist as collaborator, it is still possible for an ethnologist to strike out on his or her own and to reveal something of the evolutionary processes that have characterized the past. In this connection, I will present two examples of how the quantification of cultural data can assist in this endeavor.

The Quantification of Cultural Evolution

In *First Principles*, his systematic analysis of the concept of evolution, Herbert Spencer (1896:387–388) wrote as follows:

> the general advance of Science in definiteness, is best shown by the contrast between its qualitative stage, and its quantitative stage. At first the facts ascertained were, that between such and such phenomena some connexion existed—that the appearances *a* and *b* always occurred together or in succession; but it was known neither what was the nature of the relation between *a* and *b*, nor how much of *a* accompanied so much of *b*. The development of Science has in part been the reduction of these vague connexions to distinct ones. . . . we have learned to infer the amounts of the antecedents and consequents . . . with exactness.

The instrument by which the relationship between phenomena—cultural as well as physical—has been reduced to the greatest exactness is, of course, mathematics. The application of mathematics to an evolutionary (or any other) problem involves two stages. First, the relevant variables are identified and either measured or counted. Then the numerical relationship between them is determined and expressed, most precisely, by means of an equation.

The quantification of variables and their mathematical manipulation in the field of cultural evolution is still in its infancy. Nonetheless, it is a goal toward which evolutionists strive. In this connection, in 1970 I proposed a theory of the origin of the state that advanced the idea that early states—"archaic states"—arose first in areas of circumscribed agricultural land, where competition over land, as it filled with settlements, led to warfare, with the conquest of one group by another (Carneiro 1970a). The successively larger political units thus formed, continuing to elaborate their structure as they grew, eventually reached a complexity of organization that warranted their being called states.

This theory was stated in *qualitative* terms. And it was not predictive. It did not say *when* a state would arise in any particular circumscribed area. The variables involved in the process, though identified, were not quantified. Two years later, however, at Spencer's bidding, one might say, I devised an equation that, if numerical values could be assigned to the variables, would predict how long it would take (from some base period) for the onset of state formation to occur (Carneiro 1972:244–247).

However, a far more elegant and sophisticated application of mathematics to cultural evolution occurs in Robert Bates Graber's *A Scientific Model of Social and Cultural Evolution* (1995). The focus of this book, as in the paper just cited, is on population pressure and circumscription theory as they relate to the rise of the state. And in this connection, Graber's work was discussed earlier when dealing with theories of population pressure as a determinant of cultural evolution. Here I will limit myself to citing Graber's work as an example of the precision of thought that can be gained when cultural evolution is subjected to mathematical analysis by someone with intellectual acuity and a command of the requisite mathematical tools.

Graber sees his book as offering a "generalized model of the process underpinning—and in part constituting—sociocultural evolution" (1995:1). It is based on his conviction that "our current state of knowledge is indeed advanced enough to allow us to begin formulating elegant *quantitative* theories of sociocultural evolution" (1995:3). More specifically, Graber states that a significant aim of the book "is to demonstrate that valuable concepts (e.g., circumscription, population, flux) hitherto handled qualitatively can be formulated and interrelated quantitatively" (1995:12).

Graber's work points the way to future advances waiting to be made by ethnologists in the study of cultural evolution once they abandon their fixation on "alterity," "reflexivity," and the like, and turn instead to an assessment of real and important objective problems, and to the application of some hard thinking and rigorous quantitative methods to their solution.

Cultural Evolutionism and the Sociologists

Cultural evolutionism, trimmed down perhaps to *social* evolutionism, has proved too large a subject to be contained within anthropology alone. It has spilled over into the other social sciences, especially sociology.

Curiously enough, sociology has always lagged behind anthropology in its attitude toward social evolutionism. It took some fifteen years after anthropology had forsaken evolutionism for sociology to reject it as well. (The diffusion of ideas between the two disciplines has evidently been slow.) And sociology was again as long in reembracing evolutionism once anthropology had restored it to life.

In his earlier writings, Talcott Parsons, regarded in his day as the leading American sociologist, viewed Herbert Spencer, the great apostle of social evolutionism, disdainfully. Thus Parsons began his best-known work, *The Structure of Social Action* (1937), by quoting Crane Brinton's remark, "Who now reads Spencer?" agreeing that "Spencer is dead" (Parsons 1937:3).

However, apparently getting wind that cultural anthropology was turning to evolutionism once again, Parsons, in what his fellow sociologist Robert Perrin called "one of the most remarkable conversions in intellectual history" (1993:5), did a complete about-face on Herbert Spencer and came to espouse his social evolutionism. In 1961 he wrote the introduction to a reissue of Spencer's *The Study of Sociology*. Then, in a small book entitled *Societies: Evolutionary and Comparative Perspectives* (1966), Parsons dealt with social evolutionism in a positive way. (See also Parsons 1964, 1977.)

Among sociologists, Talcott Parsons was followed by Gerhard Lenski, whose book *Human Societies* (1970) was in several ways a pioneering work in modern sociology. It included an informed discussion of revivified social evolutionary theory, and followed that by tracing the general development of human societies, from small, simple bands to large and complex states.

By all odds, though, the most impressive work on social evolutionism by a present-day sociologist is that of Stephen K. Sanderson. His three books, *Macrosociology* (1988), *Social Evolutionism* (1990), and *Social Transformations* (1999), are a formidable trilogy. They deal with the history of evolutionary theory, not only in sociology but in anthropology as well. Indeed, Sanderson is more familiar with this history than are most anthropologists. But Sanderson's work is not limited to a historical survey of other theorists' ideas; he propounds a good many of his own. In fact, his expressed aim is to account for cultural evolution with robust, materialist theory. This, however, is not the place to go more deeply into Sanderson's writings on social evolutionism or his contributions to it. My aim here is only to bring his work to the attention of anthropologists, who have much to learn from it.

Summary

And now for a final summation of this survey of the checkered history, the ups and downs, of cultural evolutionism. This was the perspective with which anthropology started life. And during the last three decades of the nineteenth century it gave purpose and direction to the young discipline.

But around the turn of the century, a strong reaction against evolutionism ensued, and it carried the day. For more than fifty years it held sway, and the period of its dominance was one of overt and intense hostility to evolutionism, an opposition that served to stultify the discipline.

Then, about the time of the Darwin centennial in 1959, a sea change took place in anthropology that saw evolutionism climb back into favor and reinvigorate the discipline. Once again, though, a countercurrent set in, and although this time evolutionism was not swept away, it was severely curtailed and eroded, and only a few staunch islands of it remained. Still, to paraphrase Leslie White, cultural evolutionism is too valid and fruitful an approach to an understanding of culture not to remain a central tenet of anthropology.

After all, the most salient feature in human history is the fact that, beginning as small, simple Paleolithic bands, human societies were eventually transformed into the large, powerful, and complex states of today. And tracing the course of this transformation—this *evolution*—and laying bare the factors and forces that brought it about, remains the most challenging and rewarding task any anthropologist can undertake.

References Cited

Ackerman, Robert
1987   *J. G. Frazer, His Life and Work.* Cambridge University Press, Cambridge.
1991   "Frazer, Sir James George." *International Directory of Anthropologists,* ed. by Christopher Winters, pp. 216–217. Garland Publishing Company, New York and London.

Adams, Robert McC.
1960   "Factors Influencing the Rise of Civilization in the Alluvium: Illustrated by Mesopotamia." In *City Invincible,* ed. by Robert McC. Adams and Carl H. Kraeling, pp. 24–34. University of Chicago Press, Chicago.
1966   *The Evolution of Urban Society.* Aldine Publishing Company, Chicago.
2001   "Complexity in Archaic States." *Journal of Anthropological Archaeology,* Vol. 20, pp. 345–360.

Alland, Alexander, Jr.
1967   *Evolution and Human Behavior.* The Natural History Press. Garden City, N.Y.

Allen, Grant
1890   "The Gospel According to Herbert Spencer." *The Pall Mall Gazette,* April 26, pp. 1–2.

Bagehot, Walter
1867   "Physics and Politics. No. 1." *The Fortnightly Review,* n.s., Vol. 2, pp. 518–538.
1868   "Physics and Politics. No. 2." *The Fortnightly Review,* n.s., Vol. 3, pp. 452–471.

Baldus, Herbert
1968   "Bastian, Adolf." In *International Encyclopedia of the Social Sciences,* Vol. 2, pp. 23–24. The Macmillan Company and The Free Press, New York.

Barrett, Michèle
1985   Introduction to *The Origin of the Family, Private Property and the State,* by Friedrich Engels, pp. 7–30. Penguin Books, Harmondsworth.

Bastian, Adolf
1881   *Die Vorgeschichte der Etnologie.* Harrwitz und Gossmann, Berlin.

Bawden, Garth
1989   "The Andean State as a State of Mind." *Journal of Anthropological Research,* Vol. 45, pp. 327–332.

Beardsley, Richard K., *et al.,* eds.
1956   "Functional and Evolutionary Implications of Community Patterning." *Seminars in Archaeology. Memoirs of the Society for American Archaeology,* No. 11, pp. 129–156.

Benedict, Ruth
1931   "The Science of Custom." In *The Making of Man,* ed. by V. F. Calverton, pp. 805–817. Random House, New York.
1934   *Patterns of Culture.* Houghton Mifflin, Boston.

Bennett, John W.
 1998   *Classic Anthropology.* Transaction Publishers, New Brunswick, N.J.
Bennett, Wendell C.
 1948   "The Peruvian Co-Tradition." In *A Reappraisal of Peruvian Archaeology,* assembled by Wendell C. Bennett, pp. 1–7, Memoir No. 4, Society for American Archaeology.
Berlin, Brent, and Paul Kay
 1969   *Basic Color Terms, Their Universality and Evolution.* University of California Press, Berkeley and Los Angeles.
Berndt, Catherine H., and Ronald M. Berndt
 1973   *The Barbarians; An Anthropological View.* Penguin Books, Harmondsworth.
Bidney, David
 1946   "On the So-Called Anti-Evolutionist Fallacy: A Reply to Leslie A. White." *American Anthropologist,* Vol. 48, pp. 293–297.
 1953   *Theoretical Anthropology.* Columbia University Press, New York.
Binford, Lewis R.
 1962   "Archaeology as Anthropology." *American Antiquity,* Vol. 28, pp. 217–225.
 1972   *An Archaeological Perspective.* Seminar Press, New York.
Bird, Junius B.
 1964   Preface to the Second Edition. *Andean Culture History,* by Wendell C. Bennett and Junius B. Bird, pp. vii–xii. American Museum Science Books, The Natural History Press, Garden City, N.Y.
Blanton, Richard E.
 1975   "The Cybernetic Analysis of Human Population Growth." *Memoirs of the Society for American Archaeology,* No. 30, pp. 116–126.
 1983   Review of *The Transition to Statehood in the New World,* ed. by Grant D. Jones and Robert R. Kautz. *American Antiquity,* Vol. 48, pp. 204–205.
Blanton, Richard E., S. A. Kowalewski, Gary M. Feinman, and J. Appel
 1981   *Ancient Mesoamerica: A Comparison of Change in Three Regions.* Cambridge University Press, Cambridge.
Boas, Franz
 1896a "The Child and Childhood in Folk-Thought." *Science,* Vol. 3, pp. 741–742.
 1896b "The Limitations of the Comparative Method of Anthropology." *Science,* Vol. 4, pp. 901–908.
 1904   "The History of Anthropology." *Science,* Vol. 20, pp. 513–524.
 1930   "Anthropology." In *Encyclopedia of the Social Sciences,* Vol. 1, pp. 73–110. The Macmillan Company, New York.
 1936   "History and Science in Anthropology: A Reply." *American Anthropologist,* Vol. 38, pp. 137–141.
 1945   *Race and Democratic Society.* J. J. Agustin, New York.
 1949   *Race, Language and Culture.* The Macmillan Company, New York. (Originally published in 1940.)
 1962   *Anthropology and Modern Life.* W. W. Norton & Company, New York. (Originally published in 1928.)
 1974   "The History of Anthropology." In *A Franz Boas Reader,* ed. by George W. Stocking, Jr., pp. 23–36. University of Chicago Press, Chicago. (Originally published in 1904.)
 1982   *Race, Language and Culture.* University of Chicago Press, Chicago. (Originally published in 1940.)
Boserup, Ester
 1965   *The Conditions of Agricultural Growth.* Aldine Publishing Company, Chicago.
Bowden, Edgar
 1969   "A Dimensional Model of Multilinear Sociocultural Evolution." *American Anthropologist,* Vol. 7, pp. 864–870.

Boyd, Robert, and Peter J. Richerson
  1985 *Culture and the Evolutionary Process*. University of Chicago Press, Chicago.
  1992 "How Microevolutionary Processes Give Rise to History." In *History and Evolution*, ed.
        by Matthew H. Nitecki and Doris V. Nitecki, pp. 179–209. State University of New York
        Press, Albany.
Braidwood, Robert J., and Gordon R. Willey, eds.
  1962 "Conclusions and Afterthoughts." In *Courses Toward Urban Life*, ed. by Robert J. Braid-
        wood and Gordon R. Willey, pp. 330–359. Aldine Publishing Company, Chicago.
Brinton, Daniel G.
  1895 "The Aims of Anthropology." *Science*, n.s., Vol. 2, pp. 241–252.
  1902 *The Basis of Social Relations*. Putnam, New York.
Brose, David E.
  1973 "The Northeastern United States." In *The Development of North American Archaeology*, ed.
        by James E. Fitting, pp. 84–115. Anchor Press/Doubleday, Garden City, N.Y.
Brown, Kenneth L.
  1982 "Prehispanic Demography Within the Central Quiché Area, Guatemala." In *The Histor-
        ical Demography of Highland Guatemala*, ed. by Robert M. Carmack, John Early, and
        Christopher Lutz, pp. 35–47. Institute for Mesoamerican Studies, State University of
        New York at Albany, Publication No. 6.
Brumfiel, Elizabeth M.
  1976 "Regional Growth in the Eastern Valley of Mexico: A Test of the 'Population Pressure'
        Hypothesis." In *The Early Mesoamerican Village*, ed. by Kent V. Flannery, pp. 234–250.
        Academic Press, New York.
Buckle, Henry Thomas
  1857 *History of Civilization in England*, Vol. 1. John W. Parker and Sons, London.
Bunzel, Ruth
  1938 "Art." In *General Anthropology*, ed. by Franz Boas, pp. 535–588. D. C. Heath and Com-
        pany, Boston.
Cachel, Susan
  1989 "The Theory of Punctuated Equilibria and Evolutionary Anthropology." In *The Dy-
        namics of Evolution*, ed. by Albert Somit and Steven A. Peterson, pp. 187–220. Cornell
        University Press, Ithaca.
Caldwell, Joseph R.
  1959 "The New American Archaeology." *Science*, Vol. 129, pp. 303–307.
Campbell, Donald T.
  1965 "Variation and Selective Retention in Socio-Cultural Evolution." In *Social Change in
        Developing Areas*, ed. by Herbert E. Barringer, George I. Blanksten, and Raymond W.
        Mack, pp. 19–49. Shenkman Publishing Company, Cambridge, Mass.
Carlyle, Thomas
  1935 *On Heroes, Hero-Worship, and the Heroic in History*. Oxford University Press, London.
Carneiro, Robert L.
  1960 Review of *The Evolution of Culture*, by Leslie A. White. *Natural History*, Vol. 69, No. 2,
        pp. 4–7.
  1968 "Ascertaining, Testing, and Interpreting Sequences of Cultural Development." *South-
        western Journal of Anthropology*, Vol. 24, pp. 354–374.
  1969 "The Measurement of Cultural Development in the Ancient Near East and in Anglo-
        Saxon England." *Transactions of the New York Academy of Sciences*, Series II, Vol. 31, pp.
        1013–1023.
  1970a "A Theory of the Origin of the State." *Science*, Vol. 169, pp. 733–738.
  1970b "Scale Analysis, Evolutionary Sequences, and the Rating of Cultures." In *A Handbook of
        Method in Cultural Anthropology*, ed. by Raoul Naroll and Ronald Cohen, pp. 834–871.
        The Natural History Press, Garden City, N.Y.

1972   "From Autonomous Village to the State, a Numerical Estimation." In *Population Growth: Anthropological Implications,* ed. by Brian Spooner, pp. 64–77. MIT Press, Cambridge, Mass.

1974   "The Four Faces of Evolution." In *Handbook of Social and Cultural Anthropology,* ed. by John Honigmann, pp. 89–110. Rand McNally and Company, Chicago.

1987   "Cross-currents in the Theory of State Formation." Review article of *Development and Decline: The Evolution of Sociopolitical Organization,* ed. by Henri J. M. Claessen, Pieter van de Velde, and M. Estellie Smith. *American Ethnologist,* Vol. 14, pp. 756–770.

1992a   "Point Counterpoint; Ecology and Ideology in the Development of New World Civilizations." In *Ideology and Pre-Columbian Civilizations,* ed. by Arthur A. Demarest and Geoffrey W. Conrad, pp. 175–203. School of American Research Press, Albuquerque.

1992b   "The Calusa and the Powhatan, Native Chiefdoms of North America." *Reviews in Anthropology,* Vol. 21, pp. 27–38.

1992c   "The Role of Natural Selection in the Evolution of Culture." *Cultural Dynamics,* Vol. 5, pp. 113–140.

1995   "Godzilla Meets New Age Anthropology: Facing the Post-Modernist Challenge to a Science of Culture." *Europaea; Journal of the Europeanists* (Cagliari, Italy), Vol. 1, pp. 3–22.

1996   "Cultural Evolution." In *Encyclopedia of Anthropology,* ed. by David Levinson and Melvin Ember, Vol. 1, pp. 271–277. Henry Holt and Company, New York.

2000   "The Transition from Quantity to Quality: A Neglected Causal Mechanism in Accounting for Social Evolution." *Proceedings of the National Academy of Sciences,* Vol. 97, pp. 12926–12931.

Cauvin, Jacques
2000   *The Birth of the Gods and the Origins of Agriculture,* translated from the French by Trevor Watkins. Cambridge University Press, Cambridge.

Cavalli-Sforza, L. L.
1971   "Similarities and Dissimilarities of Sociocultural and Biological Evolution." In *Mathematics in Archaeological and Historical Sciences,* ed. by F. R. Hodson, D. G. Kendall, and P. Tautu, pp. 535–541. Edinburgh University Press, Edinburgh.

Cavalli-Sforza, L. L., and M. W. Feldman
1981   *Cultural Transmission and Evolution: A Quantitative Approach.* Princeton University Press, Princeton.

Chang, Kwang-chih
1968   *The Archaeology of Ancient China,* revised edition. Yale University Press, New Haven.

Chick, Garry
1997   "Cultural Complexity: The Concept and Its Measurement." *Cross-Cultural Research,* Vol. 31, pp. 275–307.

Childe, V. Gordon
1935   *New Light on the Most Ancient East.* Kegan Paul, London.
1942   *What Happened in History.* Penguin Books, Harmondsworth.
1944   *Progress in Archaeology.* Watts & Co., London.
1946   "Archaeology and Anthropology." *Southwestern Journal of Anthropology,* Vol. 2, pp. 243–251.
1951a   *Man Makes Himself.* The New American Library, New York. (Originally published in 1936.)
1951b   *Social Evolution.* Watts & Co., London.

Clark, Grahame
1946   *From Savagery to Civilization.* Cobbett Press, London.

Coe, Michael D.
1968   "San Lorenzo and the Olmec Civilization." In *Dumbarton Oaks Conference on the Olmec,* ed. by E. P. Benson, pp. 41–71. Dumbarton Oaks Research Library and Collection, Washington, D.C.

Comte, Auguste
   1852   *Cours de Philosophie Positive*, Vol. 1. Borrani et Droz, Libraires, Paris.
   1875   *System of Positive Philosophy*, 4 Vols., translated from the French by John Henry Bridges. Longmans, Green, London.
Condorcet, Antoine-Nicolas de
   1955   *Sketch for a Historical Picture of the Progress of the Human Mind*, translated from the French by June Barraclough, Introduction by Stuart Hampshire. The Noonday Press, New York.
Conrad, Geoffrey W.
   1992   "Inca Imperialism: The Great Simplification and the Accident of Empire." In *Ideology and Pre-Columbian Civilizations*, ed. by Arthur A. Demarest and Geoffrey W. Conrad, pp. 159–174. School of American Research Press, Santa Fe, N.M.
Conrad, Geoffrey W., and Arthur A. Demarest
   1984   *Religion and Empire: The Dynamics of Aztec and Inca Expansionism*. Cambridge University Press, Cambridge.
Coon, Carleton S.
   1948   *A Reader in General Anthropology*. Henry Holt and Company, New York.
Cowgill, George L.
   1975   "On Causes and Consequences of Ancient and Modern Population Changes." *American Anthropologist*, Vol. 77, pp. 505–525.
Darwin, Charles
   1871   *The Descent of Man*, 1st ed., 2 Vols. John Murray, London.
   1872   *The Origin of Species*, 6th ed. John Murray, London.
   n.d   *The Descent of Man*, 2nd ed. D. Appleton and Company, New York.
Demarest, Arthur A.
   1992   "Archaeology, Ideology, and Pre-Columbian Cultural Evolution; The Search for an Approach." In *Ideology and Pre-Columbian Civilizations*, ed. by Arthur A. Demarest and Geoffrey W. Conrad, pp. 1–13. School of American Research Press, Santa Fe, N.M.
Demarest, Arthur A., and Geoffrey W. Conrad, eds.
   1992   *Ideology and Pre-Columbian Civilizations*. School of American Research Press, Santa Fe, N.M.
Diamond, Stanley
   1974   *In Search of the Primitive*. Transaction Books, New Brunswick, N.J.
Dobres, Marcia-Anne, and John E. Robb
   2000   "Agency in Archaeology, Paradigm or Platitude?" In *Agency in Archaeology*, ed. by Marcia-Anne Dobres and John E. Reed, pp. 3–14. Routledge, New York.
Downie, R. Angus
   1940   *James George Frazer, the Portrait of a Scholar*. Watts & Co., London.
Drennan, Robert D.
   1991   "Cultural Evolution, Human Ecology, and Empirical Research." In *Profiles in Cultural Evolution*, ed. by A. Terry Rambo and Kathleen Gillogly. Anthropological Papers, Museum Of Anthropology, University Of Michigan, No. 85, pp. 113–135.
Driver, Harold E.
   1973   "Cross-Cultural Studies." In *Handbook of Social and Cultural Anthropology*, ed. by John J. Honigmann, pp. 327–367. Rand McNally and Company, Chicago.
Duncan, David
   1904   *Life and Letters of Herbert Spencer*, 2 Vols. D. Appleton and Company, New York.
Dundes, Alan
   1986   "The Anthropologist and the Comparative Method in Folklore." *Journal of Folklore Research*, Vol. 23, pp. 125–146.

Dunnell, Robert C.
1980   "Evolutionary Theory and Archaeology." *Advances in Archaeological Method and Theory,* Vol. 9, pp. 35–99.
1988   "The Concept of Progress in Cultural Evolution." In *Evolutionary Progress,* ed. by Matthew H. Nitecki, pp. 169–194. University of Chicago Press, Chicago.
Dunnell, Robert C., and Robert J. Wenke
1980   "An Evolutionary Model of the Development of Complex Societies." Paper presented at the annual meeting of the American Anthropological Association, San Francisco, 1980.
Durham, William H.
1979   "Toward a Coevolutionary Theory of Human Biology and Culture." In *Evolutionary Biology and Human Social Behavior,* ed. by Napoleon A. Chagnon and William Irons, pp. 39–59. Duxbury Press, North Scituate, Mass.
1991   *Coevolution: Genes, Culture, and Human Diversity.* Stanford University Press, Stanford, Calif.
1992   "Applications of Evolutionary Culture Theory." *Annual Review of Anthropology,* Vol. 21, pp. 331–355.
Durkheim, Émile
1954   *The Elementary Forms of the Religious Life,* translated from the French by Joseph Ward Swain. The Free Press, Glencoe, Ill.
Eaton, Theodore H., Jr.
1951   *Comparative Anatomy of the Vertebrates.* Harper & Co., New York.
Edmonson, Munro S.
1958   *Status Terminology and the Social Structure of North American Indians.* American Ethnological Society. University of Washington Press, Seattle.
Eggan, Fred
1950   *Social Organization of the Western Pueblos.* University of Chicago Press, Chicago.
1957   Foreword to *A Natural Science of Society,* by A. R. Radcliffe-Brown, pp. ix–xii. The Free Press, Glencoe, Ill.
1965   "Some Reflections on Comparative Method in Anthropology." In *Context and Meaning in Cultural Anthropology,* ed. by Melford E. Spiro, pp. 357–372. The Free Press, New York.
1966   *The American Indian: Perspectives for the Study of Social Change.* Aldine, Chicago.
Ember, Carol R., and Melvin Ember
2001   *Cross-Cultural Methods.* Altamira Press, Walnut Creek, Calif.
Ember, Carol R., and David Levinson
1991   "The Substantive Contribution of Worldwide Cross-Cultural Studies Using Secondary Data." *Behavior Science Research,* Vol. 25, pp. 79–140.
Ember, Melvin
1963   "The Relationship Between Economic and Political Development in Nonindustrialized Societies." *Ethnology,* Vol. 2, pp. 228–248.
1991   "Murdock, George Peter." *International Dictionary of Anthropologists,* ed. by Christopher Winters, pp. 493–494. Garland Publishing, New York.
Emerson, Ralph Waldo
1940   "History." In *The Complete Essays and Other Writings of Ralph Waldo Emerson,* pp. 123–144. The Modern Library, New York.
Engels, Frederick
1942   *The Origin of the Family, Private Property and the State.* International Publishers, New York.
Evans-Pritchard, E. E.
1951   *Social Anthropology.* Cohen & West Ltd., London.
1969   *Essays in Social Anthropology.* Faber and Faber, London. (First published in 1950.)

Fagan, Brian
 1999 *Archaeology, a Brief Introduction,* 7th ed. Prentice Hall, Upper Saddle River, N.J.
Feinman, Gary M.
 2000 "Cultural Evolutionary Approaches and Archaeology: Past, Present, and Future." In *Cultural Evolution: Contemporary Viewpoints,* ed. by Gary M. Feinman and Linda Manzanilla, pp. 3–12. Kluwer Academic/Plenum Publishers, Norwell, Mass., and New York.
Feinman, Gary M., and Jill Neitzel
 1984 "Too Many Types: An Overview of Sedentary Prestate Societies in the Americas." In *Advances in Archaeological Method and Theory,* ed. by Michael B. Schiffer, Vol. 7, pp. 39–102. Academic Press, Orlando, Fla.
Ferguson, Adam
 1819 *An Essay on the History of Civil Society.* A. Finley, Philadelphia.
Firth, Raymond
 1929 *Primitive Economics of the New Zealand Maori.* Routledge, London.
Fiske, John
 1891 "The Doctrine of Evolution: Its Scope and Influence." *The Popular Science Monthly,* Vol. 39, pp. 577–599.
Flannery, Kent V.
 1968 "Archeological Systems Theory and Early Mesoamerica." In *Anthropological Archeology in the Americas* [ed. by Betty J. Meggers], pp. 67–87. Anthropological Society of Washington, Washington, D.C.
 1972a "The Cultural Evolution of Civilizations." *Annual Review of Ecology and Systematics,* Vol. 3, pp. 399–426.
 1972b "Culture History v. Cultural Process: A Debate in American Archaeology." In *Contemporary Archaeology,* ed. by Mark P. Leone, pp. 102–107. Southern Illinois University Press, Carbondale, Ill.
 1976 "Analyzing Patterns of Growth." In *The Early Mesoamerican Village,* ed. by Kent V. Flannery, pp. 225–227. Academic Press, New York.
 1983 "Archaeology and Ethnology in the Context of Divergent Evolution." In *The Cloud People: Divergent Evolution of the Zapotec and Mixtec Civilizations,* ed. by Kent V. Flannery and Joyce Marcus, pp. 361–362. Academic Press, New York.
 1994 "Childe the Evolutionist, a Perspective from Nuclear America." In *The Archaeology of V. Gordon Childe,* ed. by David R. Harris, pp. 101–119. University of Chicago Press, Chicago.
 1995 "Prehistoric Social Evolution." In *Research Frontiers in Anthropology.* Simon and Schuster, Needham Heights, Mass.
 1998 Introduction to the Second Edition. In *The Archaeology of Society in the Holy Land,* ed. by Thomas E. Levy, pp. xvii–xx. Leicester University Press, London and Washington.
 1999 "Process and Agency in Early State Formation." *Cambridge Archaeological Journal,* Vol. 9, pp. 3–21.
Ford, James A.
 1952 *Measurements of Some Prehistoric Design Developments in the Southeastern States. Anthropological Papers of the American Museum of Natural History,* Vol. 44, Part 3, pp. 309–384.
Fortes, Meyer, and E. E. Evans-Pritchard, eds.
 1940 *African Political Systems.* Oxford University Press, London.
Fothergill, Philip G.
 1952 *Historical Aspects of Organic Evolution.* Hollis & Carter, London.
Fox, Robin
 2000 Introduction to *Ancient Society,* by Lewis Henry Morgan, pp. xv–liii. Transaction Publishers, New Brunswick, N.J.

Frazer, James G.
    1905   *Lectures on the Early History of Kingship.* Macmillan, London.
    1913a   *Psyche's Task,* 2nd ed. Macmillan, London.
    1913b   *Balder the Beautiful,* 2 Vols. Macmillan, London.
    1918   *Folk-lore in the Old Testament,* 3 Vols. Macmillan, London.
Freeman, Derek
    1974   "The Evolutionary Theories of Charles Darwin and Herbert Spencer." *Current Anthropology,* Vol. 15, pp. 211–237.
Freeman, Edward A.
    1873   *Comparative Politics.* Macmillan, London.
Freeman, Linton C., and Robert F. Winch
    1957   "Societal Complexity: An Empirical Test of a Typology of Societies." *American Journal of Sociology,* Vol. 62, pp. 461–466.
Fried, Morton H.
    1966   "On the Concept of 'Tribe' and Tribal Society." *Transactions of the New York Academy of Sciences, Series II,* Vol. 28, pp. 527–540.
    1967   *The Evolution of Political Society.* Random House, New York.
Friedman, Jonathan, and Michael J. Rowlands
    1978   "Notes Towards an Epigenetic Model of the Evolution of Civilisation." In *The Evolution of Social Systems,* ed. by Jonathan Friedman and Michael J. Rowlands, pp. 201–276. University of Pittsburgh Press, Pittsburgh.
Froude, James Anthony
    1909   "The Science of History." In *Short Studies on Great Subjects,* by James Anthony Froude, pp. 7–36. Scribners, New York.
Gailey, Christine W.
    1992   "Introduction: Civilization and Culture in the Work of Stanley Diamond." In *Dialectical Anthropology: Essays in Honor of Stanley Diamond,* ed. by Christine W. Gailey, Vol. l, *Civilization in Crisis,* pp. 1–25. University Press of Florida, Gainesville.
Gailey, Christine W., and Thomas C. Patterson
    1987   "Power Relations and State Formation." In *Power Relations and State Formation,* ed. by Thomas C. Patterson and Christine W. Gailey, pp. 1–26. Archeology Section/American Anthropological Association, Washington, D.C.
Gernet, Jacques
    1968   *Ancient China, from the Beginnings to the Empire,* translated from the French by R. Rudorff. Faber and Faber, London.
Giddens, Anthony
    1984   *The Constitution of Society.* Polity Press, Cambridge.
Gillin, John P.
    1948   *The Ways of Men.* Appleton-Century-Crofts, New York.
Gilman, Antonio
    1995   "Prehistoric European Chiefdoms." In *Foundations of Social Inequality,* ed. by T. Douglas Price and Gary M. Feinman, pp. 235–251. Plenum Press, New York.
Ginsberg, Morris
    1953   *The Idea of Progress.* Methuen & Co. Ltd., London.
    1961   *Essays in Sociology and Social Philosophy,* Vol. 3, *Evolution and Progress.* William Heineman Ltd., London.
Gluckman, Max
    1965   *Politics, Law and Ritual in Tribal Societies.* The New American Library, New York.
Godelier, Maurice
    1978   "Economy and Religion: An Evolutionary Optical Illusion." In *The Evolution of Social Systems,* ed. by Jonathan Friedman and M. J. Rowlands, pp. 3–11. University of Pittsburgh Press, Pittsburgh.

Goldenweiser, Alexander
    1922   *Early Civilization.* F. S. Crofts, New York.
    1925a "Cultural Anthropology." In *The History and Prospects of the Social Sciences,* ed. by Harry Elmer Barnes, pp. 210–254. Alfred A. Knopf, New York.
    1925b "Diffusionism and the American School of Historical Ethnology." *American Journal of Sociology,* Vol. 31, pp. 19–38.
    1927   "Anthropology and Psychology." In *The Social Sciences and Their Interrelations,* ed. by William F. Ogburn and Alexander Goldenweiser, pp. 69–88. Houghton Mifflin, Boston.
    1930   "Bastian, Adolf." In *Encyclopedia of the Social Sciences,* Vol. 2, p. 476. The Macmillan Company, New York.
    1931   "Evolution, Social." In *Encyclopedia of the Social Sciences,* ed. by E. R. A. Seligman and Alvin Johnson, Vol. 5, pp. 656–662. The Macmillan Company, New York.
    1933   *History, Psychology and Culture.* Alfred A. Knopf, New York.
Goldfrank, Esther S.
    1978   *Notes on an Undirected Life; as One Anthropologist Tells It.* Queens College Publications in Anthropology, No. 3. Queens College Press. Flushing, N.Y.
Goldman, Irving
    1955   "Status Rivalry and Cultural Evolution in Polynesia." *American Anthropologist,* Vol. 57, pp. 680–697.
Goldschmidt, Walter
    1948   "Social Organization in Native California and the Origin of Clans." *American Anthropologist,* Vol. 50, pp. 444–456.
    1959   *Man's Way.* World Publishing Company, Cleveland.
    1966   *Comparative Functionalism.* University of California Press, Berkeley and Los Angeles.
Goodenough, Ward H.
    1996   "Murdock as Bridge: From Sumner to HRAF to SCCR." *Cross-Cultural Research,* Vol. 30, pp. 275–280.
Goody, Jack
    1971   *Technology, Tradition, and the State in Africa.* International African Institute. Oxford University Press, London.
Gould, Richard A.
    1980   *Living Archaeology.* Cambridge University Press, Cambridge.
Graber, Robert Bates
    1995   *A Scientific Model of Social and Cultural Evolution.* Thomas Jefferson University Press, Kirksville, Mo.
    1997   "A Rigorous Approach to Population Pressure's Contribution to Cultural Evolution." In *Integrating Archaeological Demography: Multidisciplinary Approaches to Prehistoric Population,* ed. by Richard E. Paine, pp. 263–284. Center for Archaeological Investigations, Occasional Papers, No. 24. Southern Illinois University Press, Carbondale, Ill.
Gumplowicz, Ludwig
    1899   *The Outlines of Sociology,* translated from the German by Frederick W. Moore. American Academy of Political and Social Science, Philadelphia.
Haag, William G.
    1959   "The Status of Evolutionary Theory in American Archeology." In *Evolution and Anthropology: A Centennial Appraisal* [ed. by Betty J. Meggers], pp. 90–105. Anthropological Society of Washington, Washington, D.C.
Haddon, Alfred C.
    1902   *Evolution in Art.* Walter Scott, London.
    1934   *History of Anthropology.* Watts & Co., London.
Hallpike, C. R.
    1988   *The Principles of Social Evolution.* Clarendon Press, Oxford.

Harding, Thomas G.
    1964   "Morgan and Materialism: A Reply to Professor Opler." *Current Anthropology*, Vol. 5, p.
            109.
Harner, Michael J.
    1970   "Population Pressure and the Social Evolution of Agriculturalists." *Southwestern Jour-
            nal of Anthropology*, Vol. 26, pp. 67–86.
Harris, Marvin
    1968   *The Rise of Anthropological Theory*. Thomas Y. Crowell Company, New York.
    1969a   "Author vs. Reviewer." *Natural History*, Vol. 78, No. 1, January, p. 72.
    1969b   "Monistic Determinism: Anti-Service." *Southwestern Journal of Anthropology*, Vol. 25,
            pp. 198–206.
    1979   *Cultural Materialism: The Struggle for a Science of Culture*. Random House, New York.
    1994   "Cultural Materialism Is Alive and Well and Won't Go Away Until Something Better
            Comes Along." In *Assessing Cultural Anthropology*, ed. by Robert Borofsky, pp. 62–76.
            McGraw-Hill Book Company, New York.
Hassan, Fekri
    1978   "Demographic Archaeology." In *Advances in Archaeological Method and Theory*, Vol. 1,
            pp. 49–103. Academic Press, New York.
Hegel, Georg W. F.
    1956   *The Philosophy of History*, translated from the German by J. Sibree, Introduction by C.
            J. Friedrich. Dover Publications, New York.
Heine-Geldern, Robert
    1956   "The Origin of Ancient Civilizations and Toynbee's Theories." *Diogenes*, Vol. 13, pp.
            81–99.
Helm, June
    1962   "The Ecological Approach in Anthropology." *American Journal of Sociology*, Vol. 67, pp.
            630–639.
Herskovits, Melville J.
    1952   *Economic Anthropology*. Alfred A. Knopf, New York.
    1960   "On Accuracy in Scientific Controversy." *American Anthropologist*, Vol. 62, pp.
            1050–1051.
    1973   *Cultural Relativism*. Random House, New York.
Hill, James N.
    1977a   Introduction to *Explanation of Prehistoric Change*, ed. by James N. Hill, pp. 1–16. Uni-
            versity of New Mexico Press, Albuquerque.
    1977b   "Systems Theory and the Explanation of Change." In *Explanation of Prehistoric Change*,
            ed. by James N. Hill, pp. 59–103. University of New Mexico Press, Albuquerque.
Hobhouse, Leonard T.
    1915   *Morals in Evolution*. Chapman & Hall, London.
Hobhouse, Leonard T., G. C. Wheeler, and Morris Ginsberg
    1930   *The Material Culture and Social Institutions of the Simpler Peoples*. Chapman & Hall,
            London. (Originally published in 1915.)
Hodder, Ian
    1986   *Reading the Past*. Cambridge University Press, Cambridge.
    1999   *The Archaeological Process: An Introduction*. Blackwell Publishers, Oxford.
Hudson, Charles
    1988   "A Spanish–Coosa Alliance in Sixteenth-Century North Georgia." *The Georgia Histori-
            cal Quarterly*, Vol. 72, pp. 599–626.
    1990   *The Juan Pardo Expedition*. Smithsonian Institution Press, Washington, D.C.
Huxley, Julian
    1962   "Higher and Lower Organisation in Evolution." *Journal of the Royal College of Surgeons
            of Edinburgh*, Vol. 7, pp. 163–179.

Ingold, Tim
    1986   *Evolution and Social Life.* Cambridge University Press, Cambridge.
Jacobs, Melville
    1948   "Further Comments on Evolutionism in Cultural Anthropology." *American Anthropologist,* Vol. 50, pp. 564–568.
James, William
    1890–1891 "The Importance of Individuals." *The Open Court,* Vol. 4, pp. 2437–2440.
Jarvie, I. C.
    1969   *The Revolution in Anthropology.* Henry Regnery Company, Chicago.
Johnson, Allen W., and Timothy Earle
    1987   *The Evolution of Human Societies.* Stanford University Press, Stanford, Calif.
Johnson, Matthew
    1999   *Archaeological Theory; An Introduction.* Blackwell Publishers, Oxford.
Kant, Immanuel
    1969   "The Idea of a Universal History from a Cosmopolitan Point of View," translated from the German by W. Hastie. In *Ideas of History,* Vol. 1, *Speculative Approaches to History,* ed. by Ronald H. Nash, pp. 50–66. E. P. Dutton, New York.
Kaplan, David
    1960   "The Law of Cultural Dominance." In *Evolution and Culture,* ed. by Marshall D. Sahlins and Elman R. Service, pp. 69–92. University of Michigan Press, Ann Arbor.
Kaplan, David, and Robert A. Manners
    1972   *Culture Theory.* Prentice-Hall, Englewood Cliffs, N.J.
Kardiner, Abram, and Edward Preble
    1961   *They Studied Man.* The New American Library, New York.
Keeley, Lawrence H.
    1988   "Hunter-Gatherer Economic Complexity and 'Population Pressure': A Cross-Cultural Analysis." *Journal of Anthropological Archaeology,* Vol. 7, pp. 373–411.
    1996   *War Before Civilization.* Oxford University Press, New York.
Kehoe, Alice Beck
    1998   *The Land of Prehistory; A Critical History of American Archaeology.* Routledge, New York.
Keller, Albert G.
    1915   *Societal Evolution.* The Macmillan Company, New York.
    1931   *Societal Evolution,* revised edition. The Macmillan Company, New York.
    1933   *Reminiscences (Mainly Personal) of William Graham Sumner.* Yale University Press, New Haven.
Kingsley, Charles
    1860   *The Limits of Exact Science as Applied to History.* Macmillan, London.
Kirch, Patrick V
    1980   "Polynesian Prehistory: Cultural Adaptation in Island Ecosystems." *American Scientist,* Vol. 68, pp. 39–48.
    1984   *The Evolution of Polynesian Chiefdoms.* Cambridge University Press, Cambridge.
Kluckhohn, Clyde
    1939   "The Place of Theory in Anthropological Studies." *Philosophy of Science,* Vol. 6, pp. 328–334.
Köbben, André
    1970   "Comparativists and Non-Comparativists in Anthropology." In *A Handbook of Method in Anthropology,* ed. by Raoul Naroll and Ronald Cohen, pp. 581–596. The Natural History Press, Garden City, N.Y.
Krieger, Alex
    1955   "Comments on Problems of Historical Approach: Methods." In *An Appraisal of Anthropology Today,* ed. by S. Tax, L. Eiseley, I. Rouse, and C. Voegelin, pp. 247–250. University of Chicago Press, Chicago.

Kristiansen, Kristian, and Michael Rowlands
  1998   *Social Transformations in Archaeology.* Routledge, London.
Kroeber, A. L.
  1920   Review of *Primitive Culture,* by Robert H. Lowie. *American Anthropologist,* Vol. 22, pp. 377–391.
  1923   *Anthropology,* 1st ed. Harcourt, Brace and Company, New York.
  1931   "Diffusionism." In *Encyclopedia of the Social Sciences,* ed. by E. R. A. Seligman and Alvin Johnson, Vol. 5, pp. 139–142. The Macmillan Company, New York.
  1935   "History and Science in Anthropology." *American Anthropologist,* Vol. 37, pp. 539–569.
  1939   *Cultural and Natural Areas of Native North America.* University of California Press, Berkeley and Los Angeles.
  1944   *Configurations of Culture Growth.* University of California Press, Berkeley and Los Angeles.
  1946   "History and Evolution." *Southwestern Journal of Anthropology,* Vol. 2, pp. 1–15.
  1948   *Anthropology,* new edition. Harcourt, Brace and Company, New York.
Kroeber, A. L., and Clyde Kluckhohn
  1952   *Culture; A Critical Review of Concepts and Definitions.* Papers of the Peabody Museum of American Archaeology and Ethnology, Harvard University, Vol. 47, No. 1.
Kuper, Adam
  1988   *The Invention of Primitive Society.* Routledge, London.
Lamarck, Jean Baptiste
  1873   *Philosophie Zoologique,* 2 Vols. Libraire F. Savy, Paris.
Larco Hoyle, Rafael
  1948   *Cronología Arqueológica del Perú.* Sociedad Geográfica Americana, Buenos Aires.
  1966   *Peru,* translated from the Spanish by James Hogarth. World Publishing Company, Cleveland and New York.
Laufer, Berthold
  1918   Review of *Culture and Ethnology,* by Robert H. Lowie. *American Anthropologist,* Vol. 20, pp. 87–91.
  1930   Review of *Are We Civilized?* by Robert H. Lowie. *American Anthropologist,* Vol. 32, pp. 161–165.
Leach, Edmund
  1957   "The Epistemological Background to Malinowski's Empiricism." In *Man and Culture, an Evaluation of the Work of Bronislaw Malinowski,* ed. by Raymond Firth, pp. 119–137. The Humanities Press, New York.
  1965   Comment. *Current Anthropology,* Vol. 5, p. 299.
  1982   *Social Anthropology.* Oxford University Press, New York.
Leacock, Eleanor Burke
  1961   Comment on Elizabeth Hoyt's "Integration of Culture: A Review of Concepts." *Current Anthropology,* Vol. 2, pp. 407–414.
  1964   Comment on Morris E. Opler's "Morgan and Materialism: A Reply to Leacock." *Current Anthropology,* Vol. 5, pp. 109–110.
  1972   Introduction to *The Origin of the Family, Private Property and the State,* by Friedrich Engels, pp. 7–67. International Publishers, New York.
Leibniz, Gottfried Wilhelm
  1898   *The Monadology and Other Philosophic Writings,* translated from the German with Introduction and Notes by Robert Latta. Clarendon Press, Oxford.
Lenski, Gerhard
  1970   *Human Societies; A Macrolevel Introduction to Sociology.* McGraw-Hill Book Company, New York.
Leone, Mark P.
  1972   "Issues in Anthropological Archaeology." In *Contemporary Archaeology,* ed. by Mark P. Leone, pp. 14–27. Southern Illinois University Press, Carbondale, Ill.

Lesser, Alexander
  1985a "Evolution in Social Anthropology." In *History, Evolution, and the Concept of Culture; Selected Papers of Alexander Lesser,* ed. by Sidney W. Mintz, pp. 78–89. Cambridge University Press, Cambridge.
  1985b "Social Fields and the Evolution of Society." In *History, Evolution and the Concept of Culture: Selected Papers of Alexander Lesser,* ed. by Sidney W. Mintz, pp. 92–99. Cambridge University Press, Cambridge.
Lévi-Strauss, Claude
  1967 *Structural Anthropology.* Doubleday & Company, Garden City, N.Y.
Lewis, Herbert S.
  1968 "Typology and Process in Political Evolution." In *Essays on the Problem of Tribe,* ed. by June Helm, pp. 101–110. University of Washington Press, Seattle.
Lewis, Herbert S., and Sidney M. Greenfield
  1983 "Anthropology and the Formation of the State: A Critical Review and an Alternate Formulation." *Anthropology* (Stony Brook, N.Y., SUNY), Vol. 7, pp. 1–16.
Lillios, Katina
  2001 Review of *Social Transformation in Archaeology: Global and Local Perspectives,* by Kristian Kristiansen and Michael Rowlands. *Journal of Anthropological Research,* Vol. 57, pp. 239–240.
Linton, Ralph
  1936a *The Study of Man.* Appleton-Century, New York.
  1936b "Error in Anthropology." In *The Story of Human Error,* ed. by Joseph Jastrow, pp. 292–321. D. Appleton and Company, New York.
  1938 "The Present Status of Anthropology." *Science,* Vol. 87, pp. 241–248.
  1940 "Crops, Soils, and Culture in America." In *The Maya and Their Neighbors* (no ed.), pp. 32–40. D. Appleton and Company, New York.
  1955 *The Tree of Culture.* Alfred A. Knopf, New York.
Lippert, Julius
  1931 *The Evolution of Culture,* translated and edited by George P. Murdock. The Macmillan Company, New York.
Longacre, William A.
  1970 "Current Thinking in American Archeology." In *Current Directions in Anthropology,* ed. by Ann Fischer, pp. 126–138. American Anthropological Association, Washington, D.C.
Lovejoy, Arthur O.
  1936 *The Great Chain of Being.* Harvard University Press, Cambridge, Mass.
Lowie, Robert H.
  1917 *Culture and Ethnology.* Douglas C. McMurtrie, New York.
  1920 *Primitive Society.* Boni and Liveright, New York.
  1927 *The Origin of the State.* Harcourt, Brace and Company, New York.
  1929 *Culture and Ethnology.* Peter Smith, New York. (Originally published in 1917.)
  1931 "Social Organization." In *Encyclopedia of the Social Sciences,* ed. by E. R. A. Seligman and Alvin Johnson, Vol. 14, pp. 141–148. The Macmillan Company, New York.
  1937 *The History of Ethnological Theory.* Farrar & Rinehart, New York.
  1940a *Introduction to Cultural Anthropology,* 2nd ed. Farrar & Rinehart, New York.
  1940b "American Culture History." *American Anthropologist,* Vol. 42, pp. 409–428.
  1940c "Cultural Development." Review of *Race, Language and Culture,* by Franz Boas. *Science,* Vol. 91, pp. 598–599.
  1946 "Evolution in Cultural Anthropology: A Reply to Leslie White." *American Anthropologist,* Vol. 48, pp. 223–233.
  1947 *Primitive Society.* Liveright Publishing Company, New York. (Originally published in 1920.)

1948   *Social Organization.* Rinehart & Company, New York.

Lubbock, John (Lord Avebury)

1870   *The Origin of Civilisation and the Primitive Condition of Man.* D. Appleton and Company, New York.

1911   *Marriage, Totemism and Religion: An Answer to Critics.* Longmans, Green, London.

1913   *Prehistoric Times,* 7th ed. Williams and Norgate, London.

Lyell, Charles

1830   *Principles of Geology,* Vol. 1. John Murray, London.

1832   *Principles of Geology,* Vol. 2. John Murray, London.

Lyman, R. Lee, Michael J. O'Brien, and Robert C. Dunnell

1997   *The Rise and Fall of Culture History.* Plenum Press, New York.

Macaulay, Thomas Babington

1877   "Dryden." In *Critical, Historical, and Miscellaneous Essays,* by Thomas Babington Macaulay, Vol. 1, pp. 321–375. Hurd and Houghton, New York.

Macdonald, William K.

1978   "Population Pressure, Ecological Anthropology, and Social Evolution Among the Kalinga." A review of *Societal Ecology in Northern Luzon,* by Robert Lawless. *Philippine Quarterly of Culture and Society,* Vol. 6, pp. 172–186.

Maine, Henry Sumner

1871   *Ancient Law.* Scribners, New York.

1880   *Lectures on the Early History of Institutions,* 3rd ed. John Murray, London.

1883   *Dissertation on Early Law and Custom.* John Murray, London.

Mair, Lucy

1962   *Primitive Government.* Penguin Books, Baltimore.

1970   *An Introduction to Social Anthropology.* Oxford University Press, New York.

Malinowski, Bronislaw

1929a   *The Sexual Life of Savages of North-Western Melanesia.* Routledge, London.

1929b   "Social Anthropology." In *Encyclopaedia Britannica,* 14th ed., Vol. 20, pp. 862–870. Encyclopaedia Britannica, Chicago.

1931   "Culture." In *Encyclopedia of the Social Sciences,* ed. by E. R. A. Seligman and Alvin Johnson, Vol. 4, pp. 621–646. The Macmillan Company, New York.

1935   *Coral Gardens and Their Magic,* 2 Vols. George Allen & Unwin, London.

1937   Foreword to *Coming into Being Among the Australian Aborigines,* by M. F. Ashley-Montagu, pp. xix–xxxv. George Routledge & Sons, Ltd., London.

Manners, Robert A.

1965a   Letter to the Editor. *Current Anthropology,* Vol. 6, pp. 1–2.

1965b   "Reply." *Current Anthropology,* Vol. 6, pp. 19–320.

1966   "Reply." *Current Anthropology,* Vol. 7, p. 355.

Marcus, Joyce

1992   "Dynamic Cycles of Mesoamerican States." *National Geographic Research & Exploration,* Vol. 8, pp. 392–411.

1993   "Ancient Maya Political Organization." In *Lowland Maya Civilization in the Eighth Century A.D.,* ed. by Jeremy A. Sabloff and John S. Henderson, pp. 111–183. Dumbarton Oaks Research Library and Collection, Washington, D.C.

1998   "The Peaks and Valleys of Ancient States." In *Archaic States,* ed. by Joyce Marcus and Gary M. Feinman, pp. 59–94. School of American Research Press, Santa Fe, N.M.

2002   Comment on "The Role of Shamanism in Mesoamerican Art," by Cecelia F. Klein *et al. Current Anthropology,* Vol. 43, pp. 383–419.

Marcus, Joyce, and Gary M. Feinman

1998   Introduction to *Archaic States,* ed. by Joyce Marcus and Gary M. Feinman, pp. 3–13. School of American Research Press, Santa Fe, N.M.

Marcus, Joyce, and Kent V. Flannery
    1996   *Zapotec Civilization; How Urban Society Evolved in Mexico's Oaxaca Valley.* Thames and Hudson, London.

Marsh, Robert M.
    1967   *Comparative Sociology.* Harcourt, Brace & World, New York.

Mayr, Ernst
    1959   "Darwin and the Evolutionary Theory in Biology." In *Evolution and Anthropology: A Centennial Appraisal* [ed. by Betty J. Meggers], pp. 1–10. Anthropological Society of Washington, Washington, D.C.

McCabe, Joseph
    1921   *The ABC of Evolution.* Putnam, New York.

McLennan, Joseph F.
    1876   *Studies in Ancient History,* First Series. Bernard Quaritch, London.
    1896   *Studies in Ancient History,* Second Series. Macmillan, London.

McNett, Charles W., Jr.
    1970   "A Settlement Pattern Scale of Cultural Complexity." In *Handbook of Method in Cultural Anthropology,* ed. by Raoul Naroll and Ronald Cohen, pp. 872–886. The Natural History Press, Garden City, N.Y.

Mead, Margaret
    1943   "The Role of Small South Sea Cultures in the Post-War World." *American Anthropologist,* Vol. 45, pp. 193–196.
    1964   *Continuities in Cultural Evolution.* Yale University Press, New Haven.

Meggers, Betty J. [ed.]
    1959   *Evolution in Anthropology: A Centennial Appraisal.* Anthropological Society of Washington, Washington, D.C.
    1960   "The Law of Cultural Evolution as a Practical Research Tool." In *Essays in the Science of Culture in Honor of Leslie A. White,* ed. by Gertrude E. Dole and Robert L. Carneiro, pp. 302–316. Thomas Y. Crowell, New York.
    1991   "Cultural Evolution in Amazonia." In *Profiles in Cultural Evolution,* ed. by A. Terry Rambo and Kathleen Gillogly, pp. 191–216. Anthropological Papers, Museum of Anthropology, University of Michigan, No. 85.

Meggitt, Mervyn
    1977   *Blood Is Their Argument.* Mayfield Publishing Company, Palo Alto, Calif.

Miall, L. C.
    1912   *The Early Naturalists; Their Lives and Work (1530–1789).* Macmillan, London.

Mill, John Stuart
    1846   *A System of Logic,* 1st ed. Harper, New York.
    1886   *A System of Logic,* 8th ed. Longmans, Green, London.

Monboddo, Lord (James Burnett)
    1779–1799   *Ancient Metaphysics: Or, the Science of Universals,* 6 Vols. J. Balfour, Edinburgh.

Moore, Omar Khayyam
    1957   "Divination: A New Perspective." *American Anthropologist,* Vol. 59, pp. 69–74.

Morgan, Lewis Henry
    1871   *Systems of Consanguinity and Affinity of the Human Family. Smithsonian Contributions to Knowledge,* Vol. 17. Smithsonian Institution, Washington, D.C.
    1950   *Montezuma's Dinner.* New York Labor News Company, New York.
    1964   *Ancient Society,* ed. by Leslie A. White. Belknap Press/Harvard University Press, Cambridge, Mass.

Munro, Thomas
    1963   *Evolution in the Arts and Other Theories of Culture History.* Cleveland Museum of Art, Cleveland.

Murdock, George Peter
    1934   *Our Primitive Contemporaries.* The Macmillan Company, New York.
    1937a   "Editorial Preface." In *Studies in the Science of Society,* ed. by George P. Murdock, pp. vii–xx. Yale University Press, New Haven.
    1937b   "Correlations of Matrilineal and Patrilineal Institutions." In *Studies in the Science of Society,* ed. by George P. Murdock, pp. 445–470. Yale University Press, New Haven.
    1949   *Social Structure.* The Macmillan Company, New York.
    1954   "Sociology and Anthropology." In *For a Science of Social Man,* ed. by John Gillin, pp. 14–31. The Macmillan Company, New York.
    1957   "Anthropology as a Comparative Science." *Behavioral Science,* Vol. 2, pp. 249–254.
    1965   *Culture and Society.* University of Pittsburgh Press, Pittsburgh.
    1966   "Cross-Cultural Sampling." *Ethnology,* Vol. 5, pp. 97–114.
Murdock, George P., and Caterina Provost
    1973   "Measurement of Cultural Complexity." *Ethnology,* Vol. 12, pp. 379–392.
Murdock, George P., and Douglas R. White
    1969   "Standard Cross-Cultural Sample." *Ethnology,* Vol. 8, pp. 329–369.
Murphree, Idus L.
    1961   "The Evolutionary Anthropologists: The Progress of Mankind." *Proceedings of the American Philosophical Society,* Vol. 105, pp. 265–300.
Murphy, Robert F.
    1971   *The Dialectics of Social Life.* Columbia University Press, New York.
    1979   *An Overture to Social Anthropology.* Prentice-Hall, Englewood Cliffs, N. J.
    1994   "The Dialectics of Deeds and Words." In *Assessing Cultural Anthropology,* ed. by Robert Borofsky, pp. 55–61. McGraw-Hill Book Company, New York.
Murphy, Robert F., and Julian H. Steward
    1956   "Tappers and Trappers: Parallel Process in Acculturation." *Economic Development and Cultural Change,* Vol. 4, pp. 335–355.
Nadel, S. F.
    1951   *Foundations of Social Anthropology.* Cohen & West, London.
Naroll, Raoul
    1956   "A Preliminary Index of Social Development." *American Anthropologist,* Vol. 58, pp. 687–715.
Netting, Robert
    1977   *Cultural Ecology.* Cummings Publishing Company, Menlo Park, Calif.
Nisbet, Robert A.
    1969   *Social Change and History.* Oxford University Press, New York.
Oberg, Kalervo
    1955   "Types of Social Structure Among the Lowland Tribes of South and Central America." *American Anthropologist,* Vol. 57, pp. 472–487.
O'Laughlin, Bridget
    1975   "Marxist Approaches in Anthropology." *Annual Review of Anthropology,* Vol. 4, pp. 341–370.
Opler, Morris E.
    1962   "Integration, Evolution, and Morgan." *Current Anthropology,* Vol. 3, pp. 478–479.
    1963   "Testing Evolutionary Theory." *Human Organization,* Vol. 22, pp. 159–162.
    1964a   "Reply." *Current Anthropology,* Vol. 5, pp. 110–114.
    1964b   "Cause, Process, and Dynamics in the evolutionism of E. B. Tylor." *Southwestern Journal of Anthropology,* Vol. 20, pp. 123–144.
    1965a   "Cultural Dynamics and Evolutionary Theory." In *Social Change in Developing Areas,* ed. by H. R. Barringer, G. I. Blanksten, and R. W. Mack, pp. 68–96. Schenkman Publishing Company, Cambridge, Mass.
    1965b   "The History of Ethnological Thought." *Current Anthropology,* Vol. 6, p. 319.

1966 "More on the History of Ethnological Thought." *Current Anthropology,* Vol. 7, p. 355.

Osborn, Henry Fairfield

1927 *From the Greeks to Darwin,* 2nd ed. Scribners, New York.

Otterbein, Keith F.

1970 *The Evolution of War.* HRAF Press, New Haven.

Parsons, Talcott

1937 *The Structure of Social Action,* 2 Vols. McGraw-Hill Book Company, New York.

1961 Introduction to *The Study of Sociology,* by Herbert Spencer, pp. v–x. University of Michigan Press, Ann Arbor.

1964 "Evolutionary Universals in Society." *American Sociological Review,* Vol. 29, pp. 339–357.

1966 *Societies: Evolutionary and Comparative Perspectives.* Prentice-Hall, Englewood Cliffs, N.J.

1977 *The Evolution of Societies.* Prentice-Hall, Englewood Cliffs, N.J.

Peckham, Morris

1959 *The Origin of Species by Charles Darwin; A Variorum Text.* University of Pennsylvania Press, Philadelphia.

Pederson, Holger

1931 *The Discovery of Language; Linguistic Science in the 19th Century,* translated from the Danish by John Webster Spargo. Harvard University Press, Cambridge, Mass.

Peel, J. D. Y.

1969 "Spencer and the Neo-Evolutionists." *Sociology,* Vol. 3, pp. 173–191.

Perrin, Robert G.

1993 *Herbert Spencer, a Primary and Secondary Bibliography.* Garland Publishing, New York and London.

Perry, William J.

1923 *The Children of the Sun.* Methuen, London.

Piddocke, Stuart

1965 "The Potlatch System of the South Kwakiutl: A New Perspective." *Southwestern Journal of Anthropology,* Vol. 21, pp. 244–264.

Pitt-Rivers, Lt.-Gen. A. Lane-Fox

1906 *The Evolution of Culture and Other Essays,* ed. by J. L. Myres. Clarendon Press, Oxford.

Powell, John Wesley

1885 "From Savagery to Barbarism." *Transactions of the Anthropological Society of Washington,* Vol. 3, pp. 173–196.

1888 "Competition as a Factor in Human Evolution." *American Anthropologist,* Vol. 1, pp. 297–323.

Radcliffe-Brown, A. R.

1929 "The Sociological Theory of Totemism." *Papers of the 4th Pacific Science Congress,* Vol. 3, *Biological Papers,* pp. 295–305.

1931a "The Social Organization of Australian Tribes." *Oceania Monographs,* Vol.. 1, No. 4, Melbourne.

1931b "The Present Position of Anthropological Studies." *Proceedings, British Association for the Advancement of Science,* pp. 141–171.

1937 *The Nature of a Theoretical Natural Science of Society.* Mimeographed. The University of Chicago.

1941 "The Study of Kinship Systems." *Journal of the Royal Anthropological Institute,* Vol. 71, pp. 1–18.

1947 "Evolution, Social or Cultural?" *American Anthropologist,* Vol. 49, pp. 78–83.

1952 *Structure and Function in Primitive Society.* The Free Press, Glencoe, Ill.

1953 Letter to Claude Lévi-Strauss. In *An Appraisal of Anthropology Today,* ed. by Sol Tax *et al.,* p. 109. University of Chicago Press, Chicago.

1957   *A Natural Science of Society.* The Free Press, Glencoe, Ill.
1971   Foreword to *Military Organization and Society,* by Stanislav Andreski, 2nd ed., pp. v–vii. University of California Press, Berkeley and Los Angeles.

Radin, Paul
1933   *The Method and Theory of Ethnology.* McGraw-Hill Book Company, New York.
1939   "The Mind of Primitive Man." *The New Republic,* Vol. 98, pp. 300–303.

Rambo, A. Terry
1991   "The Study of Cultural Evolution." In *Profiles in Cultural Evolution,* ed. by A. Terry Rambo and Kathleen Gillogly. Anthropological Papers, Museum of Anthropology, University of Michigan, No. 85, pp. 23–109.

Randall, John Herman
1926   *The Making of the Modern Mind.* Houghton Mifflin, Boston.

Rappaport, Roy A.
1967a   "Ritual Regulation of Environmental Relations Among a New Guinea People." *Ethnology,* Vol. 6, pp. 17–30.
1967b   *Pigs for the Ancestors; Ritual in the Ecology of a New Guinea People.* Yale University Press, New Haven.

Rapport, Nigel, and Joanna Overing
2000   *Social and Cultural Anthropology: The Key Concepts.* Routledge, London.

Rathje, William L.
1972   "Praise the Gods and Pass the Metates: A Hypothesis of the Development of Lowland Rainforest Civilizations in Mesoamerica." In *Contemporary Archaeology,* ed. by Mark P. Leone, pp. 365–392. Southern Illinois University Press, Carbondale, Ill.

Ratzel, Friedrich
1896   *The History of Mankind,* translated from the German by A. J. Butler, Vol. 1. Macmillan, London.

Redfield, Robert
1934   "Culture Change in Yucatan." *American Anthropologist,* Vol. 36, pp. 57–69.
1941   *The Folk Culture of Yucatan.* University of Chicago Press, Chicago.
1953   *The Primitive World and Its Transformation.* Cornell University Press, Ithaca.
1955   *The Little Community.* University of Chicago Press, Chicago.

Redman, Charles L.
1991   "Distinguished Lecture in Archaeology: In Defense of the Seventies—The Adolescence of New Archeology." *American Anthropologist,* Vol. 93, pp. 295–307.

Reichenbach, Hans
1951   "Probability Methods in Social Science." In *The Policy Sciences,* ed. by Daniel Lerner and Harold D. Lasswell, pp. 121–128. Stanford University Press, Stanford.

Renfrew, Colin
1976   *Before Civilization.* Pelican Books, Harmondsworth, England. (First published in 1973.)
1987   "An Interview with Lewis Binford." *Current Anthropology,* Vol. 28, pp. 683–694.

Rindos, David
1984   *The Origin of Agricultural Systems: An Evolutionary Perspective.* Academic Press, New York.
1985   "Darwinian Selection, Symbolic Variation, and the Evolution of Culture." *Current Anthropology,* Vol. 26, pp. 65–88.

Rivers, W. H. R.
1911   "The Ethnological Analysis of Culture." In *Report of the Eighty-First Meeting of the British Association for the Advancement of Science,* pp. 490–499.
1914   *The History of Melanesian Society.* Cambridge University Press, Cambridge.

Roscoe, Paul B.
1993   "Practice and Political Centralization: A New Approach to Political Evolution." *Current Anthropology,* Vol. 34, pp. 111–140.

Ross, Edward A.
   1915   *Foundations of Sociology.* The Macmillan Company, New York.
Rountree, Helen C.
   1989   *The Powhatan Indians of Virginia: Their Traditional Culture.* University of Oklahoma Press, Norman.
Rousseau, Jérôme
   1985   "The Ideological Prerequisites of Inequality." In *Development and Decline; The Evolution of Sociopolitical Organization,* ed. by Henri J. M. Claessen, Pieter van de Velde, and M. Estellie Smith, pp. 36–45. Bergin and Garvey Publishers, South Hadley, Mass.
Rowe, John Howland
   1946   "Inca Culture at the Time of the Spanish Conquest." In *Handbook of South American Indians,* ed. by Julian H. Steward, Vol. 2, *The Andean Civilizations,* pp. 183–330. *Bureau of American Ethnology Bulletin* 143. U.S. Government Printing Office, Washington, D.C.
Sabloff, Jeremy
   1989   *The Cities of Ancient Mexico.* Thames and Hudson, New York.
Sahlins, Marshall D.
   1958   *Social Stratification in Polynesia.* University of Washington Press, Seattle.
   1960   "Evolution: Specific and General." In *Evolution and Culture,* ed. by Marshall D. Sahlins and Elman R. Service, pp. 12–44. University of Michigan Press, Ann Arbor.
   1972   *Stone Age Economics.* Aldine Publishing Company, Chicago.
Sahlins, Marshall D., and Elman R. Service, eds.
   1960   *Evolution and Culture.* University of Michigan Press, Ann Arbor.
Sanders, William T., and Barbara J. Price
   1968   *Mesoamerica: The Evolution of a Civilization.* Random House, New York.
Sanders, William T., and David Webster
   1978   "Unilinealism, Multilinealism, and the Evolution of Complex Societies." In *Social Archaeology,* ed. by Charles L. Redman, pp. 249–302. Academic Press, New York.
Sanderson, Stephen K.
   1988   *Macrosociology, an Introduction to Human Societies.* Harper & Row, Publishers, New York. (3rd edition 1995.)
   1990   *Social Evolutionism; A Critical History.* Basil Blackwell, Cambridge, Mass.
   1999   *Social Transformations,* expanded edition. Rowman and Littlefield Publishers, Lanham, Md.
Sapir, Edward
   1920   Review of *Primitive Society,* by Robert H. Lowie. *The Freeman,* Vol. 1, pp. 377–379.
   1927   "Anthropology and Sociology." In *The Social Sciences and Their Interrelations,* ed. by William F. Ogburn and Alexander Goldenweiser, pp. 97–113. Houghton Mifflin, Boston.
Schiffer, Michael B.
   1983   Review of *Cultural Materialism,* by Marvin Harris. *American Antiquity,* Vol. 48, pp. 190–194.
Service, Elman R.
   1960   "The Law of Evolutionary Potential." In *Evolution and Culture,* ed. by Marshall D. Sahlins and Elman R. Service, pp. 93–122. University of Michigan Press, Ann Arbor.
   1962   *Primitive Social Organization: An Evolutionary Perspective.* Random House, New York.
   1968a   "War and Our Contemporary Ancestors." In *War: The Anthropology of Armed Conflict and Aggression,* ed. by Morton Fried, Marvin Harris, and Robert Murphy, pp. 160–167. The Natural History Press, Garden City, N.Y.
   1968b   "Cultural Evolution." In *International Encyclopedia of the Social Sciences,* Vol. 5, pp. 221–227. The Macmillan Company and The Free Press, New York.
   1968c   Review of *The Rise of Anthropological Theory,* by Marvin Harris. *Natural History,* Vol. 77, No. 10, December, pp. 74–75.

1968d "The Prime-Mover of Cultural Evolution." *Southwestern Journal of Anthropology,* Vol. 24, pp. 396–409.

1971a *Primitive Social Organization: An Evolutionary Perspective,* 2nd ed. Random House, New York.

1971b *Cultural Evolutionism, Theory in Practice.* Holt, Rinehart and Winston, New York.

Shanks, Michael, and Christopher Tilley

1987   *Social Theory and Archaeology.* Polity Press, Cambridge.

1992   *Re-Constructing Archaeology; Theory and Practice,* 2nd. ed. Routledge, London.

Shedd, William G. T.

1857   *Lectures upon the Philosophy of History.* W. F. Draper, Andover, Mass.

Smith, G. Elliot

1923   *The Ancient Egyptians and the Origin of Civilization.* Harper & Brothers, London and New York.

1933   *The Diffusion of Culture.* Watts & Co., London.

Smith, Philip E. L., and T. Cuyler Young, Jr.

1972   "The Evolution of Early Agriculture and Culture in Greater Mesopotamia: A Trial Model." In *Population Growth: Anthropological Implications,* ed. by Brian Spooner, pp. 1–59. MIT Press, Cambridge, Mass.

South, Stanley

1955   "Evolutionary Theory in Archaeology." *Southern Indian Studies,* Vol. 7, pp. 1–24.

South, Stanley, and Halcott P. Green

2002   "Evolutionary Theory in Archaeology at Mid-century and at the Millennium." Unpublished manuscript.

Spaulding, Albert C.

1960   "The Dimensions of Archaeology." In *Essays in the Science of Culture in Honor of Leslie A. White,* ed. by Gertrude E. Dole and Robert L. Carneiro, pp. 437–456. Thomas Y. Crowell Company, New York.

Spencer, Charles

1987   "Rethinking the Chiefdom." In *Chiefdoms in the Americas,* ed. by Robert D. Drennan and Carlos A. Uribe, pp. 369–389. University Press of America, Lanham, Md.

1990   "On the Tempo and Mode of State Formation: Neoevolutionism Reconsidered." *Journal of Anthropological Archaeology,* Vol. 9, pp. 1–30.

Spencer, Herbert

1851   *Social Statics.* John Chapman, London.

1857   "Progress: Its Law and Cause." *The Westminster Review,* Vol. 67, pp. 445–485.

1863   *First Principles,* 1st ed. Williams and Norgate, London.

1872   "The Survival of the Fittest." *Nature,* Vol. 5, pp. 263–264.

1883   *The Principles of Psychology,* 3rd ed., 2 Vols. D. Appleton and Company, New York.

1886   *The Study of Sociology.* D. Appleton and Company, New York.

1890   *The Principles of Sociology,* Vol. I, 3rd ed. D. Appleton and Company, New York.

1891a "The Development Hypothesis." In *Essays: Scientific, Political, & Speculative,* Vol. 1, pp. 265–307. Williams and Norgate, London.

1891b "The Social Organism." In *Essays: Scientific, Political, & Speculative,* Vol. 1, pp. 265–307. Williams and Norgate, London.

1891c "Reasons for Dissenting from the Philosophy of M. Comte." In *Essays: Scientific, Political, & Speculative,* Vol. 2, pp. 118–144. Williams and Norgate, London.

1895   "Lord Salisbury on Evolution." *The Nineteenth Century,* Vol. 38, pp. 740–757.

1896   *First Principles,* 4th ed. D. Appleton and Company, New York.

1897   *The Principles of Sociology,* Vol. 3. D. Appleton and Company, New York.

1899   *The Principles of Sociology,* Vol. 2. D. Appleton and Company, New York.

1908   "The Filiation of Ideas." In *Life and Letters of Herbert Spencer,* by David Duncan, Vol. 2, pp. 304–365. D. Appleton and Company, New York.

1926   *An Autobiography,* 2 Vols. Watts & Co., London.

1937   *First Principles,* 6th ed. Watts & Co., London.

1967   *The Evolution of Society; Selections from Herbert Spencer's Principles of Sociology,* edited and with an introduction by Robert L. Carneiro. University of Chicago Press, Chicago.

Spoehr, Alexander
1950   "Observations on the Study of Kinship." *American Anthropologist,* Vol. 52, pp. 1–15.

Spooner, Brian, ed.
1972   *Population Growth: Anthropological Implications.* MIT Press, Cambridge, Mass.

Starcke, C. N.
1889   *The Primitive Family.* D. Appleton and Company, New York.

Starr, Harris E.
1925   *William Graham Sumner.* Henry Holt and Company, New York.

Steinmetz, S. R.
1898–1899   "Classification des Types Sociaux." *L'Année Sociologique,* Vol. 3, pp. 43–147.

Steponaitis, Vincas P.
1978   "Location Theory and Complex Chiefdoms: A Mississippian Example." In *Mississippian Settlement Patterns,* ed. by Bruce D. Smith, pp. 417–453. Academic Press, New York.

Stern, Bernhard J.
1928   "Lewis Henry Morgan: American Ethnologist." *Social Forces,* Vol. 6, pp. 344–357.

1931   *Lewis Henry Morgan, Social Evolutionist.* University of Chicago Press, Chicago.

Steward, Julian H.
1937   "Ecological Aspects of Southwestern Society." *Anthropos,* Vol. 32, pp. 87–104.

1938   "Basin-Plateau Aboriginal Sociopolitical Groups." *Bureau of American Ethnology Bulletin* 120.

1948   "A Functional-Developmental Classification of American High Cultures." In *A Reappraisal of Peruvian Archaeology,* assembled by Wendell C. Bennett, pp. 103–104. Memoir No. 4, Society for American Archaeology.

1949   "Cultural Causality and Law: A Trial Formulation of the Development of Early Civilizations." *American Anthropologist,* Vol. 51, pp. 1–27.

1950   Review of *The Science of Culture,* by Leslie A. White. *Scientific Monthly,* Vol. 70, pp. 208–209.

1953a   "Evolution and Process." In *Anthropology Today: An Encyclopedic Inventory,* prepared under the chairmanship of A. L. Kroeber, pp. 313–326. University of Chicago Press, Chicago.

1953b   Review of *Social Evolution,* by V. Gordon Childe. *American Anthropologist,* Vol. 55, pp. 240–241.

1955   *Theory of Culture Change.* University of Illinois Press, Urbana.

1956   "Cultural Evolution." *Scientific American,* Vol. 194, pp. 69–80.

Stocking, George W., Jr.
1963   "Matthew Arnold, E. B. Tylor, and the Uses of Invention." *American Anthropologist,* Vol. 65, pp. 783–799.

1965   "'Cultural Darwinism' and 'Philosophical Idealism' in E. B. Tylor: A Special Plea for Historicism in the History of Anthropology." *Southwestern Journal of Anthropology,* Vol. 21, pp. 130–147.

Strong, William Duncan
1953   "Historical Approaches in Anthropology." In *Anthropology Today, an Encyclopedic Inventory,* prepared under the chairmanship of A. L. Kroeber, pp. 386–397. University of Chicago Press, Chicago.

Sumner, William Graham
1889   "Sketch of William Graham Sumner." *The Popular Science Monthly,* Vol. 35, pp. 257–268.

1906   *Folkways.* Ginn and Company, Boston.

1918   *The Forgotten Man and Other Essays,* ed. by Albert G. Keller. Yale University Press, New Haven.

Sumner, William Graham, and Albert G. Keller
1927–1928   *The Science of Society,* 4 vols. Yale University Press, New Haven.

Swanton, John R.
1905   "The Social Organization of American Tribes." *American Anthropologist,* Vol. 7, pp. 663–673.

Tax, Sol
1955a   "Some Problems of Social Organization." In *Social Organization of North American Tribes,* ed. by Fred Eggan, pp. 3–32. University of Chicago Press, Chicago.
1955b   "From Lafitau to Radcliffe-Brown: A Short History of the Study of Social Organization." In *Social Organization of North American Tribes,* ed. by Fred Eggan, enlarged edition, pp. 445–481. University of Chicago Press, Chicago.

Taylor, Walter W.
1971   *A Study of Archaeology.* Southern Illinois University Press, Edwardsville. (Originally published in 1948.)

Thomas, David Hurst
1979   *Archaeology,* 1st ed. Holt, Rinehart and Winston, New York.
1998   *Archaeology,* 3rd. ed. Harcourt Brace College Publishers, Fort Worth, Texas.

Townsend, Joan B.
1985   "The Autonomous Village and the Development of Chiefdoms." In *Development and Decline: The Evolution of Sociopolitical Organization,* ed. by Henri J. M. Claessen, Pieter van de Velde, and M. Estellie Smith, pp. 141–155. Bergin and Harvey, South Hadley, Mass.

Tozzer, Alfred Marston
1925   *Social Origins and Social Continuities.* The Macmillan Company, New York.

Trigger, Bruce
1978   *Time and Traditions; Essays in Archaeological Interpretation.* Columbia University Press, New York.
1984   "Archaeology at the Crossroads: What's New?" *Annual Review of Anthropology,* Vol. 13, pp. 275–300.
1989   *A History of Archaeological Thought.* Cambridge University Press, Cambridge.
1998   *Sociocultural Evolution.* Blackwell Publishers, Oxford.

Turgot, Anne Robert Jacques
1949   "On the Successive Advances of the Human Mind." In *The Idea of History,* ed. by Frederick J. Teggart and George H. Hildebrand, pp. 242–259. University of California Press, Berkeley and Los Angeles.

Tylor, Edward B.
1861   *Anahuac: Or Mexico and the Mexicans, Ancient and Modern.* Longmans, Green, Longmans, and Roberts, London.
1870   *Researches into the Early History of Mankind,* 2nd ed. John Murray, London.
1871   *Primitive Culture,* 1st ed., 2 Vols. John Murray, London.
1878   "Anthropology." In *Encyclopaedia Britannica,* 9th ed., Vol. 2, pp. 107–123. Samuel L. Hall, New York.
1879   "On the Game of Patolli in Ancient Mexico, and Its Probably Asiatic Origin." *Journal of the [Royal] Anthropological Institute,* Vol. 8, pp. 116–131.
1882   "The Study of Customs." *Macmillan's Magazine,* Vol. 46, pp. 73–86.
1889   "On a Method of Investigating the Development of Institutions; Applied to Laws of Marriage and Descent." *Journal of the [Royal] Anthropological Institute,* Vol. 18, pp. 245–269.
1910   "Anthropology." In *Encyclopaedia Britannica,* 11th ed., Vol. 2, pp. 108–119. Samuel L. Hall, New York.
1916   *Anthropology.* D. Appleton and Company, New York.

1920   *Primitive Culture*, 6th ed., 2 Vols. John Murray, London.

Vayda, Andrew P.
1967   Foreword to *Pigs for the Ancestors*, by Roy A. Rappaport. Yale University Press, New Haven.
1969   "An Ecological Approach in Cultural Anthropology." *Bucknell Review*, Vol. 17, pp. 112–119.

Waitz, Theodor
1863   *Introduction to Anthropology*, ed. by J. Frederick Collingwood. Longmans, Green, Longmans, and Roberts, London.

Wallace, Alfred Russel
1872   Review of *Primitive Culture*, by E. B. Tylor. *The Academy*, Vol. 3, pp. 69–71.

Ward, Lester F.
1885   "Moral and Material Progress Contrasted." *Transactions of the Anthropological Society of Washington*, Vol. 3, pp. 121–130.

Wauchope, Robert
1966   *Archaeological Survey of Northern Georgia. Memoirs of the Society for American Archaeology*, No. 21.

Webster, David
1977   "Warfare and the Evolution of Maya Civilization." In *The Origins of Maya Civilization*, ed. by Richard E. W. Adams, pp. 335–372. University of New Mexico Press, Albuquerque.

Wenke, Robert J.
1981   "Explaining the Evolution of Cultural Complexity." *Advances in Archaeological Method and Theory*, Vol. 4, pp. 79–127.
1999   *Patterns in Prehistory*, 3rd ed. Oxford University Press, New York.

Westermarck, Edward
1901   *The History of Human Marriage*, 3rd ed. Macmillan, London.
1921   *The History of Human Marriage*, 5th ed. Macmillan, London.

White, Leslie A.
1931   Review of *Lewis Henry Morgan, Social Evolutionist. American Journal of Sociology*, Vol. 37, p. 483.
1943   "Energy and the Evolution of Culture." *American Anthropologist*, Vol. 45, pp. 335–356.
1944   "Morgan's Attitude Toward Religion and Science." *American Anthropologist*, Vol. 46, pp. 218–230.
1945a   "History, Evolutionism, and Functionalism: Three Types of Interpretation of Culture." *Southwestern Journal of Anthropology*, Vol. 1, pp. 221–248.
1945b   "Diffusion vs. Evolution: An Anti-Evolutionist Fallacy." *American Anthropologist*, Vol. 47, pp. 339–356.
1947   "Evolutionary Stages, Progress, and the Evaluation of Cultures." *Southwestern Journal of Anthropology*, Vol. 3, pp. 165–192.
1948   "Lewis Henry Morgan: Pioneer in the Theory of Social Evolution." In *An Introduction to the History of Sociology*, ed. by Harry Elmer Barnes, pp. 138–154. University of Chicago Press, Chicago.
1949a   *The Science of Culture*. Farrar, Straus and Company, New York.
1949b   "Ethnological Theory." In *Philosophy for the Future: The Quest of Modern Materialism*, ed. by Roy Wood Sellars, V. J. McGill, and Marvin Farber, pp. 357–384. The Macmillan Company, New York.
1953   Comments on "Problems of the Historical Approach: Theory." In *An Appraisal of Anthropology Today*, ed. by Sol Tax, Loren C. Eiseley, Irving Rouse, and Carl F. Voegelin, pp. 67–84. University of Chicago Press, Chicago.
1957   Review of *Theory of Culture Change*, by Julian H. Steward. *American Anthropologist*, Vol. 59, pp. 540–542.

1959   *The Evolution of Culture.* McGraw-Hill Book Company, New York.

1960   Foreword to *Evolution and Culture,* ed. by Marshall D. Sahlins and Elman R. Service, pp. v–xii. University of Michigan Press, Ann Arbor.

1973   *The Concept of Culture.* Burgess Publishing Company, Minneapolis. (With Beth Dillingham.)

1987   *Ethnological Essays,* ed. by Beth Dillingham and Robert L. Carneiro. University of New Mexico Press, Albuquerque.

White, Leslie A., A. L. Kroeber, *et al.*

1960   "Panel Five: Social and Cultural Evolution." In *Evolution After Darwin,* Vol. 3, *Issues in Evolution,* ed. by Sol Tax and Charles Callender, pp. 207–243. University of Chicago Press, Chicago.

Whiting, John W. M.

1970   "The Cross-Cultural Method." In *Readings in Cross-Cultural Methodology,* ed. by Frank W. Moore, pp. 287–300. HRAF Press, New Haven.

1986   "George Peter Murdock (1897–1985)." *American Anthropologist,* Vol. 88, pp. 682–686.

Willey, Gordon R.

1946   "The Chiclín Conference for Peruvian Archaeology." *American Antiquity,* Vol. 12, pp. 132–134.

1953   *Prehistoric Settlement Patterns in the Virú Valley, Peru. Bureau of American Ethnology Bulletin* No. 155.

1961   Review of *Evolution and Culture,* by Marshal D. Sahlins and Elman R. Service. *American Antiquity,* Vol. 26, pp. 441–443.

1976   "Mesoamerican Civilization and the Idea of Transcendence." *Antiquity,* Vol. 50, pp. 205–225.

Willey, Gordon R., and Philip Phillips

1958   *Method and Theory in American Archaeology.* University of Chicago Press, Chicago.

Willey, Gordon R., and Jeremy A. Sabloff

1974   *A History of American Archaeology,* 1st ed. W. H. Freeman and Company, San Francisco.

1993   *A History of American Archaeology,* 3rd ed. W. H. Freeman and Company, New York.

Wissler, Clark

1923   *Man and Culture.* Thomas Y. Crowell Company, New York.

Wittfogel, Karl

1957   *Oriental Despotism.* Yale University Press, New Haven.

Wright, Henry T., and Gregory A. Johnson

1975   "Population, Exchange, and Early State Formation in Southwestern Iran." *American Anthropologist,* Vol. 77, pp. 267–289.

Yengoyan, Aram A.

1991   "Evolutionary Theory in Ethnological Perspective." In *Profiles in Cultural Evolution,* ed. by A. Terry Rambo and Kathleen Gillogly, pp. 3–21. Anthropological Papers, Museum of Anthropology, University of Michigan, No. 85.

Yoffee, Norman

1979   "The Decline and Rise of Mesopotamian Civilization: An Ethnoarchaeological Perspective on the Evolution of Social Complexity." *American Antiquity,* Vol. 44, pp. 5–35.

1993   "Too Many Chiefs? (or, Safe Texts for the '90s)." In *Archaeological Theory: Who Sets the Agenda?* ed. by Norman Yoffee and Andrew Sherratt, pp. 60–78. Cambridge University Press, Cambridge.

Index